Education Law, Strategic Policy and Sustainable Development in Africa

A.C. Onuora-Oguno · W.O. Egbewole
T.E. Kleven
Editors

Education Law, Strategic Policy and Sustainable Development in Africa

Agenda 2063

palgrave
macmillan

Editors
A.C. Onuora-Oguno
Faculty of Law
University of Ilorin
Ilorin, Nigeria

T.E. Kleven
Texas Southern University
Houston, TX, USA

W.O. Egbewole
Faculty of Law
University of Ilorin
Ilorin, Nigeria

ISBN 978-3-319-85221-8 ISBN 978-3-319-53703-0 (eBook)
DOI 10.1007/978-3-319-53703-0

Printed on acid-free paper

This Palgrave Macmillan imprint is published by Springer Nature
The registered company is Springer International Publishing AG
The registered company address is: Gewerbestrasse 11, 6330 Cham, Switzerland

To every African child denied access to quality education

Foreword

Towards a New Era of Human Rights: The Right to Education in Africa

A famous African human rights scholar has suggested that the age of human rights is over.[1] He argues that, although, at no point in history, there have been more norms, processes and institutions seeking to promote human rights, human rights have lost their moral force. A number of factors are said to have contributed to this erosion of the idea of human rights. On the one hand, human rights have been abused as part of a civilising mission of the West against former colonies to "deliver primitive peoples into the Age of Europe", pursued with the same mindset with which the colonial powers already undertook their colonising mission, thus leading to large-scale aversion to the idea of human rights in the countries concerned.[2] On the other hand, the West has never quite lived up to human rights standards itself, "preaching water, but drinking wine", hence undermining the credibility of those advocating human rights. The so-called war on terror led by the USA, for example, has served to justify human rights violations on a grand scale in Afghanistan, Iraq, Libya, etc.[3] Human rights are said, in many ways, to have remained an essentially Western construct, rejected in many non-Western societies, notably in Asia and the Near East.[4] To this, one may further add that the human rights movement has generally "overpromised, but underperformed". The level of privation resulting from war or unbridled capitalism has made the future of many in war-torn or poorer countries look bleaker than ever, with the rest of the world paralysed and unable to do anything.[5]

There may be substantial truth to these sobering observations. However, even the author of these sentiments goes on to admit that "[t]he internationalisation—universalisation—of human rights principles and tenets is so deeply embedded in the psyches of states and cultures around the world that it is irreversible".[6] Hence, when the African Union in its Agenda 2063 aspires towards "[a]n Africa of good governance, democracy, respect for human rights, justice and the rule of law",[7] I suppose the only option available is to work with that concept—the concept of human rights—but to try to accomplish a reinvigoration of the human rights idea and to ensure that human rights are taken seriously. The question, of course, is how this should be achieved. This book focuses on the right to education—a so-called hybrid right, evidencing characteristics of civil and political, economic, social and cultural, and group or solidarity rights, therefore of all three generations of human rights.[8] It covers classical freedoms, such as the absence of indoctrination in schools, the right to establish private schools or academic freedom. It further encompasses positive duties of the state to make education available, accessible, acceptable and adaptable at all levels of the education system. However, it also implicates the right to development as entitling a nation as a whole to socio-economic and political progress. The right to education is, moreover, what has been termed an "empowerment right", i.e. a human right itself whose enjoyment only makes the exercise of most other human rights possible. It constitutes the basis for each person's political enlightenment, facilitates his or her socio-economic success in life and makes it possible for that person to take part in cultural life.[9] How then can the right to education reclaim its moral significance as a human right in the African context and be taken seriously in what appears to be a post-human rights era? Among the possible solutions, three may perhaps be singled out.

One of the reasons for the failure of human rights in non-Western societies has been that they have been experienced as an alien construct superimposed on such societies. No effort has been made to embed human rights in the specific context in which they were to operate. This remains the primary obstacle to the acceptance of human rights in the Near East and Asia. Although this used to be true for Africa too, significant steps have been taken to make human rights a "home-grown" achievement, at least at the regional level.[10] The regional African human rights system, with its norms (the African Charter on Human and

Peoples' Rights (Banjul Charter) of 1981, the Protocol thereto on the Rights of Women in Africa of 2003, the African Charter on the Rights and Welfare of the Child of 1990, etc.) and its institutions (African Commission on Human and Peoples' Rights, African Court on Human and Peoples' Rights, African Committee of Experts on the Rights and Welfare of the Child), has been used as the basis for this process. Its norms ensure "greater normative legitimacy by addressing the specific real-life concerns of Africans and African cultural conceptions of human rights",[11] and its institutions, specifically the African Commission, have shown themselves to be relatively effective in protecting human rights.[12] Although Article 17(1) of the Banjul Charter provides only rather succinctly that "[e]very individual shall have the right to education", this right has been elaborated on by Article 11 of the African Children's Rights Charter.[13] Article 11 broadly includes the essential elements of Articles 28 and 29 of the U.N. Convention on the Rights of the Child, the corresponding provisions in the Charter's international counterpart, but adds a distinct "African" flavour. Education is thus to be directed to "the preservation and strengthening of positive African morals, traditional values and cultures", "the preservation of national independence and territorial integrity" and "the promotion and achievements of African Unity and Solidarity".[14] The African Committee of Experts on the Rights and Welfare of the Child, the body of independent experts supervising implementation of the African Children's Rights Charter, has further started addressing the right to education in Article 11 in its first two General Comments, pointing out the importance of education for the children of incarcerated and imprisoned parents and caregivers,[15] and the urgency of realising the right to birth registration, name and nationality in Article 6, *inter alia* to guarantee access to education.[16] It has also started adjudicating on the right to education under its communication procedure. In its second decision in the case of *Children of Nubian Descent v. Kenya*, the Committee found children of Nubian descent to have suffered *de facto* inequality in their access to available educational services and resources as a result of their lack of confirmed status as Kenyan nationals, in violation of Article 11.[17] All this goes to confirm that the right to education is in the process of becoming a genuinely "African" right within the African human rights system. It is crucial that the future sees enhanced activity of this sort at the regional, but also at the national level in Africa to strengthen the moral cogency of the right to education and other human rights on the continent and beyond.

Another reason for the general demise of human rights at the international level is that they have been relegated to play purely "technical" legal role in U.N. and regional human rights procedures not enjoying prominent publicity and media coverage. The discourse at centre stage, rather than focusing on the realisation of human rights, turns around meeting human needs, eradicating poverty and achieving sustainable development. In the field of education, the right to education has thus been superseded by the lofty goal of "[e]nsur[ing] inclusive and equitable quality education and promot[ing] lifelong learning opportunities for all" by 2030.[18] While international human rights treaties such as the International Covenant on Economic, Social and Cultural Rights of 1966, or the U.N. Convention on the Rights of the Child of 1990, or the African Children's Rights Charter of 1990 create clear legal obligations for states, individually and jointly, to realise the right to education, a second strand of documents—notably the Jomtien World Declaration on Education for All of 1990, the Dakar Framework for Action of 2000, the U.N. Millennium Declaration of 2000, the 2030 Agenda for Sustainable Development of 2015, and the Incheon Declaration and Framework for Action of 2015[19]—in which political commitments replace those of a legal nature, has shifted into the spotlight now. These documents are very different from the human rights treaties long since in place and sufficient to stipulate what is expected of states: They focus on only aspects of the right to education addressed in the treaties (for example, neglecting higher education or freedom in education), sometimes they openly contradict human rights law (the minimum core obligation of international law to achieve free and compulsory primary education for all without delay[20] becomes an obligation subject to progressive realisation), and they fail to clearly identify duty bearers, who, if targets are not met, are responsible for having committed a violation of the right to education. In the words of a former U.N. Special Rapporteur on the Right to Education, "[t]he difference which human rights bring can be expressed in one single word—violation. The mobilising power of calling a betrayed pledge a human rights violation is immense".[21] This is true also with regard to the right to education and other economic, social and cultural rights, whose realisation, as is well known, depends on state resources, which, more often than not, are scarce. Not describing the failure to satisfy, at the very least, minimum essential levels of these rights as a prima facie human rights violation, renders these rights legally and morally irrelevant.[22] In a situation where clear human rights obligations of states become pledges whose fulfilment is vaguely assigned to a multitude of actors—states, intergovernmental agencies, NGOs, the private sector, or "the education community"[23] —and whose realisation, in the absence of the language of "violations", is more discretionary than mandatory, pledges will be betrayed time and time again. It is no wonder that the Incheon Declaration and Framework for Action of 2015 needs to provide for "a single, *renewed* education agenda that is holistic, ambitious and aspirational, leaving no one behind",[24] as previous ones necessarily had to fail.[25] Obviously, in these circumstances, where global development endeavours in a populist, yes, messianic fashion promise prosperity, but properly remain beyond the realm of human rights, and where genuine human rights work performed by expert bodies and tribunals is accorded a subordinate significance not enjoying any public attention, human rights will not only not be fulfilled, but also will lose their lustre.

The final observation made here relates to the need for adding a perspective which so far has been lacking in international human rights law. In a globalised word, where many actions of states affect the human rights of those beyond their borders—and may prevent the realisation of human rights in other states—human rights under international law must be recognised to give rise to extraterritorial obligations. A neglect to add this missing dimension is one of the major reasons why human rights are perceived to be failing in the present world. The Maastricht Principles on Extraterritorial Obligations of States in the Area of Economic, Social and Cultural Rights of 2011, a document prepared by a group of experts in international law, recognise that "[a]ll States have obligations to respect, protect and fulfil human rights, including civil, cultural, economic, political and social rights, both within their territories and extraterritorially".[26] Extraterritorial obligations encompass: "(a) obligations relating to the acts and omissions of a State, within or beyond its territory, that have effects on the enjoyment of human rights outside of that State's territory; and (b) obligations of a global character that are set out in the Charter of the United Nations and human rights instruments to take action, separately, and jointly through international co-operation, to realise human rights universally".[27]

Consequently, states, in devising, implementing and monitoring bilateral development co-operation policies and programmes, are obliged to comply with the right to education. A failure to do so constitutes a human rights violation. The International Monetary Fund—although its loans to low-income countries now include social spending targets, covering education—has recently been shown, in a large number of cases, not to have ensured countries under its tutelage are able in practice to meet these targets.[28] The World Bank supports the development of a multinational chain of low-fee profit-making private primary schools targeting poor families in Kenya and Uganda; these schools use highly standardised teaching methods, untrained low-paid teachers and aggressive marketing strategies to target poor households, while, on the other hand, it (the Bank) has not invested in free public primary education in these countries.[29] States, as members of the IMF and the World Bank, may not hide behind these organisations' institutional veil. As a member of an international organisation, a state remains responsible for its conduct in relation to its international human rights obligations within its territory and beyond, and it must take all reasonable steps to ensure that the international organisation concerned acts in accordance with its (the state's) pre-existing obligations under international human rights law.[30] Under international human rights law, states are required to use maximum available resources to provide public education of a high quality.[31] Primary education must be compulsory and free, secondary and higher education must be made progressively free.[32] Likewise, any liberalisation of trade in education services, whether at the primary, secondary, or higher education level, under the WTO General Agreement on Trade in Services (GATS) or any other bilateral or multilateral trade agreement, which impinges on free or progressively free public education of high quality, or any intellectual property protection under the WTO Agreement on Trade-Related Aspects of Intellectual Property Rights (TRIPS) or any other bilateral or multilateral trade agreement, which restricts access to textbooks or digital content in a way detrimental to the provision of free or progressively free public education of high quality, constitutes a human rights violations. There is an obligation of states to elaborate, interpret, and apply international agreements and standards in a manner consistent with their human rights obligations.[33] The realisation of the right to education, as that of other economic, social and cultural rights, depends on the availability of resources. When human rights treaties thus provide for the use of maximum available resources and recourse, where necessary, to international assistance and co-operation in this regard,[34] this implicates legal obligations of an extraterritorial nature. Hence, for states that are in a position to allocate 0.7 % of their gross national product to official development assistance, failure to do so must be held to constitute a prima facie human rights violation.[35] As underlined by the Maastricht Principles, "a state has obligations to … fulfil economic, social and cultural rights" in situations in which the State "is in a position … to take measures to realise economic, social and cultural rights extraterritorially".[36]

In my view, the three courses of action outlined here—domesticising human rights in the specific context in which they are to operate, debunking the approach in terms of which "all we (whoever that is) need to do is try our best, over the next 15 years or so, to satisfy certain human needs, without fearing any consequences in case we fail to achieve success" in favour of a clear violations approach, and appreciating that, taking human rights seriously, must entail the recognition of state obligations to respect, protect, and fulfil human rights also beyond national borders—will go some way towards restoring faith in human rights, including the right to education, and reinstating such rights as a compelling moral category, globally and also in Africa. The African Union's aspiration in its Agenda 2063 towards "[a]n Africa of good governance, democracy, respect for human rights, justice and the rule of law" may perhaps constitute the appropriate context for making human rights relevant on the continent again, and for adopting a perspective incorporating a wider and more robust understanding of human rights, as advocated here. In this sense, a book commenting on the importance of human rights to development in Africa in the light of that continent's complex history, the need for a proactive judiciary in the realisation of human rights and the crucial role of the right to education in advancing the AU's Agenda 2063 is most welcome and may, in its modest way, encourage Africans and others to embark on the journey into a new human rights era.

Klaus D. Beiter
B.Iur. LL.B. (UNISA, Pretoria), Dr. iur. (LMU Munich);
Associate Professor, North-West University (Potchefstroom Campus),
Faculty of Law, South Africa

Notes

1. M. Mutua, "Is the Age of Human Rights Over?," in: S.A. McClennen & A. Schultheis Moore (eds.), *The Routledge Companion to Literature and Human Rights* (Routledge, 2015), 450–458.
2. Ibid., at 455.
3. Ibid., at 452.
4. Ibid., at 452–453.
5. Ibid., at 454–455.
6. Ibid., at 455–456.
7. African Union, Agenda 2063, Aspiration 3.
8. See K.D. Beiter, *The Protection of the Right to Education by International Law: Including a Systematic Analysis of Article 13 of the International Covenant on Economic, Social and Cultural Rights* (Martinus Nijhoff, 2006), 37–43.
9. See Ibid., at 28–30.
10. See Mutua, note 1, at 453. Domesticisation implies, of course, that "new" regional norms must complement, but not contradict, corresponding global norms. See F. Viljoen, "Human Rights in Africa: Normative, Institutional and Functional Complementarity and Distinctiveness," *South African Journal of International Affairs*, 18(2) (2011), 191–216.
11. Viljoen, note 10, at 209.
12. Ibid., at 200–201.
13. Attempts to concretise the content of Article 17(1) of the Banjul Charter have, however, been made in Paragraph 8 of the Pretoria Declaration on Economic, Social and Cultural Rights in Africa (2004), Part IV.D. Right to Education (Article 17), paras. 68–71, of the Principles and Guidelines on the Implementation of Economic, Social and Cultural Rights in the African Charter on Human and Peoples' Rights (2010).
14. Art. 11(2)(c), (e), (f).
15. See General Comment No. 1 (Article 30 of the African Charter on the Rights and Welfare of the Child) on "Children of Incarcerated and Imprisoned Parents and Primary Caregivers," 2013, paras. 4, 12, 20, 26, 27.
16. See General Comment No. 2 (Article 6 of the African Charter on the Rights and Welfare of the Child) on "Right to Birth Registration, Name and Nationality," 2014, paras. 17, 31, 44, 54, 71, 85, 86.
17. See Institute for Human Rights and Development in Africa (IHRDA) and Open Society Justice Initiative on behalf of Children of Nubian Descent in Kenya v. Government of Kenya, 22 March 2011, Communication No. 2/2009.
18. U.N. General Assembly, A/Res/70/1, 2030 Agenda for Sustainable Development, Sustainable Development Goal 4.

19. World Declaration on Education for All and Framework for Action to Meet Basic Learning Needs of 1990; Education for All: Meeting our Collective Commitments: The Dakar Framework for Action of 2000; the United Nations Millennium Declaration (U.N. General Assembly, A/Res/55/2, 2000), the 2030 Agenda for Sustainable Development (U.N. General Assembly, A/Res/70/1, 2015); Incheon Declaration and Framework for Action for the Implementation of Sustainable Development Goal 4 of 2015.
20. See U.N. Committee on Economic, Social and Cultural Rights, General Comment No. 13, The Right to Education (Article 13 of the International Covenant on Economic, Social and Cultural Rights), U.N. Doc. E/C.12/1999/10, paras. 51, 57, or Principles and Guidelines on the Implementation of Economic, Social and Cultural Rights in the African Charter on Human and Peoples' Rights (2010), paras. 16, 71(a), (b).
21. K. Tomaševski, *Removing Obstacles in the Way of the Right to Education* (Novum Grafiska AB, 2001) (Right to Education Primers No. 1), 10.
22. See U.N. Committee on Economic, Social and Cultural Rights, General Comment No. 3, The Nature of States Parties' Obligations (Article 2(1) of the International Covenant on Economic, Social and Cultural Rights), U.N. Doc. E/1991/23, para. 10, or the Principles and Guidelines on the Implementation of Economic, Social and Cultural Rights in the African Charter on Human and Peoples' Rights (2010), para. 17, both documents – even if the latter more indirectly–indicating that the failure to satisfy, at the very least, minimum essential levels of economic, social and cultural rights constitutes a prima facie human rights violation.
23. On commitments of "the education community," see the Incheon Declaration and Framework for Action, for the Implementation of Sustainable Development Goal 4 of 2015 para. 2.
24. Incheon Declaration for the Implementation of Sustainable Development Goal 4 of 2015, para. 5. Own italics.
25. UNESCO's *Global Education Monitoring Report 2016: Education for People and Planet: Creating Sustainable Futures for All* thus finds that "only 64 countries met [the] 2015 target on primary education, while 40% will not achieve [the] 2030 goal on secondary education until 2100." K. Hodal & J. Holder, "Poorest Countries Hit Hardest as World Lags Behind on Global Education Goals," *The Guardian*, 6 September 2016, https://www.theguardian.com/global-development/2016/sep/06/poorest-countries-hit-hardest-world-lags-behind-global-education-goals-unesco-report.
26. Maastricht Principles, Principle 3. See O. De Schutter et al., "Commentary to the Maastricht Principles on Extraterritorial Obligations of States in the Area of Economic, Social and Cultural Rights," *Human Rights Quarterly*, 34(4) (2012), 1084–1169, for a reproduction of and commentary to the Maastricht Principles.

27. Maastricht Principles, Principle 8.
28. See A.E. Kentikelenis, "IMF Conditionality and Development Policy Space, 1985–2014," *Review of International Political Economy*, 23(4) (2016), 543–582.
29. See Education International, "World Bank Must Support Quality Public Education, Not Private Schools!" 14 May 2015, https://www.ei-ie.org/en/news/news_details/3527. In Uganda, the government and High Court have now ordered the closure of many of these schools, found to have operated in contravention of the law. See Education International, "Uganda: For-Profit Education Chain Suffers Major Blow," 4 November 2016, https://www.ei-ie.org/en/news/news_details/4165.
30. Maastricht Principles, Principle 15. See also De Schutter et al, note 26, at 1118–1119.
31. See, e.g. Art. 13 read with Art. 2(1) of the International Covenant on Economic, Social and Cultural Rights.
32. See, e.g. Art. 13(2)(a), (b), (c) of the International Covenant on Economic, Social and Cultural Rights.
33. Maastricht Principles, Principle 17.
34. See, e.g. Art. 2(1) of the International Covenant on Economic, Social and Cultural Rights.
35. It has long since been recognised that donor states should allocate this percentage of their gross national product to official development assistance.
36. Maastricht Principles, Principle 9(c).

Preface

This book, a product of scholars and activists from across Africa, derives from three fundamental beliefs: (i) a belief that basic human rights to which everyone is entitled, and which are administered by, for and among African peoples, can contribute to thriving countries and a thriving continent; (ii) a belief that education is among the most important of all human rights and that every child deserves access to a quality education; (iii) a belief in the centrality of education to thriving democracies, where all participate on an equal basis in determining our common destinies and where all share in the fruits of our common effort.

In Africa, as throughout the world, the effort to realize human rights and a quality education for all is a work in progress. Achieving success in this effort requires commitment and active participation at all levels of society and in all its institutions—from grassroots organizing at the local level, to a political process that responds to the needs of all society's members, to a judiciary that protects human rights and prods the political process to live up to its responsibilities. The authors of this book hope that this project will help advance the cause.

Houston, USA T.E. Kleven

Acknowledgements

The editors acknowledge the Law and Society of America for providing the platform that brought the IRC in existence. Special thanks also go to the Centre for Human Rights University of Pretoria, Jurisprudence and International Law Department at the University of Ilorin.

All authors are appreciated for having to work at very close deadlines, the reviewers, copy editors and everyone at Palgrave Macmillan, especially Alina Yurova, for their efforts in ensuring that the publication was on schedule.

Contents

About the Editors

Dr. A.C. Onuora-Oguno LLB (Ilorin), NLS (Nigeria), LLM (Pretoria), LLD (Pretoria) Azubike is both a Solicitor and Advocate of the Nigerian Supreme Court and a researcher with the Centre for Human Rights University of Pretoria, South Africa. He has passion for Child's rights with particular focus on the right to basic education. He was a former clerk in the Office of the Prosecutor International Criminal Court. He has written severally on the subject of education, girl child and other areas of law. Some of the numerous publications have appeared in the Child Abuse Research Journal of South Africa (2015); University of Benin Law Journal (2014) and Human Science Research Council of South Africa Conference Proceedings (2015).

Prof. W.O. Egbewole LLB (OAU), NLS (Nigeria), LLM (OAU), PhD (Ilorin) is Professor of International Law, former Dean at Faculty of Law, University of Ilorin, Nigeria. Egbewole is an expert in judicial studies in Nigeria and a member of the America Society of International Law, Law and Society of America, Nigeria Bar Association and the International Bar Association. Egbewole is a dedicated scholar of recent development in international and astute conference speaker.

Prof. T.E. Kleven LLB (Yale) is Professor of Law at Thurgood Marshall School of Law, Texas Southern University, Houston, Texas. Professor Kleven teaches courses in property, local government, environmental law and public education, and has written extensively in those areas. His recent book, *Equitable Sharing*, posits that a principle of equitable sharing, which requires that all the benefits and detriments of social life be fairly distributed among all society's members, is central to what it means to be a democratic society.

Abbreviations

ACERWC	African Committee of Experts on the Rights and Welfare of the Child
ACHPR	African Commission on Human and Peoples' Rights
ACHPR	The African Charter on Human and Peoples' Rights (Banjul Charter) of 1981
ACRWC	African Charter on the Rights and Welfare of the Child
ASIDI	Accelerated Schools Infrastructure Delivery Initiative
AU	African Union
AUC	African Union Commission
CEDAW	Convention on the Elimination of All Forms of Discrimination Against Women
CFRN	Constitution of the Federal Republic of Nigeria
CPA	Comprehensive Peace Agreement
CRA	Child Rights Act
CSO	Civil Society Organisations
EAC	East African Community
ECOWAS	Economic Community of West African States
EFA	Education For All
EPRC	Education Policy Review Commission Report
FGM	Female Genital Mutilation
GATS	General Agreement on Trade in Services
GCE	General Certificate of Education
GDP	Gross Domestic Product
ICESCR	International Covenant on Economic, Social and Cultural Rights
ICPCR	International Covenant on Civil and Political Rights

JAMB	Joint Admissions and Matriculation Board
LFN	Laws of the Federation of Nigeria
LGBTIA	Lesbian, Gay, Bisexual, Transgender, Intersex, Allies/Asexual
LGBTQ	Lesbian, Gay, Bisexual, Trans and Queer
LPC	Liberia Peace Council (LPC)
Maputo Protocol	Protocol to the African Charter on Rights of Women
MDG	Millennium Development Goal
NABTEB	National Education Certificate and National Business and Technical Examination Certificate
NCLR	Nigerian Constitutional Law Report
NECO	National Education Certificate
NEPAD	New Partnership for Africa's Development
NESRI	National Economic and Social Rights Initiative
NGO	Non-Governmental Organisations
NPEA	National Policy on Education Act
NPE	National Policy on Education
NSCQR	Nigerian Supreme Court Quarterly Reports
NUC	National Universities Commission
OAU	Organisation for African Unity
PEN	Poets, Essayists, Novelists
RBA	Right-Based Education
REC	Regional Economic Communities
SADC	Southern African Development Community
SCNLR	Supreme Court of Nigeria Law Reports
SDG	Sustainable Development Goal (SDG)
SERAP	Social Economic Rights Accountability Project
SIAS	Screening, Identification, Assessment and Support Strategy
SMART	Specific, Measureable, Achievable, Realistic and Time-Bound
SOGIE	Sexual Orientation and Gender Identity and Expression
SSS	Senior Secondary School
TFR	Total Fertility Rate
TRC	Truth and Reconciliation Commission
TRIP	Trade-Related Aspects of Intellectual Property Rights
UBEC	Universal Basic Education Commission
UBE	Universal Basic Education
UDHR	Universal Declaration of Human Rights
UMACIS	Uganda Manufacturers Association Consultancy and Information Services
UNCRC	United Nations Convention on the Rights of the Child
UNESCO	United Nations Educational, Scientific and Cultural Organization
UNGA	United General Assembly

UNHCR	United Nations High Commissioner for Refugees
UNICEF	United Nations International Children Education Fund
UNSC	United Nations Security Council
UPE	Universal Primary Education
UTME	Unified Tertiary Matriculation Examination
WAEC	West Africa Education Certificate
WHO	World Health Organisation
WiLDAF	Women in Law and Development in Africa
WTO	World Trade Organisation

List of Tables

CHAPTER 1

Introduction

Jerusa Ali, W. O. Egbewole and T. E. Kleven

1 Agenda 2063 and the Right to Education

The right to education is clearly articulated in the following African regional human rights treaties: article 17(1) of the African Charter on Human and Peoples' Rights (1981), article 11 of the African Charter on the Rights and Welfare of the Child (1990), and article 12 of the Protocol to the African Charter on Human and Peoples' Rights on the Rights of Women in Africa (2003). Collectively, these human rights instruments have defined a uniquely African approach to the realisation of the right to education that 'must ensure, inter alia, the availability, accessibility, and acceptability of the education provided to children'.[1] In what is known as the *Talibés Case*,[2] the African Committee of Experts on the Rights and Welfare of the Child (ACERWC), drawing on the

J. Ali (✉)
Carleton University, Ottawa, Canada
e-mail: jerusa.ali@carleton.ca

W.O. Egbewole
Faculty of Law, University of Ilorin, Ilorin, Kwara, Nigeria
e-mail: eabdulwahab@unilorin.edu.ng

T.E. Kleven
Texas Southern University, Houston, TX, USA
e-mail: tkleven@tmslaw.tsu.edu

A.C. Onuora-Oguno et al. (eds.), *Education Law, Strategic Policy and Sustainable Development in Africa*, DOI 10.1007/978-3-319-53703-0_1

Children of Nubian Descendants Case,[3] underscore that '[c]hildren have responsibility to their family, society and country under article 31 of the Charter; and, as such, they can discharge these obligations only when they get the necessary education'.[4] The implications are manifold: it places the right to education as a foundational right fundamental to the realisation of other rights, and to the discharge of obligations to family, society, and state.

How does the 'right to education' relate to the African Union's (AU) Agenda 2063? The 'right to education' is not explicitly referenced in the AU's Agenda 2063, yet access to education, particularly for women and girls, is recognised as being central to economic growth and sustainable development priorities. As a development plan, Agenda 2063 follows the creation of economic development strategies that began with the Lagos Plan of Action for the Economic Development of Africa 1980–2000 and culminated with the 2001 New Partnership for Africa's Development (NEPAD). NEPAD created new political, economic, and corporate governance structures resulting in an overly complex relationship between states, regional treaty-based bodies, and international organisations. By the mid-2000s, this vast array of executive, advisory, financial and decentralised institutions and bodies were tasked with redefining African economic self-sufficiency in a globalised world. Recognising that the success of economic and social development required local ownership, Agenda 2063 articulates an inclusive vision of endogenous participation in long-term sustainable development goals grounded in human rights. The right to education and other basic human rights are indirectly referenced throughout the Agenda 2063 Framework Document and in the seven interconnected development aspirations.[5] The contributors to this volume have taken up the challenge to clearly translate and interpret development goals and aspirations, and in so doing, they offer concrete examples of education law and policy.

2 African Perspectives on the Realisation of the Right to Education: Law and Policy

The authors of this book draw from their diverse backgrounds in law, policy, and activism to present original case studies from Nigeria, Ghana, South Africa, Uganda, and Liberia. The essays do not claim to cover the breadth of education legal and policy initiatives that have been taken up by African states and communities since 2013. Rather, they critically outline the challenges and opportunities of the realisation of the right to education as it relates specifically to Agenda 2063. The book is structured in two main parts that cover similar themes about the need for inclusive and participatory development in the realisation of the right to education; part one focuses on law and part two focuses on policy.

Ngozi Chuma-Umeh explores Nigeria's domestic commitment to the realisation of universal primary education and addresses the challenges of the realisation of the right of universal education in a plural, multicultural, federal state. She highlights the importance of focusing educational laws, policies, and resources on every learner, including vulnerable groups such as disabled children, and she concludes that universality and equality ought to be taken up as concomitant policy strategies towards the realisation of the right to education. Ashwanee Budoo advocates a human rights-based approach to budget allocation. She argues that the adoption of the implementing legislation for international and regional human rights law has not signalled the realisation of rights at a local level in human rights-based policies. Ashwanee relies on the provisions of the Maputo Protocol to call for an enhanced budgetary approach to the realisation of rights to education. In a jurisprudential analysis of human rights education by Mohammed Enesi Etudaiye and Muhtar Adeiza Etudaiye, they discuss the mainstreaming of human rights education, according to an endogenous perspective on the right of access to the right 'type' of education. Their focus on Nigerian legal institutions exposes the present-day limits of Human Rights and Constitutional Law education, which has thus far excluded African Jurisprudence and the African nature of human rights and development. Understanding the central role teachers should play in the realisation of access to education, Azubike C. Onuora-Oguno focuses on the welfare of teachers from a human rights law perspective. He draws on sources from international human rights law and policy and advocates for a rights-based approach to 'teacher malaise in Nigeria'. Mariam Adepeju Abdulraheem-Mustapha's contributes an empirical-based case study concerning the barriers to the realisation of the right to education in Nigerian borstal institutions. Her study provides a clear understanding of the limits of the enforceability of constitutional protected socio-economic rights, including the right to education in Nigeria. In concluding part one, Olanike Adelakun-Odewale addresses the need for inclusive education to make the focus on the girl child a priority. Her essay contends that existing cultural and religious norms and practices that favour educating boys over girls are a significant impediment to the realisation of the right to education. She presents a unique theory of 'resource sharing' of available family resources in order to remedy this gender-based practice.

Part two of the book focuses on issues of policy and strategic development. Veronica Fynn Bruey takes up the topic of the human resource development of women and children by providing a critical legal assessment of Liberia's ability to achieve good governance, democracy, and the respect for human rights, justice, and the rule of law. Her chapter outlines numerous social and political setbacks that Liberia has faced as a result of a protracted civil war, many of which have stalled Liberia's 10-year implementation plan for Agenda 2063. Michael Addaney compares the educational policies of Ghana and South Africa from a macro and micro perspective and emphasises the importance of local ownership of Agenda 2063. Sylvia Ivy Tayebwa critiques Ugandan education policies for failing to encourage the realisation of social and economic rights. She places access to education as a central tenet to the Africa 2063 vision of long-term social and economic development. In representing the minority divide and calling for greater respect for all irrespective of race, colour, or sexual orientation, David. N.C. Ikpo critically evaluates links between social exclusion and the existing Nigerian education legal framework. He evaluates practices and policies that have failed to address the effects of negative prejudices, such as homophobia.

The book's last chapter by Solomon Tekle Abegaz provides human rights perspectives on maternal and child health outcomes. He argues that improving women's access to primary education is key to reducing maternal and child mortality. Significantly, he links the right to education and the right to health through a discussion of international and regional human rights treaties.

Notes

1. Decision on the communication submitted by the Centre for Human Rights (University of Pretoria) and La Rencontre Africaine pour la Défense des Droits de l'Homme (Sénégal) versus the Government of Senegal, Decision No. 003/Com/001/2012, done at the 23rd Ordinary Session held in Addis Ababa, Ethiopia, on 15 April 2014, at 13, para 46 (African Centre for Democracy and Human Rights Studies Online Library), available at: http://

www.acdhrs.org/wp-content/uploads/2015/10/DECISION-CAEDBE_DSA-ACE-64-1047.15_English.pdf (African Centre for Democracy and Human Rights Studies Online Library 2014).

2. Ibid. Talibé is the Francophone transliteration of a student of qur'anic studies in Arabic.
3. Decision on the communication submitted by the IHRDA and OSJI (on behalf of children of Nubian descent in Kenya) versus the Government of Kenya, No. 002/2009, done at the 17th Ordinary Session held in Addis Ababa, Ethiopia, on 22 March 2011 (African Union 2011).
4. Decision on the communication submitted by The Centre for Human Rights (University of Pretoria) and La Rencontre Africaine pour la Défense des Droits de l'Homme (Sénégal) versus the Government of Senegal, Decision No. 003/Com/001/2012, Done at the 23rd Ordinary Session held in Addis Ababa, Ethiopia, on 15 April 2014, at 13, para 46 (African Centre for Democracy and Human Rights Studies Online Library), available at: http://www.acdhrs.org/wp-content/uploads/2015/10/DECISION-CAEDBE_DSA-ACE-64-1047.15_English.pdf (African Centre for Democracy and Human Rights Studies Online Library 2014).
5. African Union Commission, 'Agenda 2063 Framework Document: The Africa We Want', available at: http://www.fasngo.org/assets/files/25%20GIMAC/Final%20docs/Report%20of%20the%20Commission.pdf (African Union Commission 2016).

Bibliography

African Centre for Democracy and Human Rights Studies Online Library. 2014. Decision on the Communication Submitted by the Centre for Human Rights (University of Pretoria) and La Rencontre Africaine pour la Défense des Droits de l'Homme (Sénégal) versus the Government of Senegal, Decision No. 003/Com/001/2012, done at the 23rd Ordinary Session held in Addis Ababa, Ethiopia, on 15 April 2014, at 13, para 46. http://www.acdhrs.org/wp-content/uploads/2015/10/DECISION-CAEDBE_DSA-ACE-64-1047.15_English.pdf. Accessed 3 Nov 2016.

African Union Commission. 2016. Agenda 2063: The Africa We Want. http://agenda2063.au.int/en/documents/agenda-2063-africa-we-want-popular-version-final-edition. Accessed 3 Nov 2016.

African Union. 2011. Decision on the Communication Submitted by the Institute for Human Rights and Development in Africa (IHRDA) and the Open Society Justice Initiative (OSJI) (on behalf of children of Nubian descent in Kenya) versus the Government of Kenya, No. 002/2009, done at the 17th Ordinary Session held in Addis Ababa, Ethiopia, on 22 March 2011.

Authors' Biography

Jerusa Ali BSc (Georgetown), MA (Keele), LLM (Nottingham) is a PhD candidate in Law and Legal Studies at, Carleton University, Ottawa, Canada. As part of her doctoral project, she recently completed fieldwork as a scholar in residence at the Department of Jurisprudence and International Law, University of Ilorin, Nigeria.

Prof. W.O Egbewole LLB (Hons) (Ife), BL (Lagos) NLS (Nigeria), LLM (OAU), PhD (Ilorin) is Professor of International Law, former Dean at Faculty of Law, University of Ilorin, Nigeria. Egbewole is an expert in judicial studies in Nigeria and a member of the America Society of International Law, Law and Society of America, Nigeria Bar Association and the International Bar Association. He is currently the Newsletter Editor of Negligence and Damages Committee of the International Bar Association.

Prof. T.E Kleven LLB (Yale) is Professor of Law at Thurgood Marshall School of Law, Texas Southern University, Houston, Texas. Professor Kleven teaches courses in property, local government, environmental law and public education, and has written extensively in those areas. His recent book, *Equitable Sharing*, posits that a principle of equitable sharing, which requires that all the benefits and detriments of social life be fairly distributed among all society's members, is central to what it means to be a democratic society.

CHAPTER 2

Issues of Human Right to Basic Education and Equality of Educational Opportunity in Africa: A Case Study of Nigeria

Ngozi Chuma-Umeh

1 Introduction

The African region has been slow in stirring commitment towards the development of equality of opportunity in education for deserving learners and peoples in Africa. In order to address part of the constraints towards the realisation of the targeted Millennium Development Goals of 2015 in Africa, and as part of achieving the African Union's (AU) Agenda 2063, examining the issues concerning the equalisation of educational opportunity on the continent is paramount. The achievement of universal primary education was among the critical goals that needed to be engaged with in guiding plans and programmes of states towards national development in the long run. This is no doubt traceable to an appreciation of the importance of realising the right to education, which

N.C.-Umeh (✉)
Imo State University, Owerri, Imo State, Nigeria
e-mail: umehngozi@gmail.com

N.C.-Umeh
University of Pretoria, Pretoria, South Africa

A.C. Onuora-Oguno et al. (eds.), *Education Law, Strategic Policy and Sustainable Development in Africa*, DOI 10.1007/978-3-319-53703-0_2

has often been described as being central to human and national development.[1] As a result, the significance of creating equal opportunity for all learners in Nigeria, albeit in an African context, cannot be undermined.

The visibility in protecting equal educational opportunity under African regional human rights instruments is considered piecemeal. The African Charter on Human and Peoples Rights (ACHPR)[2] provides for the right to education as equal right to education for everyone in article 17. In doing so, it universalises formal equality by seeking to suggest that unequals be treated alike. However article 18(4) of the ACHPR impliedly addressed the issue of equality of opportunity by requiring states to take 'special measures of protection' (emphasis mine) that are responsive to the 'physical and moral needs of the aged and disabled persons'. In other words, article 18(4) introduced the opportunity to consider the varying needs of the aged and 'disabled persons' with regard to the provision of equal opportunity in the enjoyment of human rights, like the right to education. But the ACHPR failed to extend similar protection to other vulnerable groups as well as individuals who equally require equal educational opportunity in education.

However, the African region sought to remedy the oversight and later extended equality of opportunity in education of children and women when it adopted the African Charter on the Rights and Welfare of the Child (African Children's Charter),[3] and more recently the Protocol to the African Charter on Human and Peoples' Rights on the Rights of Women in Africa (African Women's Protocol).[4] The African Children's Charter follows the provision of the African Charter by the use of the words 'special measures of protection' while the protocol on women specifically made reference to 'equality of opportunity and access in the sphere of education and training'.[5]

In spite of this gradual visibility of the provision of equal educational opportunity for vulnerable groups such as the aged, disabled persons, children and women under the African regional system, concerns still exist. One is that the manner as well as factors to be considered in providing this protection was not specified. Secondly, the rest of the population who do not come within the protected categories seem to have been left at the whims and caprices of national jurisdictions.[6] Indeed, the oversight has serious implications for learners in Nigeria and within the region as it suggests a lack of awareness as to the urgency of securing equal opportunity in education for all learners in Africa.

Holistically, achieving equal opportunity in education for all learners in Africa must consider the social background, environment and socio-economic factors of all learners, if we are to realise the AU's Agenda 2063. What is important is to appreciate that securing equal opportunity in education cannot be assuaged by the rhetoric of rights to a selected category of citizens. It also cannot be assuaged without an articulation of the methods of implementation and distribution. The method of distribution must, of necessity, involve discriminatory distribution of educational resources in a compensatory manner. It must also be articulated to envisage all citizens that genuinely deserve it.

A commitment towards achieving equality of opportunity is synonymous with seriously taking the manner of distribution and redistribution critically. Particularly in the Nigerian context where there is huge socio-economic inequality, the realisation of equal opportunity in education for the least favoured in the society under considerations of learner's background, socio-economic and environmental factors is vital to achieve equality for all learners in Nigeria. Within this premise, Nigeria is used in this study, to reflect the region's scenario with reference to challenges regarding the provision of equal basic educational opportunity.

Nigeria is considered based on the reasoning that Nigeria has diverse linguistic groups, internally displaced persons, different cultures and a large population. Furthermore, Nigeria has an underdeveloped economy, poverty is prevalent and literacy level is very low. Comparably, it has been found that Nigeria shares most of its developmental problems with most African countries,[7] even though some African states like South Africa have begun to enact progressive education laws and valuable decisions. Reports also indicate that literacy level in most African states is still low.[8] Out of the 52 countries in Africa, only 10% has a literacy level that is above 85% while more than 35% has a literacy level of less than 50%.[9] Granted that literacy level may not be a perfect measure of educational results, but it is considerably compelling for international comparisons.

Specifically, the Federal Government of Nigeria, in a bid to further the Millennium Development Goal of achieving universal basic education for all and to consolidate its National Policy on Education, established through an Act of the National Assembly, the Universal Basic Education Act (UBE) in 2004. The objective of the UBE is that at the end of 6 years of primary school and 3 years of junior secondary school, every child in Nigeria must have acquired the relevant knowledge and skills needed for socio-economic independence and be able to contribute to national development. Basically, the UBE Act provides the legal framework for the implementation of compulsory free basic education in Nigeria. This is in view of the fact that the Nigerian Constitution failed to specifically guarantee the right to education. The vision of Nigeria's Federal Government in relation to its educational policy and the UBE Act can be seen as a move in the direction of equalisation of educational opportunities as it provides at a minimum the compulsory level to which all children in Nigeria would be educated.

However, the provision of physical access to education is not considered sufficient in terms of realising equal opportunity in basic education. It will therefore be argued that the UBE Act like the Constitution failed to provide a clear approach on how educational resources are to be distributed, in view of the realities of learners' socio-economic and diverse background for instance. This lack of a definition of a method of distribution constitutes a serious omission and poses a great challenge to the commitment of realising the right to equal education for all. The situation is even made worse when juxtaposed with the Constitution's presumption of equality of status which discounts concrete inequality in the scheme of distribution.

This chapter has four sections: the first section—the present section—is the introduction. The second section highlights the challenges that Nigeria faces in the provision of equal educational opportunity for all learners, and it also analyses pertinent concepts such as formal equality and substantive equality. Section three further advances Nigeria's approach regarding the provision of equal opportunity in education for all learners. Section four is the conclusion.

2 The Enormity of the Challenge

Presently in Nigeria, everyone seeks education. The desire is either for oneself or for one's other immediate or distant relations. This is because education has been identified in numerous literature as a sure means of socio-economic participation and mobility.[10] For instance, since after the Nigerian civil war, most educated people were able to secure jobs, skills or better social positions relatively easier than their uneducated counterparts. Thus, acquired skills, qualifications and certificates became equivalent to meal tickets.[11] Having identified education as an equaliser of opportunities among societies, the Nigerian government saw mass education as the best starting point for the achievement of its development objectives. To be able to provide equal educational opportunities for all its citizens, the Nigerian government adopted the National Policy on Education in 1977.[12]

Although the Federal Government of Nigeria stated in the policy that government will multiply and make educational and training facilities adequate and accessible to all citizens, for the purpose of providing equal educational opportunity, neither the 1977 issue of the National Policy nor the revised editions or even the present edition entrenched as a value what the state should do to advance or realise equality of opportunity in basic education.[13] It is therefore feared that since states of the federation have started to implement the National Policy on Education without a defined implementation process, each state will contrive and apply its own method. The unintended consequence will be multifaceted interpretations and practice of equal educational opportunity which might not show strong convergence with the AU's Agenda of a prosperous Africa based on inclusive growth and sustainable development.[14]

Considering the fact that the objective of the Nigerian National Policy on Education is to develop a self-reliant, free, egalitarian and democratic society with full bright opportunities for all citizens,[15] a corresponding normative ethic ought to be adopted in the distribution and redistribution of educational resources in order to achieve equal educational opportunity. In this regard, the educational resources contemplated include adequate manpower, equipment/facilities, good environment and structures, as well as funding. Thus, equal educational opportunity in this study is imagined as making the provision and process of education equal in order to ensure that each learner is provided the needed accommodations required to acquire education.[16]

Indeed, it could be argued that there are various interpretations of the meaning of equality of educational opportunity.[17] On the other hand, some authors have suggested that it might mean nothing at all.[18] Our purpose is not to undertake a detailed exploration of the various meanings of equality of opportunity.[19] Rather, the purpose is to align this discourse with the ideas of non-discrimination and equality in the context of education. The study is particularly interested in exploring understandings of formal and substantive equality in relation to the demand of equal educational opportunity, so as to secure equality of outcome or benefit.

Ultimately, equality has emerged as a fundamental principle for attending to the discrimination and marginalisation suffered by individuals or groups in the scheme of distribution.[20] Meanwhile, it does not have an agreed definition,[21] but formal equality and substantive equality approaches have become known as the core counterpoints, with each approach contending to remedy inequality in different modes and proportions.[22]

2.1 Formal Equality

Under the 1999 Constitution of the Federal Republic of Nigeria (Constitution), the idea of equality is one of its founding values.[23] To avoid inequalities between different categories of individuals in the society, the Constitution provides in section 42 that:

1. A citizen of Nigeria of a particular community, ethnic group, place of origin, sex, religion or political opinion, shall not by reason only that he is such a person:
   (a) be subjected either expressly by, or in the practical application of, any law in force in Nigeria or any executive or administrative action of the government, to disabilities or restrictions to which citizens of Nigeria of other communities, ethnic groups, place of origin, sex, religious or political opinion are not made subject; or
   (b) be accorded either expressly by, or in the practical application of, any law in force in Nigeria or any such executive or administrative action, any privilege or advantage that is not accorded to citizens of Nigeria of other communities, either groups, place of origin, sex, religion or political opinions.[24]
2. No citizen of Nigeria shall be subjected to any disability or deprivation merely by reason of the circumstances of his birth.[25]

Accordingly, a law or conduct violates the equal protection clause under the Nigerian Constitution if a differentiation not accorded to any Nigerian is made, even when it is ethically appropriate or when a rational purpose demands that differentiations be made. This provision under the Nigerian Constitution regarding equality is also characteristic of formal equality traceable to the equality conceptions of historical international human rights instruments.[26]

Formal equality according to Albertyn and Goldblatt assumes that individuals are equal and that differential conduct or idea is always inexorably suspect or unreasonable.[27] This presumption of equality of status often masks practical inequalities that exist among categories of persons in the society. It ignores, for instance, that learners are heterogeneous with respect to social and historical background, geographical development, economic status, school type, sex and disability. Formal equality does not appreciate human difference and perceives positive differentiation or discrimination in favour of vulnerable persons or groups as discriminatory and inconsistent with the right to equality. It is a conception of equality that does not consider the 'all fingers are not equal' mantra which appreciates the fact that all persons are not similarly situated.

Formal equality seeks to apply the same standards to everyone regardless of any dissimilar impact on certain individuals and groups. Because of its non-recognition of difference and assimilatory characteristics, formal equality would be inappropriate to recognise the legitimacy of treating individuals unequally, as it were, in order to realise equal educational opportunities. It turns out to be a problem when educational resources are distributed equally to learners of unequal development level or unequally to beneficiaries of equal development status. In essence, a fairly greater attention to compensate the less advantaged to benefit equally distributed educational resources as much as the dominant majority is not usually envisaged.

2.2 Substantive Equality

Against the backdrop of formal equality, substantive equality has the prospect to remedy the effects of the formal equality model. For Day and Brodsky,

> A substantive model of equality, which considers inequality in conditions and imbalances of power among groups, anticipates a deeper level of change. It posits that the functioning of institutions and the structure of relationships among groups must change significantly, and that working towards equality is a process to transformation, not a minor adjustment.[28]

Day and Brodsky separate substantive equality from formal equality, which according to them implies that

> Existing frameworks are acceptable, except that there are occasional incidents of prejudice and perhaps some marginalisation of certain groups. The situation is to conciliate between individuals when there are incidents of prejudice and to ensure that all groups are included in existing institutions by being treated the same as those that are already inside. In other words, this version of equality anticipates little change in the functioning of institutions.[29]

Contrariwise, substantive equality appreciates that genuine equality can only be realised if regard is given to the historical, social and economic circumstances of individuals in the distribution of educational resources. It imagines that barriers within the sociopolitical that prevent individuals from enjoying the right to equality are dismantled, and the responsibility to do this lies with the state general education system and not the learners. Substantive equality does not assume that everyone has the same need and the same future to be non-discriminatorily satisfied using similar measure. It therefore goes beyond similar treatment to consider justified differentiation in order to remedy past and systematic inequalities.

The difference between substantive equality and formal equality can be likened and explored in the light of Wollheim's argument concerning 'everyone having an equal right to education' and 'everyone having a right to equal education'.[30] The proposition that 'everyone has an equal right to education' countenances that 'what' education each individual has right to may be laid down by society or law as given without specifying the criterion.[31] This is hardly a realistic objective.

The second proposition that 'everyone has a right to equal education' seems to imply that everyone has a natural right to the same educational facilities and resources in relation to processes and procedures enjoyable according to individual needs. This second interpretation appears realistic and amenable to a heterogeneous society like Nigeria and other African states as it acknowledges positive discrimination and consequently confers legitimacy to substantive equality.

Philosophically, the notion of substantive equality ultimately appeals to the idea of distributing the benefits and detriments of democratic societies in a discriminatory and compensatory manner.[32] It calls for transcending conceptions of equality which require that socio-economic positions are open to all regardless of difference. In responding to both socio-economic exclusions, substantive quality seeks to bring about the substance of what Thomas Kleven, in his moral theory of social justice, has called 'equitable sharing' for a truly democratic society.[33] For Kleven, the concept of equitable sharing is imagined as a social ideal that expects the sociopolitical environment to take everyone's interest into account and fairly accommodate everyone's needs.

Kleven's point is that the imperative of securing self-determination and equality values is foundational to any democracy, which in essence requires that all aspects of social life be equitably shared among all society's members. This he further situates in the belief of the inherent equality of all people. Therefore, implicit in Kleven's argument is the appeal to an egalitarian distribution. It emphasises the need for a distribution and redistribution of the goods of social life in accordance with people's needs in order to enable all participate inclusively.[34] Ultimately, responding to people's needs require the eradication of the formal equality model so as to embrace substantive equality. A distribution and redistribution through substantive equality speaks to systematic inequality, which would otherwise be left untouched by mere equal treatment or formal equality.[35]

3 Paradox of School Creation and the Reduction of Inequality in Nigeria

There exists a dilemma in the creation and reduction of inequality through educational equality in Nigeria. Therefore, the argument is that the recognition of disparity in the plurality of individuals precipitates the ground for different and unequal treatment during the allocation of educational resources. The Compulsory Universal Primary Education Programme is a grandiose education scheme in Nigeria to equalise educational opportunity for all citizens.[36] It is considered a political interpretation of the concept of equality with a view to satisfy the legal and formal conceptions attached to constitutional right of all citizens to equal and adequate educational opportunities at all levels.[37]

It is, however, observed that the magnanimous provisions under Nigeria's 2004 UBE Act and the Revised National Policy on Education of 2013 (NPE) have not resulted in the imagined equitable objective envisaged. The UBE Act and the NPE have not enjoyed popular commendations as a result of the discrimination implicit in their contrivance and issuance. First, comparable equal achievement or outcome, difference in individual abilities and capacities, social and family background, parents' economic status, geographical location, language, religion and culture were not contemplated. Second, upon execution heed was not paid to the individual needs of each learner.

Recognising and addressing the differences in individuals as those mentioned above is necessary for attaining equality of educational opportunity. It is also observed that assessments and examinations as a means of equalising education opportunities are biased towards strict formal practices and Western urban culture developed elsewhere. Thus, learners in the rural areas or from different socio-economic and cultural backgrounds may experience school as largely an introduction of foreign culture, directly or indirectly presented as superior to their own.[38] This type of conception implicitly sees the school as perpetuating 'hierarchical citizenship'. One feels that this fact is not unconnected with the *Boko Haram* sect conception of education in Nigeria.

Boko Haram is an Islamic extremist group in north-eastern Nigeria. The group's name *Boko Haram* is a Hausa statement, which upon translation into English means 'western education is sinful'. The group is opposed to everything that is of Western origin, especially Western education ideologies and systems. This also happened earlier in the northern part of Nigeria. According to Fafunwa, parents refused to send their children to school for fear of the children being converted to Christianity while they were Muslims.[39] The obvious dilemma in this conception of education can also be blamed on the absence of appropriate ideology regarding the normative values animating equality in education. Even in the face of Nigeria's compulsory universal primary education, it is not likely that equality of opportunity will be achieved.

The general implication is that educational syllabus, arrangements and administration do not adequately represent the interest of each learner. Thus, the need for some enlightenment and some other flexible modes of assessment and examination as a means of evaluating and equalising opportunities for learners ought to be articulated, so that the whole population can take up the opportunity of access to school, which is provided to everyone under the recognition that there are different educational needs of individuals. The school should expose learners to challenges commensurate with their identities as well as abilities, and learners should be made to appreciate the criteria for examination grades and assessments as a means of offering equal educational chance.

If equal participation in education is to have any meaning as a means towards equality of educational opportunity, there must also be an opportunity for different groups and individuals to decide what education shall be about. It is considered expedient that barriers within the sociopolitical environment which influence and limits variables to equality of educational opportunity should be identified and eliminated accordingly, for the realisation of equal life chances. Educational resources ought to be presented in a manner that harmonises the background of learners of all classes.

The premise is that inequalities in education should be remedied. But there often exists a serious paradoxical problem in the equality interpretations adopted for this needed remedy. Almost every African country engages in educational reform. However, the main thrust is usually in the direction of closing widening disparities in access to education without intensifying normative measures for achieving equality in education in law and in fact. While South Africa is an example of an African State that is decisively moving away from the conception of equality as formal equality, it can also be seen to illuminate normative conceptions of equality in their constitutional text within which all statutory documents and jurisprudence are grounded.[40]

Equality as conceived within the jurisdiction of South Africa has been described as a pervasive value and right under the South African Constitution.[41] It has also been articulated as the Constitution's key transformative value and right in the attainment of inclusive citizenship.[42] The admirable content of the right to equality under the South African Constitution and the extent to which it subscribes to inclusive citizenship and equal opportunity for every citizen can be gleaned and confirmed from the South African Constitutional Court's equality jurisprudence.

The Constitutional Court of South Africa has in several cases reiterated that the type of equality contemplated under section 9 of the Constitution is substantive equality and not just formal equality.[43] The Court's exacting approach to the determination of unfair discrimination has been stated to be particularly instructive of the Constitutional Court's approach to substantive equality.[44]

Although the Constitutional Court has borrowed its equality jurisprudence from foreign jurisdictions such as Canada and India, it has formulated its own standards and stages for determining discrimination in any circumstance in the popular case of *Harksen v Lane NO & Others.*[45] In the highlighted case, the Constitutional Court enunciated the relevant stages for determining unfair discrimination and unequal treatment against individuals. This as summarised by Ngwena[46] involves: whether there is a reasonable and legitimate justification for the policy, law or practice; whether the differentiation amounts to unfair discrimination; and if unfair discrimination is established, whether it can be justified in terms of the limitation clause under section 36 of the Constitution.

Additionally, the Court emphasised that differentiation amounted to unfair discrimination if it impairs the human dignity of the individual or group concerned.[47] On this basis, the major factor which rendered discrimination unfair was obviously the effect or impact it had on the individual or group concerned[48] and in determining the impact of discrimination, the Constitutional Court considered the following factors cumulatively relevant: (a) the position of the complaint and whether the complainant belongs to a social group that have suffered patterns of disadvantage, (b) the nature of the provision or power and the purpose it seeks to achieve and whether the provision or power is intended to achieve a worthy societal goal, and (c) the extent to which the discrimination has affected the rights or interests of the complainant and whether it has led to an impairment of the fundamental human dignity of the complainant.[49]

Indeed, this legal and juridical approach to equality within the South African jurisdiction has the attainment of substantive equality and human dignity as its objective. It not only suggests a commitment to recognising each person's worth as a human being, regardless of differences.[50] It also signifies a constitutional commitment to remedying systematic subordination and marginalisation in order to attain a type of equality which recognises human difference and inclusive citizenship. It demonstrates a significant convergence between the vision of equality of the South African Constitution and that of some foreign jurisdictions such as Canada and India that have moved to establish admirable legal and juridical background towards the attainment of concrete equality.

Even though one can argue that there are still gaps in relation to meeting the learning needs of every learner within the South African jurisdiction, the major problem within the South African system one thinks is with implementation and conduct of the state education officials as exemplified in the facts of most relevant cases identified.[51] However, the idea behind exemplifying South Africa's equality jurisprudence lies in informing useful achievements that can be emulated and mistakes that must be avoided. Care must be taken to avoid certain practices, submissions and decisions that portray attributes of restrictive equality which may serve to attenuate rather than assist in developing African states equality jurisprudence including Nigeria as far as realising equal opportunity in education for all is concerned within the region.

Comparatively, Nigeria and other African states that are yet to give positive interpretations and expressions to equality as a way of offering concrete opportunities for the attainment of equal educational opportunity can emulate the inspiring principles inherent in South Africa's equality jurisprudence. Since differences exist among learners, it is advocated that differences in treatment should be applied so that equal benefit may be realised.

4 Conclusion

The implication of the observation in this chapter is that equal distribution of educational resources by the state will enhance the opportunities for Nigerian learners as Africans to get more education and more from education in terms of access and equality. Emphasis is on schools offering quality and inclusive education in terms of achievements and outcomes. Again, differentiation should apply when educational resources are distributed to schools. It should be such that the method of distribution compensates the disadvantaged positions of schools and less advantaged learners. Each school whether in urban or rural, regular or special should offer educational training and resources in a comparably related manner.

In the Nigerian context, there is an obvious need for a conceptual definition regarding inclusive equality in education—at least one that is expressive and practicable. In popular right concept of equality of educational opportunity, no education of a people would tantamount to denial of educational opportunity—a right which is constitutional.[52] However, it has been an uphill task entrenching and achieving the somewhat universalisable concept of equality due to the failure of the Nigerian ruling class to internalise, establish and effectuate the prerequisites for successful implementation. Such neglect only brings about the stagnation of education and conscious denial of the rights in education to most learners and individuals in the society.

The idea that we are all created equal in spite of the apparent inequality within Nigeria's educational system and in the larger social context ignites considerable concern so much so that it is most difficult if not impossible to contemplate an education system that does not pay attention to the status, background and circumstances of learners. What should be really obtained is the substantive equality model where educational resources are distributed in a relevant disproportionate form. Such a method ameliorates the position of the underprivileged learners and strengthens capacities for implementation and attainment of vision 2063 in line with the shared aspiration of good governance, respect for human rights, justice and rule of law. It would also mean that each learner will be well educated, and no learner subjected to any form of discrimination.

Notes

1. UN Committee on Economic, Social and Cultural Rights (CESCR), General Comment No. 13, The Right to Education (Art. 13 of the Covenant), Adopted at the Twenty-first Session of the Economic, Social and Cultural Rights December 1999, E/C.12/1999/10; Kishore Singh, 'Promotion of the equality of opportunity in education' Report of the Special Rapporteur on the right to education (2011) United Nations General Assembly (UNGA) A/HRC/17/29.
2. Adopted on 27 June 1981, and entered into force on 21 October 1986.
3. Adopted on 11 July 1990, and entered into force on 29 November 1999.
4. Adopted on 11 July 2003, and entered into force on 25 November 2005.
5. See article 11 of the African Charter on the Rights and Welfare of the Child (n. 3 above) and article 12 of the African Charter on Human and Peoples' Rights on the rights of Women in Africa (African Women's Protocol) (n. 4 above).
6. For example, internally displaced persons, national minorities, indigenous people, HIV positive/Aids victims etc.
7. Charity Ojogwu, "The challenges of attaining millennium development goals in education in Africa by 2015", College *Student Journal* 43 (2009): 375 (Ojogwu 2009).
8. Central Intelligence Agency World Fact book (2015), http://www.cia.gov/library/publications/the-world-factbook/fields/2103.html#136, accessed 1 November 2016; The African Economist (2013), Ranking of African Countries by literacy rate, http://www.theafricaneconomist.com/ranking-of-african-countries-by-literacy-rate-zimbabwe-no-1#, accessed 29 October 2016 (Central Intelligence Agency World Fact book 2015; The African Economist 2013).
9. As above.
10. Patience U. Enaibe, "Need to promote women education and participation in politics for sustainable national development", *International Journal of Educational Research and Development* 19 (2012): 1; Peter O Ejikeme, "Education as key to national development: Issues, challenges and the way forward", *Journal of Humanities and the Social Sciences* 6 (2014): 20; Noah Berger & Peter Fisher, "A well educated workforce is key to State prosperity" (2013), *Economic Analysis and Research Network*. Washington DC: Economic policy institute, accessed 29 October, 2016, http://hdl.voced.edu.au/10707/294721 (Enaibe 2012; Ejikeme 2014; Berger and Fisher 2013).
11. Chima B. Iwuchukwu, "The Myths and Realities of equal educational opportunities in Nigeria" (PhD thesis, University of Nigeria Nsukka, 1988).

12. Nigeria National Policy on Education (1977).
13. Nigeria has adopted quite a number of policies on education. The first was the 1977 edition, which was successively followed by a revised 2nd, 3rd, and 4th editions of 1981, 1988 and 2004 respectively as well as a draft 2007 5th edition. The 2013 NPE is the 6th and latest edition, representing 10 years of basic education, 3 years of senior secondary education and 4 years of university education of 2013.
14. See the Aspiration 1 of the Vision and African Union Aspirations for 2063 as compiled in the African Union Commission Framework Document (2015) v.
15. See Nigeria National Policy on Education 6th Edition (2013) section 1; The Constitution of the Federal Republic of Nigeria as Amended, 1999 (Nigerian Constitution) section 18 (Nigeria National Policy on Education 2013; Constitution of the Federal Republic of Nigeria as Amended 1999).
16. Jones A. Akinpelu, *An introduction to philosophy of education* (London: Macmillan, 1981), 717 (Akinpelu 1981).
17. Christopher Jencks, "Whom must we treat equally for educational opportunity to be equal", *Ethics* 98 (1988): 518; Frankel Charles, "Equality of Opportunity", Ethics 81(3) (1971): 191.
18. As above.
19. Andrew Mason provides an insight into the different understandings of equality of opportunity, see Andrew Mason, "Equality of opportunities: Old and new", *Ethics 111* (2001): 761 (Mason 2001).
20. Charles G. Ngwena, "Equality for people with disabilities in the workplace: an overview of the emergence of disability as a human right issue", *Journal of Juridical Science* 29 (2004): 167 (Ngwena 2004).
21. Louis P. Pojman and Robert Westmoreland, *Equality: Selected readings* (Oxford: Oxford University Press, 1997), 1 (Pojman and Robert 1997).
22. Charles Ngwena, (n. 20 above) 169.
23. Preamble to the Nigerian Constitution.
24. Section 42 (1) (a) & (b) of the Nigerian Constitution.
25. As above, section (2)
26. For instance, the United Nations Charter is a treaty that established the United Nations and professes to protect the interest of *all* men from fear and want adopted the formal equality approach. The Charter was signed on 26th June 1945. The Universal Declaration on Human rights (UDHR) also conceive equality in terms of formal equality; Adopted 10 December 1948, GA Res. 217 A (III) Art 1 & 2 expresses that *all* human beings are born free and equal and endowed with reason. The International Bill of Human Rights, comprising of International Covenant on Civil and Political Rights (ICCPR) and International

Covenant on Economic, Social and Cultural Rights (ICESCR) similarly recognise equality for all persons as formal equality, Adopted by the UN General Assembly on 16th December 1966 G.A. Res 2200 A (XXI).
27. Cathi Albertyn & Beth Goldblatt, "Facing the challenge of transformation: Difficulties in the development of an indigenous jurisprudence of equality" *South African Journal on Human Rights* 14 (1998): 248 (Albertyn and Goldblatt 1998).
28. Shelagh Day & Gwen Brodsky, "The duty to accommodate: Who will benefit?" *Canadian Bar Review* 75 (1996): 433 (Day and Brodsky 1996).
29. As above.
30. Richard Wollheim, "Equality" *Proceedings of the Aristotelian Society* (1955–56) 56:281–300. Reprinted as "Equality and equal rights", in *Justice and social policy: A collection of essays*, ed. Frederick A. Olafson (Englewood Cliffs: Spectrum books, 1961), 111 (Wollheim 1961).
31. Drawn from a reading of Wollheim as above.
32. Thomas Kleven, *Equitable Sharing: Distributing the benefits and detriments of democratic society* (Maryland: Lexington books, 2014) (Kleven 2014).
33. As above.
34. As above, 7–21.
35. CG Ngwena, "*Western Cape Forum for intellectual Disability V Government of the Republic of South Africa*: A case study of contradictions in inclusive education" *African Disability Rights Yearbook* 1 (2013): 139 (Ngwena 2013).
36. See Nigeria National Policy on education, 6th edition (2013) Section 2 para 12. See also Nigeria Universal Basic Education Act, 2004 (Nigeria National Policy on education 2013; Nigeria Universal Basic Education Act 2004).
37. See section 18 of the Nigerian Constitution.
38. Kjell Eide, 'Some key problems of equality in education' education', in *Planning education for reducing inequalities: International Institute for Educational Planning*, ed. Mark Blaug *&* Zsuzsa Ferge (Paris: UNESCO Press, 1981), 95 (Eide 1981).
39. Aliu B. Fafunwa, *History of Education in Nigeria* 1974. (London: Macmillan 1974), 48 (Fafunwa 1974).
40. See equality guarantee under section 9 of the 1996 Constitution of the Republic of South Africa on protection against discrimination. See also the Employment Equity Act (EEA) of 1998 and the Promotion of Equality and Prevention of Unfair Discrimination Act 2000 (The Equality Act). The EEA provides protection against discrimination in the workplace for a long list of protected groups and enables affirmative action in relation to

designated groups, while the Equality Act provides comprehensive protection against unfair discrimination in the public and private spheres, apart from where the EEA is applicable. I am grateful to Sandra Fredman for this information (Employment Equity Act 1998; Promotion of Equality and Prevention of Unfair Discrimination Act 2000).

41. Charles Ngwena, (n. 35 above) 152.
42. Cathi Albertyn & Beth Goldblatt, (n. 27 above) 249–250; Marius Pieterse, 'What do we mean when we talk about transformative constitutionalism? *South African Public Law* 20 (2005): 155 (Pieterse 2005).
43. For instance, *President of the Republic of South Africa & Another v Hugo* 1997 (6) BCLR 708 (CC) para 41; *Prinsloo v Vander der Linde & Another* 1997 (6) BCLR 759 (CC); *Harksen v Lane NO and Others* 1998 (1) SA 300 (CC) para 53, *National Coalition for Gay and Lesbian Equality & Others v Minister of Home Affairs & Others* 2000 (1) BCLR 39 (CC) para 62; *Minister of Finance v Van Heerden* 2004 (6) SA 121 (CC) para 26.
44. Charles Ngwena, (n. 35 above) 153.
45. *Harksen v Lane NO and Others* 1998 (1) SA 300 (CC).
46. Charles Ngwena (n. 35 above) 153.
47. *Harksen v Lane NO and Others* (n. 45 above) para 51.
48. As above.
49. *Harksen v Lane NO and Others* (n. 45 above) para 51–53.
50. Prinsloo v Van der Linde 1997 6 BCLR 759 (CC) para 31.
51. *Western Cape Forum for Intellectual Disability v Government of the Republic of South Africa & Another* 2011 5 SA 87 (WCC); *Tripartite Steering Committee and Another v Minister of Basic Education and Others* (2015) 3 ALL SA 718.
52. See section 18 of the Nigerian Constitution.

Bibliography

Books

Akinpelu, Jones A. 1981. *An Introduction to Philosophy of Education*. London: Macmillan.

Fafunwa, Aliu Babatunde. 1974. *History of Education in Nigeria*. London: Macmillan.

Kleven, Thomas. 2014. *Equitable Sharing: Distributing the Benefits and Detriments of Democratic Society*. Maryland: Lexington Books.

Pojman, Louis P., and Westmoreland Robert. 1997. *Equality: Selected Readings*. Oxford: Oxford University Press.

Chapters of a Book

Eide, Kjell. 1981. Some Key Problems of Equality in Education. In *Planning Education for Reducing Inequalities: International Institute for Educational Planning*, ed. Mark Blaug and Zsuzsa Ferge, 95–115. Paris: UNESCO Press.

Wollheim, Richard. 1961. 'Equality' *Proceedings of the Aristotelian Society* (1955–1956) 56: 281–300. Reprinted as 'Equality and Equal Rights' in Frederick A Olafson *Justice and Social Policy: A Collection of Essays*, ed. Frederick A Olafson, 111–127. Englewood Cliffs, NJ: Spectrum Book.

Journals

Albertyn, Cathi, and Beth Goldblatt. 1998. Facing the Challenge of Transformation: Difficulties in the Development of an Indigenous Jurisprudence of Equality. *South African Journal on Human Rights* 14: 248–276.

Day, Shelagh, and Gwen Brodsky. 1996. The Duty to Accommodate: Who will Benefit? *Canadian Bar Review* 75: 433–473.

Ejikeme, Peter O. 2014. Education as Key to National Development: Issues, Challenges and the Way Forward. *Journal of Humanities and the Social Sciences* 6: 20–26.

Enaibe, Patience U. 2012. Need to Promote Women Education and Participation in Politics for Sustainable National Development. *International Journal of Educational Research and Development* 19: 1–5.

Jencks, Christopher. 1988. Whom must we Treat Equally for Educational Opportunity to be Equal. *Ethics* 98: 518–533.

Frankel, Charles. 1971. Equality of Opportunity. *Ethics* 81 (3): 191–211.

Mason, Andrew. 2001. Equality of Opportunities: Old and New. *Ethics* 111 (4): 760–781.

Ngwena, Charles G. 2004. Equality for People with Disabilities in the Workplace: An Overview of the Emergence of Disability as a Human Rights Issue. *Journal for Juridical Science* 29: 167–197.

Ngwena, Charles G. 2013. Western Cape Forum for Intellectual Disability V Government of the Republic of South Africa: A Case Study of Contradictions in Inclusive Education. *African Disability Rights Yearbook* 1: 139–164.

Ojogwu, Charity. 2009. The Challenges of Attaining Millennium Development Goals in Education in Africa by 2015. *College Student Journal* 43: 375–383.

Pieterse, Marius. 2005. What do we Mean When we Talk About Transformative Constitutionalism? *South African Public Law* 20: 155–166.

International human rights instruments, declarations, guidelines and other statements

African Charter on Human and Peoples' Rights, OAU DocCAB/LEG/67/3/ Rev.5 Adopted on 27 June 1981, and Entered into Force on 21 October 1986.

African Charter on the Rights and Welfare of the Child (African Children's Charter) OAU Doc CAB/LEG/24.9/49 Adopted 1990 Entered into Force 29 November 1999.

African Union Commission Agenda 2063 Framework Document: The Africa we want September 2015.

International Covenant on Economic, Social and Cultural Rights, 993 UNTS 3, Adopted on 16 December 1966, and Entered into Force on 3 January 1976.

Promotion of the Equality of Opportunity in Education, Report Prepared by Kishore Singh the Special Rapporteur on the Right to Education (2011) United Nations General Assembly (UNGA) A/HRC/17/29.

United Nations Committee on Economic, Social and Cultural Rights (CESCR), General Comment No. 13: The Right to Education (Art.13 of the CESCR) Adopted by the Committee on Economic, Social and Cultural Rights at the 21st Session, UN Doc E/C.12/1999/10, December 1999.

United Nations Convention on the Rights of Persons with Disabilities GA Res. 61/611, Adopted on 13 December 2006, and Entered into Force on 3 May 2008.

United Nations Convention on the Rights of the Child, GA Res. 44/25, Adopted on 20 November 1989, and Entered into Force on 2 September 1990.

Universal Declaration of Human Rights, Adopted and Proclaimed by General Assembly Resolution 217 A (III) of 10 December 1948.

Cases Cited

Harksen v Lane NO 1998 (1) SA 300 (CC) Constitutional Court of South Africa.

National Coalition for Gay & Lesbian Equality v Minister of Justice. 1998 (12) BCLR 1517 (CC) Constitutional Court of South Africa.

President of the Republic of South Africa v Hugo 1977 (6) BCLR 708 (CC) Constitutional Court of South Africa.

Prinsloo v Van der Linde, 1997 (6) BCLR 759 (CC) Constitutional Court of South Africa.

Tripartite Steering Committee and Another v Minister of Basic Education and Others, (2015) ZAECGHC 67 Eastern Cape High Court.
Western Cape Forum for Intellectual Disability v Government of the Republic of South Africa & Another 2011 5 SA 87 (WCC) Western Cape High Court.

Domestic legislation, regulations and policy guidelines: Nigeria

Constitution of the Federal Republic of Nigeria as Amended, 1999.
Nigeria National Policy on Education, 1st Edition (1977).
Nigeria National Policy on Education, 6th Edition (2013).
Nigeria Universal Basic Education Act, 2004.

Domestic legislation, regulations and policy guidelines: South Africa

Constitution of the Republic of South Africa No 108 of 1996.
Employment Equity Act No 55 of 1998.
Promotion of Equality and Prevention of Unfair Discrimination Act 4 of 2000.

Internet publications

Central Intelligence Agency World Fact book. 2015. http://www.cia.gov/library/publications/the-world-factbook/fields/2103.html#136. Accessed 30 Oct 2016.
Berger, Noah, and Peter Fisher. 2013. A Well Educated Workforce is Key to State Prosperity. *Economic Analysis and Research Network*. Washington, DC: Economic Policy Institute. http://hdl.voced.edu.au/10707/294721. Accessed 29 Oct 2016.
The African Economist. 2013. Ranking of African Countries by Literacy Rate. http://www.theafricaneconomist.com/ranking-of-african-countries-by-literacy-rate-zimbabwe-no-1#. Accessed 29 Oct 2016.

Thesis/Dissertation

Iwuchukwu, Chima. 1988. The Myths and Realities of Equal Educational Opportunities in Nigeria. PhD thesis, University of Nigeria Nsukka.

Author Biography

Ngozi Chuma-Umeh holds an LLB (Hons) from Imo State University and an LLM from Abia State University. She is a Doctor of Laws (LLD) candidate at the Centre for Human Rights University of Pretoria. Her doctoral thesis is on the right to inclusive primary education for learners with disabilities in Nigeria. She has published legal articles and has won distinguished awards and prices for academic excellence, positive leadership qualities and monumental contributions to the development of the Nigerian state. She is an upwardly mobile legal practitioner and an academic. She is presently a law teacher at Imo State University Owerri, Nigeria, with a special interest in human rights.

CHAPTER 3

Adoption of a Human Rights Approach to Budgeting as a Step to Realise the Right to Education in African Countries

Ashwanee Budoo

1 Introduction

The right to education is protected both at the international and at the regional level. Nevertheless, despite the provisions of these laws, Africa as a continent still faces challenges in ensuring access to education. For instance, in 2011, Sub-Saharan Africa had the lowest adult literacy rate compared to other regions.[1] Similarly, for the same period, Sub-Saharan Africa had the lowest youth literacy rate.[2] By 2014, most African countries were heading in the right direction to reach the target for primary school enrolment but, however, completion of education and low-quality education remained a challenge across the continent.[3] There is, therefore, a need for African countries to take concrete and effective steps to ensure that the right to education is realised across the continent.

One of the objectives of Agenda 2063 is to come up with a 'global strategy to optimize the use of Africa's resources for the benefits of all Africans'.[4] Such a use of the resources can be made towards the

A. Budoo (✉)
Centre for Human Rights, University of Pretoria, Pretoria, South Africa
e-mail: sheetal6189@yahoo.com

A.C. Onuora-Oguno et al. (eds.), *Education Law, Strategic Policy and Sustainable Development in Africa*, DOI 10.1007/978-3-319-53703-0_3

realisation of the right to education. Furthermore, UNESCO has recommended states to allocate 26% of their budget to education. Thus, African states have to use their resources for the benefits of those requiring an education. Recognising the link between budgetary resources and education, African states have been allocating a substantial amount of their budget to education. For instance, Africa, as a continent, has allocated the highest percentage of its budget to education at 18.4%, followed by East Asia and the Pacific.[5] However, these budgetary allocations are not sufficient to meet Africa's education target.

One of the means to maximise resources for the realisation of the right to education is to adopt a human rights approach to budgeting. The current chapter purports to study whether the adoption of a human rights approach to budgeting can ensure a better realisation of the right to education across the African continent. The objective is to present a human rights approach to budgeting as a means through which African governments can efficiently allocate their resources to realise the right to education.

The chapter firstly studies the different provisions of the law at the regional level which provides for the right to education and for the allocation of resources to realise the right to education. Secondly, it provides for the benchmark against which the realisation of the right to education can be measured. Thirdly, it explains a human rights approach to budgeting to realise the right to education in African countries while highlighting the challenges which arise during such a process before concluding.

2 African States' Obligations to Allocate Resources to Realise the Right to Education

The right to education is enshrined in several international[6] and regional instruments. However, since the current book focuses on Agenda 2063 of the African Union, this section focuses on the African regional instruments. The study of these instruments is done with the aim of establishing the obligations of African states to allocate resources to realise the right to education.

2.1 African Charter on Human and Peoples' Rights

In the 1960s, Africa initiated discussions for the drafting of a regional document which will concentrate on human rights and which will establish an institution for overseeing the implementation of the rights provided for by the document.[7] However, the then Organization of the

African Unity (OAU)[8] had other priorities including 'decolonisation, racial discrimination, economic development and African Unity' and the African Charter on Human and Peoples' Rights (African Charter) was adopted more than 2 decades after the discussions started.[9]

The African Charter was adopted in 1981 and it entered into force in 1986. It is a unique human rights instrument since it incorporates civil and political rights, economic, social and cultural rights, and individual and peoples' rights in one single document. In relation to the right to education, article 17(1) of the African Charter provides that '[e]very individual shall have the right to education'. It is to be noted that there is no express provision of the African Charter which provides for African states to allocate resources to realise the right to education.

However, article 1 of the African Charter requires states to take 'legislative and other measures' to give effect to the rights therein. Yeshanew has interpreted other measures as 'non-legislative steps'[10] that African states must adopt for the full realisation of the rights protected by the African Charter. The non-legislative steps include financial steps as per General Comment 3 of the ICESCR Committee.[11] In addition, the proposition by Yeshanew, the African Commission on Human and Peoples' rights (African Commission) has adopted rules and principles which interpret budgetary allocation of resources as one of the steps states have to take. Such rules and principles were adopted in accordance with article 45(1)(b) of the African Charter[12] and include the Pretoria Declaration on Economic, Social and Cultural Rights 2004, the Guiding Principles on Economic, Social and Cultural Rights in the African Charter 2011, and general comments of the African Commission.

As such, despite the fact that the African Charter does not expressly state that African states have to adopt budgetary measures to give effect to the rights protected therein, the interpretations given to the words 'other measures' implies that the African Charter requires African states to allocate sufficient resources. In relation to the right to education, therefore, African states have to allocate sufficient resources which ensure that the right to education is realised.

2.2 *African Charter on the Rights and Welfare of the Child*

The African Charter on the Rights and Welfare of the Child (African Children's Charter) was motivated by the fact that the Convention on the Rights of the Child did not take into account the local situations that prevail in Africa.[13] The African Children's Charter tried to tackle issues that were more of concern to the African child. The African Children's Charter contains provisions which concern resource allocation for the realisation of the right to education.

In the first instance, with regard to the right to education, article 11(1) of the African Children's Charter provides for the right to education for every child. States are required to take 'special measures' to ensure that 'female, gifted and disadvantaged children' have equal access to education. In addition, concerning children who fall pregnant before completing their education, article 11(6) of the African Children's Charter imposes an obligation on states to 'take all appropriate measures' to ensure that the child has the opportunity to pursue their education.

Concerning resource allocation, the first article of the African Children's Charter imposes an obligation on states to take 'necessary steps... to adopt such legislative or other measures as may be necessary to give effect to the provisions of this Charter'.[14] The African Committee of Experts on the Rights and Welfare of the Child (African Children's Committee) has interpreted the other measures to be adopted to include a budgetary allocation to realise children's rights at the national level.[15] For instance, in the concluding recommendations for South Africa, it has urged the state to 'allocate the necessary budget for the promotion and protection of children's rights and ensuring its effective and efficient use'[16] and to adopt a 'child rights sensitive budgeting and expenditure'.[17] Similarly, Burkina Faso was recommended to allocate an adequate budget for programmes and policies for the realisation of the rights and welfare of the child.[18]

The above provisions of the African Children's Charter and their interpretation by the African Children's Committee, therefore, point out to the fact that African states have to provide budgetary resources to realise the right to education.

2.3 The Protocol to the African Charter on the Rights of Women in Africa

The Maputo Protocol entered into force in 2005 and it provides for women's human rights in Africa. Article 12 of the Maputo Protocol imposes an obligation on states to take appropriate steps to ensure the right to education and training of women in Africa. In relation to allocation of resources to realise the right to education in the Maputo

Protocol, its article 26(2) provides that 'States Parties undertake to adopt all necessary measures and in particular shall provide budgetary and other resources for the full and effective implementation of the rights herein recognised'. The above two articles of the Maputo Protocol, therefore, requires African states to allocate resources to realise the right to education.

2.4 *The African Youth Charter*

The African Youth Charter came into force in 2009[19] and it provides for the rights of young persons in Africa. Generally, it requires states to adopt a National Youth Policy which ensures that youth is mainstreamed in all planning and decision-making processes.[20] Its article 13 elaborates on the obligations that states have towards education and skills development of young persons. Article 13(1) of the African Youth Charter more specifically provides that '[e]very young person shall have the right to education of good quality'. States are further required to 'provide free and compulsory basic education' and to make 'all forms of secondary education more readily available and accessible'.[21] Article 13 of the African Youth Charter additionally imposes an obligation on states to '[a]llocate resources to upgrade the quality of education delivered and ensure that it is relevant to the needs of contemporary society and engenders critical thinking rather than rote learning'.[22]

The above articles demonstrate that the African Youth Charter imposes an obligation on states to take steps towards the provision of education to the youth. Allocation of resources forms part of the steps that states are required to adopt to that end. As such, the African Youth Charter provides for the obligation to allocate resources to realise the right to education.

The above legal instruments of the African Union have established that African states have to allocate resources to realise the right to education. However, as noted in the introduction part of this chapter, African states still face challenges in realising the right to education of its citizens. This chapter puts forward that a human rights approach to public budgeting can enable countries to more effectively allocate their resources towards the realisation of the right to education. Before studying the human rights approach to public budgeting, this chapter expands on the benchmark which determines whether a state is abiding by its obligations to realise the right to education.

3 Benchmarks to Determine Whether a State is Realising the Right to Education[23]

A state's compliance with its global, regional and sub-regional obligations to realise the right to education can be assessed by studying the availability, accessibility, adequacy and adaptability (4-As)[24] of education. In terms of availability, the policies and programmes in place by the government should be 'available in sufficient quantity within the jurisdiction of the state party'.[25] For instance, in the context of the right to education, the state has the obligation to ensure that there is the availability of quality education for the population. The state has to take into account the financial implications of the above measures and has to provide for this expenditure in its budget.

Accessibility implies that the service should be 'accessible to everyone, without discrimination' and accessibility is achieved when there is non-discrimination, physical accessibility and economic accessibility.[26] In the context of access to education, for example, the state has to ensure that the law prohibits discrimination on the basis of sex while accessing education. At the same time, it has to ensure that schools are set up in areas that are close to communities so that children face no challenge to go to school. The state has to ensure that there are no school fees so that children who come from a poor background can have access to education. The above measures referred to require the state to spend and, therefore, require resource allocation in the public budget.

The service that is being provided by the state has to be in a form that is accepted by the citizens. For instance, the services concerning education will not be considered as acceptable if the language used to instruct the children is foreign to them. The state has to ensure that the education provided is in a language that is understood. To do so, it either has to provide language courses for instructors who use a foreign language or it has to provide training courses for persons who are already conversant with the language. The state will be required to include this additional cost when allocating expenditure to the Ministry of Education so that the latter can undertake the above measures.

Finally, adaptability means that the service 'has to be flexible so it can adapt to the needs of changing societies and communities and respond to the needs' of the people 'within their diverse and cultural settings'.[27] For instance, in some communities, girls still have the traditional role of looking after the family and doing the household chores.

The government can come up with programmes where it provides education for the girl child in the hours where she is expected to be free from her household duties. This will require the state to pay additionally for resource persons who will undertake that task and this will require budgetary allocations.

The 4-As formula is important for the study of a human rights approach to public budgeting, since budget framers can use them as a yardstick to allocate their resources to different sectors. As can be noted from the above discussion, while ensuring that it is abiding by all 4-As, states have to incur expenditure. Therefore, resource allocation at the national level needs to ensure that the 4-As are respected.

States' compliance with the obligation to realise the right to education through the allocation of sufficient budgetary resources can be assessed by adopting a human rights approach to public budgeting. Having established the yardstick that can be used to assess whether a state is complying with its obligation to allocate sufficient budgetary resources to realise the right to education, this chapter now moves to the human rights approach to public budgeting.

4 Human Rights Approach to Public Budgeting[28]

A budget whose policies and programmes positively impact on human rights is a pro human rights budget.[29] Tracking human rights aspects in the budget has been referred to as 'detective work' because analysts have to work on the budget to assess what has been done in favour of the advancement of human rights and what else could have been done.[30] This activity has been termed as human rights budgeting. Human right budgeting is, in simple terms, 'work that seeks to relate human rights to government budgets, and budget work to human rights work'.[31] The public budget is important for Civil Society Organisations (CSOs) to assess how much resources a government is allocating to realise human rights.[32]

States have international obligations to realise the rights provided by the international legal instruments that they have ratified. It has been argued that the mere existence of international and domestic laws does not lead to the realisation of the rights and that there is a need to adopt policies for the implementation of the laws.[33] National budgets reflect those policies adopted and are imperative for the relevant stakeholders to assess whether the government is translating its commitments in concrete actions.

A human rights approach to public budgeting enables the government to abide by its human rights commitments at the global, regional and domestic level. To know whether a government is respecting its international obligations under the international legal instruments that it has ratified, one can turn towards its public budget and assess its 'revenue, allocations and expenditures'.[34] The analysis of a national budget from a human rights perspective can be done either through revenue or through expenditure analysis.

4.1 Context of a Human Rights Approach to Public Budgeting

In a perfect market, equilibrium in terms of resources is reached when supply meets demand without any need of involvement on behalf of the government.[35] There are, however, some types of goods which the private market does not provide because they are not profitable. For instance, the private sector will not be able to control who benefits from street lights. Public finance scholars view the state as the 'organization that either does or should correct market failures through providing public goods and correcting for misallocations created by externalities'.[36]

In that instance, the government has to intervene to make provision for those goods and services. Crowding out theorists have stated that there is a need for government intervention in the case of public goods since the private sector will not provide for them as they do not earn any profit and because they cannot single out someone from using it.[37] Government intervenes in the market through public expenditure during the public budgeting process.

Through public finance, states change the resource allocations that the market economy would have had.[38] It is to be noted that states are not agents of 'intervention' but they rather are a platform which allows people having certain goals to interact and devise ways to achieve them.[39]

Taxes collected by the government, for the purposes of budgeting, are not viewed as a private property.[40] Once they are collected by the government, they are collective property which need to be distributed among the citizens. Thus, in a state where taxes are collected, it has to make provisions for goods and services that give effect to its international human rights commitments. Education is one of the services that the government has to offer to its citizens and therefore a human rights budget has to take into account expenditure on education.

4.2 *A Human Rights Approach to Public Budgeting at the Expenditure Level*

As noted above, a human rights approach to public budgeting can be done either at the expenditure level or at the revenue level. This chapter is concerned with expenditure to realise the right to education and as such, the focus is on a human rights approach to public budgeting at the expenditure level.

By studying the different budget initiatives around the world, NESRI has broken down the different types of human rights approaches to budgeting at the national level and they are studied in this section.[41] The rights-based or normative budgeting includes a human rights approach while allocating resources to the budget items and it includes human rights budgeting, equality budgeting, gender budgeting, and advocacy and mobilisation for a social justice budget. This includes the alternative budget approach which assesses the impact on different line items if the expenditure pattern is changed.

The next type of human rights approach to the national budget is participatory budgeting. This concept was coined in Brazil in the 1980s,[42] but it is to be noted that there is still no definition of the term. In simple terms, it is a process which 'allows the participation of non-elected citizens in the conception and/or allocation of public finances'.[43] Five criteria are central to participatory budgeting and they are as follows[44]:

1. The discussion of 'the financial and/or budgetary dimension' since it is a process which concerns limited resources;
2. The involvement of stakeholders from the city level and the involvement of 'a (decentralized) district with an elected body and some power over administration';
3. The holding of several meetings where stakeholders can express their view;
4. The creation of a platform where members from the public can express their concerns to the institutions responsible for the budget preparation; and
5. Accountability on the steps taken to give effects to the provisions of the budget.

Therefore, a participatory national budget has to give opportunities to all relevant stakeholders and members of the public to discuss the allocation of resources.

The NESRI Background Paper also mentions institutionalisation and enforceability of budgeting guidelines and initiatives. For instance, UK was mentioned where the Equality and Human Rights Commission has the powers to ensure that equality policies are implemented. As such, in the event the government does not implement the contents of the national budget, the Equality and Human Rights Commission has the mandate to bring a case to the Court to impose an obligation on the state to execute the provisions of the budget. Another example can be that of Ireland where they set up an advisory council to guide the policies which realise economic and social rights.

This section depicts the different types of a human rights approach to public budgeting at the expenditure level. This chapter elaborated on mainly two types of a human rights approach to budgeting, namely rights-based or normative approach to budgeting and participatory budgeting. The current chapter proposes a combination of both for the realisation of the right to education.

4.3 Challenges for the Adoption of a Human Rights Approach to Budgeting to Realise the Right to Education

The link between a human rights approach to public budgeting and a more efficient resource allocation has led the international human rights system to encourage states to adopt a human rights lens in their resource allocation process. This has been done through treaty provisions or soft law.[45] A human rights approach to public budgeting enables the population and CSOs to participate in the resource allocation process.

A human rights approach to public budgeting further allows stakeholders to assess whether the state is abiding by its obligations in the international human rights instruments it has ratified.[46] The literature on human rights approach to budgeting makes reference to mostly the pros of adopting the same. For instance, it has been argued that a human rights approach to public budgeting can enable the population to assess whether the government is fulfilling its obligation to allocate the maximum of its available resources to progressively realise human rights.[47] A briefing by Free Legal Advice Centres listed the benefits of a human rights approach to public budgeting as follows: progressive realisation of rights; protection of minimum core of rights; assessment of whether rights are adequate, affordable and accessible; information about whether states are abiding by their obligation to immediately realise some rights; analysis of whether the state is making use of the maximum of its available resources; whether there is non-retrogression in the protection of the human rights; and it provides for information which can enable relevant stakeholders to make impact assessments.[48] CSOs can make use of the public budget prepared through a human rights approach to assess whether the government is abiding by its international obligations by exploiting the international law principles such as 'consultations (participation), transparency, accountability, minimum core provision, and equality and non-discrimination'.[49]

Despite the benefits of a human rights approach to public budgeting, states still hesitate to engage in this process. There is not much literature that explains the reasons as to why states hesitate to adopt a human rights approach to public budgeting. As pointed out by Kuosmanen, there is a lack of analysis to explain the cognitive challenges that governments face in adopting a human rights approach to public budgeting.[50] His work focuses on the epistemic challenges in the inclusion of a human rights approach in public budgets. Kuosmanen does not expressly elaborate on the challenges and instead identifies the factors that contribute to an 'imperfect knowledge' of a to public budgeting.[51] This section refers to those factors as challenges instead of factors that contribute to an imperfect knowledge. The motivation for such a stand is that the factors identified by Kuosmanen can be analysed broadly as challenges in the adoption of a human rights approach to public budgeting even if the 'imperfect knowledge' aspect is ignored.

In addition to Kuosmanen's propositions, Allison, in his work concerning the adoption of a human rights approach to fisheries policies,[52] advanced some arguments against the adoption of a human rights approach to public budgets. This section makes reference to these two works to highlight the challenges in the adoption of a human rights approach to public budgeting.

Complex Nature of the Public Budgeting Process

Kuosmanen firstly identifies the concept of polycentricism as a challenge to a human rights approach to public budgeting.[53] According to him, the public budget has several complicated policies that are aimed at realising human rights which include 'the specific needs of right bearers, the inherent qualities of human rights and the nature of the broader circumstances within which public budgeting takes place'.[54] These complex issues complicate the adoption of a human rights approach to public budgeting and as a result act as a challenge.

The current chapter concerns the realisation of the right to education through the adoption of a human rights approach to public budgeting. It is thus proposed that to overcome this challenge of a human rights approach to public budgeting, budget framers consider the shortcomings of the government in terms of expenditure on education. Education is a fundamental human right and as such the government has to take into account the steps, including budgetary steps, it is taking to ensure the realisation of the right to education.

Ambiguous and Controversial Nature of Human Rights

Kuosmanen secondly identifies the ambiguous and controversial nature of human rights as a hurdle for the adoption of a human rights approach to public budgeting.[55] Despite the fact that human rights are universal, he states that different entities still have different interpretations of human rights. Allison's work expands on the challenges that the adoption of a human rights approach to budgeting faces as a result of the ambiguous and controversial nature of human rights.[56] He gives examples of the excuses that governments are able to create as a result of the controversial nature of human rights. Allison identified that governments who fail to adopt a human rights approach to public budgeting often put forward the excuse that human rights is a Western concept that promotes individual rights at the expense of the collective national interests and that it does not take into account that citizens also have responsibilities.[57]

Allison uses two arguments to refute the above proposition.[58] His first reference is to the work of Sen[59] who argued that Asian values are inventions of Asian leaders who do not want to give up power and use the cultural differences between the West and Asia to justify non-respect of their obligations. Similarly, in the context of this research, African leaders have endorsed African regional instruments and they cannot use the excuse of the Western world imposing their concepts in Africa.

Allison's second rebuttal is that the right to development, which encompasses various economic, social and cultural rights, finds its roots in the third world and non-realisation of these rights cannot be justified by invoking the fact that they are rights that concern only the Western world. This research focuses on the realisation of the right to education in Africa through the allocation of sufficient budgetary resources. It derives its legitimacy from the obligations that African states have by virtue of ratifying African Union treaties which make reference to the provision of budgetary resources to realise the right to education. Therefore, the argument of a human rights approach to public budgeting being a Western concept does not apply as the obligation to allocate sufficient budgetary resources to realise the right to education emanates from African treaties. The provisions of the African Union treaties that impose an obligation on states to allocate sufficient budgetary resources to realise women's human rights indicate that the African continent has accepted a human rights approach to public budgeting as a means to realise human rights. Thus, African governments cannot take advantage of the controversial and ambiguous nature of human rights to escape from their obligation to provide resources to realise the right to education.

Cognitive Factors
Kuosmanen thirdly advances cognitive factors as a challenge in the adoption of a human rights approach to public budgeting.[60] According to him, human beings are prone to make mistakes while taking decisions and this can affect the public budgeting process. He states that the public budgeting process is a collective endeavour which can be biased by the inputs of the different parties.

The observations by Allison are relevant for this section. He makes reference to political behaviour and biasness as a challenge for the adoption of a human rights approach to public budgeting. Allison advances that law and policy making are political and that the realisation of rights might require challenging the abuse of power by the more powerful.[61] In many countries, corruption is at the root of non-realisation of human rights and a human rights approach to public budgeting can expose such corruption as such governments are reluctant to give the population the chance to question them.

Allison also points out that the non-adoption of a human rights approach to public budgeting prevents international organisations from being too political.[62] The adoption of a human rights approach to public budgeting will reveal the lacunas of the state in terms of realisation of the human rights of its citizens. International organisations do not want to be viewed as being 'political' by questioning the state about its resource allocation process. They, sometimes, refrain from interfering in the public budgeting process of a country and give aid nevertheless. This acts as a disincentive for countries to adopt a human rights approach to public budgeting because they are aware that as long as they fulfil certain conditions, they will get the aid required.

The above two examples given by Allison demonstrate that cognitive factors influence the adoption of a human rights approach to public budgeting. However, in the context of a human rights approach to public budgeting to realise the right to education, governments have ratified several African Union instruments which provide for the obligation to allocate resources to realise the right to education. African countries are accountable to the African Commission and the African Children's Committee, which are the monitoring bodies of the different treaties, when it comes to the implementation of this obligation. As such, they cannot let the budgeting processes to be influenced by their bias.

Concerning international organisations, Allison has argued that this can be remedied by a partnership between international organisations and CSOs which advocates for the adoption of a human rights approach to public budgeting. CSOs can further pressurise international organisations to take interest in budgetary allocations for the realisation of human rights. Moreover, budget support programmes can be linked to policies that influence human rights. In the context of this chapter, budget support can be aimed at policies which promote access to education.

Methodological Factors

Kuosmanen fourthly identifies that the methodologies adopted can act as a challenge in the adoption of a human rights approach to public budgeting.[63] A human rights approach to public budgeting requires methods from the areas of economics and human rights. Such a combination might be difficult to achieve since most of the times one has either experience in human rights or in economics. Economics and human rights are different fields with different jargons, and as a result, one might not be successful in combining both.

However, he gives examples of situations where human rights impacts assessments were required for economic decisions. For the purposes of this chapter, it is presumed that such methodological challenges can be overcome by training budget framers on the importance of human rights considerations during the preparation of the budget with a particular accent on education.

Resources

Kuosmanen's fifth and final challenge relate to resources.[64] He puts forward that resources affect all the previous issues discussed and that imperfect knowledge of resources can lead to the non-adoption of a human rights approach to public budgeting. His argument can be interpreted to imply that resources are an important part of a human rights approach to public budgeting and that insufficient resources act as a challenge for the adoption of the same.

Allison also considers the issue of resources and states that the process of a human rights approach is usually slow and expensive.[65] A human rights approach to public budgeting takes time as it involves more stakeholders. Moreover, there is a need to assess the impact of the expenditure of each line item and as such the process can be expensive. It has been argued that there is a set off between the resources in terms of time and finance invested in a human rights approach against economic growth.[66] Nevertheless, as rightly highlighted by Allison, this argument can be countered by the fact that human rights realisation will have a positive impact on economic growth: he gives the example of the realisation of education and its link with economic growth. As such, even if integrating a human rights approach to public budgeting is slow and requires resources, it has a positive long-term impact on the country's development.

In a nutshell, the works of Kuosmanen and Allison represent the arguments that have been put forward for the non-adoption of a human rights approach to public budgeting but each of them has a counter argument. Most of the counter arguments highlight the fact that a human rights approach to public budgeting is the proper channel to ensure that governments allocate their resources efficiently to realise the human rights of its citizens. As such, African states can adopt a human rights approach to public budgeting to ensure that sufficient resources are allocated to realise the right to education.

5 Conclusion and Recommendations

Recognising that education is an important tool, several regional instruments have imposed an obligation on African states to undertake steps to realise the right to education. As expanded upon, one of the steps that African states have to adopt to realise the right to education is to allocate resources. However, many African countries are still lacking in fulfilling their obligations to allocate resources to realise the right to education.

This chapter studied the adoption of human rights approaches to budgeting as a means to realise the obligation to allocate resources to realise the right to education. Such a step is not exclusive of challenges but as highlighted, these challenges do not hold ground. Therefore, the adoption of human rights approaches to public budgeting can contribute towards the allocation of resources to realise the right to education.

Notes

1. UNESCO Institute for Statistics, *Adult and Youth Literacy: National, Regional and Global Trends, 1985–2015*, (Quebec: UNESCO, 2013), 8 (UNESCO Institute for Statistics 2013).
2. Ibid., 16.
3. United Nations Economic Commission for Africa, *Assessing Progress in Africa Towards the Millennium Development Goals: Analysis of the Common African Position on the Post-2015 Development Agenda* (Addis Ababa: United Nations Economic Commission for Africa, 2014), xv (United Nations Economic Commission for Africa 2014).
4. African Union, 'Agenda 2063 Vision and Priorities' (African Union, 13 October 2015), http://agenda2063.au.int/en//vision (African Union 2015).
5. The Africa-America Institute, *State Education in Africa Report 2015: A Report Card on the Progress, Opportunities and Challenges Confronting the African Education Sector'* (New York: The Africa-America Institute, 2015), 12 (The Africa-America Institute 2015).
6. Article 13 of the ICESCR; article 28 of the CRC; article 24 of the CRPD; articles 10 and 14 of the CEDAW; article 5 of the ICERD; and article 30 of the International Convention on the Protection of the Rights of all Migrant Workers and Members of their Families.
7. Germain Baricako, 'The African Charter and the African Commission on Human and Peoples' Rights', in *The African Charter on Human and Peoples' Rights: The System in Practice, 1986–2006*, ed. Malcom Evans and Rachel Murray (Cambridge: Cambridge University Press, 2008), 1 (Baricako 2008).
8. Frans Viljoen, *International Human Rights Law in Africa* (Oxford: Oxford University Press, 2012), 156–169 for the journey from the OAU to the AU (Viljoen 2012).
9. Baricako, 'The African Charter and the African Commission on Human and Peoples' Rights', 1–2 (Baricako 2008).
10. Sisay Yeshanew, *The Justiciability of Economic, Social and Cultural Rights in the African Regional Human Rights System* (Cambridge: Intersentia, 2013), 283 (Yeshanew 2013).
11. ESCR Committee General Comment 3 on article 2(1) of the ICESCR 'The nature of States parties' obligations' adopted at the fifth session in 1990.

12. Article 45(1)(b) of the African Charter: 'The functions of the Commission shall be ... [t]o formulate and lay down, principles and rules aimed at solving legal problems relating to human and peoples' rights and fundamental freedoms upon which African Governments may base their legislations'.
13. Thoko Kaime, *The African Charter on the Rights and Welfare of the Child: A Socio-Legal Perspective* (Pretoria: Pretoria University Law Press, 2009), 1–3 (Kaime 2009).
14. Article 1(1) of the African Children's Charter.
15. Paragraphs 6 and 31(b) of the African Committee concluding recommendations on the combined initial, first, second and third periodic reports of Ethiopia adopted during its first extraordinary session (6–11 October 2014); page 8 of the African Committee concluding recommendations on the initial report of Mali adopted during its 14th session (16–19 November 2009); paragraph 6 of the African Committee concluding recommendations on the initial report of Mozambique adopted during its 1st extra-ordinary session (6–11 October 2014).
16. Paragraph 7 of the African Committee concluding recommendations on the initial report of South Africa adopted during its first extraordinary session (6–11 October 2014).
17. Paragraph 9 of the African Committee concluding recommendations on the initial report for South Africa.
18. Page 8 of African Committee concluding recommendations on the initial report for Burkina Faso adopted during its 14th session (16–19 November 2009); paragraph 9 of the African Committee concluding recommendations on the initial report of Guinea adopted during its first extraordinary session (6–11 October 2014); see also generally the African Committee concluding recommendations on the first periodic report for Kenya adopted during its 1st extraordinary session (6–11 October 2014).
19. African Union, 'OAU /AU Treaties, Conventions, Protocols and Charters' (African Union, 2 June 2016), http://www.au.int/en/treaties/status (African Union 2016).
20. Article 12(1)(c) of the African Youth Charter.
21. Articles 13(4)(a) and 13(4)(b) of the African Youth Charter.
22. Article 13(4)(i) of the African Youth Charter.
23. This section is part of the author's research towards her doctoral thesis. African Union, 'OAU/AU Treaties, Conventions, Protocols and Charters' (African Union, 2 June 2016), http://www.au.int/en/treaties/status.
24. Preliminary report of the former Special Rapporteur on the right to education submitted to the Commission on Human Rights at its 55th session in 1999 E/CN.4/1999/49 (United Nations, 4 August 2016), https://documents-dds-ny.un.org/doc/UNDOC/GEN/G99/101/34/PDF/

G9910134.pdf?OpenElement: To demonstrate the state obligations concerning the realisation of the right to health, the report came up with the 4-A's formula; and General Comment 13 of ESCR Committee on article 13 of the ICESCR 'The right to education' adopted during its 21st session in 1999 E/C.12/1999/10, paragraph 6, available at, http://www1.umn.edu/humanrts/gencomm/escgencom13.htm (accessed on 26 February 2015): expanded upon the 4-As.

25. General Comment 13 of the ESCR Committee paragraph 6(a).
26. General Comment 13 of the ESCR Committee paragraph 6(b).
27. General Comment 13 of the ESCR Committee paragraph 6(d).
28. This section is part of the author's research towards her doctoral thesis.
29. Katherine Willoughby, *Public Budgeting in Context: Structure, Law, Reform, and the Results* (San Francisco: Jossey-Bass, 2014), 381 (Willoughby 2014).
30. Ann Blyberg, 'The Case of the Mislaid Allocation: Economic and Social Rights and Budget Work', *SUR-International Journal on Human Rights* 6, no. 11 (2009): 123 (Blyberg 2009).
31. Ibid., 125.
32. Institute for Socio-Economic Studies, 'Budget and Rights: Developing a Budget Analysis Method from the Perspective of Human Rights', 2009, 2 (Institute for Socio-Economic Studies, 26 August 2015), http://www.inesc.org.br/library/technical-notes/NT.%20157%20-%20%20Budget%20and%20rights.pdf (Institute for Socio-Economic Studies 2009).
33. Ibid., 3.
34. Helena Hofbauer et al. 'Dignity Counts: A Guide to Using Budget Analysis to Advance Human Rights', 2004, 1 (26 August 2014), http://internationalbudget.org/wp-content/uploads/Dignity-Counts-A-Guide-to-Using-Budget-Analysis-to-Advance-Human-Rights-English.pdf (Hofbauer 2004).
35. Centre for Aid and Public Expenditure, 'The Basic Budgeting Problem: Approaches to Resource Allocation in the Public Sector and their Implications for Pro-Poor Budgeting' (London: Oversees Development Institute, 2001), 6 (Centre for Aid and Public Expenditure 2001).
36. Richard Wagner, *Fiscal Sociology and the Theory of Public Finance: An Exploratory Essay* (Cheltenham: Edward Elgar Publishing Ltd, 2007), 3 (Wagner 2007).
37. Trish Kelly, 'Public Expenditures and Growth,' *Journal of Development Studies* 34, no. 1 (2007): 62 (Kelly 2007).
38. Wagner, *Fiscal Sociology and the Theory of Public Finance*, 179 (Wagner 2007).
39. Wagner, *Fiscal Sociology and the Theory of Public Finance*, 180 (Wagner 2007).

40. Wagner, *Fiscal Sociology and the Theory of Public Finance*, 25 (Wagner 2007).
41. NESRI Background paper, 'Moving towards Human Rights Budgeting: Examples from Around the World' (2011) (NESRI, 26 August 2015), http://www.nesri.org/sites/default/files/Moving_Toward_Human_Rights_Budgeting.pdf (NESRI Background paper. 2011).
42. Yves Sintomer et al., Transnational Models of Citizen Participation: The Case of Participatory Budgeting', *Journal of Public Deliberation* 8, no. 2 (2012): 4 (Sintomer et al. 2012).
43. Ibid 2.
44. Yves Sintomer et al. Participatory Budgeting in Europe: Potentials and Challenges', *International Journal of Urban and Regional Research* 32, no. 1 (2008): 168 (Sintomer et al. 2008).
45. See Chap. 2 for more information about the international law and a human rights approach to public budgeting.
46. Hofbauer et al., 'Dignity Counts' (Hofbauer et al. 2004).
47. Institute for Socioeconomic Studies 'Budgets and Rights' 7.
48. Free Legal Advice Centres Briefing 'A Human Rights Approach to Budgeting' (2014): 2–6 (Free Legal Advice Centres Briefing 2014).
49. Ibid., 7.
50. Jaakko Kuosmanen, 'Human Rights, Public Budgets, and Epistemic Challenges', *Human Rights Review* 17, no. 2 (2016): 247 (Kuosmanen 2016).
51. Ibid., 251–260.
52. Edward Allison, 'Should States and International Organizations Adopt a Human Rights Approach to Fisheries Policy', *Maritime Studies* 10, (2011): 2 (Allison 2011).
53. Kuosmanen 'Human Rights, Public Budgets, and Epistemic Challenges', 252 (Kuosmanen 2016).
54. Ibid.
55. Kuosmanen 'Human Rights, Public Budgets, and Epistemic Challenges', 254 (Kuosmanen 2016).
56. Allison 'Should States and International Organizations Adopt a Human Rights Approach to Fisheries Policy', 2 (Allison 2011).
57. Allison 'Should States and International Organizations Adopt a Human Rights Approach to Fisheries Policy', 105 (Allison 2011).
58. Ibid.
59. Amartya Sen, 'Human Rights and Asian Values', during the 16th Morgenthau Memorial lecture on ethics and foreign policy (1997) (Sen 1997).
60. Kuosmanen 'Human Rights, Public Budgets, and Epistemic Challenges', 255 (Kuosmanen 2016).

61. Allison 'Should States and International Organizations Adopt a Human Rights Approach to Fisheries Policy', 107 (Allison 2011).
62. Allison 'Should States and International Organizations Adopt a Human Rights Approach to Fisheries Policy', 107–108 (Allison 2011).
63. Kuosmanen 'Human Rights, Public Budgets, and Epistemic Challenges', 256 (Kuosmanen 2016).
64. Kuosmanen 'Human Rights, Public Budgets, and Epistemic Challenges', 258 (Kuosmanen 2016).
65. Allison 'Should States and International Organizations Adopt a Human Rights Approach to Fisheries Policy', 106 (Allison 2011).
66. Ibid.

Bibliography

African Union. 2015. Agenda 2063 Vision and Priorities. http://agenda2063.au.int/en//vision. Accessed 13 Oct 2015.

African Union. 2016. OAU/AU Treaties, Conventions, Protocols and Charters. http://www.au.int/en/treaties/status. Accessed 2 June 2016.

Allison, Edward. 2011. Should States and International Organizations Adopt a Human Rights Approach to Fisheries Policy. *Maritime Studies* 10 (2): 95–116.

Baricako, Germain. 2008. The African Charter and the African Commission on Human and Peoples' Rights. In *The African Charter on Human and Peoples' Rights: The System in Practice, 1986–2006*, ed. Malcom Evans and Rachel Murray. Cambridge: Cambridge University Press.

Blyberg, Ann. 2009. The Case of the Mislaid Allocation: Economic and Social Rights and Budget Work. *SUR-International Journal on Human Rights* 6 (11): 123–139.

Centre for Aid and Public Expenditure. 2001. *The Basic Budgeting Problem: Approaches to Resource Allocation in the Public Sector and their Implications for Pro-Poor Budgeting*. London: Oversees Development Institute.

Free Legal Advice Centres Briefing. 2014. A Human Rights Approach to Budgeting.

Hofbauer, Helena, et al. 2004. Dignity Counts: A Guide to Using Budget Analysis to Advance Human Rights, 1. http://internationalbudget.org/wp-content/uploads/Dignity-Counts-A-Guide-to-Using-Budget-Analysis-to-Advance-Human-Rights-English.pdf. Accessed 26 Aug 2014.

Institute for Socio-Economic Studies. 2009. Budget and Rights: Developing a Budget Analysis Method from the Perspective of Human Rights, 2. http://www.inesc.org.br/library/technical-notes/NT.%20157%20-%20%20Budget%20and%20rights.pdf. Accessed 26 Aug 2015.

Kaime, Thoko. 2009. *The African Charter on the Rights and Welfare of the Child: A Socio-Legal Perspective*. Pretoria: Pretoria University Law Press.

Kelly, Trish. 2007. Public Expenditures and Growth. *Journal of Development Studies* 34 (1): 60–84.

Kuosmanen, Jaakko. 2016. Human Rights, Public Budgets, and Epistemic Challenges. *Human Rights Review* 17 (2): 247–267.

NESRI Background paper. 2011. Moving Towards Human Rights Budgeting: Examples from Around the World. http://www.nesri.org/sites/default/files/Moving_Toward_Human_Rights_Budgeting.pdf. Accessed 26 Aug 2015.

Sintomer, Yves, et al. 2008. Participatory Budgeting in Europe: Potentials and Challenges. *International Journal of Urban and Regional Research* 32 (1): 164–178.

Sintomer, Yves, et al. 2012. Transnational Models of Citizen Participation: The Case of Participatory Budgeting. *Journal of Public Deliberation* 8 (2): 1–32.

Sen, Amartya. 1997. "Human Rights and Asian Values", During the 16th Morgenthau Memorial Lecture on Ethics and Foreign Policy.

The Africa-America Institute. 2015. *State Education in Africa Report 2015: A Report Card on the Progress, Opportunities and Challenges Confronting the African Education Sector'*. New York: The Africa-America Institute.

UNESCO Institute for Statistics. 2013. *Adult and Youth Literacy: National, Regional and Global Trends, 1985–2015*. Quebec: UNESCO.

United Nations Economic Commission for Africa. 2014. *Assessing Progress in Africa Towards the Millennium Development Goals: Analysis of the Common African Position on the Post-2015 Development Agenda*. Addis Ababa: United Nations Economic Commission for Africa.

Viljoen, Frans. 2012. *International Human Rights Law in Africa*. Oxford: Oxford University Press (156–169 for the Journey from the OAU to the AU).

Wagner, Richard. 2007. *Fiscal Sociology and the Theory of Public Finance: An Exploratory Essay*. Cheltenham: Edward Elgar Publishing.

Willoughby, Katherine. 2014. *Public Budgeting in Context: Structure, Law, Reform, and the Results*. San Francisco: Jossey-Bass.

Yeshanew, Sisay. 2013. *The Justiciability of Economic, Social and Cultural Rights in the African Regional Human Rights System*, 283. Cambridge: Intersentia.

Author Biography

Ashwanee Budoo is a programme manager for the LLM/MPhil in Human Rights and Democratisation in Africa programme at the Centre for Human Rights, University of Pretoria and holds an LLD from the University of Pretoria.

CHAPTER 4

Mainstreaming Human Rights Education: Africa and the Challenge of a General Jurisprudence Towards Sustainable Development

Muhtar Adeiza Etudaiye and Mohammed Enesi Etudaiye

1 Introduction

The Constitution is unarguably the most important document in the existence of a State. It is the basic law which grants recognition to both individual laws and a State's legal structure as well as order the power relations in the State. This therefore underlines the importance of Constitutional Law. The subject of human rights is unarguably one of the most important aspects of individual and communal existence. However, there can be little realisation of the benefits of human rights

M.A. Etudaiye (✉)
Department of Jurisprudence and International Law,
University of Ilorin, Ilorin, Nigeria
e-mail: muhtaretudaiye@yahoo.com

M.E. Etudaiye
Department of Public and International Law,
University of Abuja, Abuja, Nigeria
e-mail: mohammedetudaiye@yahoo.com

A.C. Onuora-Oguno et al. (eds.), *Education Law, Strategic Policy and Sustainable Development in Africa*, DOI 10.1007/978-3-319-53703-0_4

without a sound knowledge of its scope and attributes. But human rights exist in the context of Constitutional Law. Indeed, human rights constitute a critical part of a constitution,[1] and as such, equally fundamental is knowledge of its constitutional coefficient. This knowledge invariably, if not entirely inevitably, requires education. The connection between human rights and education has been established at least since the making of the international human rights treaties. That is not all because there is invariably also a connection between human rights and development although this real connection has only belatedly been acknowledged. The crucial question then is—if education is a sine qua non to human rights and the idea of human rights is in turn inextricably linked to development how have states, particularly the Nigerian state, approached the imperative issues of Constitutional Law and human rights education? Given the performance of constitutionalism and human rights in the African continent and Nigeria in particular, many questions arise as follows: Is this education adequate in content and methodology? Does it take into contemplation this non-performance and the reasons for it? These are the questions, among others, that this chapter seeks to address.

They are questions that are critical in the context of the African Union Commission Agenda 2063 Framework Document of September 2015 and its shared set of interconnected aspirations of "an Africa of good governance, respect for human rights, justice and the rule of law"; of "a peaceful and secure Africa"; of "an Africa with a strong cultural identity, common heritage, values and ethics", etc. In this regard, this study is designed, among others, to assist in the development of strong institutions as well as instigate competent human resources and consequently visionary and purposeful leadership in the justice and human rights sector; to reconfigure law curricula in Nigeria's educational structure in a way that welds human rights and constitutional law into Africa's morals, values and ethics and improves the management of Nigeria's many diversities; while at the same time elevating the equitable and, where appropriate, equal entitlement of Africa's women and female children in the allocation of rights and resources in all spheres of life.

Consequently, Sect. 2 of this chapter analyses the significance of education for human rights. Section 3 examines sustainable development as a concept, while Sect. 4 analyses the link between human rights and sustainable development. Sections 5, 6 and 7 analyse the deficit in human rights orientation in culturally distinct societies like Nigeria and a few, not all, of the issues which might require reorientation—issues that the curricula, as currently configured do not contemplate. Sections 8 and 9 discuss curricula and teaching at pre-tertiary levels in order to gauge the levels of preparation of students for the tertiary law programmes. Law curricula is the subject of analyses in Sect. 10. The discourses in Sects. 9 and 10 are undertaken as a measure against the usually understated highly technical nature of Constitutional Law and Human Rights Law, the latter of which is the principal feature of the study contained in Sect. 11. Section 12 concludes the paper with far-reaching recommendations tailored towards repositioning legal education in Nigeria.

2 Human Rights and Education

The interconnection between education and human rights has a long history, at least it dates as far back as the Universal Declaration of Human Rights 1948. The Declaration exhorts every State, "every individual and every organ of society" to "strive by teaching and education to promote respect for these rights and freedoms".[2] The fundamental purpose of the prescribed teaching is in order to promote respect for them.[3]

The international community regards education as "a right" and directs that "education shall be free" although it hastens to qualify this right by adding "at least in the elementary and fundamental stages".[4] It then makes elementary education "compulsory". This appears to mean that the State indeed is to force elementary education down the throat of the reluctant. Unfortunately, Nigeria has fallen far short of matching the Declaration's enthusiasm although the problem would appear to be a global one. Fereira[5] notes:

> The UN General Assembly proclaimed the year commencing on 10 December 2008 as the International Year of Human Rights Learning, to be devoted to activities to broaden and deepen human rights learning based on the principles of universality, indivisibility, interdependency, impartiality, objectivity and non-selectivity, constructive dialogue and cooperation (Resolution 62/171 of 18 December 2007). It was therefore very likely that, in 2009, unique conditions existed for launching new projects and proposing innovative activities in the field of human rights education. Still, no particularly significant initiatives seem to have been brought to the public knowledge. This is unfortunate, especially with regard to human rights education with children, as this is such an under-developed field.

It does appear, however, that from State to State, the problem has become one of degree. That being the case, it is necessary to examine the degree to which challenges have stunted Nigeria's progress towards effective human rights education.

When Article 26(1) of the Declaration states that "higher education shall be equally accessible to all on the basis of merit", it appears that the word "equally" is suggestive that all those who are qualified shall have access to higher education.[6] Indeed, the drafting in the International Covenant on Economic, Social and Cultural Rights (ICESR) appears to settle the issue[7] on two counts: first, it breaks Article 26(1) of the Universal Declaration down into its varying paragraphs and classifications; secondly, by providing that "technical and vocational secondary education, shall be made generally available and accessible to all by every appropriate means…"[8] and that "Higher education shall be made equally accessible to all…"[9] There is the insertion of the word "made" before the phrase "equally available". These two alterations to the original couching in the Universal Declaration would at first tend to confirm that the requirement of these international instruments is that higher education is afforded to every person. The difficulty, however, is with the words "equally accessible to all, on the basis of capacity". There are two (2) possible meanings: do the words "equally accessible" simply mean equal *opportunity* on the basis of the capacity of the qualified citizens? Or does "on the basis of capacity" mean on the basis of the capacity of each State party? Either way, it appears that unwilling State parties have pitched tents with the latter construction and taken full advantage to minimise the "capacity" available for higher education. Indeed, such States, like Nigeria, have taken it further by excluding from their national constitutions the right to free education at the primary level. In a country in which 53% of the population live in rural areas[10] and unemployment, by charitable statistics, stands at 12.1% in the first quarter of 2016 with poverty levels, according to the National Bureau of Statistics, at over 60% of the population[11] and as much as 70% of the population living on less than US$1.25 a day, it is not clear what percentage of the population can realistically send their school age children to school. This will be compounded by the fact that only a small fraction of Nigeria's secondary school graduates who are qualified to get into tertiary institutions actually make it there. Tertiary gross enrolment ratio continues to hover around 10% of eligible candidates.

There is another snag—if they have to make it there "on the basis of capacity" (a phrase that will shortly be expounded upon), there is usually a lot of disappointment. There is the Federal Character principle established by the Nigerian Constitution by virtue of which governmental appointments and placement in public institutions must reflect the federal character of Nigeria. According to the Constitution[12]:

> The composition of the Government of the Federation or any of its agencies and *the conduct of its affairs* shall be carried out in such a manner as to reflect the federal character of Nigeria and the need to promote national unity, and also to command national loyalty, thereby *ensuring that there shall be no predominance of persons from a few States or from a few ethnic or other sectional groups in that Government or in any of its agencies.*[13]

The permissions for employing the Federal Character principle in admissions into tertiary institutions are to be found in the above-italicised portions of the provision. The schools are agencies of government created by statute and, in any case, since they are government institutions, the conduct of their affairs must be governed by the Federal Character principle. Given Nigeria's multiethnic composition, this is a critical provision. It would make initial sense to argue that the provision being harboured in Chap. 2 of the Constitution is by virtue of the Constitution itself non-justiciable.[14] However, this does not appear to be the case given that the ouster provision[15] commences with the opening phrase, "shall not except as otherwise provided by this Constitution". The all-but clear implication of this phrase is that if a subject matter or an aspect of a subject matter contained in Chap. 2 occurs elsewhere in the Constitution, non-justiciability with respect to that subject or aspect of it is defeated.[16] And so the Constitution proceeds to create a Federal Character Commission[17] although in the Schedule to the Constitution where the membership and powers of the Commission appear,[18] there is nothing at all to suggest that the Commission has any scope beyond the "distribution of *all cadres of posts* in the public service of the Federation and of the States, the armed forces of the Federation, the Nigeria Police Force and other government security agencies, government owned companies and parastatals of the states" (emphasis added). Again, however, that impression would appear to be negated by the words "In giving effect to the provisions of section 14(3) and (4) of this Constitution, the Commission shall have the power to..." at the beginning of the Article.[19]

The implication is that Article 8(1) does not circumscribe the scope of section 14(3) and (4) of the Constitution, which appears wide enough to cover even student enrolment in tertiary institutions. From this, it may be inferred that the powers set out in Article 8(1) are in respect of certain portions of the intendment of section 14(3) and (4) and not necessarily the entire gamut of its scope. In other words, these powers are not exhaustive but are relevant only where the issue of distribution of posts arise. Indeed given that the Commission may exercise other powers with respect to student enrolment, some have had cause to be aggrieved by this side of capacity.[20]

Having established the aptness of the Commission's powers with regard to intake into tertiary institutions, there is the issue of its impact. The implication of the Federal Character principle is to do away with total adherence to merit as a sacrifice for national unity. Thus, although applicant A may score higher marks than applicant B, applicant B may yet obtain admission into a tertiary institution while applicant A misses out. In practice, it appears that how it works is that the best student from each state must first be admitted in which case although applicant B's score may only have qualified him for seventh place in another state, he gets admitted ahead of students who are better than him because he is the best student from his State. A fundamental lacuna in the Constitution is the lack of a requirement for the federal government or "educationally disadvantaged states" for that matter to periodically give proof of their accomplishments towards bridging the gap such that this accepted essentially does not meetphenomenon of "disadvantage" can be phased out eventually perhaps on an incremental basis. It ought not to be the intention of the Nigerian Constitution that a state with capacities for development should be perpetually disadvantaged or classified as such. Indeed, given those dynamics, it is arguable that an educationally advantaged state could evolve to be an educationally disadvantaged state in comparison with a previously educationally disadvantaged state. The dynamics are many and it is a wonder that the Constitution has laid this foundation for sterility.

There are other considerations one of which is "catchment area". In ordinary English lexicon, the expression simply means the area from which a particular school or hospital will accept patients or pupils as the case may be. If this were the case, the "catchment area" of tertiary institutions in Nigeria would be the entire federation. In Nigeria, however, it refers to the geographical areas located closer to the tertiary institution. Catchment areas also get their share in disregard to merit.

These are merely more qualifications to the requirement of "capacity" (depending on what meaning is adopted) in the international rights instruments.

There is another important factor which invariably ensures that "capacity" is not the basis upon which students are admitted to read the best courses, law inclusive. Corruption is better known in Nigeria as "The Nigerian Factor" although it would be better still to christen it "the Nigerian Nightmare" given the throes into which it has thrown her. Nigeria is generally agreed to be a State that is unwilling and/or unable to fight corruption[21] and is one of the most corrupt countries in the world. Although the Transparency International's Corruption Perception Index (CPI) released in December 2014 ranks Nigeria as the 39th most corrupt country in the world,[22] this is considered by many Nigerians, never mind observers the world over, as particularly charitable to the Nigerian State. In 2008, Transparency International rated Nigeria as the most corrupt place on earth[23] and then for several years as one of the most corrupt countries in the world.[24] In the view of many, this is a more accurate evaluation of the status of corruption in Nigeria today[25] although there is hope that the new administration of President Muhammadu Buhari, elected on the anti-corruption platform as it is, has already set about addressing this deep rooted problem. The initial assessment of the Transparency International in the administration's first half-year is that little impact has been made as it still ranks Nigeria 136th in the 2015 Index.[26] Tertiary institution management condescends to being dictated to by influential persons with respect to who these institutions should admit. The consideration may be monetary or simply some other, usually unspoken, quid pro quo understanding. The Minister of Education or other ministers, Permanent Secretary or the numerous directors and deputy directors in the innumerable ministries, the National Universities Commission (NUC), the Joint Admissions and Matriculation Board (JAMB) will often be required to do favours, even offer protection—better to concession *a few* entry spaces. Nepotism also sets in. A dimension of this latter ill is what is often referred to as "staff request", i.e. the process by which members of staff of the tertiary institution put in admission requests usually on behalf of barely qualified candidates who are then preferred to better qualified candidates who have no one to make a case for them.

These many factors already impose their limitations on both the capacity for absorbing qualified applicants and the imperative of merit in the exercise before a consideration of the adequacy or otherwise of the available education, meaning—many of the best available minds do not have the benefit of the right kind of education that exposes them to the rudiments of both constitutional law and human rights education.

The Nigerian constitution makers have chosen to consign this right to the Fundamental Objectives and Directive Principles of State Policy, i.e. Chap. 2,[27] which is rendered unenforceable by the Constitution itself[28] although the ICESR requires that primary education is made both compulsory and available free.[29] In other words, the Constitution has batched primary education together with the other levels of education (i.e. secondary and higher education) for which progressive introduction of free education is permitted by the international instruments.[30] Curiously, education at the fundamental stages which the UDHR makes free[31] had, by its evolution to the ICESR, been downgraded to a component which "shall *be encouraged or intensified as far as possible* for those persons who have not received or completed the whole period of their primary education"[32] (emphasis added). Even more curious, the Nigerian constitution found a middle ground by making this form of education as described in Article 13(2)(d) of the ICESR (although the Constitution describes it as "adult literacy programme") free but as and when practicable[33] and therefore non-justiciable.[34] In passing, the point may also be made that this latter class has little or no chance of any meaningful Constitutional Law or Human Rights Law education.

As Fereira observes, "one of the main target groups of human rights education is undoubtedly constituted by children".[35] As such, there has followed some international treaties perhaps the most significant of which is the International Convention on the Rights of the Child.[36] This treaty does not only make education for the child a right,[37] its domestic derivative, the Child Rights Act[38] has also followed suit.[39] The Act further provides that every child shall have a right to free, compulsory and universal basic education and that it shall be *the duty* of the Government to provide such education.[40] There are two questions arising from this. The first ultimately superfluous question is the effect of its insertion as a right in the international treaty under Nigerian law. That is easily answered by the Constitution which stipulates that international treaties must be domesticated before they are operative in Nigeria.[41] The Child Rights Act essentially does not meet that requirement in that it is not domestication strictu sensu in the sense that the African Charter on Human and Peoples Rights (Ratification and Enforcement) Act[42] is a domestication of the African Charter on Human and Peoples Rights.[43] The latter is a wholesale transplant while the former is a selective enactment of parts of the Convention on the Rights of the Child. To put it differently, while the legislative authority of the African Charter would appear to be Sect. 12 of the Constitution, the National Assembly's authority for enacting the Child Rights Act would appear to be a combined reading of section 4(2),[44] Item 60(a) of the Exclusive Legislative List as contained in the Part I of Second Schedule to the Constitution[45] and section 17(3)(f).[46] The Supreme Court has permitted and approved this manner of construction in a series of decisions.[47] This should perhaps also explain why the Federal Government did not require to proceed to the various State houses of assembly to seek their ratification pursuant to relevant provisions of the Constitution[48]; whereas had the African Charter been domesticated during a civilian democratic dispensation, this would have been an obligatory step. Item 31 on the Exclusive Legislative List with respect to "implementation of treaties relating to matters on the" Exclusive Legislative List would appear to have no bearing on the discourse given that neither human rights, children's rights nor anything closely resembling them is listed in the aforesaid Exclusive Legislative List.

The second question, of course, is the efficacy of the right to free education, as inserted in the Child Rights Act, in the light of the constitutional consignment to the unenforceable Chap. 2 of the Constitution. It has been opined, on account of the supremacy provisions of the Constitution,[49] that it is a largely unhelpful right:

> ...the right under section 15 of the Act for a free and compulsory universal basic education up to at least junior secondary level is a largely ineffectual right given that the right to a free education is not a fundamental right under the Constitution of the Federal Republic. As the provision of the Act giving effect to free education is therefore contrary to the Constitution, it is void to the extent of its inconsistency.[50]

This does not positively construe the relevant provisions and would appear to be an erroneous view given that the political motivation behind the inclusion of Item 60(a) of the Exclusive Legislative List in the Constitution against the background of the non-justiciability of Chap. 2 was to ensure that the representatives of the people are given the opportunity to deliberate solemnly before activating the rights contained in the chapter. This is given the huge financial outlay and infrastructural imperatives of the "rights" contained in the chapter. Therefore, once the *latent* right in Chap. 2 is activated as done by the Child Rights Act,[51] it becomes a legal right. The issue, therefore, is really whether the aforesaid section 15(1) of the Child Rights Act is contrary to the Constitution (i.e. the non-justiciable section 18). The answer to that would be that the Act was enacted by the National Assembly pursuant to Item 60(a) of the Exclusive Legislative List to give "life" to a "dormant" right provided for in Chap. 2. The only surprise then would be that Nigerians have not flooded the courtrooms demanding government implementation of this right to *a free and compulsory universal basic education up to at least junior secondary school level.* It appears that it is one more thing that the Nigerian legislature has unwittingly done and Nigerians, perhaps in a state of shock have failed to take advantage of the "blunder". It is not a habit for the State to *consciously* give these socio-economic rights to Nigerians.

The theme of this work is also articulated in Article 26 of the Universal Declaration of Human Rights. The education contemplated under Article 26 shall be designed to ensure that the pursuit and advancement of human rights is at the forefront of a State party's policy goals. Thus, human rights education is to "be directed … to the strengthening of respect for human rights and fundamental freedoms".[52] The ICESR merely substantiates this approach. The issues, therefore, relate to the extent or level of human rights education that is available and whether, in the second place, they are purposed at reinforcing reverence for human rights and basic freedoms.

The African Charter follows through on this theme by enacting not just that States parties like Nigeria shall endeavour to teach it but, taking it a step further, to ensure that they are "understood"[53]:

> States parties to the present Charter shall *have the duty to promote and ensure through teaching, education and publication, the respect of the rights and freedoms contained in the present Charter* and *to see to it that these freedoms and rights as well as corresponding obligations and duties are understood* (emphasis added).

It is, therefore, deeply incumbent on every State party to the Charter to ensure that human rights is not only taught but understood by its citizens. This makes this chapter imperative in its examination of the effort made by the Nigerian State to ensure that human rights is taught, in the first place, and understood in the second.

3 Sustainable Development

In discussing sustainable development, there is a need to first embark on a conceptual analysis of the term "development". What is development itself? Development is a term which suggests a process of continuous evolution and change. In other words, the thing to be developed is in an unfinished, imperfect and incomplete state and what human society is not? It involves a process of change for the better in terms of size, strength, efficiency and advancement. The United Nations Declaration on the Right to Development[54] passed by resolution A/RES/41/128 on 4 December 1986 at the General Assembly's 97th Plenary Meeting depicts development as a comprehensive economic, social, cultural and political process that aims at "the constant improvement of the well-being of the entire population" on the basis of their vigorous, free and significant contribution in the process of development.[55] It is the responsibility of all human beings individually and collectively to work for development but, however, taking into account the necessity for absolute deference to their rights and fundamental freedoms.[56]

The Brundtland Commission defines sustainable development as "development that meets the needs of the present generation without compromising the needs of future generations".[57] The implication is that it is only worthwhile development if it can be sustained, and perhaps improved upon, for the entire duration of the life of a nation. If it cannot be sustained, then it is not a development that is worthwhile.

There is such a thing as the right to development. The United Nations has declared that the "right to development is an inalienable right"[58] designed to guarantee the right of the individual to the economic and social development and well-being.[59] The Declaration stresses the duties of everyone towards the enjoyment of rights but also controversially, in terms of a multicultural world, the universality of rights. It also underlines the inevitability of the interdependence of rights particularly stating that "the satisfaction of economic, social and cultural rights is a guarantee for the enjoyment of civil and political rights".[60] This portends great implications for the theme of this paper in that without the effective implementation of the right to development (and generally the economic, social and cultural rights); the civil and political rights are essentially vain pursuits. Education, therefore, which is an essential socio-cultural right, is a necessary tool for bringing to reality the human rights of the people.

The question is—Exactly what status does the right to development occupy? It is clearly an "inalienable human right" right,[61] but it appears that the fulfilment of that right must take into account the need for full respect, not for the *other*, but for human rights and fundamental freedoms.[62] Exactly what then is the relationship between the right to development and other human rights and fundamental freedoms? This seeming ambiguity may explain the reason that it appears it is made submissive to *other* human rights and fundamental freedoms. This approach would appear to have been adopted by the Nigerian constitution as well since the non-justiciable Chap. 2 espouses the ideas that "the security and welfare of the people shall be the primary purpose of government"[63]; the State "shall harness the resources of the nation and promote national prosperity and an efficient, a dynamic and self-reliant economy"[64] and particularly that the "State shall direct its policy towards ensuring the promotion of a *planned and balanced economic development*" (emphasis added).[65] Thus in many modern constitutions, including Nigeria's, it is hardly "inalienable" and its status as a legal right is entirely non-existent. This explains, therefore, why African governments, including successive Nigerian governments, have paid such lip service to development in spite of the abundant natural and manpower resources available to them.

The question then is—How is the law student to be prepared, as a human being, to optimally participate in and contribute to the development of the Nigerian state?

4 The Connection Between Human Rights and Sustainable Development

Some opinions have stated that human rights and development were separate and mutually exclusive spheres.[66] While development was attended to by economists, the matter of human rights was seen as the sole preserve of the lawyer.[67] Part of the responsibility for this state of affairs has been placed at the doorstep of the United Nations.[68] This state of affairs appeared to exist right up to the Cold War before the merging.[69] This convergence[70] became a mainstay of international policy but, it must be opined, was rather belated. This view is consequent upon the fact that this relationship should have been activated at the very inception of the United Nations.[71] A careful study of all the integral rights embedded within the human rights template demonstrates that human rights and development had an inexorable connection that was clear.

5 Constitutional and Human Rights Law—Concepts and Issues for Reorientation

There are many issues that have emerged in Constitutional Law and Human Rights Law. The curricula appear to be completely oblivious of these new issues because the curricula were designed several years ago and have not been adequately updated. The principle of affirmative action, for instance, is one that is unfamiliar to many undergraduate students.

Although the subject of human rights is taught in the universities, there is no evidence that this teaching contemplates the peculiar characteristics of African societies. The focus is usually and predominantly on the Western concepts of rights jurisprudence which are also manifested in the international human rights regime. This can only be the case given that the substructure and early aspects of this regime[72] were configured at times when the African continent, the Nigerian state inclusive, were either under colonial rule and consequently had no sovereign voice in international law terms or were freshly out of colonial rule[73] and were therefore ideologically still attached to the apron strings of their "mother" countries. The subsequent rights documents were agreed with rather ineffectual participation from delegates from sub-Saharan African states. Many arrived without delegates specialised in or representative of the many cultures of their countries. Although it is awkward to come to the conclusion that human rights should be taught from indigenous, traditional or customary perspectives, it is not entirely unreasonable that a dual approach to teaching human rights can fulfil aspects not only of law as it is but as it ought to be. Unfortunately, it is unlikely that manifestations of human rights in customary law systems has been hinted at, let alone taught, in a Constitutional Law or human rights law class. Indeed, a fundamental lacuna in the curricula of these courses is the absence of customary law perspectives on human rights.

De Villiers,[74] for instance, cautions against what has been the wholesale assimilation of these principles without pausing to find "a philosophical African 'home' or rationale for human rights which is based on African beliefs, experiences, values and expectations". He further notes that even the African Charter has been described as of "near irrelevance to Africa's political life". Among the issues he raises is the uncertain place of customary law vis-à-vis modern legal principles and the need for deciphering what African values should be projected in the construction of bills of rights. It is easy to see the point, and these conflicts project themselves increasingly in the debates relating to abortion (given the value attached to human life and behavioural morality in Africa), female circumcision (given the value attached to morality), euthanasia (given the sociocultural and religious value attached to human life)[75] and gay–lesbian relationships (given the value attached to morality and the sanctity of heterosexual matrimony). Polygamy, a firm fact of African social reality, is another. With respect to it, the Maputo Protocol states that monogamy shall be the preferred form of marriage.[76] In an African society? Many would consider that it smirks of an elitist plot to ram its preferences down the throat of everyone else regardless of cultural individualism. They raise issues that may generally be classified into the North and South human rights philosophies which, although they may have complementarities, are also laden with substantial contradictions and inconsistencies. This culminates into what should be the distinction between general and particular Jurisprudence.

The contemporary textbook by Twining[77] offers a different perspective of general jurisprudence from early jurisprudential works, i.e. that as society has become more cosmopolitan, a "truly cosmopolitan general jurisprudence"[78] is an imperative.[79] In his view, an insistence on the universalism of jurisprudence results in "reductionist or essentialist tendencies" to which he objects.[80] Specifically, as it relates to Africa, universalism is now generally perceived "as a Western hegemonic view with European practice as the norm and African cultural practices as deviant".[81] This hostility is not unconnected with Western jurisprudence's ignorance or dismissal of values that are not its own.[82] This deficiency has inspired scholars such as Twining to seek to overhaul the concept of jurisprudence. As he submits[83]:

> Why do I talk of 'reviving' general jurisprudence, when some prominent modern jurists, for example Hart and Raz, have claimed to have been doing 'general jurisprudence'? A brief answer is that, while much of their work can be treated as examples of general jurisprudence, their conception of 'general jurisprudence' is quite narrow in being largely confined to

> state law viewed from what is essentially a Western perspective… my conception of general jurisprudence is intended to challenge tendencies (often latent) to project parochial preconceptions onto non-Western legal orders, cultures, and traditions.

As the title of Twining's work suggests, it analyses Jurisprudence from a global perspective in terms of projecting the views of Jurisprudence from both the Northern and the Southern divides. Towards this objective, he devotes an entire chapter to discussing views on human rights from the developing world.[84] This is because of his recognition of "the diversity, the complexity and the fluidity of the phenomena" with which the scholar is or *should* be concerned.[85] That discussion reveals many aspects of the sociocultural and ideological conflicts that or should inundate human rights discourses in the region as differentiated from discourses elsewhere.

The questions, then, are whether there can be general rights jurisprudence and whether the time has not come for particular jurisprudence. In other words, is relativism better suited to a multicultural universe than universalism? Is a universal concept desirable, even attainable? Indeed, is relativism desirable, even attainable? What options exist for an amicable but just resolution of these conflicts? How have curricula, even teachers, integrated these perspectives of African jurisprudence and projected them on the international human rights regime? How do the human rights law curricula address these concerns? There is no evidence that they do.

6 Issues for Reorientation—Human Rights as Politics

It may be argued with substantial validity that human rights is essentially politics. As a result, human rights performance is essentially a feature of which of any particular divide a State is at any particular time in the evolution of the universe. During the Cold War era, the international community generally presented the socialist bloc's legal systems as not meeting the minimum standards of human rights laid down by the international human rights regime. This is despite the non-existent human rights portfolio during the same period of such West-leaning authoritarian regimes as those of Mobutu Sese Seko in the then Zaire (Democratic Republic of the Congo), Anwar Sadat's Egypt and Ferdinand Marcos's The Philippines. It was the habit of the international community to play down rights abuses in the latter countries while magnifying abuses in the Communist bloc. With the passing of the Cold War, more decentralised focus has been placed on the remnants of the Soviet/Communist/Socialist bloc—North Korea, Libya, Iraq, Syria, Cuba and China, for instance. These debates continue today. The Arab Spring and where it led? With the softening diplomatic attitude of the Chinese, the Iranians and the Cubans, even more focus will be shed on the vestiges of "radical" Arab States—Syria, for instance.

These inconsistencies also permeate through to Constitutional Law issues. The right to freedom of expression is a case in point. Is there a right for faiths to protect icons and belief? In Islam, for instance, it is a taboo to depict the Prophet of Islam in any form. In 2005 when a Danish newspaper[86] published cartoons of a person purported to be the Prophet Muhammad as a terrorist with a bomb, it was hailed, sometimes even commended by Western and Western—inclined rights activists and States as a victory for press freedom and the right to freedom of expression despite the protestation of the Muslim world. On the other hand, the response to ISIL when they take over shrines of traditional religious practices in Syria and destroy them (or the Taliban when they destroy Buddhist temples and sculptures in Afghanistan) is different—it is condemned vociferously. Are icons not expressions of faith and therefore deserving of protection as freedoms regardless of politics? When is it ever taught in Nigerian schools that apprehension of fundamental rights *could be* a matter of political perception? That there could, in fact, be a Nigerian perception, if not an African one.

7 Issues for Reorientation—Human Rights as Ethnocentrism/Matter of Opinion

There are other perspectives on human rights that need teaching in Nigerian law faculties that are today largely glossed over. For instance, ethnocentrism would appear to have forayed into the field of jurisprudence. Twining,[87] for instance, observes:

> Normative jurisprudence has experienced a lively period in recent years, but most enquiries and controversies have taken place within the framework of Western traditions of thought and with explicit or implicit reference either to Western societies or to international relations perceived from Western points of view.[88]

This appears to be even more the case in the West-versus-the-developing-world dichotomy in the field of human rights and which has resulted in retardation in its global development.[89] Even the history of human rights and the idea that human rights are a result of Western activism are largely considered as ethnocentric.[90] Indeed, it can logically be argued that the whole idea of human rights has not only been designed from a Western standpoint[91] but also that "international law consistently attempts to obscure its colonial origins, its connection with the inequalities and exploitation inherent in the colonial encounter".[92] Several factors are responsible for this. First, international law had already been shaped by the West before the events of the twentieth century that culminated in both world wars. According to Anghie,[93] "The expansion of European empires ensured that the entire globe was encompassed by one European system of international law by the conclusion of the nineteenth century". In addition, the first international human rights instrument, the Universal Declaration of Human Rights, which has formed the basis of every subsequent rights treaty, was passed as a resolution of the United Nations General Assembly in 1948, long before the Western colonies in Africa, Nigeria inclusive, gained independence. As they (including Nigeria) were not sovereign States, they were not members of the United Nations. As such, there were little or no consultations at all with the indigenous inhabitants of the continent as the colonial masters negotiated the Declaration. Shortly after the independence in 1960 (in the case of Nigeria, for example), treaties such as the International Covenant on Civil and Political Rights and the International Covenant on Economic, Social and Cultural rights were agreed[94] ostensibly with little input from the newly independent States.[95] There is the question of the manner in which subsequent human rights treaties were negotiated and the level of participation of the developing States (particularly sub-Saharan African States), which is near non-existent. The universalised secularism[96] that has been forced on the international and domestic human rights regimes and expositions are a wild figment of the imagination. Tradition and religion continue to be compelling belief systems in much of the Southern political hemisphere. Thus, African perspectives, culture and morality are almost entirely glossed over in the regime. What percentage of the international human rights regime is African or holds an African input? The curricula are silent on the need to embark on a multicultural cosmology. Thus, the teachers are unfamiliar with these perspectives having been taught themselves with perhaps even less dynamic, near extinct curricula.

Contemporary students, therefore, are victimised by teachers because in the popular cliché, "you cannot give what you do not have".

In sum, the need to localise human rights jurisprudence is not contentious largely because Nigeria operates a jurisprudence in which there is uncritical adherence to the law as it is. Thus, it is no wonder that there is no writing or debate at all on the impact of cultural imperialism and ethnocentrism in her rights regime; never mind what, in international law terms, she must acquiesce in—relativism, pluralism or monism; why the *hijab* should be outlawed in a multicultural society in which Muslims constitute at least 50% of the population or why the right to be nude in a culturally conservative society is advanced to the suppression of the right to conceal your private parts. Indeed, there might be no problem if everyone was allowed to exercise their freedoms: the freedom to conceal and the freedom to be nude. The problem arises when advocates of the right to nudity seek to impose what is after all just a right (i.e. an entitlement) on persons who do not wish to exercise the right. There are other unaddressed culture-related questions and issues: for instance, why LGBTQ Rights are to be advanced in a culturally conservative society to which it is largely alien but not polygyny rights in a society of which it is culturally a part and parcel; the idea, now perfected in Western jurisprudence, that homosexuality is, without more a question of rights or whether it is a question of morality as most Africans prefer to view it; the right to choose sexuality; the right to abortion and foetal rights; equality of spouses in the family; the role of powers—be they media, financial, political. Multiculturalism must be a critical factor in these discourses and, by extension, in the curricula.

The question is—How has the educational system in Nigeria, at the primary, post-primary and tertiary stages, catered to the(se) needs of the human rights discourse?

8 Teaching at the Primary and Secondary School Levels

At primary and secondary school levels, the teaching of fundamental rights is rather basic. Consequently, there appears to be little or no doubt that crash nature of the education, application of human rights and constitutional principles by officials in public life is also limited, oppressive and devoid of proper principles. At these levels, the relevant subjects are

Government and Civic Education. Civic Education is offered across the board, i.e. by Science and Arts students in primary, junior secondary and senior secondary schools. On the other hand, Government is offered only by students in senior secondary school who have opted for the Arts.[97] This study has undertaken to embark on a review of a couple of texts on Civic Education and Government to help ascertain the level of preparedness of students of law when they venture into tertiary education.

For the purpose of this study, two books have been chosen for partial review. The first is a widely used book on the subject of Civic Education, a subject that is compulsory for all students. In this case, a book for the use of all senior secondary school students, i.e. from I to III written by Saleh, Ademola and Damulup.[98] The Civic Education curriculum for senior secondary schools *appears* rather impressive, and this is evidenced by the work of Saleh et al.[99] The book covers an impressive array of constitutional and human rights law topics including, at Senior Secondary School I, citizenship, representative democracy, the rule of law, human rights, strong institutions of government—the executive, the legislature and the judiciary, federalism and law and order. At Senior Secondary School II, it discusses citizenship (again), democracy and national development, capitalist democracy, human rights (again) and period of emergency. At Senior Secondary School III, it discusses human rights (again), political apathy, public service in a democracy, civil society and popular participation, constitutional democracy (again) and the rule of law (again).

The initial problem, however, is the terminology "human rights" with the work consistently referring to it as "human right". Thus in Theme 6, Senior Secondary School I, there is titled "Human Right" and "Limitation of Human Right" (sic) at Senior Secondary School II. At some point, it even becomes clear that "human rights" and "human right" are employed interchangeably. It is hardly surprising that during Constitutional Law and Human Rights Law lectures and examinations, 200-Level students consistently refer to "human right" when in fact they mean "human rights". Indeed, it is probably a definition of how impressionable they are that this streak inculcated in them in secondary school abides with them till some of them graduate after seven academic sessions in spite of the effort of the lecturer to convince them that there are human rights but that the term "human right" is employed singularly and with respect to a discussion of *a* human right.[100]

The work is bedevilled by all kinds of editing and grammar problems. A topic is headed "Structures of Government in Citizenship"[101] before the opening paragraph discloses that the "three arms of government have structures as *having* been defined by the Constitution" (emphasis added).

There are also complications in the structural or chapter outlay of the work with questionable instances of placing the cart before the horse. It is awkward to be discussing the history and content of the Universal Declaration of Human Rights under Theme 6 at Senior Secondary School I before an insight into the definition, classifications, categories and characteristics of human rights in Theme 1 at Senior Secondary School III as it is to be discussing limitations of human rights at Senior Secondary II before the definition, classifications, categories and characteristics of human rights in Theme 1 at Senior Secondary School III.

The fact that the book's back cover highlights the lead author as "a lawyer" who "is prominent in the socio political circle (sic) and has brought her wealth of experience to bear on this all important book" appears to explain many things but not many others. Looking at the table of contents, the book laudably discusses many subjects relevant to Constitutional and Human Rights Law. At Senior Secondary School I level, it discusses Citizenship with sub-topics such as ways of acquiring citizenship dual citizenship, renunciation of citizenship, deprivation of citizenship.[102] The initial problem is that when one gets to what is supposed to be the "goals of citizenship",[103] what one actually finds is the "goals of citizenship education" and although the "Topic" eventually discusses "Importance of Citizen's Rights and Duties"[104] and "Obligations and Duties",[105] it is hard to say that these discourses amount to either the "goals of citizenship" or the "goals of citizenship education" although the former seems more plausible.

But perhaps the biggest problems lie in the language and discussion of these topics. On citizenship, for instance, these are the opening statements reproduced verbatim:

> Citizenship is the right which every member of a country has or acquires. This right makes a person to become a citizen of a country with full rights. When a person is a citizen of a country the person will ordinarily be subjected to all the laws of that country. When the country runs a democratic system of government, the members must be subjected to the constitution.

> This is because the Constitution is a document which contains, the rules and regulation of the country. A constitution either Written or Unwritten is what governs a country. Some clubs, association and society are also governed by *the* constitution (emphasis added).[106]

The incoherence of it all is troubling. But to end with the suggestion that "some" clubs, associations and societies are also governed by "the constitution", not "constitutions" leads the student astray in at least two respects: one, only some associations, clubs and societies are subject to the constitution; and two, it is the national constitution that governs them as distinct from their individual constitutions which are sometimes a requirement of a State's laws.

It then sets out the three ways of "acquiring" citizenship.[107] Although it is an elementary error to suggest that citizenship by birth is acquired,[108] the "acquisition" of citizenship by birth, for instance, is described as follows:

> By Birth: A person is a citizen of Nigeria if the person was born in Nigeria before 1st October, 1960, either of whose parents or any person of whose grandparents belongs or belonged to a community indigenous to Nigeria.
>
> A person shall not become a citizen of Nigeria if neither of his parents nor any of his grand parents was born in Nigeria before 1st October, 1960.

This "appears" to be a near verbatim reproduction of section 25(1) but the reproduction is completely distorted by the insertion of the words "any person" before the words "of whose grandparents. The text then completely mangles the discussion with the addition of this incomplete sentence:

> The constitution states that every person born in Nigeria before the 1st October 1960 either of whose parents or any of whose grand parents is a citizen of Nigeria.

How are the above rather awkward writings to be interpreted to adults; never mind young persons? More importantly, it was an attempt to lift the very complex provisions of section 25 verbatim for the use of 12-year-olds already generally suffering from the effect of general poor education and incompetent use of the English language.[109]

The attempt to explain the dual citizenship provisions are just as confusing because it does not betray an adequate understanding of the provisions. The book states:

> A person shall forfeit his Nigerian Citizenship if, the person had acquired or retains the citizenship or nationality of another country than Nigeria of which he is not a citizen by birth.

The next sentence which appears to attempt to clear this confusion with an illustration[110] is merely an aggravation. Why not just, "A person shall forfeit his Nigerian citizenship by registration or naturalization if he acquires or retains the citizenship of any other country of which he is not a citizen by birth" or something as uncomplicated or inaccurate?

Apart from setting out the requirements for the grant of citizenship by naturalisation with an attempt at a near verbatim reproduction with words and phrases such as "domiciled" and "immediately preceding his application", the text makes a near complete hash of the provisions of section 27(1)(g)(i) and (ii) of the Constitution[111] in the following terms:

> The person has immediately preceding the date of his application either resided in Nigeria continuously for a period of fifteen years or the person resided in Nigeria for a continuous period of twenty years immediately preceding that period of twenty years immediately preceding that period of the twelve months has resided in Nigeria for periods amounting in the aggregate to not less than fifteen years.

How is anyone, much less 13-year-olds, to construe this intelligibly?

The book also falls victim to certain popular but unverified concepts. One example—the idea that voting at general elections is an "obligation/duty" upon the citizen.[112] The following discussion is rather ambiguous—on the one hand, voting "during an election is very important" while on the other, "The citizen of voting age *is expected* to have his voters (sic) card ready for any election in which he or she is eligible to vote" (emphasis added). The well-known principle of law is that voting is a right[113] not a duty. Indeed, section 24, which sets out the duties of the Nigerian citizen, does not indicate this as a duty. Worse convolution afflicts Obligation 5 with respect to Employment where the authors state[114]:

> Every citizen has the *right* to work. Therefore, *a citizen should engage himself in gainful employment.* No citizen should be allowed to be staying idle in the community so that he does not become a vagabond in that community (emphasis added).

Given the terms in which this "duty" has been stated, one has to wonder whether employment is a right or a duty. Indeed, the Constitution does not state this as a duty of the citizen.[115] Can the Constitution impose a duty on the citizen that is not entirely within his power and discretion to discharge? As for its being a right, the Constitution merely asks the State to "*direct its policy towards ensuring* that all citizens, without discrimination...*have the opportunity for securing adequate means of livelihood* as well *as adequate opportunity to secure suitable employment*"[116] (emphasis added). There is nothing in the italicised words to indicate that employment is a citizen's right. The Constitution then takes the extra precaution of inserting this provision in Chap. 2 of this Constitution, which it makes non-justiciable,[117] i.e. that legal action may not be brought to compel the government to do any of the things indicated in the Chapter. Since the National Assembly has also not passed an Act granting the right to employment to a citizen,[118] the question of the qualification to section 6(6)(c) stated in terms of other or contrary provision elsewhere in the Constitution does not arise. Where then does this work find its authority for teaching children that Nigerians have a right to employment?

With respect to the functions of the Judiciary, to ascribe law-making function (not of the subsidiary legislation variation)[119] to the judiciary is also worrisome essentially because at this stage the audience is not exposed to the jurisprudence of the Realist School or even of the Critical Legal Studies movement. The book writes[120]:

> Making of Laws: The judiciary is responsible for making laws through its proceedings and judgement (sic) of Superior Courts of record i.e. The High Court, Federal High Court, Court of Appeal and Supreme Court.

Functions of Government[121] discusses the functions of the executive while discussing the same executive functions at a later stage,[122] this time with additional functions. This discussion is repetitive but even here fundamental issues are missed out. The impression is given, for instance, that the President appoints ambassadors and High Commissioners without more or that he declares the State of Emergency unilaterally. This is particularly irksome because when one views the functions of the Legislature, these important functions are omitted.

The work sets out the "Sources of *the* Constitution (emphasis added).[123] Since it refers to the sources of "the", not "a", constitution, it can safely be assumed that this refers to the Nigerian constitution although when it lists "The constitution of the countries" as item 8, there is a substantial derogation from that assumption. If it is to suggest that "constitutions" derive from many sources such as the accompanying list, that would be a different matter entirely. The following is the list of the sources reproduced verbatim:

1. Past experiences of a country, for example a country's past social, economic, political, historical and geographical experiences of various people as its major sources.
2. Statutes passed by Parliament or National Assembly.
3. Decrees and edicts of the military government.
4. The intellectual works of eminent authors, jurists, historians, philosophers, essayist, politicians and statesmen.
5. Case law or judicial precedents.
6. Customs and way of life of the people.
7. Rules and conventions guiding human behaviour.
8. The constitution of the countries.
9. The deliberation of constitutional conferences or constituent Assemblies of other countries.
10. Rules of international law.

The work discusses the American constitution before this list, but it is well known that these are not the sources of the American constitution and the work does not tell us that they are. Some of the sources indicated here, such as Statutes passed by Parliament, the intellectual works of eminent authors, jurists and historians, case law or judicial precedents, customs, rules and conventions appear more suited to jurisdictions with unwritten constitutions such as the UK. The confusion etched on the impressionable minds of the students early on by these misrepresentations is undeniable. In truth, there is only one source for the Nigerian constitution—the document itself and, therefore, it is said that the Nigerian Constitution is both written and codified. If the Supreme Court had not held[124] that the statutes referred to in section 274(5) of the 1979 Constitution of Nigeria[125] do not constitute part of the Nigerian Constitution, then one might say that the Nigerian Constitution had two (2) sources and, therefore, perhaps an uncodified constitution. There is no way in which, looking at the list, that one does not wonder how a secondary school teacher, untrained in law, would make headway making these distinctions to a class of young children when the lead author, a trained "lawyer", failed to make them and which failure would invariably lead to misleading millions of children.

The discussion of the Rule of Law in Nigeria[126] is equally interesting and the lawyer part of the lead author is immediately evident. There is nothing but language to quarrel with in the opening statements:

> Rule of law is enshrined in democracy. The concept of Rule of Law is a universal concept which connotes law and order, without which life and property would be unsecured[127] in any society. The concept presupposes that the underlying principle is regularity of the law and that a man is governed by law and regulations and not by the whims and caprices of the rulers of the day.

The same is true of this discourse of the "Purpose of Rule of Law"[128]:

> The purpose of rule of law is establishing a government of laws and not of men. The rule is the principle by which the process of the government is *bound with the law*. Hence government must according to the law (sic) (emphasis added).

The above-italicised words appear to be erroneously employed but accidentally correct language given the last sentence in the quotation. The result, however, is that it becomes perhaps too technical for 13-year-olds. Bound with the law? Tied up in the law or with the ropes of the law? That is almost poetic metaphor. Why not just "bound by law"?

The book states three (3) principles of the rule of law as (i) legality; (ii) impartiality; and (iii) the right of the individual under the law. In language which is eerily close, if not identical to A.V. Dicey's language (and sometimes to Aihe and Oluyede's),[129] the book states on "Legality"[130]:

> This principle explains the absolute supremacy or predominance of regular law which excludes in its totality an existence of arbitrary power or wide discretionary use of power or influence by the government,[131] powers,

> whatever their extent, must be exercised in accordance with the ordinary law of the land. The exercise of power not backed by law is obviously arbitral (sic)...

On "Impartiality"[132] the authors state, and this is reported verbatim:

> This principle explains that no body is above the law. *It involved equal subjection of all classes to the ordinary law of the land administered by the ordinary law courts.*[133] The law is no respecter of person (sic), irrespective of rank and status in I life[134] (emphasis added).

These texts highlight an even more fundamental problem in the sometimes technical language taken directly from the original text. Although it appears too complicated for children of the ages in issue, it is complicated further by vagueness and uncertainty in the explanatory text.

On "The Right of the Individual under the Law",[135] the authors state:

> The principle defines the rights of the individual under the law. Legal rights are vested in us but not conferred on us by the government. in Nigeria, the rights or privileges of every citizen is (sic) spelt out in the constitution unlike in other countries like Britain which has an unwritten constitution.

In the first place, how are the teachers and the pupils who are not trained in law to comprehend and explain "vested in" and "conferred on"? Secondly, it is easy to understand the authors' difficulties in articulating this principle since the legal framework employed by Dicey was the unwritten UK constitution rather than the prevalent contemporary written constitutions with in-built fundamental rights.[136] This explains the authors' last sentence in the quotation. Assuming therefore that that is the case, where do the additional items (d), (e) and (f) arise from especially given that they discuss "Maximum Liberty of Citizens", "Judiciary" (with special focus on the right to fair hearing and access to justice) and Citizen's Rights"—all aspects of human rights?

The text reviewed has been approved for use by Nigeria's education authorities, and this raises many issues as it appears that they either do not know better or what much is known by them has been overtaken by some other consideration, i.e. it is not unreasonable to suspect that in Nigeria, government officials may either be authoring the books themselves or the authors (not necessarily these ones) are making under-the-counter payments for approval for use of books. Officials in individual schools also "cut deals" with authors to approve their works for use in their schools. Where is the evidence of any form of review before approval in the face of the above highlighted palpable facts that speak for themselves? If there was an oversight in the first place in letting them into the curricula, what is the evidence of their recall, if any?

This review (of a few pages of the above work, it must be added) has been undertaken in order to underline the scale of the inadequacies of texts with which Nigerian children must work in understanding constitutional and human rights law at an early age.

The second work relating to the subject of Government is in sharp contrast to the conclusions drawn on the above work. The Government, as a subject in senior secondary school, is apparently critical to preparation for a degree programme. For an assessment of the handling of this subject, a review of Dibie's brilliant book[137] is also necessary. The discussion is much more articulate, and one is hard pressed to find fault with its editing. It is particularly gratifying that the authors know the difference between "crisis" and "crises",[138] evidence of good grammar in a jurisdiction where decreasing attention is increasingly being paid to it. He discusses the types and characteristics of government including the unitary state[139] and the federal state,[140] the presidential system of government, the rule of law,[141] the appointment of judges, impeachment, checks and balances (without actually stating that the arms are separate but that they share powers). There is nothing implicitly wrong with its definition of separation of powers as "the separation or division of political powers and functions among the three arms of government—the executive, the legislature, judiciary...".[142] In discussing the demerits of separation of powers, he states, "Factors of rigidity: A rigid application of the principle of separation of powers can hinder the smooth running of government".[143] This is good information for the student although there is literally no contemporary democratic system in which separation of powers is rigidly practised. The only difficulty was in not illustrating how this permissive separation of powers is practised. A plus is the discourse on pre-colonial political systems encompassing pre-colonial judicial, legislative and executive systems,[144] although it might have been just as commendable to have discussed the human rights attributes of these pre-colonial systems. The book does not do this. He also commendably addresses such critical, current local issues as a federal character[145] and fiscal federalism.[146]

The important issue of fundamental human rights, however, gets its fullest mention in two (2) pages,[147] where it discusses among others the reasons why fundamental human rights are included in constitutions. Elsewhere, there are several brief, one-sentence, dispersed references to human rights-related topics such as, under the section on the rule of law,[148] press freedom, speedy justice, period of detention and public trial. It also elucidates "factors that can safeguard the liberty of individuals",[149] liberty,[150] civil liberty (rights of citizenship) and brief, one-or-two-sentence references to issues such as the right to life, religious freedom, education; the latter with respect to which it particularly notes, "In some states, education is not a legal right".[151] It does not, however, specify Nigeria as one of such states. Again, it accurately generalises, with respect to "the right to work", "In some countries, the legal right to work is recognised. The right to work however cannot mean the right to a particular work".[152]

With respect to education, it also states, "In some states, education is not a legal right".[153] These generalisations do not translate into the specific that these two (2) rights are not available to Nigerians as rights (legal entitlements) strictly speaking given the non-justiciability of the matters contained in Chap. 2 of the Constitution.

There are two (2) main problems, however, with the discussion of human rights topics The first is understandable, given that it is a textbook on Government, that the discussion of human rights, although pinpoint, is rather sparse. The second is the complete absence of any discussion of the rights of children.

The concomitant implication is that where an institution employs the use of these two (2) books reviewed above, it will invariably be that only the Arts students are in a position to pretend to have benefited from a somewhat adequate preparatory knowledge of Constitutional/Human Rights law issues since the text on Civic Education, which the Science students are exposed to would appear to be unarguably inadequate. Unfortunately, these Science students will develop to hold administrative positions where they invariably contend with issues relating to Constitutional and Human Rights Law and where actions would most probably be guided by emotions and sentiments rather than by the rule of (or according to) law.

9 Summing Up Pre-tertiary Preparation

The teaching of Constitutional Law itself is so inadequate that usually when students eventually veer into fields other than law, ignorance is manifested at the most elementary of levels. Graduates of banking become state governors and ask commissioners for justice to prepare laws for them so that they can sign ("promulgate") the laws into force. When the 29th of May was christened Democracy Day and declared a public holiday by the Executive in Nigeria in 1999, the Executive was apparently unaware that "public holidays" was an item on the Exclusive Legislative List over which the National Assembly must first enact legislation[154] before implementation by the Executive.

The preparedness of the 200-Level student in the Nigerian university who studies Constitutional Law tames against the background of the technical nature of the course and its significant status in legal education in Nigeria. The orientation in secondary school is demonstrably scanty—they really do think that separation of powers is a separation of powers. There is little meaningful antecedent grounding. The orientation at 100 Level is perhaps even more inadequate. At the time he or she is confronted with Constitutional Law, he or she is more often than not still struggling with basic English language and pronouncing "human right" when he really does mean "human rights"—this, especially against the background of the poor standard of education in Nigeria. A 300-Level student still spells the word "Faculty" as "F-A-C-A-U-L-T-Y" despite his lecturer's best endeavour. How then does he or she cope with the subject?

This is where a reorientation is necessary, and this may be guided by the practice in other jurisdictions. Human rights education for young children is regulated, evolving and improving constantly. An example is the fact that human rights teachers in Europe now have designed for them what is called the *Compasito*, apparently developed after the realisation that the Council of Europe's Manual on Human Rights Education with Young People between the ages of 14 and 18 was inadequate for even younger people and it "urgently needed to be complemented with another manual targeting a younger audience eager to learn about human rights".[155] According to Fereira[156]:

> *Compasito* begins by offering a framework for human right education with children, clarifying and contextualising what human rights, in particular children's rights, are, and what is specific to human rights education with

> children in terms of methodology. Furthermore, *Compasito* makes available a range of different activities on specific human rights topics, understood in a broad sense, as to encompass issues related to citizenship, democracy, discrimination, environment, family, health, peace and poverty.

Compasito even employs the use of cartoon methodology to press home its work on children who would eagerly embrace this methodology.[157]

Instructively, although the textbook by Saleh et al.[158] is targeted at children, there is not one mention of the rights of children. That is a basic problem. At a somewhat more complicated level, at what point should children begin to relate the Universal Declaration of Human Rights of 1948, which Saleh et al.[159] discussed in detail, with the fact that when this foundation for the international human rights regime was laid, virtually all African nations (including their own, Nigeria) was under colonial rule and had no input whatsoever in its configuration? This basic element of "clarifying and *contextualising* what human rights … are" (emphasis added) is missed completely by the works.

10 Law Education Curricula at the Tertiary Stage

In most Nigerian universities, the course content, particularly at 100 Level, is not too dissimilar from that of the University of Abuja. Legal method is the only law course that is offered at this stage.[160] Instead, the students offer SOC101 (Introduction to Sociology), SOC103 (Introduction to African Society and Culture), ENL104 (Introduction to Nigerian Literature), although it is a requirement that students have credit in Literature in English at O Level,[161] PHL101 (Logic and Philosophical Thought) and GST101A (Use of English). Indeed, the relevance, if not the inevitability, of these courses must be conceded although germane questions remain. For instance, what do the students really need from GST 101A (Use of English) after meeting the requirements for O Levels in both English language and Literature in English? The study of GST103 (Nigerian Peoples and Culture) also raises questions. Indeed, the student is more often than not a Nigerian. While he ought to have knowledge of Nigerian culture, it would appear even more rational to remember that the student was most probably born and also lives in it. Should a curriculum devote two semesters to this course especially if the teacher is not trained to help with perhaps the most relevant aspect of Nigerian culture: its customary laws? It may be said in parenthesis, though, that if the course is taught well, the student is likely to find that the society in which the student lives is different from that which the law sometimes attempts to paint.[162] On the same grounds, SOC103 (Introduction to *African* Society and Culture (emphasis added) would appear to be even more unnecessary aside substantiating a case of duplicity. Many would consider the latter of time-consuming superfluity. The utility is even more jeopardised given the presence of Law 205 Nigerian Legal System, a 200-Level course, on the curriculum in which inklings of Nigerian culture but particularly an in-depth study of the law systems of the indigenous communities making up Nigeria are offered. As a further instance, in some other universities, the course History and Philosophy of Science is offered as a core course at 100 Level. The imperative question again—how does it help the law student, if nothing else, in his cross-examination of the medical doctor standing trial in relation to professional negligence? Every one of the borrowed courses referred to above is a core course, i.e. it is mandatory on the students. They appear to be too fringy and peripheral for the importance accorded them.

Added to these ambiguities, the teachers of these courses are borrowed from the concerned departments rather than teachers in the faculties of Law. Although this might make sense in that teachers of law courses may not have had adequate education in Political Science, Philosophy or Sociology, an even more fundamental problem is that the teachers who teach these courses (for instance, Nigerian Peoples and Culture) to law students are not legal practitioners and their brief or training is not to link culture with the concept and performance of human rights. In addition, the rather superfluous course, Use of English, is not taught with any particular reference to the construction of statutory words.

These facts present difficulties for the law teacher who has to teach students impacted upon by several challenges courses that are rather more technical than the curricula or the regulatory bodies care to concede. The challenges, among others, come in the forms of the inexperience of the students (just emerged from secondary school), limited knowledge of English language that the course "Use of English" (GST 101) is unfortunately unlikely to improve.

Against the background of two (2) interrelated factors, the compulsive focus on borrowed courses would appear to be the wrong approach. The factors relate to the place of 200-Level students as virtual greenhorns and the underestimated technical nature of Constitutional Law and Human Rights Law. These factors are the average age of students at 200 Level and the rather technical attributes of both Constitutional Law and Human Rights Law.

Constitutional Law may be viewed by some as mere "glorified Government" or "glorified Civic Education". This view could not be further from the truth, but it appears that this is the general attitude and the indifference shown by curriculum designers at both the levels of pre-tertiary schooling and the law undergraduate programme may well be evidence of this derogatory perception. What further evidence of this misperception is required when the crucial and full-fledged course of Human Rights is merely a component of the course Constitutional Law and consequently is inadequately addressed at 200 Level every academic session? By this is meant that the subject of human rights cannot be amply addressed within the context of Constitutional Law given its very wide scope. It may be vibrantly argued that Human Rights Law as a course also exists on the undergraduate law curricula but on a closer examination, this argument is unhelpful. In many universities, Human Rights Law is not a core course but an elective. At the University of Abuja, for instance, students have a choice between Human Rights Law I and II (LAW209 AND LAW210, respectively) and Introduction to Islamic Law I and II (LAW 207 and LAW208, respectively); the latter is interestingly so attractive to students that you often have three-quarters of the students in a class offering it. The question then is—Where does that leave the prospects of adequate human rights education?

11 Technical Nature of Constitutional Law and of Human Rights Law

Constitutional Law covers a wide area—it deals with supremacy; sovereignty (in more ways than one); legislative, executive and judicial powers and the "separation" of these powers; fundamental objectives and directive principles of state policy and the delicate matter of their non-justiciability; citizenship and why certain classes of persons are citizens by birth and others not; power and control over public funds and the import and specifications of the Consolidated Revenue Fund, the Federation Account (indeed the difference between both), the Contingencies Fund never mind the status of the Sovereign Wealth Fund; the command and operational use of the armed forces and when the army may be deployed for war; the ramifications of a declaration of a state of emergency; the number of votes and level of spread needed to emerge as President of the Federation and the construction of the provisions relating to fractions; the jurisdiction of the courts, e.g. the State High Courts vis-à-vis the Federal High Court or the jurisdiction of the Shari'a Court of Appeal. Each of these topics and many more embrace highly technical perspectives that naïve minds will struggle to comprehend. Even a seemingly elementary issue as the distinction between written and codified constitution and the bearing of section 315(5) of the Constitution on that discourse can prove to be subtle. A general attitude that permeates the Nigerian society and which has somehow crept into the psyche of fresh law students is the one that says, "If the President or the executive does it, it cannot be questioned"; in other words, the President is always right. Indeed, this not the truth of Nigerian Constitutional Law given the conditions of co-equality among the arms of government. It requires delicate psychology and barring meticulous care, students who come with that attitude could very well graduate with it. These are not issues to be taken for granted, and therefore the study of the Constitution needs to be undertaken by minds that can be trusted to take constitutional thought forward.

The subject of human rights is enmeshed in the same predicament. It is both technical and wide indeed. The origins and historical development of human rights is an imperative and little purpose is served in not understanding the difference between a right in the nature of a legal entitlement and a moral right and the natural law and positivist approaches (never mind the approaches of the Critical Legal Studies, Feminist Legal Criticism, the Sociological School, etc.) to understanding rights; the issue of what are human rights and what are fundamental human rights (if there are any such things in the first place); what makes *fundamental* human rights fundamental and by what selection benchmarks and processes (credible or otherwise) are the fundamental ones arrived at; should these benchmarks and processes be static and the position of human rights in relation to the indigenous legal systems[163]; the extent of derogations therefrom and the principles underlying them—these are all clever issues that require careful and incremental nurturing in young students.

At 200 Level, the students lack the necessary all-round exposure; How are they to be made to comprehend the rather complex discourses of law courses and topics as early as practically possible?

The University of Ilorin, for instance, has gone some way in finding solutions to the above highlighted problems. At 100 Level of the Common Law degree programme, students offer courses such as Introduction to Constitutional Law, Introduction to Business Law and Policing while borrowing Political Science, Sociology and Use of English. This is, however, not the case for those offering the Combined Honours programme since the students on the programme have no space for borrowing given the two (2) core Islamic law courses that they offer.

It is to be conceded that the arrangement comes with its minor problems chief among which is that although it eases matters for fresh students, direct entry students could suffer from that lack of background that not being part of the 100-Level class would have given. This is a minor problem considering the insignificant number of direct entry students into the law programmes in addition to the fact that they are presumably more experienced than the students who come in by the UTME[164] method. Even so, a solution would be to make it a requirement for direct entry students to offer these courses.

It would appear to make more sense, therefore, to cut down on, if not entirely eliminate, the borrowed courses. In place of the status quo, one would recommend the current practice at the University of Ilorin with the recommendation that even more of the borrowed courses be eliminated. The curriculum of the students who offer the combined programme need to be re-examined with a view to enabling them to benefit from these introductory courses without derogating in any way from the essential components of their field.

12 Concluding Remarks

In the circumstances, it appears that 200 Level is perhaps too early a stage for a law student to *comprehensively* come to terms with the dynamics of Constitutional Law. The question then is what measures must be taken to remedy the problem. The solution appears to go beyond merely relocating the year of study, i.e. 200 Level to another year of study. This is because the other courses that could be moved down to 200 Level could present the same challenges that Constitutional Law and Human Rights Law present at 200 Level. This makes the idea of introductory courses at 200 Level particularly attractive. There is also a need for the introduction of the clinical legal methodology in the teaching of each course in the LL.B. curriculum.

There is also a need for government to perhaps introduce an instructional material in perhaps the mould of the aforementioned Compass and the *Compasito* to guide primary and secondary schools in the teaching of issues relating to the Constitution and particularly Human Rights. There is a danger in this measure—the inclination of government to make such instructional material subjective and self-serving. If the real value of human rights is to be realised in Nigeria, the government will do well to opt for an objective design that is in total contemplation of the constitutional provisions themselves relating to human rights.

The issues of funding and corruption are critical. There is a need for free education at some level (perhaps the basic level up to secondary school) and substantially increased funding for education at all levels in Nigeria. Some might argue that the Nigerian economy could not sustain the massive financial outlay that free education entails. This argument, usually from official quarters, increasingly sounds like a premeditated, perpetual excuse that paves the way for corruption and waste of resources. The evidence is that free education is not unattainable given the sums, running into several billions of dollars that government officials have either stolen or illegally wasted on elections bribing traditional rulers and influential persons. This has always been the case, but recent evidence suggests that the infrastructure and funding required should not have been out of reach at all.

These recommendations are put forward in the fervent hope that legal education in Nigeria, particularly where Human Rights Law and Constitutional Law are concerned, meets the primacy of place that Agenda 2063 ascribes to a well-educated citizenry.

Notes

1. In Nigeria, it is contained in Chap. 4 of the Constitution of the Federal Republic of Nigeria 1999 (as amended) (The Constitution of the Federal Republic of Nigeria 1999).
2. The Preamble.
3. Ibid.
4. Article 26(1) of the *Universal Declaration of Human Rights.*
5. Fereira, Nunos, 'Human Rights Education with Children: A Review of Council of Europe's, *Compasito*' *Essex Human Rights Review* 109 (2011): 9 (Fereira 2011).

6. That is regardless that the word may be linked to the words, "Technical and professional education shall be made generally available", preceding the word "and" which is generally a conjunctive expression. If it was the intention of the article to make higher education *equally*, "generally available", it would have been unnecessary for it to subsequently employ the words "equally accessible".
7. Article 13(2).
8. Article 13(2)(b).
9. Article 13(2)(c).
10. The World Bank, "Rural Population." Accessed June 1, 2016. http://data.worldbank.org/indicator/SP.RUR.TOTL.ZS.
11. The British Broadcasting Corporation, "Nigerians Living in Poverty Rise to Nearly 61%." Accessed June 1, 2016 http://www.bbc.co.uk/news/world-africa-17015873 (The British Broadcasting Corporation 2016).
12. Section 14(3).
13. It is such a critical mechanism that a like principle is to apply in the case of the component states and local governments of the Federation. As such, section 14(4) provides, "The composition of the Government of a State, a local government council, or any of the agencies of such Government or council, and the conduct of the affairs of the Government or council or such agencies shall be carried out in such manner as to recognise the diversity of the people within its area of authority and the need to promote a sense of belonging and loyalty among all the people of the Federation".
14. Section 6(6)(c).
15. Section 6(6)(c).
16. That would be the case otherwise it would, for instance, not be imperative for the President of the Federal Republic of Nigeria to appoint at least a Minister from each state of the Federation pursuant to section 147(3) the Constitution having made a federal character provision in section 14(3), a part of its non-justiciable Chap. 2.
17. Section 153(1)(c).
18. Paragraph C of Part I of the Third Schedule.
19. Article 8(1) of Paragraph C of Part I of the Third Schedule.
20. *Badejo v. Minister of Education* (1996) 8 NWLR (Pt. 464) 15.
21. Egwemi, Victor, "Corruption and Corrupt Practices in Nigeria: An Agenda for Taming The Monster", *Journal of Sustainable Development in Africa:* 14 (2012): 72 (Egwemi 2012).
22. The Punch Newspapers. "Nigeria Now 39th Most Corrupt Nation." Accessed 29 April 2015. http://www.punchng.com/news/nigeria-now-39th-most-corruptnation-says-ti/ (The Punch Newspapers 2015).
23. Nigerian Curiosity. Accessed 26 March 2009. http://www.nigeriancuriosity.com/2008/06/r (Nigerian Curiosity 2009).

24. Transparency International Corruption Perceptions Index 2009. Accessed 12 May 2017. http://transparency.org/research/cpi/cpi/2009/0; Transparency International Corruption Perceptions Index. Accessed 12 May 2017. http://transparency.org/research/cpi2010.
25. Transparency International. "Nigeria's Corruption Challenge." Accessed 1 June 2016. http://www.transparency.org/news/feature/nigerias_corruption_challenge, observes that Global Financial Integrity estimates that more than US$157 billion of public funds has left the country illegally in the past decade. This would appear to be before the mindboggling revelations of the past one year by the Buhari Government of the depth of stealing (Transparency International 2016).
26. The News. "TI Ranks Nigeria 136th in Latest Corruption Index." Accessed 28 January 2016. http://thenewsnigeria.com.ng/2016/01/ti-ranks-nigeria-136th-in-latest-corruption-index/, on 1 June 2016 (The News 2016).
27. Section 18(3) provides only that "Government shall strive to eradicate illiteracy; and to this end Government *shall as and when practicable* provide free, compulsory and universal primary education" (emphasis added). The emphasised words indicate that no obligation is imposed on the State. This is in addition to making the chapter under which the provision falls non-justiciable under section 6(6)(c).
28. Section 6(6)(c) provides, "The judicial powers vested in accordance with the foregoing provisions of this section—(c) shall not except as otherwise provided by this Constitution, extend to any issue or question as to whether any act of omission by any authority or person or as to whether any law or any judicial decision is in conformity with the Fundamental Objectives and Directive Principles of State Policy set out in Chap. 2 of this Constitution".
29. Article 13(2)(a) provides, "(a) Primary education shall be compulsory and available free to all".
30. Articles 13(2)(b) and (c) of the ICESR.
31. Article 26(1).
32. Article 13(2)(d).
33. Section 18(3)(d).
34. Both by virtue of the words of the provision and section 6(6)(c).
35. Fereira, N. (Fereira 2011).
36. Adopted by the United Nations General Assembly in 1989.
37. Article 28(1).
38. This was signed into law in 2003.
39. Section 15(1).
40. Section 15(1).
41. Section 12(1).
42. Cap. A9 Laws of the Federation of Nigeria 2004.

43. It came into effect on 21 October 1986.
44. The section provides, "The National Assembly shall have power to make laws for the peace, order and good government of the Federation or any part thereof with respect to any matter included in the Exclusive Legislative List…".
45. The item gives the National Assembly exclusive legislative authority with respect to the establishment and regulation of authorities for the Federation "to promote and enforce the observance of the Fundamental Objectives and Directive Principles contained in" Chap. 2 of the Constitution.
46. The sub-section provides, "The State shall direct its policy towards ensuring that children, young persons and the aged are protected against any exploitation whatsoever and against moral and material neglect".
47. Federal Republic of Nigeria v. Anache (2004), 17 N.S.C.Q.R. 140.
48. Section 12(2) and (3).
49. Section 1(3) especially which provides, "If any other law is inconsistent with the provisions of this constitution, this constitution shall prevail, and that other law shall to the extent of the inconsistency be void".
50. Etudaiye, Mohammed Enesi, "The Nigerian Child as a Subject of Rights—Dovetailing the Statutory and Shari'a Law Norms in a Diverse State." *Dirasat Shari'a And Law Sciences Journal*, 41 (2014): 896 (Etudaiye 2014).
51. Section 15.
52. Article 26(2).
53. Article 25.
54. The General Assembly, The United Nations. "41/128 Declaration on the Right to Development." Accessed 3 November 2015. http://www.un.org/documents/ga/res/41/a41r128.htm.
55. Preamble.
56. Article 2.
57. The World Commission on Environment and Development in its report, "Our Common Future" published in 1987. A variation of this definition indicates that development is sustainable when it is "development that supports the security and regeneration of economic, natural, human and social resources" (see "Nigeria Population Census 1991 Analysis—Gender and Sustainable Development" Vol. 1, Abuja: National Population Commission, 2001, 4.
58. Article 1 of the United Nations Declaration on the Right to Development.
59. The Preamble.
60. Ibid.
61. Article 1.

62. Article 2.
63. Section 14(2)(b).
64. Section 16(1)(a).
65. Section 16(2)(a).
66. See The United Nations Development Programme. "Human Development Report 2000." Accessed 25 March 2009. http://www.hdr.undp.org/hdr2000/.
See also World Commission on Dams. Rajagopal, B., "Human Rights and Development: Legal and Policy Issues with Special Reference to Dams." Accessed 13 March 2009. http://www.dams.org//ins206.pdf. These two sources are agreed that the divergence was brought about by the Cold War and that there has been a convergence since the end of the Cold War (Rajagopal 2009).
67. Rajagopal, World Commission on Dams. "Human Rights and Development: Legal and Policy Issues with Special Reference to Dams" (Rajagopal 2009).
68. Rajagopal, World Commission on Dams. "Human Rights and Development: Legal and Policy Issues with Special Reference to Dams", Observes that the United Nations set up separate institutions to execute its activities each field and provided no mechanisms for the coordination of the activities of these agencies (Rajagopal 2009).
69. Rajagopal, World Commission on Dams. "Human Rights and Development: Legal and Policy Issues with Special Reference to Dams", See also "Human Development Report", op. cit. (Rajagopal 2009).
70. Rajagopal, World Commission on Dams. "Human Rights and Development: Legal and Policy Issues with Special Reference to Dams", Refers to this as 'the "developmentalization" of human rights' (Rajagopal 2009).
71. Article 1 of the United Nations Charter. In addition, the Vienna Declaration and Programme of Action declared, "Democracy, development and respect for human rights and fundamental freedoms are interdependent and mutually reinforcing".
72. This is with particular reference to the United Nations Charter of 1945 and the Universal Declaration of Human Rights 1948.
73. This is with particular reference to the International Covenant on Economic, Social and Cultural Rights and the International Covenant on Civil and Political Rights both of which were agreed in 1966.
74. De Villiers, B., "The Protection of Social and Economic Rights: International Perspectives." Paper 9 (1996) published by Centre for Human Rights, University of Pretoria. Centre for Human Rights, University of Pretoria. Accessed November 13, 2007. www.chr.up.ac.za/centre_publications/occ_papers/occ9html (De Villiers 1996).

75. The odious characterisation of suicide in Achebe, Chinua, *Things Fall Apart* (London: Heinemann, 1958) as well as the fact that it is forbidden in Islam (Achebe 1958).
76. Article 6(c).
77. Twining, William, *General Jurisprudence: Understanding Law from a Global Perspective* (Cambridge: Cambridge University Press, 2009) (Twining 2009).
78. Twining, *General Jurisprudence: Understanding Law from a Global Perspective*, 376 (Twining 2009).
79. Twining, *General Jurisprudence: Understanding Law from a Global Perspective*, 66 (Twining 2009).
80. Twining, *General Jurisprudence: Understanding Law from a Global Perspective* (Twining 2009).
81. Freeman, M., Book Review of Banda, F's Women, Law and Human Rights: An African Perspective, *International Journal of Law in Context* (Oxford: Hart Publishing, 2005), Vol. 4, No. 1 2008, 79 (Freeman 2005).
82. Twining, *General Jurisprudence: Understanding Law from a Global Perspective*, 211 quotes Tasioulas, Tasioulas, J., "Human Rights, Universality and the Values of Personhood: Retracing Griffin's Steps", *10 European Journal of Philosophy* (2002): 88 as follows, "Some cultures may not accord the same significance to autonomy and liberty as Western societies, perhaps attaching greater importance than we do to living harmoniously with others (including other species), avoiding the infliction of pain and suffering, cultivating highly refined aesthetic and religious sensibilities and so on. With respect to such cultures, we may be hard-pressed to show that judging them by reference to the familiar schedule of human rights is anything short of cultural imperialism, especially if it has a detrimental effect on their capacity to sustain valued ways of life. Are we forced to conclude that such cultures are mistaken in failing to prize autonomy and liberty sufficiently highly? Or should we, like Rawls, prune back the list of human rights in the hope of accommodating them? Or is some other response available…?" regarding the latter, should the scope of the "moral" philosophy behind the idea of human rights be broadened? (Twining 2009; Tasioulas 2002).
83. Twining, *General Jurisprudence: Understanding Law from a Global Perspective*, 21 (Twining 2009).
84. Chapter 13 of his work, which spans pp. 376–442 is titled, "Human Rights: Southern Voices".
85. Twining, *General Jurisprudence: Understanding Law from a Global Perspective* (Twining 2009).
86. Jyllands-Posten.

87. Twining, *General Jurisprudence: Understanding Law from a Global Perspective*, 123 (Twining 2009).
88. This is a point Tasioulas, J., "Human Rights, Universality and the Values of Personhood: Retracing Griffin's Steps", *10 European Jo. of Philosophy* (2002): 79 in Twining, op. cit., p. 192, also makes as follows, "The implication is that we, Eurocentric intellectuals, already know how to discriminate between genuine and bogus claimants to the title "human right", how to interpret the rights that feature on our list, how to weigh them against competing ethical considerations, including other human rights, what human rights are rights to, whether and upon whom they impose duties, how they are best institutionalised and enforced, and so on. In the light of this, what contribution could philosophy hope to make? But of course, the question is based on a false premise as no settled agreement exists on any of these questions. In neglecting the persistence of these extensive and ongoing controversies, Rorty shows himself to be disengaged from the human rights culture he purports to champion" (Tasioulas 2002; Twining 2009).
89. Okafor, "International Human Rights Fact-Finding Praxis in its Living Forms: A TWAIL Perspective", op. cit., pp. 66–67, discusses what he calls the "heaven/hell binary", "TWAIL scholars have long critiqued the tendency of international human rights praxis and discourse to foster and reproduce a *binary* dichotomy that ruptures the globe into two conceptual communities, the one 'heavenly' and the other 'hellish'; a dichotomy that draws fairly neat and bright lines between 'the Good West' and 'the Bad Third World". These scholars have also shown not just that this binary is, in fact, not based on fully appreciated reality, but that it is also harmful to the human rights struggle (e.g. by facilitating a human rights monologue rather than a dialogue, and *helping to foster or augment alienation from the human rights struggle which impedes efforts at generating a measure of mass cultural legitimacy for the human rights project*)" (emphasis added).
90. Twining, *General Jurisprudence: Understanding Law from a Global Perspective*, 433 states of Upendra Baxi as considering this form of history to be "complacent, patronising, Euro-centric or rather 'Northerncentric', top-down view of the sources of human rights, suggesting that rights are 'the gifts of the West to the Rest'. It entirely overlooks the contribution of struggles by the poor and the oppressed to the slow recognition of human rights as universal. To make sense of human rights, Baxi argues, one must see the basic ideas not as emanating from Christian natural law or the liberal Enlightenment or the reactions of Western governments to the horrors of World War II. The main

context of the production of human rights has been local communities in struggle against the diverse sources of suffering; the main impetus has been direct experience of suffering; the main authors have been those involved in grass-roots struggles" (Twining 2009).

91. Anghie, op. cit., p. 201, notes that International law is based on Western culture. Shivji, I.G., *The Concept of Human Rights in Africa* (London: CODESRIA, 1989), 3 also notes that the human rights philosophy is one of domination and a part of the imperialist design (Shivji 1989).
92. Ibid., p. 117.
93. Ibid., p. 115.
94. Both covenants were adopted in 1966, six (6) years after Nigeria's independence.
95. Anghie, ibid., p. 118, refers to the enduring character of colonial relations in the nature of neo-colonialism even after independence.
96. Twining, op. cit., pp. 431–432 observes, "Modern human rights discourse is secular. It has severed the connection between human rights discourses and religious cosmologies. This involves a radical acceptance of human finitude (no life after life/death); justifications are only of this world; it problematises custom and tradition; and creates a secular civic religion, a community of faith".
97. In some schools, all Senior Secondary School I students are required to offer Government while the school decides what field—Science or Arts—that the pupils would eventually be allocated to.
98. Saleh, J.B. et al., *Elaborate Civic Education for Senior Secondary Schools and Colleges* (Kano: New Pages Publications Ltd., 2011) (Saleh et al. 2011).
99. Saleh, J.B. et al., *Elaborate Civic Education for Senior Secondary Schools and Colleges* (Saleh et al. 2011).
100. The other plausible explanation is that they are just academically poor students.
101. Saleh, J.B. et al., *Elaborate Civic Education for Senior Secondary Schools and Colleges*, 36 (Saleh et al. 2011).
102. Saleh, J.B. et al., *Elaborate Civic Education for Senior Secondary Schools and Colleges*, 23-47 (Saleh et al. 2011).
103. Saleh, J.B. et al., *Elaborate Civic Education for Senior Secondary Schools and Colleges,* Saleh, J.B. et al., *Elaborate Civic Education for Senior Secondary Schools and Colleges*, 24 (Saleh et al. 2011).
104. Saleh, J.B. et al., *Elaborate Civic Education for Senior Secondary Schools and Colleges*, 29 (Saleh et al. 2011).
105. Saleh, J.B. et al., *Elaborate Civic Education for Senior Secondary Schools and Colleges*, 29–33 (Saleh et al. 2011).
106. Saleh, J.B. et al., *Elaborate Civic Education for Senior Secondary Schools and Colleges*, 24 (Saleh et al. 2011).

107. Saleh, J.B. et al., *Elaborate Civic Education for Senior Secondary Schools and Colleges* (Saleh et al. 2011).
108. Section 25 of the Constitution.
109. This is a problem no doubt aided by improved ICT. An example is the SMS input systems in which everything is written in shorthand: "ur", "u", "tnk", "tnx", "ur scarce ds days", etc. It is not a problem to be underestimated because in the experience of the authors, students' examination answer booklets are inundated with these expressions nowadays.
110. Saleh, J.B. et al., *Elaborate Civic Education for Senior Secondary Schools and Colleges*. The illustration reads, "For example, a person who was a Chinese citizen cannot be a Nigerian citizen and at the same time be a citizen of the United States of America" (Saleh et al. 2011).
111. It provides, "No person shall be qualified to apply for the grant of a certificate or naturalisation, unless he satisfies the President that—(g) he has, immediately preceding the date of his application, either—(i) resided in Nigeria for a continuous period of fifteen years; or (ii) resided in Nigeria continuously for a period of twelve months, and during the period of twenty years immediately preceding that period of twelve months has resided in Nigeria for periods amounting in the aggregate to not less than fifteen years".
112. Saleh, J.B. et al., *Elaborate Civic Education for Senior Secondary Schools and Colleges*, 30 (Saleh et al. 2011).
113. The Constitution substantiates this position in a number of provisions such as Sections 7(4), 77(2), 117(1), 132(5) and 178(5) and, among others, constantly refers to the *entitlement* of the citizen to vote.
114. Saleh, J.B. et al., *Elaborate Civic Education for Senior Secondary Schools and Colleges*, 30 (Saleh et al. 2011).
115. Section 24.
116. Section 17(3)(a).
117. Section 6(6)(c).
118. This would be pursuant to Item 60(a) of the Exclusive Legislative List which gives the National Assembly legislative powers over matters contained in Chap. 2 of the Constitution.
119. Under many provisions relating to the superior courts in Nigeria, the head of each court may make rules of procedure for their courts. Relevant provisions are Section 236, 248, 254, 259, 264, 269, 274, 279 and 284 of the Constitution.
120. Saleh, J.B. et al., *Elaborate Civic Education for Senior Secondary Schools and Colleges*, 35 (Saleh et al. 2011).
121. Saleh, J.B. et al., *Elaborate Civic Education for Senior Secondary Schools and Colleges*, 33 (Saleh et al. 2011).

122. Saleh, J.B. et al., *Elaborate Civic Education for Senior Secondary Schools and Colleges*, 67–68 (Saleh et al. 2011).
123. Saleh, J.B. et al., *Elaborate Civic Education for Senior Secondary Schools and Colleges*, 59 (Saleh et al. 2011).
124. *Nkwocha v. Governor of Anambra State & Ors.* (1983) 4 N.C.L.R. 719 (1984) 1 SCNLR 634 where Eso, JSC held "it is an ordinary statute which became extraordinary by virtue of its entrenchment [section 274(5)] in the Constitution, for if the Act has been made a part of the Constitution it would not have been necessary to insert in subsection (5) of section 274 the words 'Nothing in this Constitution shall invalidate' as the draftsman of the Constitution cannot make the Constitution to invalidate part of itself nor would it be necessary to have in sub-section (6) of section 274 that the Act shall continue to have effect as a 'Federal Enactment', that is a law made by the National Assembly, the Constitution itself not being a 'Federal Enactment'".
125. The section is re-enacted as section 315(5) of the Constitution of the Federal Republic of Nigeria 1999 (as amended) (The Constitution of the Federal Republic of Nigeria 1999).
126. Saleh, J.B. et al., *Elaborate Civic Education for Senior Secondary Schools and Colleges*, 52–53 (Saleh et al. 2011).
127. One thought the word "unsecured" was more aptly employed in the discussion of loans.
128. Saleh et al., op. cit., p. 52 (Saleh et al. 2011).
129. Aihe, D.O., and Oluyede, P.A., *Cases and Materials on Constitutional Law in Nigeria* 9. Ibadan, Oxford University Press, 1979), 23 (Aihe and Oluyede 1979).
130. Most people would consider this principle to be the supremacy of law rather than merely "legality".
131. Dicey, A.V., *Law of the Constitution* (10th ed.), 202 as reproduced in Aihe and Oluyede, op. cit., wrote, "It means the absolute supremacy or predominance of regular law as opposed to the influence of arbitrary power, and excludes the existence of arbitrariness, of prerogative, or even of wide discretionary authority on the part of the government" (Aihe and Oluyede 1979).
132. Most people would consider this principle to be "equality before the law", rather than just "impartiality".
133. Dicey, A.V., *Law of the Constitution* (10th ed.), 202–203 wrote, "[It] means equality before the law, or the equal subjection of all classes to the ordinary law of the land administered by the ordinary law courts; the 'Rulke of Law' excludes the idea of any exemption of officials or others from the duty of obedience to the law which governs other citizens or from the jurisdiction of the ordinary tribunals".

134. Indeed, these words also appear to be borrowed from Aihe and Oluyede, 24 who state with respect to this second component after the statement contained in footnote 110, "Briefly put, this means equality before the law. In short, *law is no respecter of persons. Any person, irrespective of his rank and status in life*, is subject to the ordinary law of the land" (emphasis added).
135. The third main principle defined by Dicey was with respect to human rights.
136. In Dicey's explanation, the Rule of Law may be used "as a formula for expressing the fact that with us the law of the constitution, the rules which in foreign countries naturally form part of a constitutional code, are not the source but the consequence of the rights of individuals, as defined and enforced by the courts" (Dicey, ibid., p. 203).
137. Dibie, C.C., *Essentials of Government for Senior Secondary Schools* (Ibafo: Tonad Publishers Ltd., 2012) (Dibie 2012).
138. Dibie, C.C., *Essentials of Government for Senior Secondary Schools*, 205 (Dibie 2012).
139. Dibie, C.C., *Essentials of Government for Senior Secondary Schools*, 30–31 (Dibie 2012).
140. Dibie, C.C., *Essentials of Government for Senior Secondary Schools*, 31–35 (Dibie 2012).
141. Dibie, C.C., *Essentials of Government for Senior Secondary Schools*, 70 (Dibie 2012).
142. Dibie, C.C., *Essentials of Government for Senior Secondary Schools*, 75 (Dibie 2012).
143. Dibie, C.C., *Essentials of Government for Senior Secondary Schools*, 76 (Dibie 2012).
144. Dibie, C.C., *Essentials of Government for Senior Secondary Schools*, Chapter 18, 136–140 (Dibie 2012).
145. Dibie, C.C, *Essentials of Government for Senior Secondary Schools*, 34 (Dibie 2012).
146. Dibie, C.C., *Essentials of Government for Senior Secondary Schools*, 32 (Dibie 2012).
147. Dibie, C.C., *Essentials of Government for Senior Secondary Schools*, 72–73 (Dibie 2012).
148. Dibie, C.C, *Essentials of Government for Senior Secondary Schools*, paragraph 6.3, 72 (Dibie 2012).
149. Dibie, C.C., *Essentials of Government for Senior Secondary Schools*, 74 (Dibie 2012).
150. Dibie, C.C., *Essentials of Government for Senior Secondary Schools*, paragraph 6.5, 73 (Dibie 2012).

151. Dibie, C.C., *Essentials of Government for Senior Secondary Schools*, 73 (Dibie 2012).
152. Dibie, C.C., *Essentials of Government for Senior Secondary Schools* (Dibie 2012).
153. Dibie, C.C., *Essentials of Government for Senior Secondary Schools* (Dibie 2012).
154. Item 51.
155. Fereira, Nunos, "Human Rights Education with Children: A Review of Council of Europe's *Compasito*".
156. Fereira, Nunos, "Human Rights Education with Children: A Review of Council of Europe's *Compasito*" (Fereira 2011).
157. Fereira, Nunos, "Human Rights Education with Children: A Review of Council of Europe's *Compasito*" (Fereira 2011).
158. Fereira, Nunos, 'Human Rights Education with Children: A Review of Council of Europe's *Compasito*' (Fereira 2011).
159. Fereira, Nunos, 'Human Rights Education with Children: A Review of Council of Europe's *Compasito*' (Fereira 2011).
160. At a private university, Madonna University, a fresh student who was admitted during the 2007/2008 academic session would have to offer LAW 112 (Nigerian Legal Method), GES 115 (Introduction to Logic and Philosophy), GES 113 (Nigerian Peoples and Culture), ECC 111 (Principles of Economics; this should help with understanding the economic analysis of law, one supposes but for the fact that that would come four (4) years later in the study of Jurisprudence at 500 Level), PSY 111 (Introduction to Psychology), GES 112 (History and Philosophy of Science), GES104 (Literature in English having passed it at Ordinary Level and an NUC prerequisite for admission into the undergraduate law programmes), GES 111 (Use of English; having passed it at credit level at Ordinary Level). Indeed, during second semester, they also have the liberty to offer such core courses as GES 122 (Advanced Communication in English) at the same time they are offering Use of English and have passed English at Ordinary Level (the intensity with respect to studying English language is such that one is unsure whether foreign students studying in the UK are confronted with such at entry point—would interpretation of statutes be better as a course on its own although this is offered as part of Nigerian Legal System and Jurisprudence). Also, they have to offer GES 117 (Introduction to *French*) French (not Latin for emphasis)—something to ponder.
161. Such is the stringency of the requirement, that a Professor of Political Science (with expertise in International Law and Diplomacy) who applied to read Law, in a Nigerian university was denied admission.

162. For instance, when the Maputo Protocol, a part of African International Human Rights Law prescribes in its Article 15 for a polygynous continent like Africa that "monogamy ... as the preferred form of marriage".
163. De Villiers, B. (1996) 'The Protection of Social and Economic Rights: International Perspectives', Paper 9 addresses his concerns over these two issues (De Villiers 1996).
164. University and Tertiary Matriculation Examination, that students coming into Nigerian universities must undergo.

Bibliography

Achebe, Chinua. 1958. *Things Fall Apart*. London: Heinemann.

Aihe, D.O., and P.A. Oluyede. 1979. *Cases and Materials on Constitutional Law in Nigeria*. Ibadan: Oxford University Press.

Badejo, V. 1996. Minister of Education 8 NWLR (Pt. 464) 15.

De Villiers, B. 1996. The Protection of Social and Economic Rights: International Perspectives. Paper 9 (1996) published by Centre for Human Rights, University of Pretoria. Centre for Human Rights, University of Pretoria. www.chr.up.ac.za/centre_publications/occ_papers/occ9html. Accessed 13 Nov 2007.

Dibie, C.C. 2012. *Essentials of Government for Senior Secondary Schools*. Ibafo: Tonad Publishers Ltd.

Egwemi, Victor. 2012. Corruption and Corrupt Practices in Nigeria: An Agenda for Taming The Monster. *Journal of Sustainable Development in Africa* 14: 72.

Etudaiye, Mohammed Enesi. 2014. The Nigerian Child as a Subject of Rights—Dovetailing the Statutory and Shari'a Law Norms in a Diverse State. *Dirasat Shari'a And Law Sciences Journal* 41: 896.

Federal Republic of Nigeria v. Anache. 2004. 17 N.S.C.Q.R. 140.

Fereira, Nunos. 2011. Human Rights Education with Children: A Review of Council of Europe's Compasito. *Essex Human Rights Review* 109: 9.

Freeman, M. 2005. Book Review of *Women, Law and Human Rights: An African Perspective. International Journal of Law in Context* 4 (1) (2008), by Banda, F. Oxford: Hart Publishing.

International Covenant on Economic, Social and Cultural Rights and the International Covenant on Civil.

Nairaland. 2009. *Broken News*. http:/www.nairaland.com/../topic-1838.0.html, http://www.brokennews.com/displaystory.asp. Accessed 26 Mar 2009.

Nigerian Curiosity. 2009. http://www.nigeriancuriosity.com/2008/06/r. Accessed 26 Mar 2009.

Nkwocha v. Governor of Anambra State & Ors. (1983) 4 N.C.L.R. 719 (1984) 1 SCNLR 634.

Okafor. *International Human Rights Fact-Finding Praxis in Its Living Forms: A TWAIL Perspective.*

Rajagopal, B. 2009. World Commission on Dams. Human Rights and Development: Legal and Policy Issues with Special Reference to Dams. http://www.dams.org/../ins206.pdf. Accessed 13 Mar 2009.

Saleh, J.B., et al. 2011. *Elaborate Civic Education for Senior Secondary Schools and Colleges.* Kano: New Pages Publications Ltd.

Shivji, I.G. 1989. *The Concept of Human Rights in Africa.* London: CODESRIA.

Tasioulas, J. 2002. Human Rights, Universality and the Values of Personhood: Retracing Griffin's Steps. *European Journal of Philosophy* 10 (1): 79–100.

The British Broadcasting Corporation. 2016. Nigerians Living in Poverty Rise to Nearly 61%. http://www.bbc.co.uk/news/world-africa-17015873. Accessed 1 June 2016.

The Constitution of the Federal Republic of Nigeria. 1999. (as amended).

The General Assembly, The United Nations. 2015. 41/128 Declaration on the Right to Development. http://www.un.org/documents/ga/res/41/a41r128.htm. Accessed 3 Nov 2015.

The News. 2016. TI Ranks Nigeria 136th in Latest Corruption Index, 1 June 2016. http://thenewsnigeria.com.ng/2016/01/ti-ranks-nigeria-136th-in-latest-corruption-index/. Accessed 28 Jan 2016.

The Punch Newspapers. 2015. Nigeria Now 39th Most Corrupt Nation. http://www.punchng.com/news/nigeria-now-39th-most-corruptnation-says-ti/. Accessed 29 Apr 2015.

The United Nations Development Programme. 2009. Human Development Report 2000. http://www.hdr.undp.org/hdr2000/. Accessed 25 Mar 2009.

The Universal Declaration of Human Rights, 1948.

The Vienna Declaration and Programme of Action.

The World Bank. 2016. Rural Population. http://data.worldbank.org/indicator/SP.RUR.TOTL.ZS. Accessed 1 June 2016.

The World Commission on Environment and Development in its Report, 'Our Common Future' published in 1987. 2001. Nigeria Population Census 1991 Analysis—Gender and Sustainable Development, vol. 1, 4. Abuja: National Population Commission.

Transparency International. 2016. Nigeria's Corruption Challenge. http://www.transparency.org/news/feature/nigerias_corruption_challenge. Accessed 1 June 2016.

Twining, William. 2009. *General Jurisprudence: Understanding Law from a Global Perspective.* Cambridge: Cambridge University Press.

United Nations Charter of 1945 and the Universal Declaration of Human Rights. 1948.

United Nations Charter.

United Nations Declaration on the Right to Development.

Authors' Biography

Muhtar Adeiza Etudaiye LL.B (Zaria), BL (Lagos), LL.M (Ile-Ife), Ph.D. (Ilorin), Associate Professor, University of Ilorin, Ilorin, Kwara State, Nigeria, Email: muhtaretudaiye@yahoo.com, is a prolific writer who has written articles in both national and international journals of repute such as the Essex Human Rights Review, Journal of Malaysian and Comparative Law, Journal Jurisprudence among others. His areas of interest include construction of statutes with emphasis on compliance guaranty mechanisms, clinical legal education, jurisprudence and legal theory as well as human rights law. His address is Department of Jurisprudence and International Law, Faculty of Law, University of Ilorin, Ilorin, Nigeria.

Mohammed Enesi Etudaiye LL.B (Zaria), BL (Lagos), LL.M (Ile-Ife), Ph.D. (Abuja), Senior Lecturer, University of Abuja, Abuja, Federal Capital Territory, Nigeria, Email: mohammedetudaiye@yahoo.com, is an accomplished writer who has written for several national and international journals of repute such as the Essex Human Rights Review, Commonwealth Law Bulletin (of which he also serves as a Reviewer). His areas of interest include human rights law, constitutional law (particularly constitutional cultural concessioning) and feminist jurisprudence. He is of the Department of Public and International Law, Faculty of Law, University of Abuja, Gwagwalada, Federal Capital Territory, Nigeria and is currently on sabbatical with the National Institute for Legislative Studies, Abuja as a Senior Research Fellow.

CHAPTER 5

Craving for the Message but Shooting the Messenger: RBA to Teacher Welfare and Quality in Basic Education in Nigeria

A.C. Onuora-Oguno

1 Introduction

Education holds a pivotal role in ensuring that the future of every child is guaranteed. In Nigeria, presently, the challenge of access to education continues to loom large with close to 10 million children assumed to be out of school.[1] With the Universal Basic Education Act (UBEA)[2] and the Universal Basic Education Commission (UBEC) coming into place, the drive to enhance access to basic education is on the increase. Considering the components of access, availability, affordability and acceptability, an often neglected component is the role of teachers. The African Union Agenda 2063 (AU agenda) acknowledges the need and role of teachers towards this realisation.[3]

Accessibility of education represents structural and financial access among other components; availability represents the numerical and proximity components, while acceptability and adaptability represent the question of curriculum efficiency and flexibility to the needs of a people.[4]

A.C. Onuora-Oguno (✉)
Faculty of Law, University of Ilorin, Ilorin, Nigeria
e-mail: azubike.onuoraoguno@gmail.com

A.C. Onuora-Oguno et al. (eds.), *Education Law, Strategic Policy and Sustainable Development in Africa*, DOI 10.1007/978-3-319-53703-0_5

Noting that this component represents the quality of education a child can access, the role of a teacher is pivotal to the actualisation of the quality component of available and accessed education.[5] Understanding the quality concept presents its own diversified challenges; however, succinctly put, quality speaks to the ability to learn basic skills. Put differently, "...poor quality of education means millions of children are not learning the basics. Around 250 million children are not learning basic skills, even though half of them have spent at least four years in school".[6]

Regrettably, a core and continued missing link is in the learning process.[7] The poor quality experienced in our schools is linked to poor learning. According to UNESCO, "access is not the only crisis—poor quality is holding back learning even for those who make it to school. One-third of primary school age children are not learning the basics, whether they have been to school or not".[8]

The role the teacher must, therefore, play in the education process is pivotal and cannot be overlooked.[9] The challenge, however, is that most often than not, attention is paid to the question of advancing and enhancing access to education but neglecting the teacher. According to Beiter and Tomasveski, approaching the role of the teacher from a right-based perspective will demand the same level of accountability from the state on teachers as currently advocated for education.[10] That the "teacher" should be construed from a right-based approach is often submerged in certain erroneous assumptions. For instance, according to Greene:[11]

> The teacher is frequently addressed as if she had no life of her own, no body, and no inwardness...when they describe a good teacher as infinitely controlled and accommodating, technically efficient, impervious to moods. They are likely to define her by the role she is expected to play in a classroom... the numerous realities in which one exists as a living person are overlooked.

Consequently, this chapter discusses the role teachers play in driving quality education and advocates that the role of the teachers be seen from the human rights prism if both education as a message and teachers as the messengers will aid the realisation of quality basic education. It is noted, therefore, that while this article does not discuss teachers' effectiveness and quality,[12] it discusses the need for the welfare, mood and human nature of teachers to be taken into consideration by states.

This will ultimately lead to ensuring the protection of teachers' welfare rights, dignity and life.

2 Understanding Education

With no definite meaning, education represents different concepts to different people. In both the African and Western philosophies, education brings to the fore certain underpinning components of advancing the personality in order to play a meaningful role in the generality of societal existence. However, the concept of education as a fundamental human right or as an economic concern laces the terrain of human rights scholars and economists. It is, however, adopted in this chapter that the intrinsic nature of education elevates it to a fundamental right and should be so treated. It has been reiterated that with the failure to realise the Millennium Development Goal (MDG) pre-2015, the trudge and aspiration towards the post-2015 goals are greatly dependent on education. Lending credence to the pivotal basis of education, the UN Secretary-General posits that:[13]

> Education is a fundamental right and the basis for progress in every country. Parents need information about health and nutrition if they are to give their children the start in life they deserve. Prosperous countries depend on skilled and educated workers. The challenges of conquering poverty, combatting climate change and achieving truly sustainable development in the coming decades compel us to work together. With partnership, leadership and wise investments in education, we can transform individual lives, national economies and our world.

Education represents a vehicle through which cultures, norms and values in a society are sustained, transformed and transmitted. It excludes the transmission of any negative learning's while sustaining only the principles and objectives that are able to drive the advancement of human dignity and sustenance of human rights. While education may be broadly classified into formal, informal and non-formal spheres, the focus of this paper is on formal education. This, however, does not preclude the fact that the concept of a teacher is identifiable in all the other forms of education.

Distilled from an understanding of the concept of education, pivotal is the question of an education that is quality laden. This is argued based on the objective and outcome of education as hinted above. Core contents of quality education span from the availability of sufficient infrastructure to curriculum efficiency. In other words, in either the main stream education or an inclusive education sphere, there is the need to ensure the availability of all that is needed to drive education.[14] The teacher's sufficiency and availability are also another major component of quality education.[15] In this wise, teacher-to-pupil ratio is of utmost importance in determining quality.[16] It has, however, been proven that there is a link between teachers' productive level and teachers' welfare.[17] With this underpinning, it is important to underscore that determining quality is as varying as determining a unified definition of education. This is captured by Stephens thus:[18]

> Defining the concept of quality is a little like trying to define 'motherhood' – it is clearly a 'good thing' but elusive and likely to be dependent on the perspective of the person attempting the definition. For many parents, for example, it may well relate to the learning outcomes, particularly end of cycle examination results, of their respective child; for the school manager or inspector quality may well embrace improved general standards of reading, or handwriting, or mathematics; *for the classroom teacher a definition of quality linking closely to improved conditions of service.*

3 The Role of Teachers in Enhancing Access to Quality Basic Education

Understanding the concept of "teacher" is better appreciated by restating the role of the teacher, thus according to Parkay:[19]

> Becoming a Teacher embraces and articulates the changing field of education, outlining ways to be an agent of change in the profession, pinpointing meaningful uses of technology in education, clarifying realities of diversity in the classroom, and clearly outlining past, present, and future thoughts on curriculum, instruction, management, philosophy, and issues in education.

From the position of Parkay, it is evident that the place of teachers is incontrovertible in achieving the desire of ensuring access to quality education. The teacher is the main resource allocator, finding balance between the learning students and ensuring apt interaction within the school environment.[20] Furthermore, it is important that the teacher's important role is seen from an enhanced perspective. Accordingly, it is important to envisage that:[21]

> The teacher is moving away from being a "transmitter of knowledge" and led more and more towards becoming a "mediator in the construction of knowledge", a facilitator and, even at times, a social worker. He or she must also foster the development of social skills and create a learning environment that will encourage young people to learn to live together and to become responsible citizens.

In addition, the teacher must well appreciate the human rights content of education in order to be able to uphold the tenets of education within the school space. For instance, the right to privacy and dignity of a child within the education sphere must be appreciated and consequently respected by the teacher. In buttressing this position, Pigozzi has found in the analysis of the CRC and education that:[22]

> Teachers need to understand the Convention and its implications for the daily lives of children and for the responsibilities that teachers have towards children both as key mentors in the learning process and as adults who serve as important role models and as protectors of children. Teachers may need to change their classroom behaviours significantly in order to respect the rights of children. They may also have to change their interactions with communities, parents, educational leaders, and educational institutions within the education system as each component changes to be more sensitive to meeting each child's right to a quality basic education.

The role of teachers in ensuring quality education therefore does not lie in simply ensuring the quality delivery of curriculum to the child, but also in ensuring that the fundamental rights of the child are respected in the education sphere. Achieving this would mean that the child is appropriately modelled by a mentor who respects and upholds human rights and would invariably lead to the child respecting and promoting the human rights of others.

Having established that the teacher has an obligation of human rights in guaranteeing quality education, it is also important to take into cognisance that the teacher also has some inherent rights and this is discussed next in the paper.

4 Human Rights of Teachers

A right-based approach (RBA) to the question of teachers like any other RBA simply suggests the need to view the concerns of teachers from the prisms of the Universal Declaration of Human Rights (UDHR) and other instruments that are represented in the International Human Rights Bill of Rights.[23] Primarily, it is assumed herein that such rights like the right to life, freedom from discrimination and torture are all basic rights which teachers like other professionals ought to enjoy. However, the core concern of this paper in the respect of RBA is centred on the question of participation and equality. Furthermore, UDHR provides that:[24]

1. Everyone has the right to work, to free choice of employment, to just and favourable conditions of work and to protection against unemployment.
2. Everyone, without any discrimination, has the right to equal pay for equal work.
3. Everyone who works has the right to just and favourable remuneration ensuring for himself and his family an existence worthy of human dignity, and supplemented, if necessary, by other means of social protection.
4. Everyone has the right to form and to join trade unions for the protection of his interests.

The above provision brings to the fore certain elements that are neglected in the matrix of teachers' treatment. This chapter construes the right to participation and equality in terms of equality in comapred renumeration and participation of teachers in decisons making mechanisms in the education sphere. Questions of favourable remuneration and right to join trade unions and have the protection of interests are of particular concern. To examine the rights of teachers from a right-based analysis behoves the appreciation of the fact that the state of education particularly at the basic level is at its lowest ebb. It has been found that:[25]

> Most primary schools in Sub-Saharan Africa suffer from very poor conditions for learning: dilapidated or half-completed buildings, insufficient desks, overcrowded classrooms, few or no learning materials, poorly educated and motivated teachers, and choral recitation as the dominant mode of instruction.

The questions of poor motivation along intimidation from the state when demands are made through the trade unions violate the rights of teachers. For instance, it is on record that remuneration of teachers' salary aside being poor in Nigeria remains inconsistent, leading to several loss of human resource in teaching profession.[26] More often than not teachers embark on strike actions because of the refusal of the government to pay their meagre salaries.[27] Threats of no work no pay greet the efforts of teachers to enforce their rights as enshrined in the UDHR.[28] In some circumstances, teachers have been sacked in the process of demanding their rights. It is, therefore, argued that if construed from a RBA, the respect of teacher's right will be better protected.

In addition, in a research carried out in Lagos state by SERAP, it was found out that the promotion of teachers is epileptic and when done, is not matched with the corresponding remuneration enhancement. The effect of this is the low motivation of teachers in the quest of ensuring the delivery of quality basic education.

Furthermore, leveraging on the position of Heneveld, the infrastructure situation in schools with respect to teachers' accommodation is in a dismal stage and violates the right to a friendly workplace. The poor sanitary condition affects the female teacher just as the girl child in schools. In a report for the World Health Organisation (WHO), it was found that:[29]

> Girls and boys are likely to be affected in different ways by inadequate water, sanitation and hygiene conditions in schools, and this may contribute to unequal learning opportunities. *Sometimes, girls and female teachers are more affected than boys because the lack of sanitary facilities means that they cannot attend school during menstruation.*

There is, therefore, the need to ensure that the condition of facilities that have the capability of influencing teachers' output is put in the right perspectives and treated as a right-based necessity. Comparing the sanitary condition for female teachers in schools simply suggests some lack of value accorded to the teaching position. The reasoning here is that other professionals are perhaps treated in a much dignified manner than teachers who are generally treated. Consequently, a continued denial of the provision of adequate sanitary conditions in schools for teachers would ultimately lead to the abuse and violation of their right to dignity and the right to life.[30]

An RBA approach to the teacher will have the effect of ensuring that teachers are able to hold the state responsible individually or through the teachers' union for violation of their rights as individuals and as teachers collectively. According to Gill and Macmillan, teachers' rights can be summarised into the following headings:[31]

1. I have the right to physical, emotional, social, intellectual, creative and sexual safety.
2. I have the right to respect from students, colleagues, leaders and parents.
3. I have the right to teach in an atmosphere of order and attention.
4. I have the right to demand social structures within the school that guarantee respect for my rights.
5. I have the right to ask for help when needed.
6. I have the right to fair, just and effective leadership on the part of the school principal and vice-principal.
7. I have the right to express any need or grievance I may have.
8. When any of my rights are violated, I have the right to have recourse to social structures within and outside the school that protect those rights.

The right of teachers as envisaged in Gil and Macmillan brings to the fore challenges that confront teachers. It is disheartening to note that the Nigeria teacher is basically denied of all the rights contained therein. For instance, teachers are known victims of parents and community aggression when a pupil is either punished or called to order.[32] The teacher in most circumstances is used as a multiple tool of duty beyond the terms of the teachers' teaching rights.[33] Specifically construed by Bruce, the teacher should have freedom from doing clerical work, latrine and ushering.[34]

5 Enhancing Teacher Quality—The Human Rights Question

The need to enhance the quality of teacher received concern, when UNESCO in recognising "the essential role of teachers in educational advancement and the importance of their contribution to the development of man and modern society" in its recommendation on teachers[35] laid out the basis for the respect for the rights of teachers and the profession. Consequently, it is important to note that the provisions of the UNESCO recommendation speak expressly to the fundamental rights of teachers, ranging from freedom to associate and among other human rights.

The implication of a human right question to an enhanced teacher quality is further buttressed by the fact that "a good teacher matters".[36] Providing a teacher with adequate human right safeguard would invariably ensure the optimal performance of the teacher. This assertion finds credence in the preamble of the African Charter on Human and Peoples' Rights which in its preamble provides that "Considering that the enjoyment of rights and freedoms of rights and freedoms also implies the performance of duties on the part of everyone".[37]

Furthermore, a direct link between teacher and education quality has been grounded by scholars.[38] Consequently, ensuring an optimal quality education is needful to be grounded in ensuring that the human rights of teachers are well protected, especially in the school space.

With the direct link between performance in school and respect for teachers' human rights, what then are the needful things that must be embraced to ensure the respect for both the messenger and the message of education in the school space?

6 Enhancing Respect for the Teacher: What Must Be Done?

The first step to be adopted in enhancing respect for teachers is to follow a human rights perspective to teacher education. It is important that the process of teacher education must include a curriculum that will educate the teacher to the human rights obligation and protection that accrues to the profession. To achieve this, there is the need to further ensure that a balance is struck between the teachers training environment and also ultimately in the school space. Consequently, there is the urgent need to review the laws that regulate teacher education and professionalisation.[39]

Another important factor that must be taken into consideration is to ensure that remuneration of teachers meets the minimum standard. While there is no uniform basis for the analysis of what teachers should be paid, UNESCO has recommended that:[40]

> Teachers' salaries should: reflect the importance to society of the teaching function and hence the importance of teachers as well as the responsibilities of all kinds which fall upon them from the time of their entry into the service; compare favourably with salaries paid in other occupations requiring similar or equivalent qualifications; provide teachers with the means to ensure a reasonable standard of living for themselves and their families as

> well as to invest in further education or in the pursuit of cultural activities, thus enhancing their professional qualification; take account of the fact that certain posts require higher qualifications and experience and carry greater responsibilities.

In Nigeria, for instance, the salary of teachers is nothing to be compared to that of teachers in places like South Africa; however, it is noted that remuneration for teachers is generally low and discouraging in sub-Saharan Africa.[41] According to UNESCO, poor salary for teachers has a directive correlation with the quality of input teachers put into their job.[42] The state of teacher's welfare in Nigeria remains a huge course of concern, especially with regard to level of pay, promotion and unpaid wages.[43] Some states in Nigeria are yet to adopt the minimum salary proposed for teachers and, in some cases, are yet to promote teachers in over 5 years. These continuing worrisome situations have led to a call that "teachers and indeed all workers must fight for a better living standard by compelling government to pay adequate wages".[44]

It is, therefore, argued that for the teacher as the messenger of the education, message must be treated optimally in terms of ensuring that earned salary and allowances are commensurate with what is acceptable and not denied promotion as at and when due. A failure to achieve this will continue to affect the quality of teachers and willingness of individuals wanting to join the profession. This position is further buttressed by UNESCO when it found in a study that:[45]

> As in all jobs requiring a qualification that leads to access to different career paths, the conditions of service offered to teachers, including their salaries and pay scales, have a significant impact on the composition of the teaching force and upon the quality of teaching. The relative level of teachers' salaries and the availability of salary increases during the course of their careers can affect the decision by qualified individuals to enter, or to remain in, the teaching profession.

Aside from the question remuneration, safety within the school zone is another major concern. The insecurity in the school space remains a violation of the rights of the teacher, and the government is thus obligated to ensure that the school space is sufficiently safe for teachers.

Increasingly in the recent times in Nigeria, teachers have been subject of attacks from the *boko haram* group.[46] Nigeria is also not alone in this quagmire that targets messengers of education; for instance, in other areas, teachers have continued to be under attack by terrorist and militant groups that are against the concept of western education.[47] Aside from the attacks by militia groups on teachers, it is also a common occurrence that teachers have been attacked in Nigeria school space. It is on record that members of the National Youth Service Corps that are engaged to alleviate the shortage of teachers in remote communities have in time past been attacked and killed.[48] It is also noted that the growing space of attack on teachers has now included attacks from not just communities and militia groups but also of students. A recent example of student attack occurred in Britain.[49]

7 Conclusion

This chapter concludes that the realisation of the aspiration of African Union as contained in Agenda 2063 is laudable. It recognises that education is pivotal to the realisation of the aspiration. However, the chapter has argued that for education target of the aspiration to be realised, the place of teachers as agents of education must be well protected. It has projected that teachers' welfare must be construed from a right-based approach so as to enshrine the welfare of teachers. Consequently, the conclusion of the chapter is that the quality of teachers must be improved, the protection of teachers within the education sphere must be ensured and the enumeration of teachers must be improved. It is then that the goal of education can be achieved. Finally, the need to ensure that not only the message of education, but also the place of teachers as messengers of education is protected forms the basic conclusion of this chapter.

Notes

1. See generally UNESCO factsheets, accessed 10 June 2015, http://www.uis.unesco.org/FactSheets/Documents/fs-28-out-of-school-children-en.pdf; "Out of school children and child labor", accessed 10 June 2015, http://globalmarch.org/sites/default/files/Policy-Paper.pdf.
2. "UBE ACT 2004 Law of the Federation of Nigeria", accessed 10 June 2015, https://www.ilo.org/dyn/natlex/docs/ELECTRONIC/87623/99979/F606926563/NGA87623.pdf.

3. Agenda 2063 Framework Document, accessed October 29, http://agenda2063.au.int/en/sites/default/files/Final%20Draft%20Agenda%20 2063%20Framework%20-Formatted%20TOC-1.pdf.
4. See generally Fons Coomans, "Clarifying the Core Elements of the Right to Education", accessed 10 June 2015, http://www.uu.nl/faculty/leg/NL/organisatie/departementen/departementrechtsgeleerdheid/organisatie/onderdelen/studieeninformatiecentrummensenrechten/publicaties/simspecials/18/Documents/18-03.pdf; Katrina Tomaševski, Free and compulsory education for all children: The gap between promise and performance Right to Education Primers No. 2 (2001) accessed 27 October 2016, http://www.campanaderechoeducacion.org/justiciabilidad/downloads/documentosCLAVE/documentosanaliticos/free_and_compulsory_education_tomasevski.pdf. Stu Woolman and Brahm Fleisch, eds., The Constitution in the Classroom: Law and Education in South Africa, 1994–2008 (Pretoria: Pretoria University Law Press, 2009) (Coomans 2015; Tomaševski 2001a; Woolman and Fleisch 2009).
5. Adrian M. Vespoor, "The challenge of learning: improving the quality of basic education in sub-Saharan African", in *The changing landscape of education in Africa: quality, equality and democracy,* edited by David Johnson, 33–38. Oxford, Symposium books 2008 (Vespoor 2008).
6. UNESCO, "Teaching and learning: achieving quality for all summary", EFA global monitoring report 2013/2014; Johnson further describes this situation to include poor quality of teachers and poor utilisation of poor resources that are available in education delivery. See generally David Johnson, "Improving the quality of education in Nigeria: a comparative evaluation of recent policy imperatives", in T*he changing landscape of education in Africa: quality, equality and democracy,* edited by David Johnson 45. Oxford, Symposium books 2008 (Johnson 2008).
7. The process talked about here includes the perception of the child in the education sphere; Tomasveski has argued that the child must be seen as the object of any education and not a subject. See Katrina Tomaševski, removing obstacles in the way of the right to education, *Primers No.1* (2001) 44; another core aspect of the process is the method of delivery of available curriculum, see generally Godswill Obioma, "Continuous Assessment Practices of Primary and junior secondary school teachers in Nigeria", accessed 9 June 2016, http://www.iaea2008.cambridgeassessment.org.uk/ca/digitalAssets/180437_Obioma.pdf (Obioma 2016; Tomaševski 2001b).
8. UNESCO, "Teaching and learning: achieving quality for all summary", EFA global monitoring report 2013/2014.
9. The AU recognised that majority of African Countries employ unqualified teachers and this has affected outcome of the expected output from the education sector. See general Agenda 2063 Framework Document,

accessed October 29, http://agenda2063.au.int/en/sites/default/files/Final%20Draft%20Agenda%202063%20Framework%20-Formatted%20TOC-1.pdf. 35.

10. See generally, Klaus D. Beiter, The Protection of the Right to Education by International Law (Netherlands: Martinus Nijhoff, 2006); Katrina Tomaševski, Removing obstacles in the way of the right to education, *Primers No 1* (2001); John O. Afe, "Reflections on becoming a teacher and the challenges of teacher education", accessed 10 June 2015, http://www.nuc.edu.ng/nucsite/File/ILS%202002/ILS-69.pdf (Beiter 2006; Afe 2015).
11. Maxine Greene, The teacher as a stranger, accessed 4 November 2014, http://bama.ua.edu/~jpetrovi/504web/readings/Greene.pdf (Greene 2014).
12. See generally Rabinowitz, William, and Robert M.W. Travers. "Problems of defining and assessing teacher effectiveness". *Educational Theory* 3, no. 3 (1953): 212–219. Rabinowitz and Travers 1953).
13. Ban Ki-Moon, "Sustainable development post-2015 begins with education", accessed 16 June 2016, http://unesdoc.unesco.org/images/0023/002305/230508e.pdf (Ki-Moon 2016).
14. Adegbesan, Sunday O. "Establishing quality assurance in Nigerian education system: Implication for educational managers". *Educational Research and Reviews* 6, no. 2 (2011): 147 (Adegbesan 2011).
15. The European Union identifies teacher training and empowerment as a core component of quality education, see indicators on the quality of school education, accessed 16 June 2015, http://europa.eu/legislation_summaries/education_training_youth/lifelong_learning/c11063_en.htm; see also Pigozzi, Mary Joy. "Education in emergencies and for reconstruction: a developmental approach". *New York: UNICEF, available at* http://www.unicef.org/girlseducation/files/EducEmerg.pdf, *last accessed* 1, no. 07 (1999): 06 (Pigozzi 1999).
16. Adrian M. Vespoor, "The challenge of learning: improving the quality of basic education in sub-Saharan African", in *The changing landscape of education in Africa: quality, equality and democracy,* edited by David Johnson, 33-38. Oxford, Symposium books 2008.
17. Stephens, David. "Quality of basic education". *Paper for EFA Global Monitoring Report,* http://unesdoc.unesco.org/images/0014/001469/146968e.pdf. (2003) (Stephens 2003).
18. Stephens, David. "Quality of basic education". *Paper for EFA Global Monitoring Report,* http://unesdoc.unesco.org/images/0014/001469/146968e.pdf (2003). Emphasis added.
19. Parkay, Forrest W., Beverly Hardcastle Stanford, and Thomas Douglas Gougeon. *Becoming a teacher.* Pearson/Merrill, New Jersey 2010 (Parkay et al. 2010).

20. Heneveld, Ward. "Planning and Monitoring the Quality of Primary Education in Sub-Saharan Africa. AFTHR Technical Note No. 14". (1994) (Heneveld 1994).
21. Discussion paper: IBE, in collaboration with EI and UNESCO "Quality Education and the Key Role of Teachers", accessed 20 October 2016, http://www.ibe.unesco.org/International/ICE47/English/Organisation/Workshops/Workshop4CompENG.pdf.
22. Pigozzi, Mary Joy. "Education in emergencies and for reconstruction: a developmental approach". *New York: UNICEF*, available at http://www.unicef.org/girlseducation/files/EducEmerg.pdf, last accessed 1, no. 07 (1999): 06.
23. "Orientation to a right-based approach", accessed 19 October 2016 http://insightshare.org/sites/insightshare.org/files/A%20Rights-Based%20Approach%20to%20Participatory%20Video%20-%20toolkit%20(CHAPTER%202).pdf.
24. UDHR article 23.
25. Heneveld, Ward, "Planning and Monitoring the Quality of Primary Education in Sub-Saharan Africa. AFTHR Technical Note No. 14" (1994).
26. Inusah Salifu and Joseph Seyram Agbenyega, "Teacher motivation and identity formation: issues affecting professional practice", MIER Journal of Educational Studies, Trends & Practices (2013: 58) Vol. 3; Smithers, Alan, and Pamela Robinson, "Factors affecting teachers' decisions to leave the profession (2003)" (Smithers and Robinson 2003; Salifu and Seyram 2013).
27. Public Schools in Abuja Shut Down as FCT Chapter of Nigerian Union of Teachers Embarks on Strike, accessed 26 June 2016, http://www.bellanaija.com/2015/05/25/public-schools-in-abuja-shut-down-as-fct-chapter-of-nigerian-union-of-teachers-embarks-on-strike/; Ogun schools shut as teachers embark on strike, accessed 29 July 2016, http://dailypost.ng/2015/01/16/ogun-schools-shut-teachers-embark-strike/; Nigerian Teachers To Strike Again, accessed 29 July 2016, http://www.teachersolidarity.com/blog/nigerian-teachers-to-strike-again.
28. See generally Nigeria's teachers under pressure to end strike, accessed 16 August 2016, http://www.news24.com/Africa/News/Nigerias-teachers-under-pressure-oto-end-strike-20131107.
29. World Health Organization. *Water, sanitation and hygiene standards for schools in low-cost settings.* Edited by John Adams, Jackie Simms, Yves Chartier, and Jamie Bartram. World Health Organization, 2009. Emphasis mine; see also Lidonde Rose, School Sanitation and Hygiene Education Symposium, The Way Forward: Construction is not Enough! 8–10 June 2004, Delft, the Netherlands Scaling Up School Sanitation and Hygiene Promotion and Gender Concerns, accessed 16 August 2016,

http://www.wsp.org/Hygiene-Sanitation-Water-Toolkit/Resources/Readings/Global-Lidonde-Scalingup.pdf (Lidonde 2004; World Health Organization 2009).

30. We Can't Wait for Improved Sanitation. We Must Act Now, accessed 20 October 2016, http://worldtoilet.org/documents/WecantWait.pdf.
31. http://www.gillmacmillan.ie/help/teachers/the-rights-of-teachers, accessed 25 October 2016.
32. Classrooms no safe haven for Nigerian teachers: 171 killed since 2009, accessed 25 July 2016, http://www.ei-ie.org/en/news/news_details/3020.
33. B. McDowell, "A Bill of rights for classroom teachers", The Phi Delta Kappan, Vol. 40, No. 8 (May, 1959) (McDowell 1959).
34. B. McDowell, "A Bill of rights for classroom teachers", The Phi Delta Kappan, Vol. 40, No. 8 (May, 1959) 330.
35. http://portal.unesco.org/en/ev.php-URL_ID=13084&URL_DO=DO_TOPIC&URL_SECTION=201.html, accessed 16 July 2016.
36. Liston, Dan, Hilda Borko, and Jennie Whitcomb, "The teacher educator's role in enhancing teacher quality." *Journal of Teacher Education* 59, no. 2 (2008): 111–117 (Liston et al. 2008).
37. See the preamble of the African Charter, accessed 23 September 2016, http://www.achpr.org/instruments/achpr/.
38. See generally King-McKenzie Ethel, Bantwini Bogani and Barry Bogan, "Supporting Teachers to Enhance Students Success in the USA and South Africa" International Journal of Humanities and Social Science (2013), accessed 29 July 2016, http://www.ijhssnet.com/journals/Vol_3_No_15_August_2013/3.pdf (King-McKenzie et al. 2013).
39. Catahan, Marcelino D. *Enhancing Competency of Teachers: A Teaching-and-Learning Enhancement Guide.* AuthorHouse, Bllominghton, Indiana 2015 (Catahan 2015).
40. http://portal.unesco.org/education/en/ev.php-URL_ID=6140&URL_DO=DO_TOPIC&URL_SECTION=201.html. Accessed 19 June 2016.
41. Teachers and Educational Quality: Monitoring Global Needs for 2015, accessed 28 July 2016, http://www.uis.unesco.org/Library/Documents/teachers06-en.pdf. 41.
42. Teachers and Educational Quality: Monitoring Global Needs for 2015, accessed 28 July 2016, http://www.uis.unesco.org/Library/Documents/teachers06-en.pdf 45; Siniscalco M. T., "The Quality Imperative Teachers' salaries" Background paper prepared for the Education for All Global Monitoring Report 2005, available at http://unesdoc.unesco.org/images/0014/001466/146696e.pdf (accessed 19 June 2015).
43. World Teachers Day: Teachers decry poor salaries, available at http://www.punchng.com/education/wtd-teachers-decry-poor-salaries/ (accessed 19 June 2015).

44. Nigeria: Implement teacher's salary scale in Osun State now! Available at http://www.pambazuka.net/en/category.php/advocacy/57591 (accessed 19 June 2015).
45. Siniscalco Maria Teresa, "The Quality Imperative Teachers' salaries", background paper prepared for the Education for All Global Monitoring Report 2005, accessed 31 August 2016, http://unesdoc.unesco.org/images/0014/001466/146696e.pdf.
46. Boko Haram: Nigeria teacher training college attacked, accessed 19 June 2016, http://www.bbc.com/news/world-africa-29244107; female suicide bomber attacks Nigerian teaching college 19 June 2016, http://www.dailymail.co.uk/wires/afp/article-2831560/Blast-rocks-teaching-college-NW-Nigeria.html; deaths in attack on Nigeria teachers' college 19 June 2016, http://www.aljazeera.com/news/africa/2014/09/deaths-attack-nigeria-teachers-college-2014917194449334646.html.
47. According to human rights watch, majority of attacks are in conflict situations; however, this is generally not the case in some situations. See generally Coursen-Neff Z., and Sheppard B. Schools as Battle grounds Protecting Students, Teachers and Schools from Attack, 19 June 2016, http://www.hrw.org/world-report-2011/schools-battlegrounds; a video documentary evidence from human rights watch is also available, 19 June 2016, http://www.hrw.org/node/116217 (Coursen-Nef and Sheppard 2016).
48. See generally Akwei Adotei Education under attack in Nigeria, 19 June 2016, http://blog.amnestyusa.org/africa/education-under-attack-in-nigeria/; Protecting schools from attack in Nigeria and beyond: how to support community-based responses, 19 June 2016 http://protectingeducation.org/news/protecting-schools-attack-nigeria-and-beyond-how-support-community-based-responses (Akwei 2016).
49. Bradford school stabbing: Vincent Uzomah desperately tried to stem bleeding after attack, 19 June 2016, http://www.mirror.co.uk/news/uk-news/bradford-school-stabbing-vincent-uzomah-5867501.

Bibliography

Adegbesan, Sunday O. 2011. Establishing Quality Assurance in Nigerian Education System: Implication for Educational Managers. *Educational Research and Reviews* 6 (2): 147.

Afe, John O. 2015. Reflections on Becoming a Teacher and the Challenges of Teacher Education. http://www.nuc.edu.ng/nucsite/File/ILS%202002/ILS-69.pdf. Accessed 10 May 2017.

African Charter on Human and Peoples 'Rights.

Agenda 2063 Framework Document. http://agenda2063.au.int/en/sites/default/files/Final%20Draft%20Agenda%202063%20Framework%20-Formatted%20TOC-1.pdf. Accessed 29 Oct.

Akwei, Adotei. 2016. Education Under Attack in Nigeria June 19, 2016. http://blog.amnestyusa.org/africa/education-under-attack-in-nigeria/.

Beiter, Klaus D. 2006. *The Protection of the Right to Education by International Law*. Netherlands: Martinus Nijhoff.

Boko Haram: Nigeria Teacher Training College Attacked. http://www.bbc.com/news/world-africa-29244107. Accessed 19 June 2016.

Bradford School Stabbing: Vincent Uzomah Desperately Tried to Stem Bleeding After Attack. http://www.mirror.co.uk/news/uk-news/bradford-school-stabbing-vincent-uzomah-5867501. Accessed 19 June 2016.

Catahan, Marcelino. 2015. *Enhancing Competency of Teachers: A Teaching-and-Learning Enhancement Guide*. Bloomington: AuthorHouse.

Classrooms no Safe Haven for Nigerian Teachers: 171 Killed Since 2009. http://www.ei-ie.org/en/news/news_details/3020. Accessed 25 July 2016.

Coomans, Fons. 2015. Clarifying the Core Elements of the Right to Education. http://www.uu.nl/faculty/leg/NL/organisatie/departementen/departementrechtsgeleerdheid/organisatie/onderdelen/studieeninformatiecentrummensenrechten/publicaties/simspecials/18/Documents/18-03.pdf. Accessed 10 June 2015.

Coursen-Neff Z., and B. Sheppard. 2011. Schools as Battle Grounds Protecting Students, Teachers, and Schools from Attack. http://www.hrw.org/world-report-2011/schools-battlegrounds. Accessed 19 June 2016.

Deaths in Attack on Nigeria Teachers' College. http://www.aljazeera.com/news/africa/2014/09/deaths-attack-nigeria-teachers-college-2014917194449334646.html. Accessed 19 June 2016.

European Union Identifies Teacher Training and Empowerment as a Core Component of Quality Education. *Indicators on the Quality of School Education*. http://europa.eu/legislation_summaries/education_training_youth/lifelong_learning/c11063_en.htm. Aceessed 16 June 2015.

Female Suicide Bomber Attacks Nigerian Teaching College. http://www.dailymail.co.uk/wires/afp/article-2831560/Blast-rocks-teaching-college-NW-Nigeria.html. Accessed 19 June 2016.

Greene, Maxine. The Teacher as a Stranger. http://bama.ua.edu/~jpetrovi/504web/readings/Greene.pdf. Accessed 4 Nov 2014.

Heneveld, Ward. 1994. Planning and Monitoring the Quality of Primary Education in Sub-Saharan Africa. AFTHR Technical Note No. 14.

http://www.gillmacmillan.ie/help/teachers/the-rights-of-teachers. Accessed 25 Oct 2016.

IBE. 2016. Quality Education and the Key Role of Teachers. Collaboration with EI and UNESCO. http://www.ibe.unesco.org/International/ICE47/English/Organisation/Workshops/Workshop4CompENG.pdf. Accessed 20 Oct 2016.

Johnson, David. 2008. Improving the Quality of Education in Nigeria: A Comparative Evaluation of Recent Policy Imperatives. In *The Changing*

Landscape of Education in Africa: Quality, Equality and Democracy, ed. David Johnson. Oxford: Symposium books.

Ki-Moon, Ban. 2016. Sustainable Development Post-2015 Begins with Education. http://unesdoc.unesco.org/images/0023/002305/230508e.pdf. Accessed 16 June 2016.

King-McKenzie, Ethel, Bogani Bantwini, and Bogan Barry. 2013. Supporting Teachers to Enhance Students Success in the USA and South Africa. *International Journal of Humanities and Social Science*. http://www.ijhssnet.com/journals/Vol_3_No_15_August_2013/3.pdf. Accessed 29 July 2016.

Lidonde, Rose. 2004. School Sanitation and Hygiene Education Symposium The Way Forward: Construction is not Enough! June 8–10. Delft, The Netherlands Scaling up School Sanitation and Hygiene Promotion and Gender Concerns. http://www.wsp.org/Hygiene-Sanitation-Water-Toolkit/Resources/Readings/Global-Lidonde-Scalingup.pdf. Accessed 16 Aug 2016.

Liston, Dan, Hilda Borko, and Jennie Whitcomb. 2008. The Teacher Educator's Role in Enhancing Teacher Quality. *Journal of Teacher Education* 59 (2): 111–117.

McDowell, B. 1959. A Bill of Rights for Classroom Teachers. *The Phi Delta Kappan* 40 (8): 330–332.

Nigeria: Implement Teacher' Salary Scale in Osun State now! http://www.pambazuka.net/en/category.php/advocacy/57591. Accessed 19 June 2015.

Nigerian Teachers To Strike Again. http://www.teachersolidarity.com/blog/nigerian-teachers-to-strike-again. Accessed 29 July 2016.

Obioma, Godswill. 2016. Continuous Assessment Practices of Primary and junior secondary school teachers in Nigeria. http://www.iaea2008.cambridgeassessment.org.uk/ca/digitalAssets/180437_Obioma.pdf. Accessed 9 June 2016.

Ogun Schools Shut as Teachers Embark on Strike. http://dailypost.ng/2015/01/16/ogun-schools-shut-teachers-embark-strike/ Accessed 29 July 2016; Nigerian Teachers To Strike Again. http://www.teachersolidarity.com/blog/nigerian-teachers-to-strike-again. Accessed 29 July 2016.

Orientation to a Right Based Approach. http://insightshare.org/sites/insightshare.org/files/A%20Rights-Based%20Approach%20to%20Participatory%20Video%20-%20toolkit%20(CHAPTER%202).pdf. Accessed 19 Oct 2016.

Out of School Children and Child Labor. http://globalmarch.org/sites/default/files/Policy-Paper.pdf. Accessed 10 June 2015.

Parkay, Forrest W., Beverly Hardcastle Stanford, and Thomas Douglas Gougeon. 2010. *Becoming a Teacher*. New Jersey: Pearson/Merril.

Pigozzi, Mary Joy. 1999. Education in Emergencies and for Reconstruction: A Developmental Approach. New York: UNICEF. http://www.unicef.org/girlseducation/files/EducEmerg.pdf. Accessed May 10 2017.

Protecting Schools from Attack in Nigeria and Beyond: How to Support Community-based Responses. http://protectingeducation.org/news/

protecting-schools-attack-nigeria-and-beyond-how-support-community-based-responses. Accessed 19 June 2016.

Public Schools in Abuja Shut Down as FCT Chapter of Nigerian Union of Teachers Embarks on Strike. http://www.bellanaija.com/2015/05/25/public-schools-in-abuja-shut-down-as-fct-chapter-of-nigerian-union-of-teachers-embarks-on-strike/. Accessed 26 June 2016.

Rabinowitz, William, and Robert M. W., Travers. 1953. Problems of Defining and Assessing Teacher Effectiveness. *Educational Theory* 3 (3): 212–219.

Salifu, Inusah, and Joseph Seyram Agbenyega. 2013. Teacher Motivation and Identity Formation: Issues Affecting Professional Practice. *MIER Journal of Educational Studies, Trends & Practices* 3: 58.

Smithers, Alan, and Pamela Robinson. 2003. Factors Affecting Teachers' Decisions to Leave the Profession.http://dera.ioe.ac.uk/4759/1/RR430.pdf. Accessed May 10 2017

Stephens, David. 2003. Quality of basic education. *Paper for EFA Global Monitoring Report*. http://unesdoc.unesco.org/images/0014/001469/146968e.pdf.

Teachers and Educational Quality: Monitoring Global Needs for 2015. http://www.uis.unesco.org/Library/Documents/teachers06-en.pdf. 45. Accessed 28 July 2016.

Teachers under pressure to end strike. http://www.news24.com/Africa/News/Nigerias-teachers-under-pressure-oto-end-strike-20131107. Accessed 16 Aug 2016.

Teresa Siniscalco Maria. 2005. The Quality Imperative Teachers' salaries. *Background paper prepared for the Education for All Global Monitoring Report*. http://unesdoc.unesco.org/images/0014/001466/146696e.pdf. Accessed 31 Aug 2016.

Tomaševski, Katrina. 2001a. Free and Compulsory Education for all Children: The gap Between Promise and Performance Right to Education. *Primers No. 2.*

Tomaševski, Katrina. 2001b. Removing Obstacles in the Way of the Right to Education *Primers No. 1*, 44.

UBE ACT 2004. Law of the Federation of Nigeria. Accessed 10 May 2017.

UNESCO Factsheets. http://www.uis.unesco.org/FactSheets/Documents/fs-28-out-of-school-children-en.pdf. Accessed 10 June 2015.

UNESCO. Teaching and Learning: Achieving Quality for all Summary. *EFA global monitoring report 2013/2014.* Johnson further Describes This Situation to Include Poor Quality of Teachers and Poor Utilisation of Poor Resources that are Available in Education Delivery.

UNESCO. Teaching and Learning: Achieving Quality for all Summary. *EFA Global Monitoring Report 2013/2014.*

Universal Declaration on Human Rights.

Vespoor, Adrian M. 2008. The Challenge of Learning: Improving the Quality of Basic Education in Sub-Saharan African. In *The Changing Landscape of Education in Africa: Quality, Equality and Democracy* ed. David Johnson, 33–38. Oxford: Symposium Books.

Video Documentary Evidence from Human Rights Watch. http://www.hrw.org/node/116217. Accessed 19 June 2016.

We Can't Wait for Improved Sanitation. We must Act now. http://worldtoilet.org/documents/WecantWait.pdf. Accessed 20 Oct 2016.

Woolman, Stu, and Fleisch Brahm, (eds.). 2009. The Constitution in the Classroom: Law and Education in South Africa, 1994–2008. Pretoria: Pretoria University Law Press.

World Health Organization. 2009. *Water, Sanitation and Hygiene Standards for Schools in Low-cost Settings,* ed. John Adams, Jackie Simms, Yves Chartier, and Jamie Bartram. World Health Organization

World Teachers Day: Teachers Decry Poor Salaries. http://www.punchng.com/education/wtd-teachers-decry-poor-salaries/. Accessed June 19 2015.

Author Biography

Dr. A.C Onuora-Oguno LLB (Ilorin), BL (Nigeria), LLM (Pretoria), LLD (Pretoria) Azubike is a Solicitor and Advocate of the Nigerian Supreme Court and a researcher with the Centre for Human Rights, University of Pretoria, South Africa. He has passion for Child's rights with particular focus on the right to basic education. He was a former clerk in the Office of the Prosecutor International Criminal Court. He has written extensively on the subject of education, girl child and other areas of law. Some of the previous publications have appeared in the Child Abuse Research Journal of South Africa (2015); University of Benin Law Journal (2014) and Human Science Research Council of South Africa Conference Proceedings (2015).

CHAPTER 6

The Legal Framework for Achieving the Goal of "Education for All" in Africa: A Case Study of the Vulnerable Students in the Nigerian Borstal Institutions

Abdulraheem-Mustapha Mariam Adepeju

1 Introduction

Arguably, it is assumed that rights are benefits or entitlements inherent in every human being irrespective of gender, religion, origin, race and colour. for which the government of a country has the responsibility to protect. These rights were put together by the United Nations General Assembly on 10 December 1948, agreed upon and published as "the Universal Declaration of Human Rights" (UDHR). The rights in UDHR broadly cover a wide range of rights to wit the "economic, social and cultural rights" and "the civil and political rights". Thus, right to education falls within the purview of the economic and social rights under UDHR.

However, the right to education as one of the socio-economic rights remains a challenge in many African countries including Nigeria. This may generally be attributed to the inadequacy of a particular country's

A.-M.M. Adepeju (✉)
University of Ilorin, Ilorin, Kwara State, Nigeria
e-mail: mariamadepeju78@gmail.com

A.C. Onuora-Oguno et al. (eds.), *Education Law, Strategic Policy and Sustainable Development in Africa*, DOI 10.1007/978-3-319-53703-0_6

legal framework in some African countries or lack of political will to implement it. In Nigeria, the question of whether right to education is construed as less important or not begs for an answer when considering the constitutional framework in particular, the provision of Chap. 2 of the Constitution of the Federal Republic of Nigeria 1999 (as amended). Unfortunately, right to education in Nigeria has been embodied in Chap. 2 of the 1999 Constitution which deals with the "fundamental objectives and directive principles of state policy" that are ordinarily not enforceable as against Chap. 4 which deals with fundamental human rights. This chapter therefore posits that the inclusion of the right to education in Chap. 2 thereof instead of Chap. 4 poses a threat to the achievement of the goal of "Education for All", especially for the vulnerable children in the Nigerian Borstal institution.

Given the importance of education to human life, this chapter therefore seeks to examine the legal framework for achieving the goal of "Education for All" by undertaking empirical assessment of the issue of whether or not the vulnerable students' rights to education is easily achievable in the Nigerian Borstal institutions when this right is not within the scope of fundamental human rights entrenched in the Nigerian Constitution, 1999 (as amended). In achieving this objective, this chapter firstly examines the research methodology adopted with an overview of the historical context of Borstal institution in Nigeria. It follows with the Nigeria's responsibility under national, regional and international legal instruments on education. Findings from the empirical verification were discussed as part of this chapter. The chapter closes by proffering plausible strategies for more effective educational system that offers the Borstal students the prospect of more fulfilling and sustainable futures outside of the institution with a view to stimulating processes to reform in Nigeria.

2 Methodology

The explanatory and qualitative research design was adopted using specifically a case study type. According to Keith,[1] Sonia[2] and Creswell,[3] explanatory and qualitative study is concerned with stating the reason for what happened or how things are proceeding or what something is like for the purpose of identifying the strength and weakness of certain phenomenon. As far as this study is concerned, explanatory and qualitative design is used to explain the views of certain stakeholders on the legal framework for achieving the goal of "Education for All" in Africa by taking vulnerable children in the Nigerian Borstal institution as a case study. The researcher has a strong conviction that there must be an element of fit between the research to be carried out and the method to be used in carrying out the research.[4] It was this conviction which inspired the selection of a case study as the preferred strategy. Case studies are multi-perspective analysis. Multiple sources of data were employed in order to elicit views from participants. To achieve the objective of this study, information and evidence necessary were obtained through one-on-one interview, as well as focus group discussion (participants' observation) to gain insights into the educational opportunity given to the students of Nigerian Borstal institution. Rather than selecting a large number of people, the qualitative researcher, like this researcher, identified and recruited a small number of samples that provide in-depth information about the central phenomenon. Ultimately, the researcher secured 15 key informants[5] in each of the three Borstal institutions in Nigeria and two focus group sessions (both groups comprised six participants each).[6]

Background information of participants				
Participants	*Unit of analysis*	*Occupation*	*Location*	*Qualifications*
Key informants 1–15	Academic and administrative staff and Borstal students	Head of teaching staff, head of administrative staff, record officer, welfare officer, head of vocation training, head of medical section, heads of library and laboratory, chief security officer, class monitors in junior and senior classes 1, 2 and 3 and headman of each of the vocation units	Kaduna, Ilorin and Abeokuta	National Certificate in Education (NCE), National Diploma (ND), Higher National Diploma (HND), Bachelors of Education and Sciences (B.Ed. and B.Sc.) and Primary School Holders

(continued)

(continued)

Background information of participants				
Participants	*Unit of analysis*	*Occupation*	*Location*	*Qualifications*
Focus group session '1'	General duty section	Teaching and training staff	Kaduna, Ilorin and Abeokuta	National Certificate in Education (NCE), National Diploma (ND), Higher National Diploma (HND), Bachelors of Education and Sciences (B.Ed. and B.Sc.) and Primary School Holders
Focus group session '2'	Borstal students	Learning and vocation trainees	Kaduna, Ilorin and Abeokuta	Junior Secondary School (JSS) Certificates, Primary School Leaving Certificates and no formal education

3 An Overview of the Historical Context of Borstal Institution in Nigeria

An attempt to cater for young offenders in Prison brought the establishment of Borstal institution in Nigeria.[7] The word Borstal can be traced to a town in England near Chatham where in 1902, an attempt was made to separate young prisoners from associating with adult offenders by grouping them apart in a wing of the convict Prison at Borstal.[8] Instead of confining the youths to solitary confinement, the Borstal sought to stimulate the young offender to his/her best through large workshops by a system of marks and privileges. The Borstal institution seeks to "turn around the youths mostly from ages sixteen to twenty-one by instilling in them habits of industry, self-respect and self-control through the technique of manual labour, games, physical training, mental education, the incentive of useful and interesting trade and carefully planned series of rewards".[9]

The Nigerian corrective institution in the delivery of criminal justice system is fashioned after the English model. The first known attempt at establishing Borstal institution in Nigeria was at a wing of the Enugu Prison in 1937.[10] This, however, did not produce the expected results. It was not until 1960 that the first law on Borstal institution in Nigeria was passed as "Borstal Institutions and Remand Centre Act".[11] By Section 3 of the Borstal Institution and Remand Centres Act, 1960, the purpose of the institution is to

> bring to bear upon the inmates every good influence which may establish in them the will to lead a good and useful life on release and to fit into do so by fullest development of his/her character, capacities, and sense of personal responsibilities.

This position is further reinforced by the provision of Section 35(1)(d) of the Constitution of the Federal Republic of Nigeria 1999 (as amended), which provides that:

> every person shall be entitled to his personal liberty, and no person shall be deprived of such liberty save in the following cases and in accordance with a procedure permitted by law:
>
> (d) in the case of a person who has not attained the age of eighteen years for the purpose of his education or welfare.

The intendment of this constitutional provision suffices in situations where a child who is adjudged to be in conflict with the law, in need of care and protection or beyond parental control is taken to Borstal institution for education, rehabilitation and reformation in order to be reintegrated into the society. In order to realize this constitutional injunction, therefore, it becomes germane to create conducive environment for the education and welfare of Borstal students. The essential welfare required for an errant child or young person is to reform his/her character and make him/her a better person.

By Section 3 of the Borstal Institution and Remand Centres Act, 2004, Borstal is "any building or place or any part thereof declared to be a Borstal Institution under Section 3 of this Act".[12] Section 3 referred to, authorized the Minister to declare any building or place a Borstal institution where "offenders who were not less than sixteen but under 21 years of age on the day of conviction may be detained and given such training and instructions as will conduce to their reformation and the prevention of crime".[13] Furthermore, the Act specifies a maximum of 3 years of institutionalization in the Borstal institution, with a possible additional 1 year of aftercare supervision.[14]

Instructively, as the scope of basic education coverage expands, the attention to extend compulsory education to other groups including vulnerable children[15] in the Prisons was also considered a priority. Thus, the Borstal institutions for vulnerable children were established[16] to cater for the Borstal students educational and vocational opportunities especially those children who are not able to pass through the process of formal educational institutions and are in need of special care and protection.

According to Milner, there are two functions of Borstal institutions in Nigeria. The first is the encouragement of a personal relationship between the Borstal staff and students through which the students are given "progressive trust-demanding personal decision, responsibility and self-control", and second is the placement of emphasis on regular educational and vocational training regimen with a demanding physical training content.[17] It is argued that the law is, however, silent on what happens to convicts below the age of 16 years. Whatever be the case, there are now three Borstal institutions in Nigeria located at Abeokuta in Ogun State, Ilorin in Kwara State and Kaduna in Kaduna State.[18] In order to realize the goal of effective reintegration of Borstal students into community after release, there were provisions for vocational training in "tailoring, photography, welding, building (masonry or bricklaying), electrical installation", etc., for obtaining Trade Test I, II or III Certificate as well as formal educational instruction, up to General Certificate of Education (GCE), West Africa Education Certificate (WAEC), National Education Certificate (NECO), Junior National Education Certificate and National Business and Technical Examination Certificate (NABTEB). However, studies have shown that by the 1980s, facilities and training had deteriorated[19] and were virtually non-existent in the 1990s.[20]

It has to be reiterated that by the provisions of UN Rules for the Protection of Juveniles Deprived of their Liberty[21] and also mostly emphasized by the Beijing Rules,[22] the institutionalization or confinement at any stage of the proceedings shall be the last resort for the shortest period of time. The rationale for this is the belief that confinement seldom protects the interests of the child. Instructively, the custodial punishment can only be imposed if the offence is of a serious nature. Thus, the custodial sentence should only be justified if the offence is of a violent nature or is a sexual crime, if it is in the opinion of the Court that a custodial punishment is necessary to protect the public from danger and if the offender refused to serve previously imposed community sentence.[23]

Instructively, Borstal institutions are intended to provide such training as would conduce to the children reformation and reintegration into the society.[24] But these institutions are very few[25] and too far apart in a federation of 36 states with a capital territory, Abuja. More importantly, with the rising wave of juvenile delinquency in Nigeria, Borstal institutions are becoming grossly inadequate for the treatment of young offenders[26] particularly in education. This study posits that the primary objective of educating Borstal students has not been achieved. Thus, the teeming vulnerable Borstal students are now languishing in adult Prisons[27] under inhuman and deplorable conditions.[28]

Also, in Nigeria, the staff of Borstal institutions are drawn from Prison staff. This is seen as a serious handicap to the reformation and rehabilitative ideals of Borstal training for students. This is in view of the fact that Prison staff are trained to handle adult criminals. Hence, the staff are not used to the "large-hearted approach" required in the case of Borstal students who should be handled as if they are in their own homes.[29]

4 Nigeria's Responsibility Under National, Regional and International Legal Instruments on Education

Significantly, the protection and promotion of rights to education as one of the socio-economic rights in Africa received tremendous support from the adoption of the African Charter on Human and Peoples' Rights, 1986.[30] This Charter makes neither distinction as to the type of rights nor distinction as to which of the rights are of less importance than others and theoretically made no distinction as to their implementation.[31] Thus, it did not create any hierarchy of rights, and this is seen as a leap beyond the ideological cleavages and disputes that led to the subjugation of socio-economic rights as being of lesser value than civil and political rights.[32] In the same vein, the African Charter on the Rights and Welfare of the Child (ACRWC), 1909, puts education forward as a premise on which the potentials of a child can be identified and enhanced. It places obligations on the child to effectively contribute to the peaceful existence of the state.[33] It is, however, submitted that where the government fails in its responsibility to provide access to quality education, the child is unable to carry out the obligations required by the Charter.[34] Internationally, the declaration of the UDHR in 1948 and the adoption of the UN Convention on the Rights of the Child (UNCRC), 1989, brought into global focus issues relating to children and this gained importance among countries that are signatory and ratified the same. They have given great visibility to issues concerning children and have served as a reference for the development of new laws and public policies.[35]

As signs of Nigeria government's commitment to the protection of the rights of the child to education, it has adopted measures in line with some regional, international treaties and declarations. For instance, the Bill of Rights under UDHR has been adequately incorporated into Chap. 4 of the Nigerian Constitution, 1999 (as amended). While the Education for All Declaration, 2000, was adopted as the National Policy on Education Act, 2004, and the Universal Basic Education Act, 2004. The UNCRC, the ACRWC, and the African Charter on Human and Peoples' Rights, 1986, were adopted as the Child Rights Act, 2003, and Cap A9 Laws of the Federal Republic of Nigeria, 2004, respectively. Instructively, the above-mentioned regional and international legal instruments required Nigeria to take proactive action towards achieving education for all. It is therefore evident from the national legal instruments that Nigerian government introduced free Universal Basic Education and put in place National Action Plan for its implementation.

Summarily, the municipal protection of the rights of the child to education is the Constitution of the Federal Republic of Nigeria (CFRN), 1999 (as amended). Chap. 4 of the CFRN enshrines several fundamental human rights which accrue to all Nigerians. In Chap. 2 of the CFRN, particularly in Section 18, the obligation of everyone to have compulsory and basic education is restated. Aside from the CFRN, other legislative Acts also exist that aim at the protection of the rights of the child to education. In addition to the Constitution, there are three major legislations of interest in this discourse—the Universal Basic Education Act,[36] the Child Rights Act[37] and the National Policy on Education Act.[38] The provisions of the mentioned Acts are "based on certain fundamental principles relating to the promotion and sustenance of child dignity and enhancement of child development".[39] Education is conceived to be laden with potentials of enhancing the dignity of an individual and enabling the child to contribute meaningfully to the community.

With the Nigerian domestication of the UNCRC and ACRWC through the enactment of the Child Rights Act (CRA) 2003,[40] it showed great resolve to protect the Nigerian child from all forms of deprivation including lack of access to education. Composed of 278 sections and 11 schedules, the Act promises a uniform standard for the concerns of the rights of children to education.[41] However, the situation is not encouraging as the applicability of CRA depends on its domestication by states in Nigeria in order to bring in uniformity as CRA is a Federal Act on a subject, which is not within the exclusive legislative competence of the federal government. CRA (with the exception of the Federal Capital Territory, Abuja, over which it has direct application) can only become binding on the states in the federation if it is approved by a simple majority or if interested state passes its own version without reference to the federal statute.[42] Currently, the CRA has been promulgated into law in 23 states out of 36 states.[43] Failure of all the 36 states of the federation to domesticate the CRA leads to ununiformed application of the provisions of the Act with particular respect to access to education.

It is reiterated here that the inability of the federal government to ensure that all states in Nigeria domesticate the CRA in their respective states continues to inform the lack of uniform attempt to pursue the goal of "Education for All". It is, however, opined that having ratified the CRC and domesticated it in Nigeria, Nigeria's obligations under the treaty cannot be abdicated by the mere refusal of some states to domesticate the CRA with their state legislation. This argument is further advanced based on the supremacy of the CFRN 1999. Thus, a state is bound to act only in line with the commitment of the government at federal level and also to respect government obligations under international law.

Arguably, Nigeria aimed at achieving the purpose set down and in the same standard with CRC through attempts to enact the Universal Basic Education Act (UBE Act) which contains the obligation of the Nigerian government to ensure that every child has access to quality basic education. The Act places obligations on parents and guardians to ensure that their children or wards attain free and compulsory education as provided by the government. The intent of the UBE Act is in consonance with the provisions of the CRA discussed above.

To further strengthen its commitment under the international and regional obligations, Nigeria made an attempt to establish policy and laws by the enactment of the National Policy on Education Act (NPEA), 2004, but the NPEA gets more complicated when considering judicial interpretation of justiciability of rights to adequate and equal education opportunities within the context of Chap. 2 of the Nigerian Constitution, 1999,[44] which constitutes fundamental objectives and directive principles of state policy (DPSP)[45] not ordinarily justiciable.[46]

Interestingly, there is a growing acknowledgement of the indivisibility and interdependency of right to education as one of the socio-economic rights with other fundamental human rights. This acknowledgement dates back to the position adopted by world leaders at the 1993s World Conference on Human Rights in Vienna, where human rights were described as "universal, indivisible and interdependent and interrelated".[47] Thus, this chapter argues for making the right to education a fundamental human right by amending the Nigerian Constitution to reflect the same as construing right to education under DPSP posits danger to the Nigeria, aligning its education system with her current developmental goals and that of the emergent global village.

More importantly, the Nigerian Supreme Court in the case of *Attorney-General of Ondo State v. Attorney-General of the Federation & 35 Ors*[48] decided that the DPSP can be enforced if the Executive and the Legislature work together in order to give expression to any objectives mentioned in Chap. 2 through appropriate enactment. Also, Section 9 of the NPEA mandated the government to take various measures to implement the policy. From the case cited above, this chapter posits that the enactments of CRA, UBE Act and NPEA have solved the issue of right to education by making it justiciable as it is interdependent and interrelated with fundamental human rights. More so, it is argued that one can interpret the cross-cutting right to education in the light of the provision of Section 35(1) (d) of the Constitution as the fundamental human right of a person under the age of eighteen years. Thus, confinement of children in the Borstal institutions for the purpose of their education should be made a fundamental human right that can be enforced in the court of law.

Despite the enactments of those Acts and policy, studies conducted by Alamika and Chukwuma[49] show that the laudable goals of the institution are not realized due to lack of proper implementation of those policies, legal and institutional frameworks for vulnerable students in the Borstal institutions. They stressed further that the objectives of the institution are compromised by lack of proper planning and implementation; lack of funding inadequate staff in qualitative and quantitative terms; and lack of necessary training facilities in the workshops and educational programmes. They confirmed further[50] that less than half of the population sampled, representing 180 (48.3%) of the Borstal students had access to education and vocational training.[51] To them, apart from counselling which was reported on a positive note, educational and vocational facilities were inadequate or non-existent. Thus, it is the contention of this chapter that for an effective rehabilitation programme,measures such as: education, vocational training, individual and group counselling, psychiatrist and psychological treatment,[52] students' personnel services,[53] student welfare services,[54] student social recreational services,[55] student library services,[56] and health services[57] must be included; otherwise, the rehabilitation objective and "Education for All" goal will not be fulfilled.

It is hereby submitted that an empirical verification is necessary to be carried out as decided in this chapter to determine the efficacy of the legal framework, and it is after such a realistic evaluation that it is possible to make recommendations for robust reforms. Similarly, in view of all the analysis of the laws and policy on education discussed above, a question that begs for an answer is whether the problems of the goal of "Education for All" are related to its non-inclusion in the Chap. 4 of the Nigerian Constitution as *grundnorm* of the country or whether the misconception of the interpretation of the Constitution and other existing laws and policy hinders the achievement of the goal. It is therefore safe to argue that none of these problems fully account for non-achievement of the goal of "Education for All" in Nigeria as this will be ascertained through the empirical findings in this chapter.

5 Findings and Discussion

While using explanatory and qualitative approaches in this study, it was revealed that students in the Borstal institutions are those children that are either in conflict with the law or beyond parental control. Key informants '1'–'15' as well as the two focus group sessions in all the three Borstal institutions claimed that all students at the institutions are below eighteen years of age. To them, 75% of the students are children acclaimed to be beyond parental control and 25% are those in conflict with the law. The participants further attested that Borstal institutions are solely for boys, and from 2010 till date, the institutions housed 734 students out of which 162 are from Ilorin, 452 from Kaduna and 120 from Abeokuta, respectively. This corresponds with the available data that delinquency and crime have strong gender associations as studies have shown[58] that from the police records, crime rates of male juvenile and male young adult offenders are more than double those of young females, and conviction rates for boys are six or seven times higher. The number of male juvenile suspects for every 100,000 members of the designated age group is more than six times the corresponding figure for females; for those in the youth category, the male–female suspect ratio is even higher at 12.5 to 1.[59]

It was also expressed by the key informants '1'–'15' interviewed that before the students leave the Borstal institution, they must have a basic vocational training or academic qualification either Junior WAEC or Senior School Certificate educational training or at least a Trade Test Certificate. It was further revealed by the key informants particularly at Kaduna and Ilorin that Borstal students are not released from the institutions until the completion of the term which spans from 6 months to 3 years. To them, upon release, there are aftercare officers who take care of the Borstal institutions' released student. Focus group 1 was of the view that those Borstal students who undergo full academic training while at the Borstal institution can sit for Junior or Senior NECO, Senior WAEC and JAMB and are admissible into higher institutions of learning. They are not regarded as ex-convicts and can live freely in society like every other person without any form of stigmatization.

However, according to the first focus group session, they lamented that despite the laudable therapeutical models, Borstal institutions are very few and that the students have not attained full educational opportunities.

For instance, they expressed deep concern about inadequate and lack of qualified teachers as most of the teaching staff have no teaching qualifications and that the institutions are at the mercy of the Youth Corp members. They also lamented on lack of equipped libraries and laboratories.

This is in tandem with the studies by Alamika and Chukwuma[60] that the objectives of the Borstal institution are compromised by lack of proper planning and implementation; lack of funding, inadequate staff in qualitative and quantitative terms; and lack of necessary training facilities in the workshops and educational programmes. A study conducted by Okagbue I[61] also shows correspondence with the findings that Borstal institutions are very few and become grossly inadequate for the treatment of child offenders. It further stressed that the institution is confronted with the problem of achieving its reformative objective. For instance, Borstal institution is hindered by the institutions' personnel who are drawn from Prison staff as they were trained to handle adult criminals. Thus, the staff are not used to the "large-hearted approach which requires handling of child offenders as if they are in their respective homes.

In addition, the study also revealed that the institutions' problems relate to lack of resource availability and management, resource control and personnel policy as well as administrative style. The participants interviewed further expressed that the institutions lack funding from the government. In particular, most if not all of the participants at Kaduna expressed in tears that more than 25% of the Borstal students in the three institutions are out without being well equipped in terms of education. This pattern of findings is similar to both the interview phase of the work and focus group sessions. Students who are in academic training have narrated terrible experiences witnessed by them in their learning as they lamented that most of them wanted to be science students, but because of inadequate laboratory equipment, they were forced to do any available subject. This was confirmed by Alamika and Chukwuma[62] in their study that less than half of the population sampled representing 180 (48.3%) of the juveniles in the Borstal institutions had access to education and vocational training.[63] Apparently, the objective of rehabilitation and equal educational opportunity for vulnerable children in the Borstal institutions was not achieved.

6 Conclusion and Recommendations

Educational opportunity is an important aspect of a child's upbringing. As used in this chapter, it refers to all forms of conventional academic training that children receive in a conventional school environment. It would also be perceived to mean all opportunities for educational advancement that a child is exposed to in the course of his/her upbringing. A detailed understanding of the findings in this study shows that Borstal institutions are meant for boys and the laws and policy on the Nigerian Borstal institutions delimit the years of committal of students into Borstal institution. Thus, a child less than 16 years is said not to be admitted into the institution, whereas the general definition of a child for the purposes of children in conflict with the law under the national, regional and international laws is "any person below the age of eighteen years".[64]

Instructively, the purpose of injunction underscored by Section 35(1)(d) of the Nigerian Constitution 1999 (as amended) has not been realized as findings in this study have shown that some Borstal institutions' students are not well equipped educationally. As education is seen as a tool in achieving the ultimate goal of reforming the Borstal students' character in order to make them better persons in Nigeria, the status of a fundamental human right should be accorded. Thus, until there is cross-cutting interpretation, education is not ordinarily enforceable in the Nigerian Courts as it falls within Chap. 2 of the Constitution of the Federal Republic of Nigeria 1999 (as amended); therefore, education of Borstal institutions' students is not ordinarily and optimally guaranteed, and as such, a Borstal student cannot ordinarily enforce his right to education unless such right is interpreted within the context of Section 35(1)(d) of the same Constitution. This chapter therefore argues that non-justiciability of this educational objective ordinarily without cross-cutting interpretation is posing a threat to the realization of the primary objective of establishing Borstal institution in Nigeria. Thus, such incarceration in the Borstal institution poses a threat to Nigeria's efforts to align itself with her current developmental goals with that of the emergent global village. It also contradicts the provision of Section 35(1) (d) of the same 1999 Constitution as same cannot be ordinarily enforced unless and until that the right to education of Borstal students is made fundamental human rights for the purpose of achieving education for all levels.

In order to make education more effective in the Borstal institutions, the government should provide enough funds, recruit professional staff and establish more Borstal training institutions in the country to bring such education closer to the people.

Alternatively, it is suggested that government should create awareness on the concept of diversion and restorative justice provided under the Child Rights Act[65] in order to achieve maximum educational opportunity for the delinquent child. The idea of restorative justice (i.e. promoting reconciliation, restitution and responsibility) through the involvement of the child, family, community and the victim will provide delinquent child the opportunity to develop his/her capacity to contribute positively to the society.

Notes

1. Keith F. Punch, *Introduction to Social Research: Quantitative and Qualitative Approaches* (London, California, India: Sage Publications, 2005), 15 (Punch 2005).
2. Sonia Ospina, "Qualitative Research", in Encyclopaedia of Leadership, vol. 1, eds. George R. Goethals, James MacGregor Burns and Georgia Sorenson (Califonia, UK, India: Berkshire Publishing Group LLC, Sage Publications, 2004), 1 (Ospina 2004).
3. John W. Creswell, Research Design: Qualitative, Quantitative and Mixed Methods Approaches (California, UK, India: Sage Publications Limited, 2009), 3 (Creswell 2009).
4. Janet Houser, *Nursing Research: Reading, Using and Creative Evidence* (Sudbury MA: Jones and Bartlett Learning, 2011), 93. See also, Peter G. Miller, John Strang and Peter M. Miller, *Addiction Research Methods* (Chichester, West Sussex, UK; Ames, Iowa: Blackwell Addiction Press, 2010), 4 (Houser 2011; Miller et al. 2010).
5. See Janet House, *Nursing Research, Using and Creative Evidence* (Sudbury MA: Jones and Bartlett Learning, 2011), 93 (Houser 2011).
6. Qualitative research requires a lot of labour. Hence, analysing a very large sample can take a lot of time and often unrealistic. Thus, '15' is said to be the normal acceptable sample for all qualitative research. See, Mason Mark, "Sampling and Saturation in Ph.D. Studies Using Qualitative Interviews", *Forum Qualitative Sozialforschung/Forum: Qualitative Social Research* 11, no. 3, Art 8 (2010), accessed 23 February 2012, url: http://www.qualitative-research.net/index.php/fqs/article/view/1428/3027. See also, Charmz Kathy, *Constructing Grounded Theory: A Practical Guide Through Qualitative Analysis* (London, California, India: Sage Publications, 2006), 114 (Mason 2010; Kathy 2006).

7. Ogbolumani, B.O.I., "Institutional Treatment of Juveniles", in *The Magistrate and the Offender,* ed. Elias, T.O. (Lagos: University Press, Lagos 1972), 122 (Ogbolumani 1972).
8. Ibid
9. Ibid.
10. Ibid.
11. Presently Cap B38 Laws of the Federation of Nigeria, 2004.
12. Ibid., Section 2.
13. The law also declares Borstal Remand Center as a place for the detention of persons not less than 16 but under 21 years of age who are remanded or committed in custody for trial or sentence.
14. See Ogbolumani, B.O.I., "Institutional Treatment of Juveniles", in *The Magistrate and the Offender,* ed. Elias, T.O. (Lagos: University Press, Lagos 1972), 122. See also, Igbo, E.U.M., *Introduction to Criminology.* (Nsukka: Afro-Orbis Publication Ltd., 2007), 85–86. See also, Alemika, E.E.O. and Chukwuma, I.C., *Juvenile Justice Administration in Nigeria: Philosophy and Practice* (Lagos: Centre for Law Enforcement Education, Lagos, 2001), 52–53. See also Crime and the Quality of Life in (Lagos: Nigeria Government of the Federal Republic of Nigeria Publication, Lagos, August 1980), 35 (Ogbolumani 1972; Igbo 2007; Alemika and Chukwuma 2001).
15. Vulnerable children are delinquent children who are not more than specified age that has violated criminal laws and engaged in disobedient, indecent or immoral conduct and is in need of treatment, rehabilitation or supervision defined by statute. See Black's Law Dictionary (Centennial ed. 1981–1991), p. 428.
16. See the Borstal Institutions and Remand Centre Act, Cap B38, Laws of the Federation of Nigeria, 2004. See also, the Prison Act, Cap P. 29, Laws of the Federation of Nigeria, 2004.
17. Milner, A., *The Nigerian Penal System,* (London: Sweet and Maxwell, London, 1972) cited in Abdul-Mumin Sa'ad, "Juvenile Justice in Nigeria", A paper presented at the Conference Session of the Research Committee on Deviant Behaviour (RC 29) during the XVI International Sociological Association (ISA) World Congress of Sociology (Durban, South Africa, 2006) (Milner 1972; Abdul-Mumin Sa'ad 2006).
18. Kaduna, Abeokuta and Ilorin. See Aduba J.N., "From Punishment to Treatment: Humane Approach to the Sentencing of Young Offenders", in *Women and Children Under the Nigerian Law* (Vol. 6, Federal Ministry of Justice Publication, 1989), 216–217. See also Ogbolumani, B.O.I., "Institutional Treatment of Juveniles", in *The Magistrate and the Offender,* ed. Elias, T.O., 117–130 (Aduba 1989; Ogbolumani 1972).

19. Ahire, P.T., "Juvenile Delinquency and the Handling of Young Prisoners in Nigerian Borstal Institutions", in *The Nigerian Prisons Service and the Public* (Nigerian Prisons Service, Abuja, 1987), 23 (Ahire 1987).
20. Human Rights Monitor, *Administration of Juvenile Justice: the Example of The Borstal Training Institution Kaduna*, 1997.
21. See Rules (1) UN Rules for the Protection of Juveniles Deprived of their Liberty.
22. Rules 13, 17 and 19 of the Beijing Rules.
23. See Stephenie J. Mill, "The Age of Criminal Responsibility in an Era of Violence: Has Britain set a Vandabult", *The Nashville University Journal of Transnational Law Vandabult* 28, no. 2 (1995): 320 (Mill 1995).
24. See Section 236 of the Child Rights Act, 2003.
25. See Okagbue, I., "The Treatment of Juvenile Offenders and the Rights of the Child", in *The Rights of the Child in Nigeria*, ed. Ayua, I.A. and Okagbue, I.E. (Nigerian Institute of Advance Legal Studies 1996), 9. See also, Alemika, E.E.O. and Chukwuma, I.C., *Juvenile Justice Administration in Nigeria: Philosophy and Practice,* 53. The first of it was established in Kaduna in the southern part of Kaduna State. In the first instance, a Borstal remand centre was established as a remand and reception centre prior to the transfer of committed juvenile offenders to the Borstal Institution in Kaduna (Okagbue 1996; Alemika and Chukwuma 2001).
26. See the Nigerian Prisons Service Annual Report for 1986, 46.
27. This can be confirmed from the report gathered from The Vanguard Newspaper of 5 September 2008 at p. 10 that "No fewer than 200 juveniles are currently languishing in Port Harcourt Prison as they have been put behind bars among over 2400 inmates, in (sic) which over 1800 of the adults and children are awaiting trial.
28. Alemika, E.E.O., "A Study of Socio-Cultural and Economic Factors in Delinquency Among Kaduna Borstal Inmates" (B.Sc. Sociology Original Essay, University of Ibadan, Ibadan Nigeria, 1978), 25 (Alemika 1978).
29. See Chinwe, R. Nwanna and Naomi E.N. Akpan, *Research Findings of Juvenile Justice Administration in Nigeria* (Chinwe and Naomi 2003).
30. The Charter in its Articles 15–24 protects a wide range of socio-economic rights such as the rights to health (Art. 16) and rights to education (Art. 17) among others.
31. See the African Commission decision, in *Purohit and Another v The Gambia* (2003) AHRLR 96. See also, Viljoen, F., *International Human Rights Law in Africa* (Oxford University Press, 2007), 240.
32. See Mbazira, C., "Enforcing the economic, social and cultural rights in the African Charter on Human and People's Rights: Twenty years redundancy, progression and significant strides", *African Human Rights Law Journal 6, no. 2* (2006): 338 (Mbazira 2006).

33. ACRWC article 11 (b).
34. ACRWC article 31.
35. It is also possible to assure that the Child Rights Convention has been enormously influential; indeed, to many, it is regarded as the touchstone for children's rights throughout the world. It constitutes the most comprehensive list of human rights created for a specific group. International bodies refer to it with approval on the basis that it can be utilized to promote a change in the way children, as individual with rights, are viewed and also to encourage their active and responsible participation within the family and society.
36. Universal Basic Education Act 2004.
37. Child Rights Act 2003.
38. National Policy on Education, 2004
39. A bill proposed by Amadi Gary Kelechi and Okpara Nnenna Joy, accessed 20 February 2015, url: http://nials-nigeria.org/proposed-bill/ENFORCEMENTOFEDUCATIONOFCHILDRENANDYOUNGPERSONSBILL.pdf.
40. The Child Rights Act is a law to consolidate and amend the legal framework relating to juveniles in conflict with law and children in need of care and protection. Section 15(1) of the Child Rights Act, 2003, provides for right to free compulsory and universal basic education, and it shall be the duty of the government in Nigeria to provide such education.
41. In Section 15 of the Act, a child is entitled to free, compulsory and universal primary education.
42. See Owosanoye, B. and Wernham, M., Street Children and Juvenile Justice System in Lagos State of Nigeria (Human Development Initiative, 2004), 11, accessed on 12 May 2013, url: http://www.gvnet.com (Owosanoye and Wernham 2004).
43. Child Rights Act has been promulgated into law in only 23 states which are Abia, Anambra, Bayelsa, Eboniyi, Ekiti, Imo, Jigawa, Kwara, Lagos, Nassarawa, Ogun, Ondo, Plateau, Rivers, Taraba, Kogi, Oyo, Benue, Osun, Edo, Delta, Cross River and Akwa Ibom, accessed on 18 December 2015, url: http://www.unicef.org/wcaro/WCARO_Nigeria_Factsheets_CRA.pdf. It leaves thirteen states without Child Rights Law and these states one way or the other are still using the Children and Young Persons Laws of their respective states.
44. See Section 18 of the Nigerian Constitution 1999.
45. The DPSPs are usually used for interpreting the provision of a Constitution. They are "related to policy or goals or directions rather than to existence or extent of legal rights vested in any individual or group normally subject to the jurisdiction of courts of law". See Okere, B.O, "Objectives and directives principles of state policy under

the Nigerian Constitution", *The International and Comparative Law Quarterly* 32 (1983): 221 (Okere 1983).

46. See Section 6(6) (c) of the Nigerian Constitution 1999.
47. Vienna Declaration and Programme of Action: UN GABOR world conference on human rights, 40th session, 2nd plenary meeting, part 1, 5: UN doc A/CONF. 157/24 (1993), reprinted in (1993) 32, *International Legal Materials* 1661. See also, Steiner, H.J., Alston, P. and Goodman, R., *International Human Rights in Context: Law, Politics, Morals*, 3rd ed. (Clarendon Press, 2008), 263; Harris-Short, S., "International human rights law: Imperialist, inept and ineffective? Cultural relativism and the UN Convention on the Rights of the Child", *Human Rights Quarterly* (2003): 131 (Steiner et al. 2008; Harris-Short 2003).
48. (2002) 9 NWLR (pt. 772) 222 at 381.
49. Alemika, E.E.O. and Chukwuma, I.C., *Juvenile Justice Administration in Nigeria: Philosophy and Practice* 39 (Alemika and Chukwuma 2001).
50. Ibid., 70, 74.
51. Ibid.
52. Paul Holland and Wallace J. Mlyniec, "Whatever Happened to the Right to Treatment? The Modern Quest for a Historical Promise", *Temple L. Rev*, 68 (1995), 1791–1836 (Holland and Mlyniec 1995).
53. Yusuf, S., "Students' Personnel Services and Academic Performance in Ilorin—South Local Government Area Secondary School. Kwara State" (M.Ed. thesis Department of Educational Management, University of Ilorin, 2011), 20 (Yusuf 2011).
54. Ibid.
55. Edem, D.A., *Introduction to Educational Administration in Nigeria* (Ibadan: Spectrum Book, 1998), 35. See also, Ojo, F., *Human resource management; theories and issues.* (Lagos: Panaf Publishing, inc., 1988), 20 (Edem 1998; Ojo 1988).
56. Adeleke, A.A., Use of library resources by academic staff in the Nigerian polytechnics. *Journal of Library Science 12, no. 2 (2005): 15–24* (Adeleke 2005).
57. Olaitan, G.I., "Relationship between Provision, Utilization of Students' Services and Academic Achievement in Secondary Schools in Ilorin Metropolis" (M.Ed. thesis Department of Educational Management, University of Ilorin, 2003), 15 (Olaitan 2003).
58. Abdulraheem-Mustapha, M.A., "An analysis of the framework for juvenile justice Administration in Nigeria" (PhD thesis, Faculty of Law, University of Ilorin, Nigeria, 2014), 150 (Abdulraheem-Mustapha 2004).
59. See Kilpatrick et al., 2003b, accessed on 2 November 2015, url: World Youth Report. (2004). "Juvenile Delinquency" http://www.un.org/esa/socdev/unyin/documents/ch07.pdf (Kilpatrick et al. 2003b).

60. Alemika, E.E.O. and Chukwuma, I.C., *Juvenile Justice Administration in Nigeria: Philosophy and Practice* 39 (Alemika and Chukwuma 2001).
61. Okagbue, I., "The Treatment of Juvenile Offenders and the Rights of the Child", in *The Rights of the Child in Nigeria*, ed. Ayua, I.A. and Okagbue, I.E. (Okagbue 1996).
62. Ibid., 70.
63. Ibid.
64. See Section 278 of the Nigerian Child Rights Act, Article 2 of the African Charter on the Rights and Welfare of the Child and Article 1 of the Convention on the Rights of the Child.
65. The Judges are empowered under Section 223 of the Child Rights Act to dispose of cases where they are satisfied that an offence has been committed, with alternatives to custodial or institutional placement. The section also provides for situations where there is sufficient evidence to prosecute and where decisions have been taken to proceed to trial that diversion must be considered in each and every case in order to meet the needs of the child and encourage the child to be accountable to the harm caused.

Bibliography

Articles in Journals

Adeleke, A.A. 2005. Use of Library Resources by Academic Staff in the Nigerian Polytechnics. *Journal of Library Science* 12 (2): 15–24.

Harris-Short, S. 2003. International Human Rights Law: Imperialist, Inept and Ineffective? Cultural relativism and the UN Convention on the Rights of the Child. *Human Rights Quarterly* 25 (1): 130–181.

Holland, Paul, and Wallace J. Mlyniec. 1995. Whatever Happened to the Right to Treatment? The Modern Quest for a Historical Promise. *Temple L. Rev* 68: 1791.

Mbazira, C. 2006. Enforcing the Economic, Social and Cultural Rights in the African Charter on Human and People's Rights: Twenty Years Redundancy, Progression and Significant Strides. *African Human Rights Law Journal* 6 (2): 333–357.

Mill, Stephenie J. 1995. The Age of Criminal Responsibility in an Era of Violence: Has Britain Set a Vandabult. *The Nashville University Journal of Transnational Law Vandabult* 28 (2): 295.

Okere, B.O. 1983. Objectives and Directives Principles of State Policy Under the Nigerian Constitution. *The International and Comparative Law Quarterly* 32 (1): 214–228.

Articles on the Internet

Kilpatrick, et al. 2003. World Youth Report (2004). Juvenile Delinquency. http://www.un.org/esa/socdev/unyin/documents/ch07.pdf. Accessed 2 Nov 2015.

Mason, Mark. 2010. Sampling and Saturation in Ph.D. Studies Using Qualitative Interviews. *Forum Qualitative Sozialforschung/Forum: Qualitative Social Research* 11 (3): Art. 8. http://www.qualitative-research.net/index.php/fqs/article/view/1428/3027. Accessed 23 Feb 2012.

Books

Aduba, J.N. 1989. From Punishment to Treatment: Humane Approach to the Sentencing of Young Offenders. In *Women and Children Under the Nigerian Law*, vol. 6. Lagos: Federal Ministry of Justice Publication.

Ahire, P.T. 1987. Juvenile Delinquency and the Handling of Young Prisoners in Nigerian Borstal Institutions. In *The Nigerian Prisons Service and the Public*. Abuja: Nigerian Prisons Service.

Alemika, E.E.O. 1978. *A Study of Socio-Cultural and Economic Factors in Delinquency Among Kaduna Borstal Inmates (B.Sc. Sociology Original Essay)*. Ibadan: University of Ibadan.

Alemika, E.E.O., and I.C. Chukwuma. 2001. *Juvenile Justice Administration in Nigeria: Philosophy and Practice*. Lagos: Centre for Law Enforcement Education, Lagos.

Chinwe, R.N., and E.N.A. Naomi. 2003. *Research Findings of Juvenile Justice Administration in Nigeria*. Lagos: Constitutional Right Project, CRP.

Creswell, W. 2009. *Research Design: Qualitative, Quantitative and Mixed Methods Approaches*. California: Sage.

Edem, D.A. 1998. *Introduction to Educational Administration in Nigeria*. Ibadan: Spectrum Book.

Houser, Janet. 2011. *Nursing Research: Reading, Using and Creative Evidence*. Sudbury, MA: Jones and Bartlett Learning.

Igbo, E.U.M. 2007. *Introduction to Criminology*. Nsukka: Afro-Orbis Publication Ltd.

Kathy, Charmz. 2006. *Constructing Grounded Theory: A Practical Guide Through Qualitative Analysis*. London: Sage.

Miller, Peter G., John Strang, and Peter M. Miller. 2010. *Addiction Research Methods*. Chichester: Blackwell Addiction Press.

Milner, A. 1972. *The Nigerian Penal System*. London: Sweet and Maxwell.

Ogbolumani, B.O.I. 1972. Institutional Treatment of Juveniles. In *The Magistrate and the Offender*, ed. T.O Elias. Lagos: University Press, Lagos.

Ojo, F. 1988. *Human Resource Management; Theories and Issues*. Lagos: Panaf Publishing.
Okagbue, I. 1996. The Treatment of Juvenile Offenders and the Rights of the Child. In *The Rights of the Child in Nigeria*, ed. I.A. Ayua and I.E. Okagbue. Nigerian: Institute of Advance Legal Studies.
Ospina, Sonia. 2004. Qualitative Research. In *Encyclopaedia of Leadership*, ed. George. R. Goethals James MacGregor Burns, and Georgia Sorenson, vol. 1. California: Berkshire Publishing Group LLC, Sage.
Owosanoye, B., and M. Wernham. 2004. Street Children and Juvenile Justice System in Lagos State of Nigeria. Human Development Initiative.
Punch, Keith F. 2005. *Introduction to Social Research: Quantitative and Qualitative Approaches*. London: Sage.
Steiner, H.J., P. Alston, and R. Goodman. 2008. *International Human Rights in Context: Law, Politics, Morals*, 3rd ed. Wotton-under-Edge: Clarendon Press.
Viljoen, F. 2007. *International Human Rights Law in Africa*. New York: Oxford University Press.

Papers Presented at Conferences, Workshops and Seminars

Abdul-Mumin Sa'ad. 2006. Juvenile Justice in Nigeria. A paper presented at the Conference Session of the Research Committee on Deviant Behaviour (RC 29) during the XVI International Sociological Association (ISA) World Congress of Sociology, in Durban, South Africa.

Theses and Monographs

Abdulraheem-Mustapha, M.A. 2014. *An Analysis of the Framework for Juvenile Justice Administration in Nigeria*. Unpublished. Ph.D. Law, University of Ilorin, Ilorin, Nigeria.
Olaitan, G.I. 2003. *Relationship Between Provision, Utilization of Students' Services and Academic Achievement in Secondary Schools in Ilorin Metropolis*, Unpublished. M.Ed. Educational Management, University of Ilorin, Ilorin Nigeria.
Yusuf, S. 2011. *Students' Personnel Services and Academic Performance in Ilorin—South Local Government Area Secondary School. Kwara State*. Unpublished. M.Ed. Educational Management, University of Ilorin, Ilorin, Nigeria.

Author Biography

Abdulraheem-Mustapha Mariam Adepeju holds a Ph.D. from University of Ilorin, LLM from Obafemi Awolowo University (OAU), Ile-Ife and LLB from Usmanu Dan Fodiyo University, Sokoto State. She is a senior Lecturer at the Department of Public Law, Faculty of Law, University of Ilorin, Nigeria. She has published articles in international, national and local journals. She is a recipient of awards from the American Council of Learned Society under the aegis of African Humanities Programme and All African Universities. She is a member of the American Law Society Association and member of many local and national professional associations in Nigeria. She attended many international and national workshops/trainings.

CHAPTER 7

Right to Inclusive Development of the Girl Child in Africa

Olanike Adelakun-Odewale

1 Introduction

Over the past few decades, there has been clamour to recognise, promote and protect the right and development of the girl child globally and with special attention on Africa. Various gatherings and discussions have taken place on the need to fight discrimination against the girl child and to ensure that the girl child enjoys her fundamental rights as much as the boy child does. Several international and regional instruments are in place to ensure that discrimination against the girl child is eradicated but despite the instruments the girl child is still largely discriminated against in Africa.

The belief that the sole responsibilities of the girl child/woman are the upkeep of the home while the boy/man is saddled with the responsibilities of market-based activities to make financial provision for the family had influenced the culture of placing high value on the boy child education in Africa. This, in turn, evolved into the dominating practice of African communities that concentrate on the education of the

O. Adelakun-Odewale (✉)
American University of Nigeria, Yola, Adamawa State, Nigeria
e-mail: nikegolden@yahoo.com

A.C. Onuora-Oguno et al. (eds.), *Education Law, Strategic Policy and Sustainable Development in Africa*, DOI 10.1007/978-3-319-53703-0_7

boy child coupled with many discriminatory norms[1] that hinder the girl child's full enjoyment of her rights.[2]

Additionally, the patrilineal culture and perception that men have the authority to make decisions with the woman as the recipient[3] had affected the rate at which girls are educated. This is, however, more pronounced in families with low income[4] and high population coupled with cultural and societal influence.[5] The belief is that the returns to a girl's parents from educating the girl are lower compared to that of the male child. This is based on the fact that a girl child will eventually get married[6] and it is perceived that any investment in a girl child will leak into another household while any investment in a boy child is perceived as a security of the lineage which maximises household utilities,[7] thus the preference for boy child education as against educating the girl child. There is the perception that investing in boys will bring higher income to the family as the boy child is likely to get a job faster and get higher pay than the girl.[8]

United Nations Educational, Scientific and Cultural Organization (UNESCO) noted on its website that gender inequality in education affects both boys and girls, men and women but girls and women are more affected by this problem. Fifty-nine million children of primary school age are not enrolled in school and more than half of these children, 30 million, live in sub-Saharan Africa with 17 million being girls.[9]

It had been established that education influences development[10] with the skills acquired in education acting as driving force for inclusive and sustainable development. If sustainable development is to be achieved in Africa, there is need to focus on inclusive development which can be achieved through quality education for all without discrimination of any form.

The issue of gender equality was enshrined in the 1948 Universal Declaration of Human Rights (UDHR) and this was further reinforced by a plethora of instruments such as the 1979 Convention on the Elimination of All Forms of Discrimination against Women (CEDAW), 1995 Beijing Declaration and Platform for Action, and at the regional level, the 1981 African Charter on Human and Peoples' Rights (ACHPR) and more specifically the 2003 Protocol to the African Charter on Human and Peoples' Rights on the Rights of Women (Maputo Protocol). The Maputo Protocol seeks to achieve enforcement of existing instruments as well as promote women's rights in Africa. The goal is to bridge the gender inequality that exists in Africa.

Despite the availability of the legal documents which most African countries have acceded to, the wide gap between boy and girl enrolment in schools has not been bridged. This chapter examines the legal framework for the rights of the girl child to inclusive development in Africa. Inclusion as to the development in the context of this chapter will be reviewed from the aspect of the right to education as it affects the girl child in Africa. Efforts are made to determine the impediments to the realisation of the right to education of the girl child in Africa. The impact of the Maputo Protocol in this respect is assessed. This chapter concludes by making a position on the possibility of realising the first aspiration of Agenda 2063 of the African Union Commission which is to have an inclusive growth and sustainable development in Africa.

2 Status of the Girl Child in Africa

In most countries of the world,[11] the girl child is accorded lower status than the boy child,[12] the situation is, however, worse in Africa. The practice was to elevate the needs of men above women and by ascribing powerful roles to men to elude women thereby creating a divide in the status of men and women and influencing a lower status accorded to women in the society.[13]

Africa may be one of the toughest places for a girl child to exist as girls (as well as women) do not have strong decision-making power. Others, predominantly males, make decisions for them thereby making the woman to be dependent on the man.[14] In terms of upbringing, the girl child is trained to handle certain chores.[15] In the same vein, the male counterpart is trained to be the "man" of the house and trained to be commanding, to take charge of activities in the absence of the parents, and so on. This, in effect, undermines the girl's self-esteem[16] and she sees herself as being inferior to the male child which is capable of affecting her economic productivity,[17] in that she will not be able to put in her best to contribute to the society if she has to submit to male dominance.

Patriarchy had been identified as one major factor responsible for the low status of girls and women in Africa. The radical feminists have identified the family as a primary source of women oppression in the society.[18] In the Shona culture of Zimbabwe for instance, Shona males are trained to see themselves as the household head and bread winner of the family while Shona females are trained to be obedient housekeepers.[19] The Shona girl is taught how to use her sexuality to satisfy her husband and benefit the male race.[20]

In Nigeria, women are marginalised and excluded from playing a significant traditional leadership role.[21] A critical example of this marginalisation is seen in the way the birth news of a male child is received compared to the way that of a female is received. The birth of a male child is celebrated with much joy and celebration; the naming ceremony is celebrated in a buoyant manner, while the birth of a female child is often not received with joy, especially if it is a family with existing female children.

Igube[22] noted that "paid employment, patriarchal relations within the household, patriarchal culture, sexuality, violence toward female, and the state" are some patriarchal structures that restrict the girl child's right to education as well as encourage male domination.

Alabi, Bahah and Alabi[23] noted two forms of patriarchy which are private and public. Private patriarchy had been described as the individual domination of women and girls within the household such that girls are socially trained to believe that they cannot take decisions concerning them on their own but by males around them. Children are trained to accept different roles based on their gender.

Public patriarchy on the other hand involves a situation where women and girls are involved in public life such as education and politics but the quality and level of involvement is generally lower to their male counterparts.[24]

To this end, an average girl child grows up believing that there are ways a woman should do things and there is a limit to which a woman is expected to behave. If not properly challenged, there is a tendency that such a girl child will limit herself and not explore her full potentials and the girl child will see herself as being inferior to the boy counterpart. The gender gap that exists in Africa today can be attributed to the long existing patriarchy embedded in African culture. This is responsible for the lower status accorded to girls and women in Africa.[25]

3 Right and Access to Education

The right to education had been seen as the enabling right to the realisation of other rights as well as a catalyst for positive social change.[26]

The move towards realisation of the importance of education and access to education to the growth of any society had led to a plethora of legal frameworks to guarantee, protect, promote and preserve education in many communities of the world. A particular attention on the need for the education of the girl child in Africa is necessitated by the vulnerability of the girl child based on her gender.

Several international treaties impose clear obligations on Member States to the treaties such that once the treaties have been domesticated by State Parties, there could be state remedies whenever a breach occurs. The right to education was recognised in Article 26(1) of the UDHR where it was provided that "everyone has the right to education". While this right to education extends to everybody by virtue of being human, it can be deduced that the main beneficiaries are children.[27] Basic education is required to be free and generally available with the requirement that higher education shall be accessible.[28]

The right to education is reflected in Articles 13 and 14 of the International Covenant on Economic, Social and Cultural Rights (ICESCR), 1966. This right was reaffirmed as it concerns girls and children in Article 10 of CEDAW. More explicitly, the right of a child to education was provided for in the United Nations Convention on the Rights of the Child, 1989.[29]

The CRC remains the most important instrument on the rights of a child, including the right to education. This instrument is unique in that it encouraged the availability and accessibility of educational and vocational information. Article 28(1) (a) is to the effect that "primary education is compulsory and available free to all". The CRC further enjoins State Parties to take measures to encourage attendance and reduce rate of drop-outs.[30] Article 28(1) places a duty on State Parties to recognise the right of a child to education with a view to achieving the right progressively on the **basis of equal opportunity**.[31]

Of importance is the UNESCO Convention against Discrimination in Education in 1960 which guarantees the right to education for all persons. This instrument defined educational discrimination as:

> any distinction, exclusion, limitation or preference which being based on race, colour, sex, language, political or other opinion, national or social origin, economic condition or birth has the purpose or effect of nullifying or impairing equality of treatment in education and in particular:
>
> a. of depriving any person or group of persons of access to education of any type or at any level;
> b. of limiting any person or group of persons to education of an inferior standard;
> c. of inflicting on any person or group of persons conditions which are incompatible with the dignity of man.[32]

Regionally, the ACHPR was adopted in June 1981 and as at 31 October 2016, all African States except South Sudan had ratified the ACHPR. Thus, this is the most important instrument on human rights in Africa. Article 2 of the Charter contains an all-embracing prohibition of discrimination of all forms. By virtue of Article 17 of the Charter, every individual shall have the right to education.

The Protocol to the African Charter on Human and Peoples' Rights on the Rights of Women in Africa (Maputo Protocol), 2003 reiterate the right to education and training. Article 12 of Maputo Protocol enjoins State Parties to take appropriate measures to:

1. eliminate all forms of discrimination against women and guarantee equal opportunity and access in the sphere of education and training;
2. eliminate all stereotypes in textbooks, syllabuses and the media, that perpetuate such discrimination;
3. protect women, especially the girl child from all forms of abuse, including sexual harassment in schools and other educational institutions and provide for sanctions against the perpetrators of such practices;
4. provide access to counselling and rehabilitation services to women who suffer abuses and sexual harassment;
5. integrate gender sensitisation and human rights education at all levels of education curricula including teacher training.[33]

The Protocol further provides that:

> States Parties shall take specific positive action to:
>
> a. promote literacy among women;
> b. promote education and training for women at all levels and in all disciplines, particularly in the fields of science and technology;
> c. promote the enrolment and retention of girls in schools and other training institutions and the organisation of programmes for women who leave school prematurely.[34]

Furthermore, the African Charter on the Rights and Welfare of the Child (ACRWC), 1990 guarantees the right of a child to education and provides that every child shall have the right to education.[35] Other regional instruments that promote the right to education include the African Youth Charter, 2006[36]; African Union Convention for the Protection and Assistance of Internally Displaced Persons in Africa (Kampala Convention), 2009[37] and Arab Charter on Human Rights, 2004.[38]

The African Commission on Human and Peoples' Rights at its 58th Ordinary Session in Banjul in April 2016 urges State Parties to guarantee the full scope of the right to education.[39] The Committee further calls on States to fulfil their duties in respect of access to education. State Parties are enjoined to address social and cultural issues that impede the girl child's equal enjoyment to the right to education. Parties are also implored to ensure that pregnant children have the opportunity to complete their education.

Scholars have argued that education is a means to an end while some say it is an end in itself, yet others argue that the end becomes the means again. Callaway[40] is of the view that "life is education and education is life" such that whatever a person becomes is largely dependent on the education she receives. Education had also been described as the process through which individuals are made functional members of their society.[41] According to Offorma, education is the "process of providing information to an inexperienced person, particularly the girl-child, to help her develop physically, mentally, socially, emotionally, spiritually, politically and economically".[42]

However, trying to define education from a classroom perspective is not encompassing as education can be said to include formal and non-formal forms of education such that culture cannot be totally departed from education; as argued that education is the art of making available to each generation the organised knowledge of the past.[43] In the African traditional society, education includes the formal and informal vocational and moral training[44] such that the basic principles of the traditional education are derived from the different cultures and methods of acquisition of training.

While Dewey had argued that the purpose of education is to provide the social conditions that support persons in having a range of experiences necessary to develop whatever capacities, interests and desires each individual might have,[45] Fafunwa holds the view that the end objective of education is to produce an individual who is honest, respectful, skilled, co-operative and who would conform to the social order.[46] Callaway on his part is of the opinion that the goal of traditional education is to discipline all the faculties of the individual to bring out his or her best human qualities at each life stage.[47]

The concept of African education is seen as encompassing as it provides no excess skill, no idle hands and no unemployment. The curriculum is not compartmentalised into separate courses that are taught on specific dates and time. Members of the society are the trainers as a result of which children never run out of teachers.[48] This concept of traditional African education where a child learns the norms, values and essential skills of a society is the acceptable form of education in most African societies.[49]

While it had been estimated that 90% of all countries in the world have legally binding documents that require children to attend school,[50] issues such as limited access to education, inability to retain enrolled students, low quality of education, inequality in education, negative cultural norms[51] and lack of political will for policy enforcement are impediments to the realisation of the provisions of these binding documents.

It has been established that over 12 million girls in Africa are at risk of not receiving education.[52] Bolaji, in the Sketch Newspaper of 9 September 2007, opined that great gender inequality exists in terms of access to education in many parts of Nigeria especially in the northern parts of the country such that many girls are not sent to school and out of those that were sent to school, a lot drop out of school before they could complete the basic stage of their education.

In the 2016 global education monitoring report,[53] the largest gender gaps in education are in Northern Africa, Western Asia and sub-Saharan Africa[54] with the disparity at the expense of girls. The report revealed that the poorest girls' access to education in Nigeria has worsened since 2000 while wide disparity remains in Ethiopia where the poorest girls are likely never to have access to education. It was noted that adverse political environments in countries such as Nigeria, Democratic Republic of Congo Central African Republic and Chad which limits the access to external expertise and financial aid have its toll in access to education.[55]

The main impediments to the realisation of the African girl's right to education are child marriage, child abuse, conflicts, sexual violence and harmful cultural practices. Coupled with these impediments are child labour, poverty, quest for wealth, bereavement, truancy and broken homes among others.[56]

Child marriage is a pandemic that Africa had been dealing with for decades. This practice had eaten deep into the African system such that the tendencies of African girls at a brighter future which could lead to economic contribution and sustenance had been jeopardised.

Agenda 2063 recognised child marriage as an impediment to regional development and prosperity.

Girls not bride noted on their website that all African countries are faced with the problem of child marriage, though with varying prevalent degrees. About 40% of girls in sub-Saharan Africa marry before they are 18 with Africa accounting for 15 out of the 20 countries where the incident of child marriage is at the peak.[57] About 77% of girls in Niger[58] and more than 60% of girls in Central African Republic and Chad marry before they are 18.[59] To this effect, Human Rights Watch projected that the number of child brides will double by 2030.

Poverty had been cited by victims and perpetrators of child marriage as a justification.[60] There is a belief by some that giving a girl away in marriage will give her a chance at having a better life.[61] Culture and religion are other factors that encourage the persistent practice of child marriage.

Child marriage directly violates the rights of the girl child as guaranteed by many international conventions and declarations as well as regional treaties. The Maputo Protocol specifically imposed the obligation on State Parties to "enact appropriate national legislative measures to guarantee that the minimum age of marriage for women shall be 18 years".[62]

In Ethiopia, child marriage and the need for the girl child to take care of her children and in-laws has been recognised as factors denying the girl child the right to be formally educated.[63] Poverty, diseases, death of mother, household chores, child marriage and cultural practices have been identified as impediments to realisation of girl child education in Kenya.[64]

Cases across Africa revealed that many girls stay out of school as a result of marriage, pregnancy or family pressure and while school administrators ought to encourage married girls to remain in school, policies of the school actually see to their expulsion from the system.[65] This educational exclusion results in persistent poverty[66] as uneducated girls and women have limited chances to financially provide for themselves and their families. Anyier[67] from South Sudan narrated to Human Rights Watch how her uncle forced her out of school to marry an older man. She cleans offices and lamented that if she was opportune to attend secondary school, she would get a better job.

While Kenya had recorded an increase in the enrolment rates across all levels in the recent years, retention and transition rates of girls have been low compared to boys.[68] This development can be attributed to harmful cultural practices, gender stereotypes giving education preference to boys, poverty, FGM, early marriages and early pregnancies.[69]

Article 5 of Maputo Protocol guarantees the elimination of harmful practices against women. There is a clear obligation on States Parties to prohibit and condemn all forms of harmful practices which negatively affect the human rights of women and that are contrary to recognised international standards. States Parties are enjoined to take all necessary legislative and other measures to eliminate such practices.[70] Article 1 of Maputo Protocol defined harmful practices to mean "all behaviours, attitudes and/or practices which negatively affect the fundamental rights of women and girls, such as their right to life, health, dignity, education and physical integrity".

FGM is specifically classified as a harmful practice. This is worthy of note as the Maputo Protocol is the first human right treaty to explicitly call for eradication of female genital mutilation (FGM).[71] Though few studies have been conducted on the correlation of FGM and access to education of school age girls, it can be safely posited that FGM could limit the girl child's access to education. In Kenya, FGM is performed on girls of school age such that they get late to school or do not attend at all during the initiation[72] and healing period as a result of which the affected girls would have missed a lot of academic activities.[73] Also, when FGM is carried out on school age girls, it is with the belief that the girls are ready for marriage[74] as a result of which they are given out in marriage and thus denied further access to education as a result of the marriage or pregnancy. Girls who have been circumcised often reject education at that point due to attitudinal change when they see themselves as adults.[75]

It had been reported that in Sierra Leone and Guinea parents pay hugely for the FGM ceremony as a result of which some could no longer afford to send their daughters to school and they are eventually withdrawn from school.[76] It is worthy of mention that in Mali and Burkina Faso, the subject of FGM had been included into school curriculum[77] and as such children can air their opinion and question the practice.

By denying the girl child access to education, the girl child is denied the required knowledge and skills necessary to advance her social and economic status[78] and thus such a girl child will become an ignorant woman and recycle the same process she went through.[79] UNESCO noted that educated mothers usually have smaller and healthier families and more likely to produce more educated children thereby developing the society economically.[80]

In the words of Oyigbenu, "Lack of access to education is indeed the end of the world, because without it there is certainly no future for the girl-child in the strict sense of full inclusion and participation in the development process, self actualisation, and self-fulfilment, and personal freedom".[81]

4 Inclusive Development

Development as a concept had been subjected to different analysis. Development was construed from the perspective of growth and increase in size, shape and structure or change in time and space.[82] To measure the development rate of any society, the economic, social and political development takes the lead in order of preference and as such, the individual quota of development becomes extremely important.

Many members of the African society are excluded from the development based on many factors such as gender, ethnicity, disability, age, poverty and educational qualification.[83] This diversity of life had resulted in the exclusion of certain persons in the development process of the African society. To achieve growth and development, all the groups in a society need to contribute their share to opportunity creation as well as benefit from the development.[84]

Inclusive development had been described in the light of growth coupled with equal opportunities.[85] Inclusive development is said to occur in a society where all members of a society participate in and contribute to the growth process equally, regardless of their individual circumstances.[86] As such, when talking about inclusive development, emphasis is always on the economic opportunities created by growth which is available to all citizens without any disparity.[87]

Development can be achieved and measured in various forms, with the most common form being the economic factor and how the benefits of such growth are shared.[88] Economic factor, especially in terms of sustainable and equitable growth, is significant to achieve inclusive development.[89] Sustainable and equitable development had been described as one that is broad-based across sectors and regions, e.g. employing the labour force in the poor and vulnerable groups of the population.[90] It had thus been noted that the economic factor encompasses providing the poor and low-income rural households with both the capacity and opportunities to benefit from economic growth.[91]

Another tool of measuring inclusive development is the social factor. Fernando noted that the social factor covers supporting the social development of poor and low-income households and disadvantaged groups, eliminating inequalities in social indicators, empowering women and providing for social safety nets for the vulnerable groups.[92] It follows therefore that to achieve inclusion in Africa, there is the need to focus on getting rid of the barriers that impede inclusion in the society as well as focus on the marginalised groups. It will be essential to build their capacity and support them to lobby for and guarantee their inclusion.

While growth is always measured in terms of economic growth, development cannot be quantified in a precise manner. Development had been referred to in the light of (i) just economic growth, (ii) changes in economic structure of production, (iii) spatial distribution of population, (iv) improvements in "social indicators" of education and health, etc.[93]

In trying to draw a link between development and education, Jekayinfa and Kolawole postulated that development refers to the changes that have taken place in the policy and practice of education in all countries of the world. The growth of educational institutions, the growth in enrolment, number of schools and students at various levels of education are to be assessed. They further stated that the growth in the number of teachers and other support staff, changes in curriculum, changes and improvements in the methods and resources for teaching must all be taken into consideration.[94]

The strong link between education and socioeconomic development can be seen in the campaigns of United Nations Educational, Scientific and Cultural Organization's Education For All, 2000; United Nations Millennium Development Goals, 2000; African Union's New Partnership for African Development agenda, 2001; and UN's Sustainable Development Goals, 2015.

According to UNICEF's report released on 11 October 2016, girls between 5 and 14 years old spend 40% more time on unpaid household chores than their male counterparts.[95] Girls bear the most burden of household chores in Burkina Faso, Yemen and Somalia. The report notes that girls' domestic work is not visible and usually undervalued. The African female child is expected to assist in the basic household chores of the house such as cooking, taking care of siblings, laundry, and so on.[96] This had been recognised as a hindering factor to the enrolment of the girl child in school.[97]

If the number of hours an African female child put into household chores and unpaid domestic labour is to be quantified economically, then there is no gainsaying that the African economy will be measured in a different perspective and the growth of the economy will be commendable.[98] It had been discovered that the more the household size increases, so does the household chores responsibilities of the older female child increase.[99]

With every stage of education, the chance of being poor is reduced. Where a girl is afforded access to an extra year of school beyond the average, her eventual age can be increased by 10–20%.[100] It had been established that education is capable of reducing mortality rate.[101] In Africa, children of mothers who receive education of 5 years or more are likely to survive beyond age 5[102] as it is shown that an educated mother is more likely to have her child immunised against childhood diseases.[103]

Thus, it can be safely said that human development without gender parity is the key to inclusive development and sustainable growth. Human development can greatly be achieved by affording all members of a society access to quality education which is capable to develop their brains and bring out their talents and potentials.

5 African Legal Framework Towards Development of the Girl Child

Having identified that women are the heart of the society and they have a great influence on children, educating girls will be one of the most important investments[104] any country can make to secure sustainable development and great future.

The ACRWC, by virtue of Article 11, places an obligation on Member States to take measures in respect to females to ensure they have equal access to education. Article 17 of the ACHPR also guarantees every individual's right to education. Article 13 of the African Youth Charter further enjoins Member States to ensure that girls as well as young women who become pregnant or gets married before completing their education are given the opportunity to continue their education.

The Southern African Development Community (SADC) is committed to gender equality. In its SADC Gender Policy, Member States are enjoined to promote participation of women, men, girls and boys in all education and training programmes and processes in order to strengthen their contribution to and benefit from regional and national educational development agendas.[105]

The African Union (AU) declared 2015 as the Year of Women Empowerment and Development towards Africa's Agenda 2063.[106]

The declaration is a display of AU's renewed political commitment and support for the women's empowerment and the gender equality agenda. One of the major aims of the seven point Agenda for 2063 is to ensure full participation, with the full engagement of women and youth particularly, in achieving common destiny under united and strong Africa.[107]

In order to achieve the aspiration on inclusive growth and sustainable development by 2063, the African Union in the Agenda 2063 sets certain goals which include: a high standard of living, well-educated citizens and transformed economies among others. To achieve people-driven development, the goal is to achieve full gender equality in all spheres of life and engagement of youth and children. Priority for this goal is on women and girls' empowerment and eradication of violence and discrimination against women and girls.[108] Africa aims to eliminate all barriers to access to quality education and health for all women and girls by 2063.

On the commitment to ensure that African women have equal access to education, the African continent has in existence some instruments, which seeks to promote the right to education, with several African countries being State Parties.[109]

Of importance in discussing steps taken is the adoption of the Maputo Protocol. In recognition of the fact women's rights are inalienable, interdependent and indivisible human rights as guaranteed by all international and regional treaties, conventions and covenants, it was noted in the Preamble of Maputo Protocol that women's rights and women's essential role in the development have been reaffirmed.[110] Maputo Protocol was necessitated by the fact that despite ratifying the ACHPR and other instruments and despite Member States commitment to eliminate all forms of discrimination and harmful practices against women, women are still victims of discrimination and harmful practices in Africa.[111]

The Maputo Protocol was originally adopted by the Assembly of the African Union on 11 July 2013 at Maputo, Mozambique and entered into force on 25 November 2005, after being ratified by the required 15 member States.[112] The instrument is binding on all countries that ratify it and Member States undertook to achieve full ratification and enforcement by 2015 and domestication by 2020.[113] However, as at September 2016, 37 States[114] have signed and ratified the Protocol, 15 States[115] have signed but have not ratified, while 3 member States[116] of the African Union had neither signed nor ratified the Protocol.[117]

The Maputo Protocol is significant in ensuring inclusive development of the girl child in Africa because the focus is not on creating new rights or repeating existing rights, rather the focus is on the enforcement of existing recognised rights as guaranteed by earlier identified instruments. Women as used in the context of the Protocol refer to the female gender, including girls.[118]

Article 5 of the Protocol calls on State Parties in a strong language to prohibit and condemn all forms of harmful practices which affect the right of the woman. State Parties are enjoined to take necessary legislative and other measures to eliminate such practices. The Protocol is the first of its kind that will specifically classify FGM as a harmful practice.[119] Article 26 of the Protocol imposes the obligation on State Parties to ensure the implementation of the Protocol at national levels. State Parties are required to submit periodic reports to indicate legislative and other measures taken to ensure the full implementation of the rights recognised in the Protocol.

It is, however, disheartening to realise that full implementation of the Maputo Protocol is not practicable due to the fact that some countries have not adopted and ratified the Protocol while some Member States made reservations on the ratification.[120]

It is also pertinent to note that while there is a call on the government to ensure adequate implementation of policies that promote girl child education, we must not forget the fact that the duty goes beyond the government alone. Non-governmental organisations, institutions such as family, cultural and religious institutions also have a role to play in ensuring that every girl child is afforded the opportunity at education.

Many African countries have taken steps to promote girl child education by having policies in place to that effect. For instance, there are Nigerian legislations that guarantee the right to education and prohibit the withdrawal of girls from school in order to ensure the completion of basic education.[121] A ministerial portfolio was also created for women affairs and child welfare. Furthermore, the issue of girl child education was approached from a right-based approach by recognising the right to access to education as well as to quality education.[122]

A major problem on the recognition of right to education in Nigeria, however, lies in the fact that Child's Rights Act is not applicable to the whole of Nigeria. Child welfare is an issue that falls on the concurrent list of the government and as such, each State of the Federation is required to domesticate her version of the law.

South Africa has series of laws and programmes[123] that seek to promote and empower the girl child. Section 29(1) of the Constitution of the Republic of South Africa 1996 guarantees the right to basic education including right to adult basic education. The South African Constitution made the right to education immediately realisable and this can be seen in the light of judicial pronouncements.[124] Quality basic education is at the centre of realisation of the national goals of reducing poverty and inequality in South Africa.[125]

Other policies that seek to guarantee quality education and development in South Africa include Language in Education Policy (1997), National Norms and Standards for School Funding (2006), Education White Paper 6: Special Needs Education (2001) and the Screening, Identification, Assessment and Support Strategy (SIAS) (2008), National Framework for Quality Education in Rural Areas (2007), Accelerated Schools Infrastructure Delivery Initiative (ASIDI) and the Quality Improvement, Development, Support and Upliftment Programme.

The overall purpose of these policies in South Africa is to ensure equal access to quality an inclusive education. Thus, South Africa had witnessed an improvement in access to education and enrolment rates have improved, reaching 98% in Grades 1–9 and 83% in Grades 10–12 in 2011.[126] World Economic Forum's 2015 Human Capital Report ranked South Africa 101 out of 142 on gender enrolment in primary schools.[127] Being ranked 42 from the bottom in the World Economic Forum's 2015 Human Capital Report, South African government admitted the need to improve access to education for girls.[128]

A major setback to achieve gender parity in education in South Africa is gender-based violence. Violence and harassment against girls in school[129] are a factor for exclusion of girls. Violence against girls and women in South African had been said to cost the economy R28.4-billion to R42.2-billion a year.[130]

Tanzania had ratified a total of 11 international instruments[131] and 3 regional instruments[132] and their various Protocols that seek to promote the right to education. On its part, the Tanzanian government has in place national laws and policies to realise the right to education. Article 11 under part II of the Constitution of the United Republic of Tanzania, 1977, recognises the right to education as a fundamental objective and directive principle of state policy.[133]

The National Education Act[134] is Tanzania's primary law on education. Article 35 of the Act guarantees compulsory primary education for every child who has reached the age of 7 years. No child shall be refused enrolment in school and parents shall ensure that the child regularly attends the primary school. Also, every child of not less than 5 years old shall be eligible to be enrolled in pre-primary education for 2 years. A non-discrimination clause[135] is included as well as education freedom.[136]

Furthermore, the Education Fund Act, 2001 establishes an Education Fund, the purpose of which is to fund the improvement of the quality, access to and equality of education at all educational levels in Tanzania and Zanzibar. The Law of the Child Act, 2009 brings together child-specific provisions from a range of national laws into one document. Child's right to education is guaranteed by Article 9 while Article 8 stipulates that parents, legal guardians and those having custody of children have the duty to provide the child with the right to education and guidance. Article 5 prohibits discrimination against children, and Articles 87–93 guarantee children's right to acquire vocational skills and training, and apprenticeships, if over the age of 14, or having completed primary education.[137]

Education policies in Tanzania include Tanzania National Development Vision 2025 and National Strategy for Economic Growth and Reduction of Poverty.[138] These policies recognise education as pertinent to improvement of the quality of life and social well-being. A program tagged "Big Results Now" focuses on six priority areas, including education. The Tanzanian Ministry of Education and Vocation Training's plan to realise Vision 2025 concentrates on improvement of quality of education and training by expanding institutional frameworks and structures; expansion of access to education and training at all levels; enhancement of equity in the provision of education and training at all levels; and capacity-building and development of the management of education and training services.[139]

Action aid reports in a research study on education for girls in Tanzania[140] that pregnancy, poverty and early marriage are the major barriers to realise the right to education by a girl child in Tanzania. Girls in rural areas were reported to attribute punishment and exclusion from school to sexual activities over which they had no control. The report noted that there was considerable silence on the issue of gender-based violence. All Africa reported on its website on 28 September 2015 that families got their daughters married because they were pregnant or because of the fear that they might get pregnant. It was further reported that many schools in Tanzania have compulsory pregnancy test policy, and the government allows schools to expel married students and students who commit offences against morality.

It was reported that gender-based violence such as male students raping female students as well as teachers seducing girls and threatening to give poor grades for non-compliance is a contributory factor to the rate at which girls drop out from schools in Tanzania.[141]

Kenya has enshrined in its Children's Act, 2001 the right to education and criminalises any act that seeks to deny any child of the right to education by section 127 which provides that "any person found guilty of negligence is liable for a maximum of five years" imprisonment or a fine of a sum not exceeding KES 200,000 or both fine and imprisonment'.[142] Also, by the 2010 Constitution of Kenya every person has a right to education[143] and by Article 53.1.b, every child has the right to free and compulsory education. In addition to this, minorities and marginalised groups are provided special opportunities in education.[144] Article 27 guarantees equality and freedom from discrimination.

As such, the right to education is an enforceable right in Kenya and every person has the right to institute court proceedings claiming that a right or fundamental freedom in the Bill of Rights has been denied, violated or infringed, or is threatened.[145] Article 22 also sets out the rules of standing, allowing individuals to bring cases in the public interest and also of associations to institute proceedings in the interest of its members. Article 23 grants the Courts of Kenya the authority to uphold and enforce the Bill of Rights which includes the power to grant appropriate relief.

The enforceability of the right to education had been demonstrated in a number of judicial pronouncements. In *Michael Mutinda Mutemi v Permanent Secretary, Ministry of Education and Ors*,[146] the High Court of Kenya determined that the government had failed to demonstrate concrete policy measures, guidelines and the progress made towards the realisation of economic rights and particularly the right to education. Also, in *Institute for Human Rights and Development in Africa (IHRDA) and Open Society Justice Initiative* on behalf of Children of Nubian Descent in *Kenya v Kenya*,[147] the African Committee of Experts on the Rights and Welfare of the Child found a violation of the right to education of children of Nubian descent where the court held that there is de facto inequality in the children's access to available educational services and resources, and this can be attributed in practice to their lack of confirmed status as nationals of the Republic of Kenya.

Additionally, the 2013 Basic Education Act guarantees the implementation of the right to free and compulsory basic education[148] and provides for the establishment of pre-primary, primary and secondary schools, adult and continuing education centre as well as special and integrated schools for learners with disabilities.[149] Tuition fees as well as admission fees are prohibited.[150] Primary and secondary education is compulsory and parent who fails to take his or her child to school commits an offence by virtue of Article 30.[151]

The Kenyan Gender in Education Policy provides a planning framework for gender-responsive education at all levels and formalises the rights and responsibilities of all people involved directly or indirectly in the education sector, and is further expected to contribute to the elimination of disparities. Teenage mothers in Kenya are allowed to go back to school and the rights of adolescent mothers are respected.[152] The State, however, has made all necessary efforts to ensure that girls who are victims of unwanted and early pregnancies are not stigmatised nor denied re-entry opportunity by school administrators.[153]

Provision of gender-sensitive facilities such as sanitary towels and building of toilets for girls in schools are further measures taken to encourage girls' enrolment in school and girl child education. Also, the State zero-rated the taxes on sanitary towels to make them cheaper and affordable.[154]

Regarding other factors that hinder the girl's right to education, the Women's Act 2010 of The Gambia had been criticised on the refusal to incorporate Article 5 of the Protocol despite incorporating all other provisions. However, section 19 of the Children's Act of Gambia prohibits all harmful traditional practices on children under the age of 18. However, FGM was expressly criminalised in The Gambia in December 2015 with a fine of $1250 or 3 years imprisonment for perpetrators of this act.[155]

FGM was criminalised for persons under age 18 in Tanzania[156] but this might pose a problem where women above 18 voluntarily submit to FGM. Ugandan enacted the Prohibition of Female Genital Mutilation Act 5 of 2010 and criminalised FGM by virtue of section 4.

Article 6 stipulates that marriageable age shall be 18. While many African countries have reflected this position in their legislations,[157] the provision was given judicial backing in Zimbabwe when the Constitutional Court[158] struck down section 22(1) of the Marriages Act which allows children of 16 to get married.

6 Conclusion

It is clear that Africa as a continent has sufficient legal framework to develop the girl child towards a sustainable environment. While some African countries had identified education as an important tool for social and economic development and had made the right to education enforceable with the will towards enforcement, other African countries are still in the realm of making the right to education a fundamental directive and thus render a plethora of legislations and policies ineffective.

A popular African adage says "educate a man and you educate an individual but educate a woman and you educate a nation".[159] This long-time adage summarises the importance of education of the girl child who is saddled with the bulk of the responsibility of passing on the values and norms of the society to her children. It is common knowledge that you can only give what you have and as such, the woman who is not enlightened and well trained in terms of the knowledge and skills she acquires from an early stage in life will also pass the same quality of education[160] on to her children. As such, while advocating for the education of the girl child, attention should be paid to the quality and standard of the education being advocated for.

Having identified formal education as the principal institutional mechanism for developing human skills and knowledge, education has many benefits for the girl child throughout every stage of her human existence. An educated female has the tendency to marry at a point when she can have a say in whoever she chooses to marry. She will have control over her child bearing pattern such that the woman that she becomes will have a better understanding on issues that could affect her health and that of her children. Education is also capable of enlightening the female child about various diseases and measures to take for prevention, treatment or management without complicating matters for herself or her loved ones.

It is also pertinent to note that investment in the girl child education will lead to increased economic productivity, improved returns, intergenerational education, social and cultural development as well as sustainability of the developmental process.[161] This in turn will have a positive effect on poverty reduction since a girl child that is educated has the chances of a better job with higher earnings. For those that choose to be self-employed, the level of exposure and education will influence the way they handle and vocation they embark on and they will add their quota by being employers too.

A step towards ensuring an inclusive development in any society will be to ensure the creation of productive and gainful employment to achieve financial and economic independence of members of the society. This can be achieved if every household realises the need to share the household income appropriately to give both the male and female children of the household equal opportunities at education and training without discrimination based on gender. It is pertinent to note that the more reliant any household is on the girl child domestic labour, the more discriminatory and inequitable that household is and the more vulnerable the household becomes. Such a household will be unable to meet its economic needs and the cycle of poverty and vulnerability of such a household will continue.

7 Recommendations

In recognition of the fact, legal frameworks play a strong role in transforming norms and having analysed the importance of the Maputo Protocol, African Countries need to put in place policies that specifically address the creation of an environment that ensure access of girls to effective and quality education. There is the need to regulate budgets to accommodate funding for access of the girl child to education. It is pertinent for the countries that have not adopted and ratified the Protocol to do so and give effect to its content.

Since the major problem in Africa lies in the enforcement of legal instruments, there is the need to encourage stakeholders to take a step further in realising the right to education of the girl child by adopting a right-based approach. Families, community leaders, NGOs, girls, law enforcement officers, school administrators and educators should be sensitised on the need to seek redress in law courts. This would give effect to existing laws and policies. There is also the need to create specific courts to deal with issues that affect girls and women in order to have speedy trials. Stakeholders should be trained on their legal responsibilities in realising the right to education for all in Africa.

Education should be transparently free without hidden costs that could hinder participation. Incentives in form of scholarships and school feeding programmes should be implemented with a focus on scholarships for girls. Instructional materials should be gender sensitive and classroom approach should encourage active learning.

National governments should have effective monitoring systems such that schools are tasked to give reports on a regular basis on the rate of enrolment and retention. The monitoring bodies should also have policies to ensure the effective safe learning environment for the girl child. National education regulatory bodies should reinforce their commitment towards education of the girl child by strategising on how to improve access to education for the girl child. Regulatory bodies should further ensure that discriminatory practices that exclude pregnant or married students from school should be eradicated. The practice of compulsory pregnancy tests for female students is also discriminatory and be stopped. Students should be reabsorbed into school after giving birth without facing stigmatisation.

There is the need to educate students themselves on their rights. This should be incorporated into schools' curriculum such that both boys and girls learn the essence of their rights so that the boys will grow up to respect the rights of women and break the discriminatory cycle.

Teachers and school administrators should be trained on handling gender imbalance in schools. There should also be gender balance in the recruitment of teachers as female teachers will serve as encouragement for girls to continue their education. Teaching materials and strategies should promote equitable behaviour. Inclusive development of the girl child using education as a tool is a responsibility for all.

Notes

1. Such as female genital mutilation, child marriage, and gender-based violence.
2. Onuora-Oguno, Azubike, "Enhancing Equality and Eliminating Discrimination: Girl Child Empowerment and Access to Quality Basic Education in Nigeria," *Yonsei Law Journal* 6: 1 (2015), 75 (Onuora-Oguno 2015).
3. Wamue-Ngare, Grace and Waithera Nancy Njoroge, "Gender Paradigm Shift within the Family Structure in Kiambu, Kenya", *African Journal of Social Sciences* 1: 3 (2011): 14 (Wamue-Ngare and Njoroge 2011).
4. Hillman, Arye L. and Eva Jenkner, "Educating Children in Poor Countries," Economic Issue 33 (2004) International Monetary Fund, http://www.imf.org/external/pubs/ft/issues/issues33/ .Accessed November 1, 2016 (Hillman and Jenkner 2004).
5. Osagiobare, Osamiro Emmanuel, Rita Osayemwenre Oronsaye and Victor Ekwukoma, "Influence of Religious and Cultural Beliefs on

Girl-Child Educational Aspiration in Nigeria," *Journal of Educational and Social Research* 5: 2(2015) 166 (Osagiobare et al. 2015).

6. Hari, Patricia, "Parents' and Community Attitudes towards Girls' Participation in and Access to Education and Science, Mathematics and Technology (SMT) Subjects", accessed November 1, 2016, http://www.unesco.org/education/educprog/ste/projects/girls%20africa/femsa/femsa6.html (Hari 2016).
7. Kambhampati, Uma S and Raji Rajan, "The 'Nowhere' Children: Patriarchy and the Role of Girls in India's Rural Economy," *The Journal of Development Studies* 44: 9 (2008): 1309, doi:10.1080/00220380802264978 (Kambhampati and Rajan 2008).
8. Department for International Development, "Girls' Education: towards a better future for all" (January 2005), accessed October 30, 2015, http://www2.ohchr.org/english/issues/development/docs/girlseducation.pdf (Department for International Development 2005).
9. UNESCO, "Left Behind," accessed October 30, 2016, http://www.uis.unesco.org/_LAYOUTS/UNESCO/no-girl-left-behind/index.html#cover-intro-4 (UNESCO 2016b).
10. UNESCO, "Education and Skills for Inclusive and Sustainable Development beyond 2015: Thematic Think Piece" (2012) 3, accessed October 30, 2016, http://www.un.org/millenniumgoals/pdf/Think%20Pieces/4_education.pdf (UNESCO 2012).
11. Specifically low-income countries such as African and Asian countries.
12. Kambarami, Maureen, "Femininity, Sexuality and Culture: Patriarchy and Female Subordination in Zimbabwe", *Africa Regional Sexuality Resource Centre* (2006): 3, accessed October 30, 2016, http://www.arsrc.org/downloads/uhsss/kmabarami.pdf (Kambarami 2006).
13. Shoola, Toni, "The Effect of the Sub-Saharan African Gender Divide on the Rights and Status of Women in a Globalized World", *International Research Scape Journal* 1(2013): 4, accessed October 2016, http://scholarworks.bgsu.edu/irj/vol1/iss1/7?utm_source=scholarworks.bgsu.edu%2Firj%2Fvol1%2Fiss1%2F7&utm_medium=PDF&utm_campaign=PDFCoverPages (Shoola 2013).
14. Kambarami, "Femininity, Sexuality and Culture", 3.
15. Such as sweeping, cooking, babysitting, and so on.
16. Osagiobare, "Influence of Religious and Cultural Beliefs" 168.
17. Parsons, Jeffery et al., "Economic Impacts of Child Marriage: A Review of the Literature", *The Review of Faith and International Affairs* 13:3(2015): 15, accessed 2 November 2016, doi:10.1080/15570274.2015.1075757 (Parsons et al. 2015).
18. Igube, R.B., "Gender Security and Advancement: the Case of Inequality and Inequity" (paper presented at the round table discourse by Higher

Link Educational Programme, The British Council, Change Managers International, University of Abuja, Abuja 8th march, 2004) (Igube 2004a).

19. Kambarami, "Femininity, Sexuality and Culture," 5.
20. Kambarami, Maureen, "Femininity, Sexuality and Culture: Patriarchy and Female Subordination in Zimbabwe", *Africa Regional Sexuality Resource Centre* (2006): 3, accessed 30 October 2016, http://www.arsrc.org/downloads/uhsss/kmabarami.pdf (Kambarami 2006).
21. R.B. Igube, *Women and Gender Studies* (Abuja: Sir Kuf Ventures Limited, 2004), 4 (Igube 2004b).
22. Igube, *Women and Gender Studies* 6.
23. Alabi, T., M. Bahah and S.O. Alabi, "The Girl-Child: A Sociological view on the Problems of Girl-Child Education in Nigeria", *European Scientific Journal* 10:2 (2014) 402 (Alabi et al. 2014).
24. Igube, "Gender Security and Advancement," 10.
25. Shoola, "Sub-Saharan African Gender Divide," 2.
26. UNESCO, "Education and Skills".
27. Beiter, Klaus Dieter, *The Protection of the Right to Education by International Law* (Leiden: Martinus Nijhoff Publishers, 2005), 20 (Beiter 2005).
28. Article 26 UDHR.
29. Article 28 CRC.
30. Article 28(1) (e).
31. Emphasis mine.
32. Article 1 of UNESCO Convention.
33. Article 12(1), Protocol to the African Charter on Human and People's Rights on the Rights of Women in Africa (Maputo Protocol), 2003.
34. Article 12(2), Maputo Protocol.
35. Article 11, ACRWC.
36. Articles 13 and 20.
37. Article 9.2(b).
38. Articles 40 and 41.
39. Resolution on the Right to Education in Africa—ACHPR/Res. 346 (LVIII) 2016.
40. Callaway H, "Indigenous Education in Yoruba Society," in *Conflict and Harmony in Education in Tropical Africa,* ed. G.G. Brown and M. Hiskett (London: George Allen & Unwin Ltd, 1975), 26–38 (Callaway 1975).
41. Ocho, Lawrence Offie, *Issues and Concerns in Education and Life* (Enugu: Institute of Development Studies, 2005), 24 (Ocho 2005).
42. Offorma, Grace C., "The Boy Child Education in the South-Eastern States of Nigeria: Problems and Prospects" (paper presented at the convention of the Unity Schools Old Students Association (USOSA), Enugu, Nigeria, 2008) (Offorma 2008).

43. Good, C.U., *ed*, *Dictionary of Education* (New York, 1945) (Good 1945).
44. Callaway, "Indigenous Education," 29.
45. Dewey, John, *Experience and Education* (London: Collier Macmillan, 1938), 86 (Dewey 1938).
46. Fafunwa, Baba A., *History of Education in Nigeria* (London: George Allen and Unwin Ltd., 1974) (Fafunwa 1974).
47. Callaway, "Indigenous Education," 29.
48. Ayandele, E.A., *African Historical Studies* (London: Frank Cass, 1979) (Ayandele 1979).
49. Ndofirepi, Amasa Philip and Elizabeth Spiwe Ndofirepi, "(E)ducation or (e)ducation in Traditional African Societies? A Philosophical Insight," *Stud Tribes Tribals* 10: 1(2012): 15 (Ndofirepi and Ndofirepi 2012).
50. UNESCO Institute for Statistics (2009).
51. "UNICEF's Girl's Education and Gender Equality," last modified 23 March 2015, http://www.unicef.org/education/bege_70640.html (UNICEF's 2015).
52. "Humanium's Right to Education: situation of children's right to education worldwide," Humanium, accessed 31 October 2016, http://www.humanium.org/en/world/right-to-education/.
53. UNESCO, "Gender Review: Creating sustainable futures for all," Global Education Monitoring Report (2016): 15, accessed on November 1, 2016, http://unesdoc.unesco.org/images/0024/002460/246045e.pdf (UNESCO 2016a).
54. UNESCO, "Gender Review".
55. UNESCO, "Gender Review".
56. Okeke, E.A.C., U.M. Nzewi and Z. Njoku, "Tracking school age children's education status in UNICEF A-Field states", in *UNICEF—a field state* (Enugu: UNICEF, 2008) (Okeke et al. 2008).
57. UNICEF, "Ending Child Marriage: Progress and Prospects," accessed 15 November 2015, http://data.unicef.org/corecode/uploads/document6/uploaded_pdfs/corecoe (UNICEF 2015).
58. UNICEF, "Ending Child Marriage".
59. UNICEF, "Ending Child Marriage".
60. Human Rights Watch, "Ending Child Marriage in Africa: Opening the Door for Girls' Education, Health, and Freedom from Violence" accessed 1 November 2016. Human Rights Watch 2016.
61. Human Rights Watch, "Ending Child Marriage".
62. Article 6(b) Maputo Protocol.
63. Offorma, "The Boy Child Education".
64. Mwangi, Elijah, "News and views from Africa," 2014, accessed 20 December 2015, http://www.newsfromafrica/indices/index_1707.html.

65. Human Rights Watch, "Ending Child Marriage".
66. UNICEF, "Early Marriage Child Spouses," *Innocenti Digest* 7 (2001), 12, accessed 13 November 2015, http://www.unicef-irc.org/publications/pdf/digest7e.pdf (UNICEF 2001).
67. Human Rights Watch interview with Anyier D., (Bor County, South Sudan, March 15, 2012), accessed 12 June 2016, https://www.hrw.org/news/2015/12/09/ending-child-marriage-africa.
68. State Report submitted to the CRC Child in 2013, CRC/C/KEN/3-5, paragraph 351.
69. State Report, CRC/C/KEN/3-5.
70. Article 2, Maputo Protocol. The measures include legislative prohibition and protection of women on certain cultural practices including female genital mutilation, awareness creation and provision of support to victims of these practices.
71. Muriithi, Caroline Muthoni, "An analysis of the Protocol to the African Charter on Human and Peoples' Rights on the Rights of Women in Africa" in *Journey to Equality: 10 Years of the Protocol on the Rights of Women in Africa* ed., Combo, Brenda, Rainatou Sow & Faiza Jama Mohamed (Equality Now, 2013), 44 (Muriithi 2013).
72. Deutsche Gesellschaft für Internationale Zusammenarbeit, "Female Genital Mutilation and Education," accessed 12 May 2016, https://www.giz.de/expertise/downloads/giz2011-en-fgm-bildung.pdf (Deutsche Gesellschaft für Internationale Zusammenarbeit 2016).
73. Ondiek, Concellia Aoko, "The Persistence of Female Genital Mutilation (FGM) and its Impact on Women's Access to Education and Empowerment: a Study of Kuria District, Nyanza Province, Kenya" (PhD diss., University of South Africa, 2010) (Ondiek 2010).
74. Deutsche Gesellschaft für Internationale Zusammenarbeit, "Female Genital Mutilation".
75. Ondiek, "Female Genital Mutilation".
76. Deutsche Gesellschaft für Internationale Zusammenarbeit, "Female Genital Mutilation".
77. Deutsche Gesellschaft für Internationale Zusammenarbeit, "Female Genital Mutilation".
78. UN Women, "The Girl Child" (Fact Sheet No. 12: United Nations Department of Public Information DPI/2035/L, May 2000), accessed 10 May 2016, http://www.un.org/womenwatch/daw/followup/session/presskit/fs12.htm.
79. UN Women, "The Girl Child".
80. Sutherland, Anna, "The Many Ways Mothers' Education Matters," 19 February 2015, accessed 12 June 2016, http://family-studies.org/the-many-ways-mothers-education-matters/ (Sutherland 2015).

81. Oyigbenu, Amirikpa, "Girl-Child Education and Nigeria's Development Agenda: a Literary Perspective", *African Research Review* 4:2 (2010) 418 (Oyigbenu 2010).
82. Jekayinfa, A.A., and D.O. Kolawole, "Conceptual Background to the History of Education in Nigeria", *Perspective on the History of Education in Nigeria* (2008), accessed January 10, 2016, https://www.unilorin.edu.ng (Jekayinfa and Kolawole 2008).
83. "UNDP's Inclusive Development," UNDP, accessed 12 June 2016, http://www.undp.org/content/undp/en/home/ourwork/povertyreduction/focus_areas/focus_inclusive_development.html.
84. "UNDP's Inclusive Development".
85. Ali, Ifzal, and Juzhong Zhuang, *Inclusive Growth toward a Prosperous Asia: Policy Implications* (ERD Working Paper 97, ADB: Manila, 2007) 3 (Ali and Zhuang 2007).
86. Rauniyar Ganesh, and Ravi Kanbur, *Inclusive Growth and Inclusive Development: A Review and Synthesis of Asian Development Bank Literature* (Asian Development Bank Occasional Paper No. 8, 2009), accessed 7 March 2016, http://www.adb.org/sites/default/files/evaluation-document/35885/files/op8-inclusive-growth-development.pdf (Rauniyar and Kanbur 2009).
87. Ali, "Inclusive Growth," 3.
88. Ali, "Inclusive Growth," 3.
89. Rauniyar, "Inclusive Growth," 3.
90. Ali, Ifzal, and Hyun Hwa Son, "Defining and Measuring Inclusive Growth: Application to the Philippines" (ERD Working Paper Series No. 98, ADB: Manila, 2007) (Ali and Son 2007).
91. Fernando, Nimal, *Rural Development Outcomes and Drivers: An Overview and Some Lessons* (Manila: Asian Development Bank, 2008) (Fernando 2008).
92. Fernando, *Rural Development*, 51.
93. Rauniyar, "Inclusive Growth," 6.
94. Jekayinfa, "Conceptual Background".
95. "UNICEF's Girls spend 160 million more hours than boys doing household chores every day," UNICEF, accessed 1 November 2016.
96. "UNICEF's Girls".
97. UN Women, "The Girl Child".
98. Edmonds, Eric V., "Understanding Sibling Differences in Child Labour", *Journal of Population Economics*, 19:4(2005), 799 (Edmonds 2005).
99. Edmonds, "Sibling Differences," 802.
100. Psacharopoulos, George, and Anthony Patrinos, "Returns to Investment in Education: A Further Update" (Washington DC: World Bank,

Policy Research Working Paper No. 2881, 2002) (Psacharopoulos and Patrinos 2002).

101. Department for International Development, "Girl's Education: Towards a Better Future for All" (2005), accessed 12 March 2016, http://www2.ohchr.org/english/issues/development/docs/girlseducation.pdf (Department for International Development 2005).
102. Summers, Lawrence H, "Investing in All the People: Educating Women in Developing Countries" (EDI Seminar Paper, No. 45. Washington DC: World Bank, 1994) (Summers 1994).
103. Gage, Anastasia; Elisabeth Sommerfelt, and Andrea L. Piani, "Household Structure and Childhood Immunization in Niger and Nigeria" *Demography*, 34: 2 (1997) 298, accessed 10 December 2015, doi:10.2307/2061706 (Gage et al. 1997).
104. Department for International Development, "Girl's Education".
105. SADC Gender Policy, Paragraph 4.3.
106. 24th Ordinary Session of the Assembly of African Union Heads of State and Government, Addis Ababa, accessed 30 October 2016, http://agenda2063.au.int/en/news/24th-ordinary-session-assembly-african-union-heads-state-and-government-begins-addis-ababa.
107. Aspiration 6 of Agenda 2063.
108. Africa Union, "Agenda 2063 framework document," accessed 30 October 2016, http://agenda2063.au.int/en/sites/default/files/Final%20Draft%20Agenda%202063%20Framework%20-Formatted%20TOC-1.pdf (Africa Union 2016).
109. Such as the ACRWC, 1990; Maputo Protocol, 2003; African Youth Charter, 2006; and Kampala Protocol, 2009.
110. In the United Nations Plans of Action on the Environment and Development in 1992, on Human Rights in 1993, on Population and Development in 1994 and on Social Development in 1995.
111. Preamble to Maputo Protocol, paragraph 12.
112. UNICEF, "Toward Ending Female Genital Mutilation," last updated 7 February 2006, accessed June 16, 2016, http://www.scoop.co.nz/stories/WO0602/S00099.htm (UNICEF 2006).
113. Asuagbor, Lucy, "Status of Implementation of the Protocol to the African Charter on Human and People's Rights on the Rights of Women in Africa," accessed 10 September 2016, http://www.peaceau.org/uploads/special-rapporteur-on-rights-of-women-in-africa-presentation-for-csw-implementation.pdf (Asuagbor 2016b).
114. Angola, Benin, Burkina Faso, Cameroon, Cape Verde, Comoros, Congo, Cote d'Ivoire, Democratic Republic of the Congo, Djibouti, Equatorial Guinea, Gabon, Gambia, Ghana, Guinea, Guinea-Bissau, Kenya, Lesotho, Liberia, Libya, Malawi, Mali, Mauritania,

Mozambique, Namibia, Nigeria, Rwanda, Senegal, Seychelles, Sierra Leone, South Africa, Swaziland, Tanzania, Togo, Uganda, Zambia and Zimbabwe.

115. Algeria, Burundi, Central African Republic, Chad, Eritrea, Ethiopia, Madagascar, Mauritius, Niger, Sahrawi Arab Democratic Republic, Sao Tome and Principe, Somalia, South Sudan, Sudan.
116. Botswana, Egypt and Tunisia.
117. ACHPR, "African Commission on Human and Peoples' Rights' Ratification Table, Protocol to the African Charter on Human and Peoples', Rights on the Rights of Women in Africa," accessed 17 June 2016, http://www.achpr.org/instruments/women-protocol/ratification/ (ACHPR 2016).
118. Article 1(k), Maputo Protocol.
119. Muriithi, "African Charter," 44.
120. Cameroon on African ethical and moral values; Kenya on Articles 10(3) & 14(2) of Maputo Protocol; Namibia on Article 6(d); South Africa on Articles 1(f) 4(j) 6(d) 6(h) & 31; Uganda on Articles 14(1)(a) & 14(2)(c); Rwanda on Article 14(2)(c).
121. Universal Basic Education Act, 2004; Child's Right Act, 2003; National Policy on Education, 2004.
122. Child's Rights Act, 2003.
123. Equality legislations, Constitution, Land Reform and Gender Policy 1997, Specific budget allocations to benefit girls and women, etc.
124. *Governing Body of Juma Musjid Primary School v Essay N.O.* (CCT 29/10) [*2011*] ZACC 13; *Section 27 and Others v Minister of Education and Another* (24565/*2012*) [*2012*] ZAGPPHC 114.
125. National Planning Commission, 2012.
126. SAHRC Charter of Children's Rights: The Right of Children to Basic Education, 2012, SAHRC 8.
127. http://reports.weforum.org/global-gender-gap-report-2014/economies/#economy=ZAF.
128. http://www.gov.za/sites/www.gov.za/files/Status_of_women_in_SA_economy.pdf.
129. http://www.sahistory.org.za/article/girl-child.
130. http://www.southafrica.info/services/rights/gender-051212.htm#.VZJSak3vpzl.
131. ICESCR, 11 June 1976; CRC, 10 June 1991; CEDAW, 20 August 1985; ICCPR, 11 June 1976; CERD, 27 October 1972; CRPD, 10 November 2009; Convention relating to the State of Refugees, 12 May 1964; UNESCO Convention against Discrimination in Education, 03 January 1979; ILO 138 Minimum Age Convention, 16 December 1998; ILO 182 Worst Forms of Child Labour Convention, 12 September 2001.

132. ACHPR—18 February 1984; ACRWC—16 March 2003; African Youth Charter—20 December 2012.
133. However, Article 41 of the Draft Constitution under consideration recognises right to education a basic right.
134. NEA, 1978, amended in 1995 and 2002.
135. Article 56.2.
136. Article 56.3.
137. Other laws in Tanzania that promotes access to education includes the Institute of Adult Education Act, 1975; Vocational Education and Training Act, 1994, revised in 2006; University Act, 2005.
138. Other policies includes Education and Training Policy, 1995; Education Sector Development Programme, (2008–2017); Primary Education Development Programme (First phase: 2002–2006; second phase: 2007–2011; third phase: 2012–2017); Secondary Education Development Programme (First phase: 2004–2009; second phase: 2010–2015); Inclusive Education Strategy (2009–2017); The Technical Education and Training Policy, 1996; Higher Education Development Programme and the National Higher Education Policy, 1999.
139. Right to Education Project Factsheet: United Republic of Tanzania, accessed August 10, 2016, available http://www.right-to-education.org/sites/right-to-education.org/files/resource-attachments/RTE_Country_Facsheet_Tanzania_January_2015.pdf.
140. Action Aid, "Transforming Education for Girls in Tanzania: Baseline Research Summary Report", accessed November 2, 2016, http://www.actionaid.org/sites/files/actionaid/aategintbaselinetanzaniafinal.pdf.
141. Action Aid Report.
142. Section 127 of the Children's Act of Kenya, 2001.
143. Article 43.1.f.
144. Article 56.
145. Article 22.
146. [2013] eKLR, Petition No. 133 of 2013.
147. [2011] communication 002/2009.
148. Part IV.
149. Article 28.
150. Articles 29 and 32.
151. Other major education legislations and policies in Kenya includes 2003 Persons with Disabilities Act; 2013 Kenya Institute of Curriculum Development Act; 2012 Teachers Service Commission Act; Kenya Vision 2030; 2012 Policy Framework for Education and Training—Reforming Education and training in Kenya; 2012 Policy Framework for Science, Technology and Innovation.

152. Right to Education: Country Factsheet, Kenya, 2004, Right to Education Project, accessed August 15, 2016, http://www.right-to-education.org/sites/right-to-education.org/files/resource-attachments/RTE_Right_to_Education_Country_Factsheet_Kenya_2014.pdf.
153. State Report submitted to the Committee on the Rights of the Child in 2013, CRC/C/KEN/3-5, paragraph 242.
154. State Report submitted to the CRC in 2013, CRC/C/KEN/3-5, paragraph 324.
155. Asuagbor, Lucy, "Inter-session Activity Report of Special Rapporteur on the Rights of Women in Africa," (58th Ordinary Session of the African Commission on Human and Peoples' Rights, 6-20 April 2016), accessed July 24, 2016, http://www.achpr.org/files/sessions/58th/inter-act-reps/254/58os_inter_session_report_asuagbor_eng.pdf (accessed 24 July 2016) (Asuagbor 2016a).
156. Penal Code ch 16 Laws of Tanzania 2002.
157. Including Burkina Faso, Rwanda, Gambia, Nigeria, Uganda, Malawi, Burundi, Cameroon, Ivory Coast, Liberia, Republic of Congo, South Africa among others.
158. In the case of *Loveness Mudzuru and Ravimbo Tsopodzi v Minister if Legal and Parliamentary Affairs and others*, Unreported, CCZ 12/2015.
159. Attributed to Ghanaian scholar Dr. James Emmanuel Kwegyir-Aggrey (1875–1927).
160. Education here refers to both formal and informal education.
161. Collins, n. 58.

Bibliography

ACHPR. 2016. African Commission on Human and Peoples' Rights' Ratification Table, Protocol to the African Charter on Human and Peoples' Rights on the Rights of Women in Africa. http://www.achpr.org/instruments/women-protocol/ratification/. Accessed 17 June 2016.

Action Aid. 2016. Transforming Education for Girls in Tanzania: Baseline Research Summary Report. http://www.actionaid.org/sites/files/actionaid/aategintbaselinetanzaniafinal.pdf. Accessed 2 Nov 2016.

Africa Union. 2016. Agenda 2063 Framework Document. http://agenda2063.au.int/en/sites/default/files/Final%20Draft%20Agenda%202063%20Framework%20-Formatted%20TOC-1.pdf. Accessed 30 Oct 2016.

Alabi, T., M. Bahah, and S.O. Alabi. 2014. The Girl-Child: A Sociological View on the Problems of Girl-Child Education in Nigeria. *European Scientific Journal* 10 (2): 393–409.

Ali, Ifzal, and Hyun Hwa Son. 2007. Defining and Measuring Inclusive Growth: Application to the Philippines. ERD Working Paper Series No. 98, ADB: Manila.

Ali, Ifzal, and Juzhong Zhuang. 2007. Inclusive Growth Toward a Prosperous Asia: Policy Implications. ERD Working Paper 97, ADB: Manila. 3.

Asuagbor, Lucy. 2016. Inter-session Activity Report of Special Rapporteur on the Rights of Women in Africa (58th Ordinary Session of the African Commission on Human and Peoples' Rights, 6–20 April 2016). http://www.achpr.org/files/sessions/58th/inter-act-reps/254/58os_inter_session_report_asuagbor_eng.pdf. Accessed 24 July 2016.

Asuagbor, Lucy. 2016. Status of Implementation of the Protocol to the African Charter on Human and People's Rights on the Rights of Women in Africa. http://www.peaceau.org/uploads/special-rapporteur-on-rights-of-women-in-africa-presentation-for-csw-implementation.pdf. Accessed 10 Sept 2016.

Ayandele, E.A. 1979. *African Historical Studies*. London: Frank Cass.

Beiter, Klaus Dieter. 2005. *The Protection of the Right to Education by International Law*. Martinus Nijhoff Publishers.

Callaway, H. 1975. Indigenous Education in Yoruba Society. In *Conflict and Harmony in Education in Tropical Africa*, ed. G.G. Brown, and M. Hiskett, 26–38. London: George Allen & Unwin Ltd.

Department for International Development. 2005. Girls' Education: Towards a Better Future for All (January 2005). http://www2.ohchr.org/english/issues/development/docs/girlseducation.pdf. Accessed 30 Oct 2015.

Deutsche Gesellschaft für Internationale Zusammenarbeit. 2016. Female Genital Mutilation and Education. https://www.giz.de/expertise/downloads/giz2011-en-fgm-bildung.pdf. Accessed 12 May 2016.

Dewey, John. 1938. *Experience and Education*, 86. London: Collier Macmillan.

Edmonds, Eric V. 2005. Understanding Sibling Differences in Child Labour. *Journal of Population Economics* 19 (4): 795–821.

Fafunwa, Baba A. 1974. *History of Education in Nigeria*. London: George Allen and Unwin Ltd.

Fernando, Nimal. 2008. *Rural Development Outcomes and Drivers: An Overview and Some Lessons*. Manila: Asian Development Bank.

Gage, Anastasia, Elisabeth Sommerfelt, and Andrea L. Piani. 1997. Household Structure and Childhood Immunization in Niger and Nigeria *Demography* 34 (2): 295–309. doi:10.2307/2061706. Accessed 10 Dec 2015.

Good, C.U. (ed.). 1945. *Dictionary of Education*. New York: McGraw-Hill.

Hari, Patricia. 2016. Parents' and Community Attitudes towards Girls' Participation in and Access to Education and Science, Mathematics and Technology (SMT) Subjects. http://www.unesco.org/education/educprog/ste/projects/girls%20africa/femsa/femsa6.html. Accessed 1 Nov 2016.

Hillman, Arye L., and Eva Jenkner. 2004. Educating Children in Poor Countries. Economic Issue 33. International Monetary Fund. http://www.imf.org/external/pubs/ft/issues/issues33/. Accessed 1 Nov 2016.

Human Rights Watch. 2016. Ending Child Marriage in Africa: Opening the Door for Girls' Education, Health, and Freedom from Violence. December 9, 2015. https://www.hrw.org/news/2015/12/09/ending-child-marriage-africa. Accessed 1 Nov 2016.

Igube, R.B. 2004. Gender Security and Advancement: The Case of Inequality and Inequity. Paper presented at the round table discourse by Higher Link Educational Programme, The British Council, Change Managers International, University of Abuja, March 8, in Abuja.

Jekayinfa, A.A., and D.O. Kolawole. 2008. Conceptual Background to the History of Education in Nigeria. *Perspective on the History of Education in Nigeria*. https://www.unilorin.edu.ng. Accessed 10 Jan 2016.

Kambarami, Maureen. 2006. Femininity, Sexuality and Culture: Patriarchy and Female Subordination in Zimbabwe. *Africa Regional Sexuality Resource Centre*. http://www.arsrc.org/downloads/uhsss/kmabarami.pdf. Accessed 30 Oct 2016.

Kambhampati, Uma S., and Raji Rajan. 2008. The 'Nowhere' Children: Patriarchy and the Role of Girls in India's Rural Economy. *The Journal of Development Studies* 44 (9): 1309–1341. doi:10.1080/00220380802264978. Accessed 13 March 2015.

Muriithi, Caroline Muthoni. 2013. An analysis of the Protocol to the African Charter on Human and Peoples' Rights on the Rights of Women in Africa. In *Journey to Equality: 10 Years of the Protocol on the Rights of Women in Africa*, ed. Combo, Brenda, Rainatou Sow and Faiza Jama Mohamed (Equality Now, 2013), 44.

Ndofirepi, Amasa Philip and Elizabeth Spiwe Ndofirepi. 2012. (E)ducation or (e)ducation in Traditional African Societies? A Philosophical Insight. *Stud Tribes Tribals* 10 (1): 13–28.

Ocho, Lawrence Offie. 2005. *Issues and Concerns in Education and Life*, Enugu: Institute of Development Studies.

Offorma, Grace C. 2008. The Boy Child Education in the South-Eastern States of Nigeria: Problems and Prospects. Paper Presented at the Convention of the Unity Schools Old Students Association, USOSA, Enugu, Nigeria.

Okeke, E.A.C., U.M. Nzewi, and Z. Njoku. 2008. *"Tracking School Age Children's Education Status in UNICEF A-Field states" in UNICEF—A Field State*. Enugu: UNICEF.

Ondiek, Concellia Aoko. 2010. The Persistence of Female Genital Mutilation (FGM) and its Impact on Women's Access to Education and Empowerment: A Study of Kuria District, Nyanza Province, Kenya. PhD dissertation, University of South Africa.

Onuora-Oguno, Azubike. 2015. Enhancing Equality and Eliminating Discrimination: Girl Child Empowerment and Access to Quality Basic Education in Nigeria. *Yonsei Law Journal* 6 (1): 75–102.

Osagiobare, Osamiro Emmanuel. 2015. Rita Osayemwenre Oronsaye and Victor Ekwukoma, "Influence of Religious and Cultural Beliefs on Girl-Child Educational Aspiration in Nigeria". *Journal of Educational and Social Research* 5 (2): 165–170.

Oyigbenu, Amirikpa. 2010. Girl-Child Education and Nigeria's Development Agenda: A Literary Perspective. *African Research Review* 4 (2): 418–432.

Parsons, Jeffery, et al. 2015. Economic Impacts of Child Marriage: A Review of the Literature. *The Review of Faith and International Affairs.* 13 (3): 12–22. doi:10.1080/15570274.2015.1075757. Accessed 2 Nov 2016.

Psacharopoulos, George, and Anthony, Patrinos. 2002. Returns to Investment in Education: A Further Update. Policy Research Working Paper No. 2881, Washington, DC: World Bank.

Igube, R.B. 2004b. *Women and Gender Studies*, 4. Abuja: Sir Kuf Ventures Limited.

Rauniyar Ganesh, and Ravi Kanbur. 2009. Inclusive Growth and Inclusive Development: A Review and Synthesis of Asian Development Bank Literature. Asian Development Bank Occasional Paper No. 8, 2009. http://www.adb.org/sites/default/files/evaluation-document/35885/files/op8-inclusive-growth-development.pdf. Accessed 7 March 2016.

Right to Education Project Factsheet: United Republic of Tanzania. 2016. http://www.right-to-education.org/sites/right-to-education.org/files/resource-attachments/RTE_Country_Facsheet_Tanzania_January_2015.pdf. Accessed 10 Aug 2016.

Right to Education: Country Factsheet, Kenya, 2004, Right to Education Project. http://www.right-to-education.org/sites/right-to-education.org/files/resource-attachments/RTE_Right_to_Education_Country_Factsheet_Kenya_2014.pdf. Accessed 15 August 2016.

Shoola, Toni. 2013. The Effect of the Sub-Saharan African Gender Divide on the Rights and Status of Women in a Globalized World. *International Research Scape Journal* 1(Article 7): 1–48. http://scholarworks.bgsu.edu. Accessed 12 Oct 2016.

Summers, Lawrence H. 1994. Investing in All the People: Educating Women in Developing Countries. EDI Seminar Paper 45, Washington, DC: World Bank.

Sutherland, Anna. 2015. The Many Ways Mothers' Education Matters, February 19. http://family-studies.org/the-many-ways-mothers-education-matters/. Accessed 12 June 2016.

UN Women. 2000. The Girl Child (Fact Sheet No. 12: United Nations Department of Public Information DPI/2035/L, May 2000). http://www.un.org/womenwatch/daw/followup/session/presskit/fs12.htm. Accessed 10 May 2016.

UNESCO. 2012. Education and Skills for Inclusive and Sustainable Development beyond 2015: Thematic Think Tiece, 3. http://www.un.org/millenniumgoals/pdf/Think%20Pieces/4_education.pdf. Accessed 30 Oct 2016.

UNESCO. 2016a. Gender Review: Creating Sustainable Futures for All. Global Education Monitoring Report (2016). http://unesdoc.unesco.org/images/0024/002460/246045e.pdf. Accessed 1 Nov 2016.

UNESCO. 2016b. Left Behind. http://www.uis.unesco.org/_LAYOUTS/UNESCO/no-girl-left-behind/index.html#cover-intro-4. Accessed 30 Oct 2016.

UNICEF. 2001. Early Marriage Child Spouses. *Innocenti Digest*, *7*: 12. http://www.unicef-irc.org/publications/pdf/digest7e.pdf. Accessed 13 Nov 2015.

UNICEF. 2015. Ending Child Marriage: Progress and Prospects. http://data.unicef.org/corecode/uploads/document6/uploaded_pdfs/corecoe. Accessed 15 Nov 2015.

UNICEF's Girl's Education and Gender Equality, last modified March 23, 2015. http://www.unicef.org/education/bege_70640.html.

Wamue-Ngare, Grace, and Waithera Nancy Njoroge. 2011. Gender Paradigm Shift within the Family Structure in Kiambu, Kenya. *African Journal of Social Sciences* 1 (3): 10–20. www.sachajournals.com. Accessed 31 Oct 2016.

Author Biography

Olanike Adelakun-Odewale Called to the Nigerian Bar as a Barrister and Solicitor of the Supreme Court of Nigeria in 2007, received a Bachelor's degree in law from Olabisi Onabanjo University, Nigeria in 2006, a Master's degree in law from University of Ibadan, Nigeria in 2010 and a Master's degree in Library and Information Science form the University of Ibadan, Nigeria in 2016. She is presently a doctoral student at the Centre for Child's Law, University of Pretoria, South Africa. Olanike is a Lecturer and Law Librarian at the American University of Nigeria where she teaches and comments on Legal Methods and Family Law. Her area of expertise lies in International Law, Child's Rights Legal Information Literacy and Legal Research.

CHAPTER 8

The African Union's Agenda 2063: Education and Its Realization

Michael Addaney

1 Introduction

The African Union's (AU) Agenda 2063 is a well-developed comprehensive plan for the structural transformation of Africa which was adopted at the AU's golden jubilee summit in 2013.[1] The heads of states and governments assembled at the summit declared their resolve to make progress in eight priority fields which are to be integrated into national development policies and plans.[2] These priority areas include African identity and renaissance, continuation of the struggle against (neo)colonialism and for the right to self-determination, African integration for socioeconomic development, peace and security, democratic governance as well as to establish and position Africa's destiny at the global level.[3] The Agenda is anchored in and driven by the development aspirations of the African peoples that were culminated through a broader continental consultative process. Various stakeholders including governments, civil society organizations, think tanks, research institutions, Africans in the Diaspora, women, children as well as the private sector were all

M. Addaney (✉)
University of Pretoria, Pretoria, South Africa
e-mail: appl.adm@gmail.com

A.C. Onuora-Oguno et al. (eds.), *Education Law, Strategic Policy and Sustainable Development in Africa*, DOI 10.1007/978-3-319-53703-0_8

consulted.[4] The regional economic communities (RECs) through their inter-ministerial sector meetings were actively involved in the process.[5]

It has been observed that Agenda 2063 is an ambitious and comprehensive blueprint for Africa.[6] But it faces major challenges such as lack of resources for its effective and efficient execution as well as lack of commitment from African leaders and the AU itself.[7] This is due to the well-established perception that African leaders publicly agree on the issues that they do not actually believe in or fully support. History reminds us of the several failed continental agendas adopted by the AU since its inception that sought to propel shared growth, security, and sustainable development through the advancement of political, economic, social, and technological transformation similar to the new Agenda. Nevertheless, the AU has successfully advanced popular concepts such adopting 'African solutions to African challenges' and 'African Renaissance which despite much contestations seems to be accepted as the way forward in building the Africa we want by 2063. However, critics point to the failure of the Trans-African Highway agenda which the African Group at the United Nations headquarters in partnership with the then Organisation for African Unity (OUA, now AU) and the Economic Commission for Africa championed in the 1970s.[8] This Agenda was stillborn and never saw the light of day despite the hype and the pledges that were made to raise funds for its realization. Much as the new Agenda is welcome, this and other failed initiatives by the AU due to lack of commitment from African leaders[9] raise skepticism about its implementation.

To overcome these hurdles, there is the need for a careful identification of the challenges ahead and the requisite solutions to address such challenges adequately. Education is touted as the key to enlightenment and transformation. It is, therefore, one of the most potent vehicles for finding effective solution to the challenges ahead as well as an 'efficient tool for the execution of the new Agenda'.[10] It has been contended that the AU through its member states needs to integrate the Agenda into their national educational plans and initiate institutional as well as policy reforms at the national level to enhance access to quality and accessible basic and higher education.[11] On this premise, through a qualitative approach, this chapter meta-analytically argues that the existing continental education systems, pedagogy, and curriculum are not responsive to the Agenda's eight point goals. Therefore, the existing education system needs to be reformed to be rights-respecting, that is context-specific as well as cogent enough to drive the successful and effective delivery of the Agenda.

It has been argued that managing the implementation of the Agenda for sustainable development impact requires that the African peoples should have the core principles of the Agenda engrained in their hearts, distilled in their minds, and skilled in their fingers through national and regional teaching and research institutions.[12] For instance, the Agenda identifies among others the prevalence and severity of extreme unpredictable weather conditions which distort normal crops patterns, reduce agricultural and industrial production as well as export earnings which affect the socio-economic development of Africans.[13] It further recognizes that climate change and natural disasters will continue to adversely impact the development of Africa for many years to come and admit Africa's limited capacity for disaster preparedness and prevention which is the resulting trail of suffering, deaths, and material destruction in every natural disaster.[14] It, therefore, seeks to achieve high standard of living, quality life, and well-being for all Africans as well as to build resilient economies and communities.[15]

The Agenda identifies strategies but without integrating these aspirations and strategies into the existing educational system, it will only remain in theoretical realms and shelves just like the other regional agendas and policies. On this premise, this chapter posits that integrating the Agenda into the existing continental and national educational systems is the durable means of achieving clarity, synergy, cooperation, and coherence among the national and regional implementation strategies to ensure that no one is left behind. DeGhetto et al. argue that there is the need to address the question of how the Agenda can be effectively and efficiently integrated and synchronized into national-level policies as well as specific legislative and policy actions are to be adopted to ensure that the integration is not only effected but well managed to make sustainable impact.[16] The chapter is divided into four sections: Section 1 introduces the chapter and is followed by a brief discussion of the Agenda 2063. Section 3 examines education as an instrument for realizing the Agenda 2063, and Section 4 concludes by recommending education as the cogent strategy and bedrock to realize the Agenda 2063.

2 This is What We Want: Agenda 2063 from a General Perspective

Agenda 2063 is an ambitious and people-centered continental vision with a carefully crafted action plan that aims to position Africa for growth over the next 50 years. It incorporates lessons and experiences from Africa's past. The core objective is to secure unity, prosperity as well as peace for all its citizens. In simple terms, Agenda 2063 is targeted at ensuring that Africa do things differently in a people-centered manner, by scaling and scoping up to ensure it is bigger as well as better in terms of governance, performance outcomes, and impact on citizens.[17] According to the Africa Union Commission, the critical success factors for the Agenda are inter alia the participation of multiple key stakeholders at all stages from preparation to implementation, a result-based management approach with SMART (specific, measureable, achievable, realistic, and time bound) strategic objectives as well as instilling the right set of African values especially in the area of attitudes, and mind sets.[18] Agenda 2063 originates from the AU Constitutive Act and vision while it also builds on continental, subregional, and national priorities.[19]

DeGhetto et al. assert that as both a continental vision and action plan, the Agenda strongly calls for positive socioeconomic transformation in Africa.[20] This is relevant since it goes beyond drivers for economic growth and shared development and demands for transparent governance, transformational change as well as shared prosperity. Achieving this requires, inter alia, human resource capacities and competencies for the management of the longitudinal, multilevel transformational change. The Agenda challenges all the citizens of Africa to take stock of and learn from Africa's past experiences for its future growth and development. It is argued that this learning is 'not a mere academic exercise of taking cognizance of the historical past but as a non-reversal as well as sustaining change of attitude at the individual, institutional, and societal levels'.[21] This type of learning requires a unique combination of human capacities and competencies in order to manage the transformational changes within African states. From this perspective, the Agenda is a clarion call for Africans to think hard and wide on how to manage its future particularly, especially across generations in the areas of politics and business, technology and innovation, as well as development and society as a whole.

2.1 Africa's Promise Future

In 2013, African heads of state and government pledged their commitment to progress in eight key priority areas, which includes African identity and renaissance, the continued struggle against colonialism and the right to self-determination, continental integration, social and economic development and transformation, peace and security, democratic governance, determining Africa's destiny, and fostering Africa's place in the world.[22] There are seven primary aspirations that comprise the Agenda 2063. These aspirations stem from the eight priority areas mentioned above. These priority areas have been further broken down into 18 goals which are further distilled into 44 priority areas. Furthermore, the 44 areas are finally watered down to 161 unique and distinctive national-level targets. Thus, the vision of Agenda 2063 is broadly comprehensive and covers the issues of identity, political independence, self-determination, and socioeconomic development in light of globalization (Table 1).

In preparing the Agenda, the African Union Commission preliminarily designed 11 multistakeholder groups for broader consultation. These included the (RECs) and all AU organs, technical experts from member states, technical experts from academia and think tanks, civil society, women and youth, the private sector, faith-based and cultural organizations, Africans in the Diaspora, Africa's eminent persons, former heads of state and government, as well as citizens through Internet-based consultations.[24] This approach empowers and challenges the ordinary African citizens to take responsibility in implementing and shaping the destiny of continent. The framework entails 12 flagship projects which are regarded as priority in implementing the Agenda. These projects include the establishment of African financial institutions, formulation of a commodities strategy as well as ending wars, civil conflicts, and gender-based violence. Other projects are an integrated high-speed train networks

Table 1 The seven-point agenda 2063[a]

Agenda	*Aspirations*
1	A prosperous Africa based on inclusive growth and sustainable development
2	An integrated continent, politically united, based on the ideals of Pan-Africanism and the vision of Africa's renaissance
3	An Africa of good governance, democracy, respect for human rights, justice, and the rule of law
4	A peaceful and secure Africa
5	An Africa with strong cultural identity, common heritage, values, and ethics
6	An Africa whose development is people driven, relying on the potential of African people, especially its women and youth, and caring for children
7	Africa as a strong, united, and influential global player and partner

Source Agenda 2063—The Africa we want, 2015

[a] African Union Commission, ***Agenda 2063: The Africa We Want,*** Popular Version, Final Edition, (Addis Ababa: African Union, 2015) (African Union Commission 2015a)

that connect all African capitals as well as commercial centers, an African e-university that offers students easy access from anywhere on the globe, and the Africa outer space strategy that aims to use outer space to bolster development in agriculture, disaster management, remote sensing, climate forecast, banking and finance, as well as defense and security.

This framework also includes national-level strategic targets such as achieving a 100% literacy rate by 2030, universal access to quality health care and services by 2030, annual GDP growth of not less than 7% during the period, 50% of all elected officials at local, regional, and national levels to be women by 2030, Africa's share in global GDP to be 15% by 2063 as well as the science, technology, and innovation centers in Africa to have at least 15% of the world's patents by 2063.[25] It boldly asserts that the proportion of aid in national development budgets in all African countries must be zero by 2030.[26] In all, there are more than 160 national-level targets captured in the framework. Undeniably, Agenda 2063 requires serious consideration and focus with substantial effects likely to be witnessed by individuals, countries and the continent as well as the world.

From conceptualization through design to its current implementation phase, Agenda 2063 appears quite different from previous continental development agendas such as the Lagos Plan of Action.[27] The Agenda is more detailed with specific goals, strategic priorities, and targets. These strategic goals and priorities are challenging but realistic and achievable. The priority areas are very critical and relevant to the continent's emerging needs, and the strategic targets are directly specific and quantified.[28] These goals, priorities, and aspirations raise important educational questions including the sustainable management of the transformations, modernization of agriculture and natural resource management and infrastructure development, climate change adaptation and mitigation and sustainable development, education and capacity building, private-sector engagement, transformative governance as well as incentives, sociopolitical buy-in and broader continental ownership.

Furthermore, there are other critical questions that are arising within the African Union member states at different levels of development as well as commitment to the vision and aspirations of the Agenda. It has been argued that the more developed African economies such as Nigeria, South Africa and Egypt may regard the Agenda differently from the less developed and/or struggling countries such as Burundi and Guinea Bissau.[29] This is because the Agenda's goals and aspirations are comprehensive and cover wide range of human development issues. Therefore, this requires multidisciplinary and integrated approaches as well as different educational and human capacity building methods.

Despite the promising nature of the vision, priorities, and action plans, there are several key issues related to the implementation of the Agenda that need to be identified and addressed. The chapter identifies education among the lot and argues that it is the bedrock for resolving all the other issues that can impede the realization of the Agenda. Quality education is needed to raise and equip the human capacity required to man the new institutional arrangements to effectively move the Agenda toward realized change, development, integration, and transformation. This is very important. Acemoglu and Robinson observe that Africa is in critical need of developing inclusive political and economic institutions.[30] It should be observed that although the Agenda rightly demands for inclusive growth and sustainable development, these are not possible without quality education and associated inclusive institutions. The experience of other developing countries elsewhere shows that it is not enough just to reform 'institutional arrangements'. There is the need for Africa to build effective institutions that are capable of balancing and protecting competing political, economic, and social interests without resorting to conflict or fragility. A critical area of importance is good governance and quality education. Indeed, the AUC asserts that previous continental agendas such the Lagos Plan of Action (Abuja Treaty) demonstrate for the Agenda 2063 to succeed, however, the citizens of Africa must own the process and drive the outcome.[31] Therefore, the issue of ownership needs to be addressed since it has significant implications for the buy-in, commitment as well as resourcing, monitoring, and sustainable implementation of the Agenda.

3 Education: An Instrument for Realizing the Agenda 2063

It has been acknowledged that implementing Agenda 2063 could be hindered by lack of human capacity.[32] Africa's most significant challenge is to invest in capacity building through enhanced education in science, technology, engineering, and mathematics.[33] This implies that there is the need for measures that enhance change in the mind-set of people as well as build the capacity of Africa's human resource through education, research, and knowledge acquisition. The need for greater clarity on the roles and obligation of regional, subregional, and national institutions in the implementation of the Agenda is underscored. This will create an avenue for the Agenda to be aligned with other existing regional, subregional and national-level frameworks and aspirations as well as strengthen ownership and domestication of the Agenda by member states. Education[34] has been variously defined. It has been described the process of becoming aware of one's environment for a better and informed decision-making. Conceptually, education is defined as entailing a lifelong formal and informal process of equipping an individual to be fully aware of his environment and to exploit, manage, and dominate same for the benefit of himself and the society at large.[35]

UNICEF argues that education is the bedrock of sustainable development and serves as the pivot around which socioeconomic and political developments as well as cultural transformation of a society revolve.[36] Lawal describes education as the process of acquiring knowledge, skills, attitudes, interest, abilities, competence, and the cultural norms of a society by people and to transmit this life to the coming generations, so as to enhance perpetual development of the society.[37] These definitions capture two things. They highlight the dynamics of education and acknowledge education as a process that different individuals can have different levels of education either formally or informally acquired over a lifetime. On the other hand, the definitions and conceptualizations unpack the essence of education 'to produce a useful citizen'.[38] It can be argued that a useful citizen is useful both to himself and play relevant role in advancing the sustainable development of the society in which he or she lives as well as to the global community.

Education 'is an indispensable key to, though not a sufficient condition for, personal and social improvement...education can help ensure a safer, healthier, more prosperous and environmentally sound world, while simultaneously contributing to social, economic, and cultural progress'.[39] The following can be deduced from the conceptual and definitional analysis above. For the purpose of this chapter, the relevant words are the following:

1. aware of his environment and,
2. for the benefit of himself and the society at large,
3. formal and informal process,
4. lifelong, and
5. to exploit, manage, and dominate same.

Therefore, in realizing Agenda 2063, the African Union must ensure that Africa's education systems are churning out useful citizens who are educated sufficiently to be aware of their environment in terms of development aspirations, and are capable of dominating and realizing the same. On this premise, the begging question is 'are the educational systems and policies in Africa designed and underpinned by the principles as discussed above'. What efforts are being made to ensure that the current educational systems are training people to be aware of their environment and to dominate same for self and society at large?

On the other hand, development has been narrowly defined as an increase in gross domestic product (GDP) of a country. This narrow understanding and conceptualization of development is misleading. Most African countries have been experiencing steady economic growth over the last decade without corresponding socioeconomic development. In Nigeria, the GDP was estimated at some miserable US$36 billion in 1999.[40] In 2015, it had risen to an estimated US$489.2 billion.[41] Ghana, Kenya and Rwanda have all been experiencing an average growth rate of more than 5% since the last decade.[42] Conversely, the poverty gaps in these countries keep widening.[43] However, it is well known that this economic growth has been associated with an increasing poverty and unemployment. Similar cases like this across the continent have created a negative spate of democratic reversals as well as the potential reversals in other smoldering cauldrons.[44] Without a carefully mapped out plan to implement the Agenda, this kind of development is what Africa will experience instead of the Africa we want. Development has therefore been contemporarily conceptualized as 'a process concerned with people's capacity in a defined area over a defined period to manage and induce positive change through predicting, planning, understanding and monitoring change as well as reducing or eliminating unwanted or unwarranted change'. This indicates that the African peoples and institutions must be informed, rational and clear about their choices, their obvious destination as well as the direction.[45] Achieving this will require that such people and institutions must have a degree of education.

Through Agenda 2063, Africa's political leadership has agreed on the need to optimize Africa's resources for the benefit of all Africans. It has been argued that achieving this requires the building of the requisite human capital as well as empowers Africa's youth, scientists, researchers, and innovators to drive the execution and realization of the Agenda.[46] Admittedly, Africa's prospects of becoming the twenty-first-century engine of growth are already emerging. The African Development Bank argues that the continent is 'undergoing four major tectonic shifts painting a paradox of prosperity and poverty, dynamism of youth and disease'.[47] It further argues that overcoming this paradox requires rapid innovative and high-impact interventions in the education and research front.[48]

The AU has ostensibly engaged high gear in taking on the enormous challenges the continent faces.[49] Nevertheless, much work needs to be done in order for the ordinary Africans to own the process of Africa's renewal and work side by side with the AU to create and build the Africa we want by 2063. To realize this, the peoples and institutions of Africa have to decide what they are best able to contribute as well as identify others with similar convictions. The implication is that the renewal of Africa pointedly articulated in the Agenda 2063 must be driven by the people. Therefore, brining on board the common people will enable ownership of the Agenda by ordinary Africans and will also facilitate grassroots participation. This will address the deeply felt grievance that the African Union is a club of dictators' who are out of touch with the needs and aspirations of the African peoples. It has been emphasized that there can be no grassroots ownership and participation in realizing the Agenda if it has not been integrated into the existing educational systems and policies.[50] Agenda 2063 needs the backing of educational and sustainable planning theories, frameworks, concepts, methods as well as tools for its effective and sustaining implementation. It is, therefore, argued that African governments as well as institutions need to integrate the Agenda into their national education plans, strategies, pedagogies, and curriculum from basic school to tertiary level.[51]

4 Education, the Way Forward to 2063

The purpose of this chapter was to inform policy makers, scholars, and practitioners interested in the transformation and development of Africa about the continent's 50-year roadmap for transformation—Agenda 2063. Of course, the details constituting Agenda 2063 are extensive. Thus, it provided breathe and concise overview of the strategic goals, priority areas, and aspirations. In addition, because Agenda 2063 is in its initial phase, the chapter discussed some key issues that need to be addressed in order for it to be realized. Considering these issues and the poor quality of education particularly research and innovation on the African context, it is recommended that the continent's educational systems is reformed toward the following: (1) building and equipping human resources, (2) strengthening national educational institutions, (3) mounting a robust regional identity among the peoples of Africa (3) leveraging existing resources and building a comparative advantage, and (4) conducting more rigorous research on the African context, focused on realizing the Agenda. It is believed that quality human resource base is required to forge strong institutions, build a strong regional identity, as well as develop comparative regional advantage based on existing resources. This will form an important building block to realize the Agenda's strategic objectives of achieving structural transformation, as well as unity, prosperity, and peace for all of Africa's citizens.

5 Conclusion

This chapter sought to inform the discourse on the relevance of education to the effective realization of Africa's 50-year roadmap and plan for transformation, Agenda 2063. Evidently, like any revolutionary agenda, the Agenda 2063 contains comprehensive documents and details. Being in its initial phase, thus, there is the need to provide a succinct synopsis of the prime spur, main strategic objectives, as well as the programmed projects and how education can be utilized to achieve these strategic intentions. Therefore, this chapter outlined the key issues that need to be considered and addressed in order to realize Africa's desired transformation as set in the Agenda. Among several issues, the chapter makes a strong case for African governments and development partners to integrate Agenda 2063 into regional and national educational policies. It argues that building strong institutions as well as forming a strong regional identity at the international pedestal to achieve the aspirations and objectives set out in the Agenda requires a robust complementary educational strategy. This is because, as discussed in the chapter, developing a home region advantage based on existing natural and human resources are imperative building blocks to realize the structural transformation, continental unity, shared prosperity, and sustainable peace for all of Africa's citizens as envisaged in the Agenda. In conclusion, it should be observed as discussed in the chapter that 'Agenda 2063 is too important and strategic to be left to the African Union alone'. The renewal of Africa must be driven by the people and governments on the continent through adopting and integrating Agenda 2063 into their national educational policies, programmes and plans and, by extension, into educational curricula to make its realization a possibility.

Notes

1. African Union Commission, *Agenda 2063: The Africa We Want* (Addis Ababa: African Union, 2015), accessed 16 August 2016, url: http://www.agenda2063.au.int/en/home (African Union Commission 2015a).
2. African Union Commission, supra note 1.
3. African Union Commission, supra note 1.
4. African Union Commission, supra note 1.
5. African Union Commission, supra note 1.
6. African Union Commission, *Agenda 2063: The critical factors for success* (Addis Ababa: African Union, 2015b), accessed 26 August 2016, http://agenda2063.au.int/en/sites/default/files/05%20Critical%20Factors%20For%20Success_pdf (African Union Commission 2015b).
7. Sahra El Fassi and Faten Aggad (2014) Implementing African development initiatives: Opportunities and challenges to securing alternative financing for the Agenda 2063. Briefing note no. 65, (Maastricht: European Centre for Development Policy Management, 2014), 8 (El Fassi and Aggad 2014).
8. Harold Acemah, "Is African Union's Agenda 2063 relevant and achievable Part I," *The Daily Monitor*, May 17, 2015, accessed 25 July 2015 url: http://www.monitor.co.ug/OpEd/Commentary/African-Union-Agenda-achievable/689364-2727230-8kjyox/index.html (Acemah 2015).
9. Bujra Abdalla. (2004). 'Pan-African political and economic visions of development from the AOU to the AU: From the Lagos Plan of Action to the New Partnership for African Development' (Addis Ababa: Development Policy Management Forum, 2004), 28 (Bujra 2004).
10. Kaitlyn DeGhetto, Jacob R. Gray and Moses N. Kiggundu, "The African Union's Agenda 2063: Aspirations, Challenges, and Opportunities for Management Research," (2016) 2 *Africa Journal of Management* 2, no. 1 (2016): 93–116 (DeGhetto et al. 2016).
11. Paul Tiyambe Zeleza, "African Higher Education Summit: Revitalizing Higher Education for Africa's Future," in *African Higher Education Summit Framing Paper*, Dakar, March 10–12, 2015 (Dakar: AAU, 2015), 13 (Zeleza 2015).
12. Omano Edigheli, "Africa: Higher education must be higher priority," *Africa Focus Bulletin*, March 17, 2015, accessed 19 August 2016, url: http://www.africafocus.org/docs15/educ1503.php (Omano 2015).
13. African Union Commission, *Agenda 2063: The Africa we want, Draft Document 6* (Addis Ababa: African Union, 2014), accessed 22 August 2016, url: http://www.nepad.org/system/files/Agenda%202063%20%20English.pdf (African Union Commission 2014).
14. African Union Commission, *supra* note 14.

15. African Union Commission, *supra* note 14.
16. Kaitlyn DeGhetto, Jacob R. Gray and Moses N. Kiggundu, *supra* note 11 at 93–116.
17. Paul Tiyambe Zeleza, *supra* note 12 at 13.
18. African Union Commission, *Agenda 2063: The critical factors for success*, Agenda 2063 Document No 5 (Addis Ababa: African Union, 2015b), accessed 26 August 2016, url: http://agenda2063.au.int/en/sites/default/files/05%20Critical%20Factors%20For%20Success_.pdf (African Union Commission 2015c).
19. African Union Commission, *Agenda 2063: Background note*, Agenda 2063 Document No. 01 (Addis Ababa: African Union, 2015a), accessed 26 August 2016, url: http://agenda2063.au.int/en/sites/default/files/01%20Agenda%202063_Background_Note_s.pdf (African Union Commission 2015d).
20. Kaitlyn DeGhetto, Jacob R. Gray and Moses N. Kiggundu, *supra* note 11 at 93–116.
21. Kaitlyn DeGhetto, Jacob R. Gray and Moses N. Kiggundu, *supra* note 11 at 93–116.
22. African Union Commission, *supra* note 14.
23. African Union Commission, *Agenda 2063: A shared strategic framework for inclusive growth and sustainable development*, (Addis Ababa: African Union, 2013), accessed 22 August 2016, url: http://agenda2063.au.int/en/sites/default/files/27%2008%20Agenda%202063%20Background%20Note%20%20Eng_6.doc (African Union Commission 2013).
24. African Union Commission, *supra* note 14.
25. African Union Commission, *supra* note 14.
26. Bujra, *supra* note 10 at 29.
27. Paul Tiyambe Zeleza, *supra* note 12 at 13.
28. Kaitlyn DeGhetto, Jacob R. Gray and Moses N. Kiggundu, *supra* note 11 at 93–116.
29. Daron Acemoğlu and James A. Robinson, *Why nations fail: The origins of power, prosperity and poverty* (New York: Crown Business, 2012) (Acemoglu and Robinson 2012).
30. African Union Commission, *supra* note 19.
31. African Capacity Building Foundation, *Securing Africa's future through capacity development* (Harare: ACBF, 2015), 3 (African Capacity Building Foundation 2015).
32. Calestous Juma, *Education, research and innovation in Africa: Forging strategic linkages for economic transformation*, Discussion paper 2016-01 (Cambridge: Belfer Centre for Science and International Affairs, 2016) 4, accessed 26 March 2016, url: http://summit.trustafrica.org/wp-content/uploads/2015/03/JumaDP-Education-Africa2.pdf (Juma 2016).

33. Kumar and Ahmad define education as the purposive, conscious or unconscious, psychological, sociological, scientific and philosophical process which brings about the development of the individual to the fullest extent and also the maximum development of society in such a way that both enjoy maximum happiness and prosperity. They summarised this definition as: the development of an individual according to his or her needs and demands of society, of which he or she is an integral part. See, Satish Kumar and Sajjad Ahmad, *Meaning, aims and process of education* (Lewes: Distant Production House University and ODL, 2014), 3, accessed 1 September 2016, url: https://sol.du.ac.in/Courses/UG/StudyMaterial/16/Part1/ED/English/SM-1.pdf (Kumar and Ahmad 2014).
34. Chinedu Ohanyido, *The Pivotal Role of Education in Africa's Development*, (The Global Education Conference Network, July 24, 2012) (Ohanyido 2012).
35. UNICEF *Early Marriage: A harmful traditional practice: A statistical exploration* (2005) 1 (UNICEF 2005).
36. Yekini Olawaiye Lawal, "Education as an Instrument for Effective National Development: Which Way Nigeria," *Business & Entrepreneurship Journal,* 2, no. 2 (2013): 27–38 (Lawal 2013).
37. Eric A. Hanushek and Ludger Woessman, "The Role of Cognitive Skills in Economic Development," *Journal of Economic Literature* 46, no. 3 (2008): 607–668 (Hanushek and Woessman 2008).
38. UNESCO, "World conference on education for all: Meeting basic needs," *Jomiten, March 5–9,* (Jomtien: UNESCO, 2010) (UNESCO 2010).
39. The World Bank, *Global Economic prospects—Forecasts: Nigeria* (Washington DC: The World Bank Group, 2016), accessed 22 June 2016, url: http://data.worldbank.org/country/nigeria (The World Bank 2016a).
40. African Development Bank Group, *Economic Report on Nigeria: 2015,* Special Edition 4, (TUNIS Belvedere: ADB, 2015) (African Development Bank Group 2015).
41. The World Bank, *Africa: Overview* (Washington DC: The World Bank Group, 2016), accessed 22 June 2016, url: http://www.worldbank.org/en/region/afr/overview (The World Bank 2016b).
42. The World Bank, *Data: Sub-Saharan Africa* (Washington DC: The World Bank Group, 2016), accessed 22 June 2016, url: at http://data.worldbank.org/region/sub-saharan-africa (The World Bank 2016c).
43. Chinedu Ohanyido, *supra* note 36.
44. Allen Thomas, 'Meanings and Views of Development' in *Poverty and Development in the 21st Century,* ed. Allen Thomas, (Oxford: Oxford University Press, 2000) (Allen 2000).
45. The African Development Bank Group, "Second Ministerial Forum on Science, Technology, and Innovation in Africa" *Rabat, October 14–17,*

2014 (Rabat: the Academy of the Kingdom of Morocco) (The African Development Bank Group 2014).

46. *Ibid.*
47. *Ibid.*
48. Paul Tiyambe Zeleza, *supra* note 12 at 13.
49. Paul Tiyambe Zeleza, *supra* note 12 at 13.
50. Paul Tiyambe Zeleza, *supra* note 12 at 13.

Bibliography

Acemah, Harold. 2015. Is African union's Agenda 2063 Relevant and Achievable Part I. *The Daily Monitor*, May 17. http://www.monitor.co.ug/OpEd/Commentary/African-Union-Agenda-achievable/689364-2727230-8kjyox/index.html. Accessed 25 July 2015.

Acemoğlu, Daron, and James A. Robinson. 2012. *Why Nations Fail: The Origins of Power, Prosperity and Poverty*. New York: Crown Business.

African Capacity Building Foundation. 2015. *Securing Africa's Future Through Capacity Development*, 3. Harare: ACBF.

The African Development Bank Group. 2014. Second Ministerial Forum on Science, Technology, and Innovation in Africa. *Rabat*, October, 14–17. Rabat: The Academy of the Kingdom of Morocco.

African Development Bank Group. 2015. *Economic Report on Nigeria: 2015*, Special Edition 4. TUNIS Belvedere: ADB.

African Union Commission. 2013. *Agenda 2063: A Shared Strategic Framework for Inclusive Growth and Sustainable Development*. Addis Ababa: African Union. http://agenda2063.au.int/en/sites/default/files/27%2008%20Agenda%202063%20Background%20Note%20%20Eng_6.doc. Accessed 22 Aug 2016.

African Union Commission. 2014. *Agenda 2063: The Africa We Want*. Draft Document 6. Addis Ababa: African Union. http://www.nepad.org/system/files/Agenda%202063%20%20English.pdf. Accessed 22 Aug 2016.

African Union Commission. 2015a. *Agenda 2063: The Africa We Want*. Addis Ababa: African Union. http://www.agenda2063.au.int/en/home. Accessed 16 Aug 2016.

African Union Commission. 2015b. *Agenda 2063: The Critical Factors for Success*. Addis Ababa: African Union. http://agenda2063.au.int/en/sites/default/files/05%20Critical%20Factors%20For%20Success_.pdf. Accessed 26 Aug 2016.

African Union Commission. 2015c. *Agenda 2063: The Critical Factors for Success*. Agenda 2063 Document No. 5. Addis Ababa: African Union. http://agenda2063.au.int/en/sites/default/files/05%20Critical%20Factors%20For%20Success_.pdf. Accessed 26 Aug 2016.

African Union Commission. 2015d. *Agenda 2063: Background Note,* Agenda 2063 Document No. 01. Addis Ababa: African Union. http://agenda2063.au.int/en/sites/default/files/01%20Agenda%202063_Background_Note_s.pdf. Accessed 26 Aug 2016.

African Union Commission. 2015e. *Agenda 2063: The Africa We Want.* Popular Version, Final Edition. Addis Ababa: African Union.

Allen, Thomas. 2000. Meanings and Views of Development. *Poverty and Development in the 21st Century,* ed. Allen Thomas. Oxford: Oxford University Press.

Bujra, Abdalla. 2004. Pan-African Political and Economic Visions of Development from the AOU to the AU: From the Lagos Plan of Action to the New Partnership for African Development, 28. Addis Ababa: Development Policy Management Forum.

DeGhetto, Kaitlyn, Jacob R. Gray, and Moses N. Kiggundu. 2016. The African Union's Agenda 2063: Aspirations, Challenges, and Opportunities for Management Research. *Africa Journal of Management* 2 (1): 93–116.

El Fassi, Sahra and Faten Aggad. 2014. Implementing African Development Initiatives: Opportunities and Challenges to Securing Alternative Financing for the Agenda 2063, 8. Briefing Note No. 65. Maastricht: European Centre for Development Policy Management.

Hanushek, Eric A., and Ludger Woessman. 2008. The Role of Cognitive Skills in Economic Development. *Journal of Economic Literature* 46 (3): 607–668.

Juma, Calestous. 2016. Education, research and innovation in Africa: Forging strategic linkages for economic transformation. Discussion paper 2016-01, Cambridge, Belfer Centre for Science and International Affairs, 4. http://summit.trustafrica.org/wp-content/uploads/2015/03/JumaDP-Education-Africa2.pdf. Accessed 26 Mar 2016.

Kumar, Satish and Sajjad Ahmad. 2014. *Meaning, Aims and Process of Education,* 3. Lewes: Distant Production House University and ODL. https://sol.du.ac.in/Courses/UG/StudyMaterial/16/Part1/ED/English/SM-1.pdf. Accessed 1 Sept 2016.

Lawal, Yekini Olawaiye. 2013. Education as an Instrument for Effective National Development: Which Way Nigeria. *Business & Entrepreneurship Journal* 2 (2): 27–38.

Ohanyido, Chinedu. 2012. *The Pivotal Role of Education in Africa's Development.* The Global Education Conference Network, July 24.

Omano, Edigheli. 2015. Africa: Higher Education must be Higher Priority. *Africa Focus Bulletin,* March 17. http://www.africafocus.org/docs15/educ1503.php. Accessed 19 Aug 2016.

The World Bank. 2016a. *Global Economic Prospects—Forecasts: Nigeria.* Washington DC: The World Bank Group. http://data.worldbank.org/country/nigeria. Accessed 22 June 2016.

The World Bank. 2016b. *Africa: Overview*. Washington DC: The World Bank Group. http://www.worldbank.org/en/region/afr/overview. Accessed 22 June 2016.

The World Bank. 2016c. *Data: Sub-Saharan Africa*. Washington DC: The World Bank Group. http://data.worldbank.org/region/sub-saharan-africa. Accessed 22 June 2016.

UNICEF. 2005. *Early Marriage: A Harmful Traditional Practice: A Statistical Exploration 1*.

UNESCO. 2010. World Conference on Education for all: Meeting Basic Needs. *Jomiten, March 5–9*. Jomtien: UNESCO.

Zeleza, Paul Tiyambe. 2015. African Higher Education Summit: Revitalizing Higher Education for Africa's Future. *African Higher Education Summit Framing Paper*, Dakar, March 10–12, Dakar, AAU, 13.

Author Biography

Michael Addaney is a Senior Research and Administrative Assistant at the Quality Assurance and Planning Unit of the University of Energy and Natural Resources in Sunyani, Ghana. Michael's research interests focus on international refugee and human rights law, urbanism and right to the city, decentralisation and waste management, and the role of higher education in Africa's development. Michael has published on selected issues in international refugee and human rights law, conflict transformation and development studies with papers in the South African Yearbook of International Law (2016), Harvard Africa Policy Journal (2016), Asian Development Policy Review (2016) and Thurgood Marshall Law Review (2017). Michael Addaney is a 2015 alumnus of the Human Rights and Democratization Programme at the University of Pretoria, South Africa and also holds an MSc degree in Strategic Planning and Management, Postgraduate Diploma in Education as well as a BSc degree in Development Planning. He is a corporate member of the Ghana Institute of Planners.

CHAPTER 9

The Impact of Education Systems on Our Socioeconomic Realities, Uganda, as a Case Study

Sylvia Ivy Tayebwa

1 Introduction

Education is the "act or process of imparting or acquiring general knowledge, developing the powers of reasoning and judgment, and generally preparing oneself or others intellectually for mature life."[1] Therefore, education imparts knowledge and skills that enable people to realize their full potential and becomes a catalyst for the achievement of other development goals. In its broader perspective, education reduces poverty, boosts job opportunities, and fosters economic prosperity. It also increases people's chances of leading a healthy life, deepens the foundations of democracy, and changes attitudes.

Education's power to accelerate the achievements of wider goals needs to be much better recognized in the post-2015 development framework.[2] Hence, to unlock the wider benefits of education and achieve development goals after 2015, the education that children receive needs to be of good quality so that they actually learn

S.I. Tayebwa (✉)
Social Entrepreneur and Founder of Fruits of Rehab, Kampala, Uganda
e-mail: sylta971@gmail.com

A.C. Onuora-Oguno et al. (eds.), *Education Law, Strategic Policy and Sustainable Development in Africa*, DOI 10.1007/978-3-319-53703-0_9

and acquire the necessary life skills. The African Union's Agenda 2063 titled "The Africa We Want" stresses that Agenda 2063 is "A call for action to all Africans and people of African descent, to take personal responsibility for the destiny of the continent and be the primary agents of change and transformation."[3] This can only be realized if "WE" the African people are well educated and trained to be able to take charge of our own destiny.

In the same spirit, African governments have generally demonstrated the commitment to the education sector because of its critical role in a country's social and economic development, and its sovereignty. Subsequently, Uganda's continuous interest in education is demonstrated through a number of education policy reviews geared toward streamlining the education system in order to meet the country's goals to attain sustainable development. However, even with all these steps in the right direction, Uganda like many African countries, continues to lag behind on the development scene. We continue to see poor access to a basic quality education, poor provision of social services, and high maternal and child mortality rates.

This chapter seeks to bring to the discussion why our education systems do not solve the problems we expect them to solve. By discussing the socioeconomic realities that generally result from the education systems we go through, education policy makers can use the contradictions to create healthier and more effective education systems that offer learners the prospect of more fulfilling and sustainable futures.

The next section provides a brief background of the Ugandan Education System, and the third section pays particular attention to the current social and economic realities in comparison with what is expected of a well-educated society. Finally, in the concluding section, I consider the different approaches in coming up with a strategic plan in terms of curriculum development.

2 Background

Historically, African educational system is characterized by colonial legacy. Most countries on the continent pattern their education systems after systems that were established during the colonial period. In Uganda, for instance, children are at primary school for 7 years (i.e., Primary 1–Primary 7), then continue through secondary school for the next 6 years (Senior 1–Senior 6), and finally join an undergraduate course to shape their future. The system follows a fairly similar pattern to that of its former colonial rule, Britain.

The first form of formal education in Uganda was introduced by missionaries who sought to spread their different religious beliefs; slowly, the catechism classes became formal class rooms and later transformed into schools. The primary aim of these classes was to spread the religious beliefs and colonial rule. Hence, the fundamental principles of this type of education system are obedience and submission, which train the students to do as they are told without asking questions.

Consequently, Ugandans have remained behind on the innovation scene and in the job market because they are best productive when taking instructions.[4] It is in this regard that the postindependence period has been characterized by a number of education policy reviews geared toward streamlining the education system in order to meet the country's need to attain sustainable development.

2.1 National Goal of Education

The national goal of education roots from the 1989 Education Policy Review Commission Report (EPRC) and the 1992 Government White Paper on Education. The 1992 Government White Paper is still the basis for policy in Uganda on which the "Education Sector Strategic Plan 2007 to 2015" is based.[5]

According to the EPRC Report of 1989 and the 1992 Government White Paper on Education, Uganda's education aims are:

1. To promote understanding and appreciation of the value of national unity, patriotism, and cultural heritage, with due consideration of international relations and beneficial interdependence;
2. To inculcate moral, ethical, and spiritual values in the individual and to develop self-discipline, integrity, tolerance, and human fellowship;
3. To inculcate a sense of service, duty, and leadership for participation in civic, social, and national affairs through group activities in educational institutions and the community;
4. To promote scientific, technical and cultural knowledge, skills, and attitudes needed to promote development;
5. To eradicate illiteracy and equip the individual with basic skills, and knowledge to exploit the environment for self-development as well

as national development, for better health, nutrition, and family life, and the capability for continued learning;

6. To contribute to the building of an integrated, self-sustaining, and independent national economy.

Although we cannot say that Uganda has attained these goals, it is time to shift these goals to those which may better propel the nation to a more sustainable future. With globalization[6] and continued dissemination of geographic borderlines, Uganda's education system should yield candidates who are able to compete favorably in a global economy.[7]

Secondly, like many African countries, Uganda has witnessed dramatic growth in the demand for education at all grade levels in recent years. However, getting access to education in the first place can be a huge challenge because of the high levels of poverty. In response to this challenge and "The Millennium Development Goal 2," in 1997, the Ugandan government introduced Universal Primary Education (the idea that all children should be able to attend primary school for free), and in 2007, Universal Secondary Education was also introduced.

Since the introduction of Universal Primary Education (UPE) in 1997, enrollment in primary education tripled from about 2.7 million in 1996 to 8.7 million in 2014.[8] Unfortunately, the demand for free education outstrips the availability of spaces at the free government schools. The key problem in general across Africa is that rapid increase in school participation has come at the cost of quality, contributing to a serious shortfall in the skills necessary for productive employment. This means that for most of the population, especially those that want a higher quality of education, their only option is private schools which also vary enormously in fees and quality. Hence, it is a seemingly impossible task for many children and their families to afford a quality education.

3 Our Social and Economic Realities

3.1 Literacy

Literacy is defined as the ability to read with understanding and write a meaningful sentence in any language.[9] Learning assessments in Africa show that most primary school students still lack basic proficiency in reading at the end of the second or third grade. In several countries, a very large proportion of primary school students are illiterate, and hence, the high investment in free primary education has not translated into learning outcomes, too many children in Primary 3–7 in Uganda are unable to complete Primary 2 level work.[10]

According to another study conducted by Uwezo, only 33% of the pupils evaluated could perform all literacy and numeracy tasks that they were given and more than 70% of Ugandan third graders could not read a single word. Such household surveys that measure numeracy and literacy are consistent with these troubling results. Even children who complete primary school have low levels of basic skills, which indicates that subjecting children to a rigid, segmented, or compartmentalized type of learning situation leaves them no chance for learning, but frustration as noted by a professional magazine produced by the department of professional studies—National Teacher's college, Kyambogo—January, 1977.

Uganda's literacy rate of 73.9% is among the lowest in the world even compared to its neighbours Kenya (78%) and Tanzania (80.3%).[11] Empirical evidence confirms that poor learning outcomes resulting from a few years of low-quality education are consequently producing individuals who are barely literate and numerate and hampering the potential for education to increase productivity even in African economies that have been performing well.

Therefore, if all these studies have been made and reports discussed over the years, how have we ignored the focus on the quality of schooling by emphasizing critical thinking skills and ensuring that our education systems deliver actual learning and life skills development?

3.2 Nutrition and Health

Nutrition and health reports in Uganda have indicated that although the country is well endowed with adequate food supplies, a large proportion of children below 5 (five) years of age are malnourished. For instance, the Uganda National Action Plan 2011–2016 states that about 2.3 million young children in Uganda today are chronically malnourished which clearly indicates that the population is not conversant with which foods to give their children despite the many years of schooling.

Education is one of the most powerful ways of improving people's health. It can save lives of millions of mothers and children; help prevent and contain disease; and also is an essential element in the efforts to reduce malnutrition. Educated people would be better informed about diseases, take preventative measures, recognize signs of illness early, and use healthcare services more often. However, despite its benefits, education is often neglected as a vital health intervention in itself and as a vital means of making other health interventions more effective.

3.3 Population and Fertility Rates

Between 2002 and 2014, Uganda's population increased from 24.2 million to 34.9 million which gives an average annual growth rate of 3.03%. At this rate of growth, the population of Uganda is projected to have increased to 35.0 million in 2015 and will further increase to 47.4 million in 2025.[12] Uganda having the youngest and most rapidly growing populations in the world and a high total fertility rate (TFR) of 6.2, a large percentage of Uganda's population is younger than 15 (52%), which is above Sub-Saharan Africa's average of 43.2%.[13] This situation translates into a high youth dependency ratio that without a proper education will pose a much greater risk in the future.

The experience of the Asian Tigers shows that in order to earn a demographic dividend, countries should prioritize investments in human capital to ensure a healthy and well-educated population; accelerate economic growth and job creation to ensure that the "surplus" labor force is gainfully employed, and the large population has a strong purchasing power; and enforce accountability and efficiency in the use of public resources and delivery of social services.[14] Africa can only harvest from its demographic dividend if her children are taught and encouraged to critically think of ways to better their lives.

3.4 Dropout and Graduation Rates

UNESCO reported that in East Africa, Uganda has a very low primary survival rate of 33% (survival rate being the number of children starting together in Primary 1, progressing through the cycle with their peers still being together when finishing the primary cycle in Primary 7). The primary survival rate in Kenya is 84%, in Tanzania 78%, and in Rwanda 81%.

Dropout rates are highest in Chad (72%), Uganda (68%), and Angola (68%), where more than two out of three children starting primary school are expected to leave before reaching the last grade. Overall, it is estimated that each year of real education a child receives (not repeating a grade) could increase his/her individual earnings by 10% and lift annual GDP globally by 0.37%.[15] Furthermore, the Global Education Digest reveals that Africa has the world's highest dropout rate, and 42% of African school children will leave school early, with about one in six leaving before Grade 2.

However, graduation statistics show that thousands of graduates from Ugandan Universities each year only to find themselves unemployed or underemployed and the ones perceived to be "lucky" are doing odd jobs in European countries. This is because many lack the means, skills, knowledge, or connections to translate their education into productive employment.

Consequently, because the quality of education is often poor, parents are forced to pay for additional tutoring to enable their children to pass tests. Hence, opportunity costs may be even larger, because while they are in school, children forego opportunities to produce income like working on the family farm or selling in the marketplace. Therefore, it is not surprising that when education investments do not result in adequate learning, or even basic literacy and numeracy, parents do not try harder to keep their children in school.

Previously, it was possible to get away with a lot of that lack of focused planning in our education system because the economy was in its infancy and the population was still quite small, so it was still possible to absorb all or most of the available labor force. For example, all graduates coming out of Makerere University in the 1970s, regardless of the qualification, were assured of jobs either in the traditional civil service or in the then flourishing parastatal corporations. The fledgling private sector was also competing to recruit from the same pool, and consequently, there was very little incentive for concerted human capital development because, in terms of skills, it was an employee's market then but things have changed now.

3.5 Poverty and Economic Development

Economic development refers to the structural transformation of human society from a subsistence economy to urban industrialism and to the sustained rise in productivity and the income that result. The transformation is seen in the structure of production, consumption, investment, and trade; in financial and other economic institutions; in occupations, educational levels, health conditions, and rural–urban residence; and in people's perceptions of the social and natural worlds and of their own agency.[16]

Regrettably, Uganda is classified by the UN as one of 48 least developed countries, which are characterized by low per capita incomes, feeble human capital, and a high degree of economic vulnerability[17] despite the country's success in increasing the school enrollment levels. These trends indicate that schooling is not necessarily learning, and deep deficiencies in the quality of education mean that the effect of schooling on productivity is far below its potential. The poor quality of education directly constrains productivity and hinders individuals from acquiring new skills. Consequently, a few years of low-quality basic education will not confer much of a gain in productivity if students are never encouraged to use their critical thinking skills in order to reach their full potential.

3.6 Employment and Unemployment

Uganda illustrates the employment challenge of many Sub-Saharan African countries. As a country with one of the youngest and fastest growing populations in the world, many young Ugandans enter the labor market each year. For example, the total labor force almost doubled from approximately 7.5 million in 1990 to around 14.5 million in 2012. Yet employment growth has only just kept pace, increasing at 2.96% versus a 3.1% growth in the labor force.[18]

More broadly, we see that as much as two-thirds of the young population are underutilized in some developing economies, meaning they are unemployed, in irregular employment, most likely in the informal sector or neither in the labor force nor in education or training.[19] And according to the Uganda National Household Survey 2012/2013, up to three-quarters of recent entrants to the labor market are employed by themselves or their families; hence, with the limited job creation in the formal sector, most take up informal employment or become underemployed. The 2009/2010 Uganda National Household Survey revealed that the unemployment rate was at 4.2% in 2009/2010 compared to 1.9% in 2005/2006. Although unemployment rates still appear low, these rates mask the scarcity of formal job opportunities.

Unemployment for Ugandan youths stands at more than 65% and the rate of underemployment is high.[20] This situation in Uganda is connected to a UNESCO report that states that "Although the current generation of Africans entering the labor force is the most educated ever, many are finding that their prospects for employment and earnings differ very little from those of their parents," and in a few countries like Uganda, they are worse.[21]

In a 2010 Economic Report of Africa entitled, "Promoting High Level sustainable growth to reduce unemployment in Africa," the United Nations Economic Forum for Africa noted that African countries can pursue several short-term and long-term policies to achieve the needed structural transformation that generates high growth with increased employment creation. These policies should be based on a comprehensive development planning framework that embodies well-designed and well-implemented macroeconomic and sectoral strategies. Regrettably, there is currently no dedicated strategy in place to achieve Ugandas employment-related goals[22]; however, high unemployment rates in Uganda are attributed to the poor education system we adopted as a country that is regarded as elitist, academic oriented, and less practical.[23]

3.7 Productivity

The World Bank and UMACIS study (2004) which ranks Uganda's labor productivity as the lowest among its Sub-Saharan African neighbours in terms of value added per worker in US($) from an average firm size (Uganda 1085; Tanzania 2016; Zambia 2680; Kenya 3457) suggests that low educational achievement and limited skills contribute to difficult transitions into work and limited employment mobility among African youth.

As seen by the massive expansion in access to education, which is adding many years of schooling (repetition of some classes), but much less learning, during childhood and youth, these deep deficiencies in the quality of education mean that the effect of schooling on productivity is far below its potential. This poor quality of education directly constrains productivity and hinders individuals from acquiring new skills. Consequently, a few years of low-quality basic education will not confer much of a gain in productivity, if students are never encouraged to use their critical thinking skills in order to reach their full potential.

Furthermore, "The East African Community Common Market Protocol" that came into force on July 1, 2010, further justifies the case for intensifying skills development, because labor productivity will become more important in determining the employability of workers, given the larger labor pool available to employers, when labor moves freely within the Common Market. Hence, rapid improvements in the quality of learning provided in school are critical to increase the productivity and earnings of our youth.

3.8 Gross Development Product (GDP) and Industrial Development

Uganda's industrial sector, representing 25.1% of GDP, grew the fastest in 2013, at an estimated rate of 6.8%. This growth primarily reflected the strong performance of the manufacturing, electricity supply, and construction segments of the economy. The manufacturing sector accounts for 8.1% of GDP. Then, the services sector, accounting for 45.7% of GDP and employing 13% of the Ugandan workforce, followed with an estimated growth rate of 4.8%.[24]

Potential employment creation opportunities are emerging as the Ugandan economy continues to grow, particularly driven by the construction and service sectors, with rural infrastructure investments, increasing Internet connectivity, online companies, trade, tourism, and commerce all offering new opportunities and the tools to participate in global value chains in all sectors. Capitalizing on these opportunities and encouraging investment to create more and better jobs will not be easy because the capacity to translate growth into productive employment depends greatly on the economy's capacity to create jobs in productive and employment-intensive sectors, which should start with a good education foundation.

If schooling provides neither the financial literacy students will need to manage the meager resources under their control, nor the guidance needed to create opportunities for securing a livelihood or building wealth, that means schooling provides little assistance to promote the physical health needed for economic stability and quality of life. These realizations are especially troubling because they suggest that school leavers have a fragile foundation on which to build more specialized skills.

Improvements in curriculum content with an emphasis on critical thinking will lay the foundation for improvements in productivity. At the same time, it will maximize young people's chances of transitioning successfully to remunerative employment; complementary actions like eliminating corruption are also required to improve the business environment and develop human capital. For example, the Korean education curriculum content is being reduced by 20% to allow more time for student-centered activities and conceptual understanding of topics covered as well as decreasing the student's workload. Components like "character building" will also be added to develop a better-rounded student.[25]

Youth joblessness also implies missed opportunities in the human resources to produce goods and services.

3.9 *Brain Drain*

Uganda, like many African countries, suffers a great deal of brain drain, and every year thousands of graduates leave their African countries in search of greener pastures in European countries only to end up doing odd jobs as opposed to building their economies back home. However, whenever this argument comes up, it is usually downplayed by the statistics of diaspora remittances. For example, the UNDP Uganda annual report of 2014 reported that diaspora remittances into Uganda contribute significantly to the country's foreign exchange earnings and are also one of the major sources of investment capital and consumption. The report further says that in 2014, remittances were estimated at $900 million, an increment from $873 million in 2013. Looking at such reports blinds us at the opportunity cost of losing our human capital to developed countries.

We should ensure that our education system is able to retain its products in order to attain sustainable development.

3.10 *Cultural Independence*

Culture can be defined as the sum total of the ways in which a society preserves, identifies, organizes, sustains, and expresses itself.[26] Culture is a defining feature of a person's identity, contributing to how they value themselves among others; it also shapes a person's thinking, behavior, and the way one looks at the rest of the world.

Language is a fundamental aspect of cultural identity, as a means of communicating values, beliefs, and customs. It is an important social function that fosters feelings of group identity and solidarity; hence, it is the means by which culture and its traditions and shared values may be conveyed and preserved. However, the long years of schooling in our education system using the English language have resulted in losing our local languages and loss of language means loss of culture and identity. In many societies throughout history, the suppression of the languages of minority groups has been used as a deliberate policy in order to suppress those minority cultures. As a result, a large number of the world's languages have been lost with the processes of colonization and migration.

With an education system that promotes the British culture as opposed to the indigenous cultures, we start to see our social structure disintegrating and in turn our economies failing because the educated citizens lack a sense of belonging in their own cultures. Therefore, it is important to preserve our cultures using our education system, for example, the Masai School in Kenya called Ekiteng Lepa School.[27]

4 Conclusion

As the above review of Uganda's socioeconomic realities illustrates that most discussions and evidence of the low quality of education focus on the school system and the lack of emphasis on critical thinking in its curriculum, many youths and adults in Uganda and Africa at large have had little or no access to proper education, yet the attention and resources given to literacy and skills development programs are much lower than what is given to schooling.

When such programs receive emphasis, it tends to be on the expansion of provision of education rather than on the quality of education, and hence, policy makers should put focus on school projects and research to be mainstreamed through out the national curriculum in order to change the trend.

Policy makers should also realize that what students in impoverished regions need are not more academic skills, but rather life skills that enable them to improve their financial prospects and well-being. These include financial literacy and entrepreneurial skills; health maintenance and management skills; and administrative capabilities, such as teamwork, problem-solving, and project management.

Although schools in Uganda have begun to include entrepreneurship and health topics in their curricular requirements especially in secondary schools, including information in basic lectures is not enough. Schools must simultaneously adopt action-oriented tutorial approaches that hone critical thinking skills and enable children to identify problems, seek out and evaluate relevant information and resources, design and carry out plans for solving these problems. This involves tackling real problems that require and empower students to take the initiative and responsibility for their own learning.

Most importantly, African and government policy makers should realize that the best way for Africa to reverse the trend is to set very long-term goals and be committed to pursue them passionately as demonstrated by the South Korean Success Story in Mathematical Education in a report by Fary Sami of Harford Community College.

Finally, the dissemination of research information to the public should be revised and social media recognized more of its ability to reach a lot of the population more easily.

Notes

1. www.dictionary.com/browse/education.
2. UNESCO EFA Global Monitoring Report 2013/2014—Teaching and learning: Achieving quality for all.
3. http://agenda2063.au.int/en/vision; http://www.nepad.org/system/files/Agenda%202063%20%20English.pdf.
4. https://www.youtube.com/watch?v=Orq4Tudqc8w.
5. The Political Economy of the Education Sector Policy Reform in Uganda by Pamela K. Mbabazi, PHD Jacklyn Makaaru Arinaitwe, PHD Godber Tumushabe.
6. Globalization described as the reality shaped by an increasingly integrated world economy, new information and communications technology (ICT), the emergence of an international knowledge network, the role of the English language, and other forces beyond the control of academic institutions.
7. The Political Economy of the Education Sector Policy Reform in Uganda by Pamela K. Mbabazi, PHD Jacklyn Makaaru Arinaitwe, PHD Godber Tumushabe.
8. Uganda Bureau of Statistics 2014 Statistical Abstract, page 18 (Uganda Bureau of Statistics 2014a).
9. Uganda Bureau of Statistics 2014 Statistical Abstract, page 24 (Uganda Bureau of Statistics 2014a).
10. Uwezo Uganda Report, 2015 (Uganda Bureau of Statistics 2015).
11. https://en.wikipedia.org/wiki/List_of_countries_by_literacy_rate.
12. National Population and Housing Census 2014—Uganda Bureau of Statistics (Uganda Bureau of Statistics 2014b).
13. Africa Development Indicators (ADI) 2008/2009, focusing on the youth and employment in Africa.
14. Population secretariat, 2014.

15. http://www.unesco.org/new/en/dakar/aboutthisoffice/singleview/news/42_of_african_school_children_will_drop_out_before_the_end_of_primary_education.
16. https://researchgate.net/publication/253441933_Population_and_development.
17. UNCTAD Least Developed Country Report, 2015 (UNCTAD 2015).
18. World Bank Report (2014).
19. ILO report—Global Employment Trends for Youth 2013—A Generation at Risk (ILO 2013).
20. State of Uganda Population Report 2014 (UNFPA 2014).
21. UNESCO report on youth and skills, "working below the poverty line is a much more widespread phenomenon than not working at all" 2012.
22. Uganda's Employment Challenge Report of November 2014 by the Economic Development Policy and Research Department, Ministry of Finance, Planning and Economic Development (The Economic Development Policy and Research Department 2014).
23. http://www.newvision.co.ug/new_vision/news/1324251/uganda-education-overhaul#sthash.ANKytx7n.dpuf.
24. Uganda Bureau of Statistics 2014 Statistical Abstract.
25. South Korea, A success story in Mathematical Education by Fary Sami, page 25.
26. The Uganda National Cultural Policy (2006).
27. http://thebranch.info/masai-school/.

Bibliography

Africa Development Indicators (ADI) 2008/2009. Focusing on the Youth and Employment in Africa.

1989 Education Policy Review Commission Report (EPRC).

http://thebranch.info/masai-school/.

http://www.newvision.co.ug/new_vision/news/1324251/uganda-education-overhaul#sthash.ANKytx7n.dpuf.

http://www.unesco.org/new/en/dakar/aboutthisoffice/singleview/news/42_of_african_school_children_will_drop_out_before_the_end_of_primary_education.

https://en.wikipedia.org/wiki/List_of_countries_by_literacy_rate.

https://www.mnnonline.org/news/uganda-has-highest-school-drop-out-rate-in-east-africa/.

https://www.unido.org>Pub_free>Productivity_Performance_in_DCs_Uganda.pdf.

ILO. 2013. Report-Global Employment Trends for Youth 2013-A Generation at Risk.

Population Secretariet. 2014.

Sekiwu, Denis, and Botha M.M. 2014. Education as a Public Good: Justification and Avenues of Values Integration into Management of Ugandan School discipline. *Global Educational Research Journal* 2 (10): 195–208, ISSN-2360-7963.

South Korea, A success story in Mathematical Education by Fary Sami.

The 1992 Government White Paper on Education.

The Economic Development Policy and Research Department. 2014. Ministry of Finance, Planning and Economic Development—Uganda's Employment Challenge Report of November, 2014.

The Uganda National Cultural Policy. 2006.

Tumushabe Godber, Jacklyn M. Arinaitwe and Pamela K. Mbabazi. The Political Economy of the Education Sector Policy Reform in Uganda.

Uganda Bureau of Statistics. 2014a. Statistical Abstract.

Uganda Bureau of Statistics. 2014b. National Population and Housing Census 2014.

Uganda Bureau of Statistics. 2015. Statistical Abstract.

Uganda National Action Plan 2011–2016.

UNCTAD. 2015. Least Developed Country Report, 2015.

UNESCO Report on Youth and Skills. 2012. Working Below the Poverty Line is a much more Widespread Phenomenon than not Working at all.

UNESCO, EFA Global Monitoring Report 2013/2014. Teaching and learning: Achieving Quality for all.

UNFPA. 2014. State of Uganda Population Report 2014. Harnessing Uganda's Demographic Dividend for Socio-Economic Transformation. https://researchgate.net/publication/253441933_Population_and_development.

Uwezo Uganda Report. 2015. 5th Uwezo Annual Learning Assessment.

World Bank Report 2014.

World Bank. 2013. The Second Uganda Economic Update. August 2013.

www.guardian.com>...>Development>Employment/feb102015.

Author Biography

Sylvia Ivy Tayebwa is a Social Entrepreneur and Founder of Fruits of Rehab—a non-governmental organization in Uganda, which aims at giving people who have gone through traumatic experiences in their lives (e.g. ex-convicts) a platform to demonstrate that they have been rehabilitated and are now better and productive members of the society through innovative means of economic empowerment.

CHAPTER 10

African Union Agenda 2063: Aspiring for Justice and the Rule of Law in Liberia

Veronica Fynn Bruey

1 Introduction

1.1 Overview

Having centralized collective efforts on decolonization, struggle against apartheid and acquisition of political independence in the last 50 years, the African Union (AU) envisions "an integrated, prosperous and peaceful Africa, driven by its own citizens, representing a dynamic force in international arena". In accomplishing this vision, on 13 May 2013, the African Union declares *Agenda* 2063 *Vision: The Africa We Want*, which is "a global strategy to optimise use of Africa's resources for the benefits of all Africans". The African Union's *Agenda 2063 Vision* identifies seven aspirations, which reflects the continent's collective desire for women and children to maximize their full potential without fear, disease and want. Aspiration #3 anticipates "an Africa of good governance, democracy, respect for human rights, justice and the rule of law". As a State recovering from a 14-year civil war, encumbered with numerous social,

V.F. Bruey (✉)
Journal of Internal Displacement, Monrovia, Liberia
e-mail: veronica.fynn@anu.edu.au

A.C. Onuora-Oguno et al. (eds.), *Education Law, Strategic Policy and Sustainable Development in Africa*, DOI 10.1007/978-3-319-53703-0_10

political and legal setbacks, the goal of this chapter is to critically assess Liberia's ability to realistically achieve Aspiration #3 based on the recommendations of the Liberia Truth and Reconciliation Commission Report released in 2009.

The chapter begins with a conceptual overview of the rule of law, exploring global, regional and sub-regional perspectives. Following is an analysis of the African Union's law-making history in testing the viability of Agenda 2063. Six key legal instruments, relating to forced migration, human rights and children and women's rights, are applied to track the integrity, accountability and enforceability of the rule of law within the African Union. The chapter further examines Liberia's progress towards achieving Aspiration #3 as a post-war recovery State, juxtaposed against the main attributes of the rule of law: access to justice, exercise of power (arbitrariness) and public confidence. Using case examples referenced in the Truth and Reconciliation Commission Report, an appraisal of the justice system is carried out to evaluate Liberia's capacity to achieve Aspiration #3 of Agenda 2063. In concluding and making recommendation, the chapter explores opportunities that post-war Liberia could explore for augmenting the rule of law and challenges it must overcome in order to effect the implementation of Agenda 2063.

1.2 Global Perspectives on the Rule of Law

With a reasonable degree of certainty, it can be agreed that the rule of law is a fundamental principle of governance, firmly established in the constitution of western democracies.[1] On the contrary, the same cannot be said for the definition of this "exceedingly elusive global idea, which give rise to rampant divergence of understandings".[2] As an "essentially contested concept"[3] that is "notoriously difficult to define and measure",[4] there is no single consensus on the definition of the term,[5] but rather contrasting convictions of what it actually is.[6] The preamble of the *Charter of the United Nations* 1945 enshrines the concept of the rule of law stating that "we the peoples of the United Nations determined to establish conditions under which justice and respect for the obligations arising from treaties and other sources of international law can be maintained…"[7] The preamble of the *Universal Declaration of Human Rights* 1949 also upholds the rule of law, "[w]hereas it is essential, if man is not to be compelled to have recourse, as a last resort, to rebellion against tyranny and oppression, that human rights should be protected by the rule of law".[8] The United Nations Secretary General refers to the rule of law as:

> a principle of governance in which all persons, institutions and entities, public and private, including the State itself, are accountable to laws that are publicly promulgated, equally enforced and independently adjudicated, and which are consistent with international human rights norms and standards. It requires, as well, measures to ensure adherence to the principles of supremacy of law, equality before the law, accountability to the law, fairness in the application of the law, separation of powers, participation in decision-making, legal certainty, avoidance of arbitrariness and procedural and legal transparency.[9]

On a unique occasion of the 67th Session of the UN General Assembly's High-level Meeting on the Rule of Law on 24 September 2012, Member States (including Liberia) committed to strengthening the rule of law, recognizing "that the rule of law applies to all States equally…and to that respect for and promotion of the rule of law and justice should guide all of their activities".[10]

Arguably, the World Justice Project purports that the rule of law is a system derived from an internationally accepted standard based on "universal" (or Western) principles.[11] These universal principles are: (1) the government and individuals are accountable; (2) even application of the law; (3) enactment process is fair and accessible; and (4) justice is delivered timely and by competent representatives. The Rule of Law Index,[12] complemented by the Open Government Index,[13] is a tool devised by the World Justice Project to capture performance indicators within a simple and coherent framework for measuring the extent to which countries attain performance indicators of the above universal principles. For the World Justice Project's Rule of Law Index, 2015, apart from Botswana (ranked at 31), Ghana (ranked at 34), South Africa (ranked at 36) and Senegal (ranked at 38), all other African countries (17 in total) are ranked at 43 or higher. Save rankings for those African countries that are not listed (i.e. a total of 34 countries). Precisely, Liberia scores 83 out of the 102 countries ranked on the Rule of Law Index.[14]

1.3 (Sub)-Regional Perspectives

Despite many challenges with measuring the rule of law, for example, "aggregating too many discrete elements into a single overarching concept",

Tom Ginsburg argues that the World Justice Project's Rule of Law Index addresses some of the measurement problems[15] by surveying some 100,000 household and experts in all of the 102 countries ranked in 2015.[16] To the end, the African Union, as a regional hub for leadership and governance, is obligated to safeguard the rights of its citizens under international law in partnership with other sub-regional organizations such as the Economic Community of West African States (ECOWAS),[17] the Southern African Development Community (SADC)[18] and the East African Community (EAC).[19] Relevance to this chapter is efforts made by the United Nations Security Council (UNSC) to assist sub-regional bodies such as ECOWAS in implementing its mandate. In a letter dated 23 December 2013, the President of the UN Security Council extended the function of the UN Office for West Africa[20] for another three years from 1 January 2014 to 31 December 2016.[21] While it is unclear whether the UN Office of West Africa would continue its role after 31 December 2016, within the stipulated period mentioned above, the UN Office for West Africa reports twice per year in the areas of "good offices, enhancing sub-regional capacities to address cross-border and cross-cutting threats to peace and security, and promoting good governance, respect for the rule of law, human rights and gender mainstreaming".[22]

1.4 *Theoretical Concepts of the Rule of Law (Access to Justice, Rule of Law)*

In his groundbreaking work, "The Rule of Law" (2010), Lord Tom Bingham boldly admits that his perspective on the rule of law is neither "comprehensive" nor "universally applicable", but rather a general exploration of the concept.[23] Having suggested eight core principles[24] that characterize the rule of law, Bingham attempts to define the rule of law as: "that all persons and authorities within the State, whether public or private, should be bound by and entitled to the benefit of laws publicly made, taking effect (generally) in the future and publicly administered in the courts".[25]

Stripped of all its technicalities, the rule of law simply means that government in all its actions is bound by rules fixed and announced beforehand.[26] Joseph Raz characterizes the rule of law as both a virtue of the legal system and a political ideal by which it is to be judged.[27] Thus, if the rule of law is not the rule of good law, then the term may lack any useful function. As the purpose of establishing the rule of law is to maintain conditions, which will uphold dignity of individuals, so then is the rule of law required to recognize and maintain civil, political, social, economic, educational and cultural rights of individuals.[28] When the rule of law is understood to mean that the government is limited by the law from infringing a cluster of rights, Edward Palmer Thomson aptly describes it as "a cultural achievement of universal significance"[29] while Brian Tamanaha coins it as the "universal human good".[30]

Raz cautions that "[t]he law can violate people's dignity in many ways".[31] For example, the law may institute slavery, racial discrimination, oppress minority groups or perpetuate sexual violence against girls and women without necessarily violating the rule of law. To this end, Raz argues that "[o]bserving the rule of law by no means guarantees that such violations do not occur".[32] It is with Raz's caveat, inter alia, that the United Nations, alongside the World Justice Project, resolves to devise a litmus test for assessing, operationalizing and implementing the rule of law as stated above. Thus, in efforts to strengthen the "rule of law" especially in developing countries that are emerging from conflict (such as Liberia), the United Nations published the "Rule of Law Indicators: Implementation Guide and Project Tools" in 2011.[33] In a nutshell, the rule of law indicators is a tool for monitoring changes in the performance and fundamental characteristics of the justice system in post-conflict situations.

Although common to Bingham's eight characteristics,[34] the United Nations' rule of law indicators[35] and the World Justice Project Rule of Law Index[36] are themes of accessibility of the law; equality before the law; transparency and accountability of government; fairness and access to justice; arbitrariness, discretion and exercise of power by authority; fundamental human rights; administration, management and competency of legal personnel and public confidence in the law; Peter Shivute[37] presents as critical viewpoint pertinent to customary Indigenous law perspectives in Africa.

Shivute doubtlessly embraces the crucial role that the rule of law plays in "safeguarding arbitrary and capricious governance and abuse of power, and to enforce limitations on the power of the State and all its institutions of government". Proposing that separation of power between the executive, legislature and judiciary is the emblem of the rule of law, Shivute argues that the constitution is a solid foundation upon which free and democratic States uphold, protect and promote of human rights and good governance.[38] However, rising number of civil unrest, corruption and lack of decentralized government services constrain access to justice for all. For example, lack of the formal justice systems in most of rural Africa compels rural dwellers to resort to Indigenous customary law, which may not necessarily conform to the universal principle of the rule of law, even though such traditions are the important sources of law.[39] Hence, Peter Ntephe, in his PhD thesis, asks whether sub-Saharan Africa needs a new kind of rule of law?[40] Adopting the Afrocentric critique of modern law, Ntephe references "coups and corruption to demonstrate that the absence of systemic fidelity to modern law in Africa, the [rule of law] orthodoxy is futile".[41] While making a case for an alternative to modern law in Africa,[42] Ntephe concludes that although "African customary law simultaneously endures and produce diverse legal cultures, it continuously undermines the successful implementation of modern law in Africa". Thus, "a form of law that is different from modern law should align with the peculiar rationalities at the core of African social realities".[43]

It is against this backdrop that Liberia's potential to achieve Aspiration #3 of the African Union's Agenda 2063 is considered in the specific context of the Liberia Truth and Reconciliation Commission Report, 2009. As monitoring and evaluation of the rule of law indicators are meant for collaborative implementation with (sub)-regional institutions and national governments,[44] the next session of this chapter first assesses the law-making process of the African Union with respect to implementation and enforcement in Member States, especially Liberia.

2 African Union and the Africa 2063 Agenda: Assessing Law-Making

Not only is Liberia a founding member of the Organization of Africa Union (OAU) (now the African Union (AU)), but also that the birthing of the OAU[45] took place on the soils of Africa's oldest republic, Liberia.[46] Prior to the signing of the OAU Charter on 25 May 1963 by Heads of States and Government of 30 independent nations in Africa,[47] there was the *Sanniquellie Declaration*.[48] Amidst disputes between newly independent African States concerning the philosophical ideology of the concept of pan-Africanism, William V. S. Tubman (then President of Liberia), Kwame Nkrumah (then President of Ghana) and Ahmed Sékou Touré (then President of Guinea) convened the Sanniquellie Conference in Nimba, Liberia on 19 July 1959.[49] Dubbed as the Monrovia Group[50] (as opposed to the Casablanca Group),[51] the Sanniquellie Conference[52] formulates six principles for the achievement of The Community of Independent African States. A key component of the Community of Independent African States' principle is that

> [e]ach State and federation, which is a member of the Community, shall maintain its own national identity and constitutional structure. The Community is being formed with a view to achieving unity among independent African States. It is not designed to prejudice the present or future international policies, relations and obligations of the States involved.[53]

In spite of the quarrels and rivalries, the *OAU Charter* 1963 which established the pan-African organization, entrenches seven fundamental principles of all Member States: (1) equal sovereignty of all Member States; (2) respect for sovereignty and territorial integrity; (3) inalienable right to independent existence; (4) peaceful settlement of disputes; (5) unreserved condemnation of political assassination; (6) absolute dedication to the total emancipation of African territories; and (7) non-alignment with regard to all power blocs. Challenges with accomplishing the objectives of the OAU,[54] through led to the *Sirte Declaration* 1999, setting the stage for the newly established (AU) with the vision of accelerating the process of integration in Africa, supporting the empowerment of the African States in the global economy and addressing the conglomerate of socio-economic and political problems facing the continent.[55]

Transitioning from the OAU to the AU, the *African Union Constitutive Act* 2000, building on the OAU Charter 1963, transposes the above principles using contemporary languages such as "interdependence among Member States", "non-interference in Member States internal affairs", "participation of the African peoples in the activities of the union", "promotion of self-reliance, gender equality and social justice", among others. Thus, having centralized collective efforts on decolonization, struggle against apartheid and acquisition of political independence in the last 50 years through the auspices of the OAU, the (AU) envisions "an integrated, prosperous and peaceful Africa, driven by its own citizens, representing a dynamic force in international arena". In accomplishing this vision, on 13 May 2013, the African Union declares *Agenda 2063 Vision: The Africa We Want*,[56] which is "a global strategy to optimise use of Africa's resources for the benefits of all Africans". The African Union's *Agenda 2063 Vision* identifies seven aspirations, which reflects the continent's collective desire for women and children to maximize their full potential without fear, disease and want.

Over the years, the OAU/AU has contributed immensely towards shaping the trajectory of international law by way of protecting rights. Without a doubt, the Member States of the African Union are making great strides to remedy the deficiency of the OAU. In particular, the AU recognizes the interconnection between democracy, the rule of law and good governance.[57] In 2002, the New Partnership for Africa's Development (NEPAD), a pan-African strategic framework for the socio-economic development of the continent, was set up to coordinate pace and impact regarding civil and political rights. More recently, *Agenda 2063* (2013), specifically Aspiration #3, expands on effective implementation of good governance, the rule of law and respect for justice. Three major areas that the OAU/AU has been instrumental in safeguarding rights are (1) forced migration, (2) human rights and (3) children and women's rights.

2.1 Forced Migration

At the time, when the UN *Convention Relating to the Status of Refugees* 1951 (hereafter the UN Refugee Convention) provided little or no protection for Africans forced to leave their places habitual residence "owing to external aggression, occupation, foreign domination or events seriously disturbing public order in either part or the whole of his country of origin or nationality, ...", the OAU created its very own *Convention Governing the Specific Aspects of Refugee Problems in Africa* 1969 (hereafter, the African Refugee Convention). As newly independent States emerging from colonial rule, it made sense for the OAU to broaden the legal definition of a refugee beyond the temporal and geographical restrictions the UN Refugee Convention imposed. Unfortunately, since 1969, in blatant violation of the *OAU Charter* 1963 and later the *AU Constitutive Act* 2002, there were a total of 188 successful and failed military *coups d'états* in Africa between 1956 and 2001.[58] Bethany Lacina and Nils Gleditsch[59] and Anke Hoeffler[60] suggest that between 1960 and 2002, approximately 1.55 million people were killed in battle in Africa alone, accounting for 40% of the global total (i.e. 3.86 million deaths). By the end of 2015, sub-Saharan Africa hosted 4.4 million

(27%) of the UNHCR's mandated 16.1 million refugees.[61] With rising death tolls and unabating violent conflict, the AU leads international law-making by creating yet another ground-breaking instrument, the AU *Convention for the Protection and Assistance of Internally Displaced Persons in Africa* 2009 (hereafter the *Kampala Convention*). Six years after the *Kampala Convention*, sub-Saharan Africa accounts for 11.9 million (29%) of the 40.8 million people displaced internally.[62] Although 40 and 25 Member States have signed and ratified the Kampala Convention, respectively, domesticating into national law is but a far-fetched goal. Post-war Liberia has neither ratified nor domesticated the *Kampala Convention.*

2.2 *Human Rights*

Since the OAU Charter 1963 imposed no specific duties on Member States to protect human rights, followed by subsequent hostility of some African States toward embracing the idea of regional human rights protection, the President of The Gambia convened two ministerial conferences on 8–15 June 1980 and 7–19 January 1981, where the draft *African Charter on Human and Peoples' Rights* (also known as The Banjul Charter) was adopted and later submitted to the OAU.[63] A point of interest here is that a preliminary draft of the African Charter was prepared during the 16th Ordinary Session of the Assembly of Heads of States and Government from 17 to 20 July 1979. However, it was at the *18th Ordinary Session of the Assembly of the Heads of State and Government* on 27 June 1981 that the Banjul Charter was adopted and entered into force on 21 October 1986. Considering the virtues of African historical tradition and civilization (see the Preamble), the Banjul Charter, stipulates essential attributes of the rule of law that "[e] very individual shall be equal before the law" (Article 3(1)) and "[e] very individual shall be entitled to equal protection of the law" (Article 3(2). A culmination of two years' work (1979–1981), Richard Gittleman describes the Banjul Charter as a "history step toward the protection of human rights in Africa"[64] and Luis Gabriel Franceshi's as an "original and innovative instrument in the field of human rights".[65] All 55 African States (with exception of South Sudan) have ratified the Banjul Charter. To complement and reinforce the function of the African Commission on Human and Peoples' Rights in protecting and promoting human rights as well as interpreting the Banjul Charter, Article 1 of the Protocol of the Banjul Charter established the African Court on Human and Peoples' Rights (hereafter the African Court) in June 1998.

The African Court never came into existence and was later merged with the AU Court of Justice[66] under Article 28 of the Protocol on the Statute of the African Court of Justice adopted by AU Assembly of Heads of States and Government in July 2008. Although the Protocol establishing the merged single court, called African Court of Justice and Human Rights should stop both the African Court and the Court of Justice from operating, the African Court still in use, while the African Court of Justice and Human Rights has yet to enter into force. Notwithstanding is novelty, the African Union human rights regime, the African Court has been criticized for being a "toothless bulldog"[67] owing to its ineffectiveness and lack of ability to enforce its decision. Based on the strongly worded language (such as sovereignty and non-interference) used in the *Constitutive Act* 2000, it is not surprising that as at February 2016, only seven (Liberia not included) of the thirty States Parties to the African Charter on Human and Peoples' Right Protocol which established the African Court, have recognized the competence of the African Court to receive cases from non-governmental organizations and individuals. Of the 90 non-advisory cases received by the Court since its creation, 60 are pending, four transferred to the African Commission, three against non-State entities and 23 are finalized. Liberia has yet to submit a contentious and advisory case to the African Court. Nonetheless, the Economic Community of West African States Court of Justice (hereafter the Community Court of Justice)[68] may offer some hope[69] to Liberia given the first[70] submission of Liberians[71] to the Community Court of Justice in 2015. Noteworthy, since 2004, the Community Court of Justice has decided a total of 114 cases, peaking at 28 cases in 2015 alone.[72]

2.3 Children and Women's Rights

Aspiration #6 of the Africa 2063 Agenda places a central focus on women stating that development of the Africa we want should be relied on and driven by its people "…especially its women and youth, and caring for children".[73] Two important pieces of instruments forms the bedrock of Aspiration #6: (1) the *African Charter on the Rights and Welfare of the Child*, (hereafter the African Children Charter) and (2) the *Protocol to the African Charter on Human and Peoples' Rights on the Rights of*

Women in Africa, 2003 (hereafter Maputo Protocol). The *African Children Charter* was adopted by the OAU 11 July 1990 and entered into force on 29 November 1999. To date, 46 of 55 AU Member States have ratified the *African Children Charter*. Subject to Article 32–46 of the African Children Charter, the African Committee of Experts on the Rights and Welfare of the Children (Committee of Experts) was established in 2002 to promote, protect, monitor the implementation and interpret the rights enshrined in the Charter. Highlighted achievements of the Committee of Experts include strengthening institutional structures, holding thematic discussions, celebrating the Day of the African Child and investigating Northern Uganda on the State of children in its conflict. Although Liberia has signed and ratified the *African Children* Charter, it is estimated that some 15,000 children fought alongside Charles Taylor's war between 1989 and 1987.[74] Coupled with suffering with all kinds of atrocities, sexual violence, disruption of school and forced displacement, a UNHCR report 2003 asserts that one out of every 10 Liberian children may have been recruited in the civil war.[75] Research conducted by Bosede Awodola (2012) argues that efforts to reintegrate thousands of former Liberian child soldiers in need of economic empowerment and psychological support is challenged by ineffective follow up mechanisms by implementing agencies.[76]

The Maputo Protocol, adopted on 11 July 2003 in Maputo, Mozambique, is appended to the African Charter. Defining "women as persons of female gender, including girls", the Maputo Protocol is closely linked to the African Children's Charter (*see* Article 1(k) of the Maputo Protocol). The Maputo Protocol owes much of its existence to the Women in Law and Development in Africa (WiLDAF), who spearheaded its drafting and signing to address lack of respect for women's human rights in Africa. To date, 36 AU Member States have signed and ratified the Maputo Protocol (NB: Liberia has signed and ratified). Women's rights guaranteed under the Maputo Protocol is legally binding and comprehensive, ranging from elimination of all forms of discrimination (Article 2), elimination of harmful practices (Article 5), participation in political decision-making process (Article 9), protection in armed conflicts (Article 11) and control over their reproductive health rights (Article 14). By virtue of the African Charter, individuals can bring complaints to the African Court on Human and Peoples Rights (Article 27); however, Frans Viljoen critiques that, "such complaints have only been invoked in a few instances and then only tangentially to other more prominent allegations".[77] For example, Benjamin de Carvalho and Niels Nagelhus Schia report that on a monthly basis, over 50 cases of rape are reported yet only a few are sent to court.[78] At this juncture, one cannot help but question: Given the persistent threat to human rights protection and access to justice, what benefit is there, if any at all, to developing beautifully worded instruments that lack capacity to be implemented and enforced?

3 Achieving Aspiration #3: The Truth and Reconciliation Commission of Liberia

There is a parable which States that a fish starts to rot from its head. It follows that if the African Union struggles continuously with enforcing and implementing its law, what more can be expected of post-war Liberia with regards to achieving of Aspiration #3? As Raz bluntly puts it, "there is no possibility of practicing good governance if there is not systematic installation of the rule of law. There is no validation of the rule of law if it has no normative consequences. Precisely, the rule of law is not legally valid if there is no legal system in force".[79] To this end, the viability of Liberia achieving Aspiration #3 of the African 2063 agenda is assessed within the context of the Truth and Reconciliation Report, 2008. But first consider a rough overview of Liberia's civil war.

Liberia is Africa's oldest republic founded by former slave settlers from the USA in the 1800s. Declaring its independence on 16 July 1847, former slave setters sought freedom and sovereignty as an independent State possessing all the rights, powers and functions of government.[80] Unfortunately, 133 years after independence, political unrest culminating into a 14-year civil war resulted in the deaths of over 250,000 people and uprooted approximately 1.3 million people,[81] with women and girls disproportionately impacted.[82] To this effect, Article XIII of the Accra *Comprehensive Peace Agreement* (CPA) 2003 paved the way for post-war recovery in Liberia. Following was the historic election of the first female president in Africa in 2005, Ellen Johnson Sirleaf.[83] Then came the arrest of former president, Charles Taylor in 2006 by the International Criminal Court, on suspicion of war crimes committed in Sierra Leone.[84] During her leadership (2005–present), President Johnson-Sirleaf struck an impressive list of milestone-making enormous strides in Liberia's post-war recovery, including revising Liberia's Penal

Code to provide for gang rape,[85] adding a Sexual and Gender-based Violence Crimes Unit to the Ministry of Justice and establishing a fast-track court to prosecute only rape cases, Criminal Court "E".[86]

The fact that post-war Liberia is ahead of eight African countries (e.g. Kenya, Egypt, Ethiopia, Uganda, Nigeria, Zimbabwe, Sierra Leone and Cameroon) on the ranking of the Rule of Law Index[87] suggests that significant progress is taking place. The UN Peace-building Fund with focus on the rule of law,[88] assisted by the American Bar Association Rule of Law Initiative,[89] in addition to national efforts including the Independent National Human Rights Commission of Liberia (2005),[90] Governance Commission (2007),[91] Liberia Anti-Corruption Commission (2008),[92] the Law Reform Commission (2009),[93] Land Reform Commission (2009),[94] LiberLII (2011),[95] Constitutional Review Commission (2012),[96] and Liberia Vision 2030 (2012),[97] among others, are promising reflection of Liberia's commitment to good governance and the rule of law. Notwithstanding, to what extent can these progresses effectively transform governance, democracy and justice for all?

3.1 Case Examples: Prosecuting War Crimes and Human Rights Violation in Liberia

Pursuant to Article XII of the CPA 2003 and *Independent National Commission for Human Rights Act* 2005, the Independent National Human Rights Commission is mandated to monitor and report on human rights violations in Liberia, including acting on the recommendations of Liberia's Truth and Reconciliation Commission (hereafter the TRC). The TRC-consolidated Final report, a 496-page document, makes a total of 60 recommendations. Of particular interest to this chapter are: (1) Recommendation 12.0: Accountability and Extraordinary Criminal Court and (2) Recommendation 14.0: Accountability and Public Sanctions Generally. Under Recommendation 12.0, Charles G. Taylor, Prince Y Johnson and George Boley are listed as leaders of warring factions who should be tried in an "Extraordinary Criminal Court for Liberia".[98] On 26 April 2012, the Residual Special Court for Sierra Leone convicted former President Taylor of war crimes committed in Sierra Leone. He is now serving a single sentence of 50 years in Britain.[99] Johnson, who is currently a senator of Nimba,[100] is named among the most notorious perpetrations during the civil war.[101] Besides testifying to the TRC about participation in the civil war, Prince Johnson has not been prosecuted and remains strong in Liberia's legislature.[102] Leader of rebel group, Liberia Peace Council (LPC) George Saigbe Boley, was finally deported from the USA on the basis that he committed human rights violation in Liberia during the civil war.[103] Boley, like Johnson, has not been tried for alleged war crimes and crimes against humanity committed in Liberia.[104]

Under Recommendation 14:0 of the TRC Report, the names of President Ellen Johnson Sirleaf, Kabineh Ja'neh and Tom Woewiyu are recorded as "the most prominent political leaders and financiers of different warring factions and armed groups…" hence should be subjected to public sanctions either by lustrations or debarment from holding public office for 30 years as of 1 July 2009.[105] To date, President Johnson-Sirleaf is still in office after a successful second-term election in 2011, even as accusation of her participation in the civil war lurks.[106] Immediately after her inauguration, President Johnson-Sirleaf appointed, Kabineh Ja'neh, a former leader of rebel group, Liberians United for Reconciliation and Democracy, as Supreme Court Justice.[107] Similar to Boley experience above, the US Customs and Immigration indicted Woewiyu for perjury having denied his membership with Taylor's rebel group, National Patriotic Front of Liberia when applying for US citizenship in 2006.[108] Worth mentioning is Charles McArthur Emmanuel Jr. (Taylor's son aka Chucky Taylor), who is also listed with individuals recommended for prosecution for economic crimes in Liberia.[109] Chucky Taylor was the first American charged and convicted under the *US Torture Victim Protection Act* 1994 by a US Federal Court. He was sentenced to 97 years in prison on 9 January 2009.[110]

3.2 Scouting Opportunities

These seven case examples illustrate major problem with applying the principles of the rule of law in Liberia. Together, these cases exemplify abuse of power by those in authority, compromise of the judiciary system, incompetence of legal personnel, unfairness and injustice, inaccessibility of the law, favouritism for those in power, arbitrariness of the law, especially when applied to those in power, lack of public confidence in the justice/legal system, corruption and overall poor governance. The fact that Taylor, Boley, Woewiyu and Taylor Jr. were tried and convicted, albeit in different jurisdictions, indicates the likelihood of prosecuting Johnson-Sirleaf, Johnson and Ja'neh for allege war crimes, crimes against humanity and human rights violation in Liberia. As a post-war country, Liberia's priority in strengthening the rule of law requires first and foremost addressing the TRC recommendations and prosecuting all those suspected of human rights violation, war crimes and crimes against humanity.[111] Until then, it remains questionable how Liberia can possibly achieve Aspiration #3 of Agenda 2063.

3.3 *Challenges and Factors Affecting Implementation*

According to Nancy Annan, several complex factors, including poverty, human rights violation, bad governance, corruption, ethnic marginalization and small arms proliferation, are responsible for the protracted nature of violent conflicts in West Africa.[112] In the case of post-war Liberia (for example), the rule of law is crucial in dispensing and accessing justice. However, in addition to Annan's complex factors listed above, post-war Liberia is challenged high illiteracy rate, high unemployment rate, high prevalence rates of disease, poor infrastructure, low economic growth and a legal education system desperately in need of reform. Legal education in Liberia is far from standard. One obvious fact is that the justice system is patriarchal and dominated by males. The only Law School in the country, Louise Arthur Grimes School of Law, is located in the capital city, which serves applicants mostly in and around the capital city. There is no clinical education program in the country, and thus law school graduates are under no obligation to gain practical experiences beyond the capital city or focus on access to justice in poor/rural communities. There are no intermediate courts (e.g., Appeals Court) between the County Court and the Supreme Court of Liberia. Since its establishment, the Supreme Court of Liberia serves as both the highest and an appellate court in the country. The problem this poses is litigants, mainly from rural Liberia with little or no access to the formal justice system, seldom progress their cases to the Supreme Court once dissatisfy with the court of first instance (e.g., the County/Circuit Courts) judgment. Detailed explanation of other constrains on the justice system in post-war Liberia is beyond the scope of this chapter. However, the key question at stake is, given the challenges listed above and more, how possible is it for Liberia to achieve Aspiration #3?

4 Conclusion and Recommendations

Agreeing on a universal definition of the rule of law is a challenging task. Albeit, there is no doubt that the rule of law is crucial for good governance and democracy. In promoting development, protection and participation, the AU's *Agenda* 2063 envisions the Africa We Want. Aspiration #3 specifically focus on creating the "an Africa of good governance, democracy, respect for human rights, justice and the rule of law". Can Liberia, as a post-war recovery nation, achieve Aspiration #3? The seven case examples presented, based on Liberia Truth and Reconciliation report recommendations, suggest that achieving Aspiration #3 is unlikely. Nevertheless, building on some progresses already made, there is a small window of opportunity Liberia can explore to augment implementation of Aspiration #3 of Agenda 2063. Herewith are four modest suggestions.

4.1 Recommendation

1. The AU must rethink the philosophical underpinnings of the Constitutive Act regarding sovereignty and non-interference. It is impossible to fully accomplish Agenda 2063 without effecting the AU Court of Human Rights and Justice where African leaders suspecting of war crimes and crimes against humanity can be prosecuted.
2. The AU must enhance and promote individual direct access to the Court of Human Rights and Justice, especially for girls and women who are disproportionately impacted by protracted violence on the continent.
3. Liberia must address all of the TRC recommendations by respecting and giving full weight to independent Human Rights Commission.
4. Reforming and overhauling civic and legal education in Liberia is way overdue. Liberia must restructure its civic and legal education by expanding and extending opportunity and access to marginalized/rural communities across the country.

Notes

1. Tom H Bingham, *The Rule of Law* (London, UK: Penguin, 2011), 29 (Bingham 2011).
2. Brian Z. Tamanaha, *On the Rule of Law: History, Politics, Theory* (Cambridge, UK: Cambridge University Press, 2004), 3 (Tamanaha 2004).
3. Jeremy Waldron, "Is the Rule of Law and Essentially Contested Concept (in Florida?)", *Law and Philosophy* 21, no. 2 (2002): 137–164 (Waldron 2002).

4. Juan Carlos Botero and Alejandro Ponce, "WJP Open Government Index™ 2015 | The World Justice Project" (Washington, DC, 20 March 2015), 10, http://worldjusticeproject.org/open-government-index (Botero and Ponce 2015).
5. Department of Peacekeeping Operations and Officer of the High Commissioner for Human Rights, "The United Nations Rule of Law Indicators: Implementation Guide and Project Tools", UN Report (Geneva, Switzerland: United Nations Publications 2011), v, http://www.un.org/en/events/peacekeepersday/2011/publications/un_rule_of_law_indicators.pdf (Department of Peacekeeping Operations, and Officer of the High Commissioner for Human Rights 2011).
6. Tamanaha, *On the Rule of Law*, 3.
7. Executive Office of the Secretary General, "United Nations and *the Rule of Law*", Text and Pictures, *United Nations and the Rule of Law* (2016), https://www.un.org/ruleoflaw/.
8. Ibid.
9. Department of Peacekeeping Operations and Officer of the High Commissioner for Human Rights, "The United Nations Rule of Law Indicators: Implementation Guide and Project Tools", v–vi; UN Security Council, "UN Secretary General Report: The Rule of Law and Transitional Justice in Conflict and Post-Conflict Societies", UN Document (Geneva, Switzerland: United Nations, August 23, 2004), para. 6, RoL & TC-a1293.
10. United Nations General Assembly, "Sixty-Seventh Session: Declaration of the High-Level Meeting of the General Assembly on the Rule of Law at the National and International Levels", in *Resolution Adopted by the General Assembly on 24 September 2012*, A/RES/67/1 (Sixty-seventh session: Agenda item 83, Geneva, Switzerland: United Nations, 2012), para. 2, http://www.un.org/en/ga/search/view_doc.asp?symbol=A/RES/67/1 (United Nations General Assembly 2012).
11. The World Justice Project, "What Is the Rule of Law?" *World Justice Project*, 9 May 2012, http://worldjusticeproject.org/what-rule-law (The World Justice Project 2012).
12. The World Justice Project Rule of Law Index is a quantitative assessment tool designed to offer a detailed and comprehensive picture of the extent to which countries adhere to the rule of law in practice. The WJP Rule of Law Index presents a portrait of the rule of law in each country by providing scores and rankings organized around nine themes: constraints on government powers, absence of corruption, open government, fundamental rights, order and security, regulatory enforcement, civil justice, criminal justice and informal justice. These country scores and rankings are based on answers drawn from more than 100,000

household and expert surveys in 102 countries and jurisdictions (see The World Justice Project, Rule of Law Index 2015, 9).

13. Botero and Ponce, "WJP Open Government Index™ 2015 | The World Justice Project", 4–5. The World Justice Project describes an open government as one that "shares information, empowers people with tools to hold the government accountable, and fosters citizen participation in public policy deliberations—is a necessary component of a system of government founded on the rule of law". The World Justice Project Open Government Index 2015 measures government openness and provides scores and rankings on four dimensions based on (1) publicized laws and government data, (2) right to information, (3) civic participation and (4) complaint mechanism. Liberia ranks 71 of the 102 countries reported, globally.
14. Mark David Agrast, Juan Carlos Botero, and Alejandro Ponce, "Rule of Law Index 2015", Private Document (Washington, DC: World Justice Project, 2015), 6, http://worldjusticeproject.org/sites/default/files/roli_2015_0.pdf (Botero and Ponce 2015).
15. Tom Ginsburg, "Pitfalls of Measuring the Rule of Law", *Hague Journal on the Rule of Law* 3 (2011): 269–280 (Ginsburg 2011).
16. Agrast, Botero, and Ponce, "Rule of Law Index 2015", 5 (Agrast et al. 2015).
17. Community Computer Centre and Directorate of Communication, "Economic Community of West African States: From an ECOWAS of States to an ECOWAS of Peoples", Regional Organization, *Home* (2016), http://www.ecowas.int/; ECOWAS Court of Justice, "Economic Community of West African States Court of Justice", Text and Pictures, *Community Court of Justice* (2012), http://www.courtecowas.org (ECOWAS Court of Justice 2012).
18. SADC, "Southern African Development Community: Towards a Common Future", Text and Pictures, *SADC Tribunal* (2016), http://www.sadc.int/about-sadc/sadc-institutions/tribun/. It is stated on SADC's website that "after several judgments ruling against the Zimbabwean government, the Tribunal was de facto suspended at the 2010 SADC Summit. On 17 August 2012 in Maputo, Mozambique, the SADC Summit addressed the issue of the suspended SADC Tribunal. The SADC Summit resolved that a new Tribunal should be negotiated and that its mandate should be confined to interpretation of the SADC Treaty and Protocols relating to disputes between Member States" (SADC 2016).
19. EAC, "East African Community: One People, One Destiny", Text and Pictures, *EAC Organs* (2016), http://www.eac.int/about/organs; Ibid.; EACJ, "The East African Court of Justice", Text and Pictures, *East African Court Of Justice* (2016), http://eacj.org/ (EAC 2016).

20. Information and Communication Technology Division, "Human Rights, Governance and Rule of Law", Text and Pictures, *United Nations Office for West Africa* (2016), https://unowa.unmissions.org/Default.aspx?tabid=802 (Information and Communication Technology Division 2016).
21. Gérard Araud, "Letter Dated 23 December 2013 from the President of the Security Council Addressed to the Secretary-General", UN Security Council, S/2013/759 (23 December 2013), http://www.securitycouncilreport.org/atf/cf/%7B65BFCF9B-6D27-4E9C-8CD3-CF6E4FF96FF9%7D/s_2013_759.pdf (Araud 2013).
22. UN Security Council, "Report of the Secretary-General on the Activities of the United Nations Office for West Africa", UN Report (Geneva, Switzerland: United Nations Security Council, 2014), para. 2, http://www.securitycouncilreport.org/atf/cf/%7B65BFCF9B-6D27-4E9C-8CD3-CF6E4FF96FF9%7D/s_2014_945.pdf (UN Security Council 2014).
23. Bingham, *The Rule of Law*, 2011, 37 (Bingham 2011).
24. According to Bingham, eight general attributes of the rule of are: (1) accessibility of the law; (2) the law not discretion; (3) equality before the law; (4) the exercise of power; (5) human rights; (6) dispute resolution; (7) a fair trial; and (8) the rule of law in the international order (see of *The Rule of Law*, 2011, 37–129).
25. Tom H. Bingham, "The Rule of Law", *The Cambridge Law Journal* 66, no. 01 (13 April 2007): 5, doi:10.1017/S0008197307000037; Bingham, *The Rule of Law*, 2011, 8 (Bingham 2011).
26. Joseph Raz, *The Authority of Law: Essays on Law and Morality* (Oxford University Press, 1979), 210 (Raz 1979).
27. Ibid., 211.
28. Ibid., 210–211.
29. Edward Palmer Thompson, *Whigs and Hunters: The Origin of the Black Act* (New York, NY: Pantheon Books, 1975), 265 (Thompson 1975).
30. Tamanaha, *On the Rule of Law*, 137.
31. Raz, *The Authority of Law: Essays on Law and Morality*, 221.
32. United Nations Human Rights, "Measuring Justice and Rule of Law", Text and Pictures, *United Nations Human Rights Office of the High Commissioner* (2016), 221, http://www.ohchr.org/EN/NewsEvents/Pages/JusticeAndRuleOfLaw.aspx (UNHCR 2016).
33. Department of Peacekeeping Operations and Officer of the High Commissioner for Human Rights, "The United Nations Rule of Law Indicators: Implementation Guide and Project Tools".
34. Bingham, *The Rule of Law*, 2011, 37–129 (Bingham 2011).
35. Department of Peacekeeping Operations and Officer of the High Commissioner for Human Rights, "The United Nations Rule of Law Indicators: Implementation Guide and Project Tools", 5–11.

36. Agrast, Botero, and Ponce, "Rule of Law Index 2015", 8–18 (Agrast et al. 2015).
37. Peter Shivute, "The Rule of Law in Sub-Saharan African: An Overview", in *Human Rights and the Rule of Law in Namibia*, ed. Nico Horn and Anton Bösl (Windhoek, Namibia: Macmillan Namibia, 2008), 213–219, http://www.kas.de/upload/auslandshomepages/namibia/HumanRights/shivute2.pdf (Shivute 2008).
38. Ibid., 213–214.
39. Ibid., 217–219.
40. Peter Ntephe, "Does Africa Need Another Kind of Law? Alterity and the Rule of Law in Sub-Saharan Africa" (PhD Thesis, University of London, School of Oriental and African Studies, 2012), 3, http://eprints.soas.ac.uk/13823/1/Ntephe_3376.pdf (Ntephe 2012).
41. Ibid., 3, 15.
42. Ibid., 73.
43. Ibid., 361.
44. United Nations Human Rights, "Measuring Justice and Rule of Law", v.
45. Anonymous, "The Birth of the OAU", *New African* 528, no. May (2013): 132–137 (Anonymous 2013).
46. Colin Legum, *Pan-Africanism: A Short Political Guide* (New York, NY: Frederick A Praeger, 1965), 45, http://www.freedomarchives.org/Documents/Finder/Black%20Liberation%20Disk/Black%20Power!/SugahData/Books/Legum.S.pdf (Legum 1965).
47. The African Union Commission, "African Union", Text and Pictures, *History of the OAU and AU* (2016), http://www.au.int/en/history/oau-and-au (African Union Commission 2016).
48. Legum, *Pan-Africanism: A Short Political Guide*, 45–47; Anonymous, "Sanniquellie Conference", *International Organization* 62, no. 16 (1962): 444–446 (Anonymous 1962).
49. Legum, *Pan-Africanism: A Short Political Guide*, 45–55.
50. Osei Boateng, "OAU and Western Penetration Efforts", *New African* 528, no. May (2013): 142–147 (Boateng 2013).
51. According to Osei Boateng (2013): leading up to the formation of the Organization of African Unity, the splinter between the Guinea, Mali and Ghana group, which later morphed into the Monrovia Group, from that of the radical Casablanca group with Egypt on board was fueled by Western countries, precisely Britain, France and the USA, who wanted African Unity by gradual means via regionalism.
52. Lolan Ekow Sagoe-Moses, "The Well Runs Dry: The Socio-Economic Costs of Political Success—Pan-Africanism as a Quest for Racial Equality through National Independence" (Bachelor Honours of Arts (Honours) Thesis, University of Virginia, 2013), 79–80 (Sagoe-Moses 2013).

53. Legum, *Pan-Africanism: A Short Political Guide*, 45.
54. Thaddeus C. B. Jahn, "The African Union: Organization of African Unity 2.0 or Regional Renaissance?" *E-International Relations*, 23 May 2014, 6, http://www.e-ir.info/2014/05/23/the-african-union-organization-of-african-unity-2-0-or-regional-renaissance/ (Jahn 2014).
55. The African Union Commission, "African Union".
56. Directorate of Strategic Policy Planning, "African Agenda 2063: General Briefing Kit" (Powerpoint, Agenda 2063, Addis Ababa, Ethiopia, 30 March 2016), http://agenda2063.au.int/en/sites/default/files/10-%20POWER-POINT%20PRESENTATION%20ON%20AGENDA%202063%2029March2016.pdf; African Union Commission, "Agenda 2063: Framework Document", Text (Addis Ababa, Ethiopia: African Union, September 2015), http://agenda2063.au.int/en/documents/agenda-2063-framework-document-ar-en-fr-po; African Union Commission, "Agenda 2063: The Africa We Want", Popular Version (Addis Ababa, Ethiopia: African Union, September 2015), http://archive.au.int/assets/images/agenda2063.pdf; African Union, "Agenda 2063: The Future We Want for Africa - About Agenda 2063", Text and Pictures, *African Union: A United and Strong Africa* (2015), http://agenda2063.au.int; African Union Commission, "Overview of Aspirations, Goals and Priority Areas of Agenda 2063" (African Union, 30 March 2016), http://agenda2063.au.int/en/documents/overview-aspirations-goals-and-priority-areas-agenda-2063 (Directorate of Strategic Policy Planning 2016; African Union Commission 2015a, b, 2016).
57. Alemu Aneme, "Introduction to the Norms and Institutions of the African Union", Text and Pictures, *Hauser Global Law School Program* (December 2010), 5, http://www.nyulawglobal.org/globalex/African_Union.html (Aneme 2010).
58. Veronica P. Fynn, *Legal Discrepancies: Internal Displacement of Women and Children in Africa* (Kusterdingen, Germany: Flowers Books, 2011), 146, https://www.amazon.com/Legal-Discrepancies-Internal-Displacement-Children/dp/1453873414 (Fynn 2011).
59. Bethany Lacina and Nils Petter Gleditsch, "Monitoring Trends in Global Combat: A New Dataset of Battle Deaths", *European Journal of Population /Revue Européenne de Démographie* 21, no. 2–3 (June 2005): 145–166, doi:10.1007/s10680-005-6851-6 (Lacina 2005).
60. Anke Hoeffler, "Dealing with the Consequences of Violence Conflicts in Africa" (Oxford, England: African Development Bank Report, March 13, 2008), 8, http://users.ox.ac.uk/~ball0144/consequences.pdf (Hoeffler 2008).
61. UNHCR, "Global Trends: Forced Displacement in 2015", UN Report (Geneva, Switzerland: United Nations High Commission

for Refugees, 2016), 66, http://www.unhcr.org/en-us/statistics/unhcrstats/576408cd7/unhcr-global-trends-2015.html (UNHCR 2016).
62. Alexandra Bilak et al., "Global Report on Internal Displacement" (Geneva, Switzerland: Internal Displacement Monitoring Centre, 2016), 27, 29, http://www.internal-displacement.org/assets/publications/2016/2016-global-report-internal-displacement-IDMC.pdf (Bilak et al. 2016).
63. African Commission, "African Commission on Human and Peoples' Rights", Regional Organization, *History of the African Charter* (2016), http://www.achpr.org/instruments/achpr/history/ (African Commission 2016).
64. Richard Gittleman, "The African Charter on Human and Peoples' Rights: A Legal Analysis", *Virginia Journal of International Law* 22, no. 4 (1982): 667–714 (Gittleman 1982).
65. Luis Gabriel Franceschi, *The African Human Rights Judicial System: Streamlining Structures and Domestication Mechanisms Viewed from the Foreign Affairs Power Perspective* (Cambridge, UK: Cambridge Scholars Publishing, 2014), 106.
66. Article 18 of the AU Constitutive Act provides for the establishment of the African Court of Justice. A protocol creating the African Court of Justice was adopted in 2003 and entered into force in 2009. The African Court of Justice is the principle judicial organ of the African Union, which resides over disputes pertaining to the AU Constitutive Act and interpretation and application of all treaties and legal instruments adopted and ratified within the AU (*see* Girmachew (2010) and http://www.au.int/en/organs/cj).
67. Franceschi, *The African Human Rights Judicial System*, 106.
68. ECOWAS Court of Justice, "Economic Community of West African States Court of Justice"; International Justice Resource Center, "Economic Community of West African States Court of Justice", *International Justice Resource Center*, 5 September 2012, http://www.ijrcenter.org/regional-communities/economic-community-of-west-african-states-court-of-justice/ (ECOWAS Court of Justice 2012).
69. Mia Swart, "Can Regional and Sub-Regional African Courts Strengthen the Rule of Law in Africa? Questions of Impact and Enforcement", in *Shielding Humanity*, ed. Olufemi Elias and Charles Jalloh (Brill, 2015), 705–725, http://booksandjournals.brillonline.com/content/books/b9789004293137_031; Community Computer Centre and Directorate of Communication, "Economic Community of West African States: From an ECOWAS of States to an ECOWAS of Peoples"; ECOWAS Court of Justice, Hissein Habre v. Republic of Senegal, Human Rights Watch (Court of Justice of the Economic Community of West African States 2010) (Swart 2015).

70. Kofi Ali Abdul-Yekin, "Who Are Our Law Makers in ECOWAS?" Text and Pictures, *GhanaWeb Feature Article* (20 April 2016), http://www.ghanaweb.com/GhanaHomePage/features/Who-are-our-law-makers-in-ECOWAS-432203 (Abdul-Yekin 2016).
71. *Han Capehart Williams & Anor c Republic of Liberia & Ors* 2015 ECW/CCJ/JUD/25/15
72. ECOWAS, "Community Court of Justice, ECOWAS", Regional Organization, *List of Decided Cases from 2004 Till Date* (2016), http://www.courtecowas.org/site2012/index.php?option=com_content&view=article&id=157&Itemid=27.
73. African Union Commission, "Agenda 2063: The Africa We Want", 2 (African Union Commission 2015b).
74. Philip Marcelo, "Rebuilding Liberia: Child Soldiers and the Youth Problem in Liberia", *Providencejournal.com*, 1 August 2013, http://www.providencejournal.com/article/20130801/SPECIAL-REPORTS/308019903; Tony Tate, "How to Fight, How to Kill: Child Soldiers in Liberia", NGO Report (New York, NY: Human Rights Watch, February 5, 2004), 1, https://www.hrw.org/reports/2004/liberia0204/liberia0204.pdf (Marcelo 2013).
75. Commission on Human Rights, "Report of the United Nations High Commissioner for Human Rights and Follow-up to the World Conference on Human Rights: Situation of Human Rights and Fundamental Freedoms in Liberia", Economic and Social Council Report (Geneva, Switzerland: United Nations Commission on Human Rights, 12 August 2003), 2, http://www.refworld.org/docid/4090ffd40.html (Commission on Human Rights 2003).
76. Bosede Awodola, "An Examination of Methods to Reintegrate Former Child Soldiers in Liberia", *Intervention* 10, no. 1 (2012): 30–40 (Awodola 2012).
77. Frans Viljoen, "An Introduction to the Protocol to the African Charter on Human and Peoples' Rights on the Rights of Women in Africa", *Washington and Lee Journal of Civil Rights and Social Justice* 16, no. 1 (2010): 11–46 (Viljoen 2010).
78. Benjamin de Carvalho and Niels Nagelhus Schia, "Sexual and Gender-Based Violence in Liberia and the Case for a Comprehensive Approach to the Rule of Law", *Journal of International Relations and Development* 14, no. 1 (January 2011): 134–141, doi:10.1057/jird.2010.26 (Carvalho and Schia 2011).
79. Raz, *The Authority of Law: Essays on Law and Morality*, 153.
80. Indiana University, "The Liberian Constitutions", Text and Pictures, *The Declaration of Independence* (2004), http://www.onliberia.org/con_declaration.htm (Indiana University 2004).

81. Commission on Human Rights, "Report of the United Nations High Commissioner for Human Rights and Follow-up to the World Conference on Human Rights: Situation of Human Rights and Fundamental Freedoms in Liberia", 2.
82. S Swiss et al., "Violence against Women during the Liberian Civil Conflict", *JAMA: The Journal of the American Medical Association* 279, no. 8 (25 February 1998): 625–629; Isis-WICCE (Organization), Liberia, and West Africa Network for Peacebuilding, *A Situation Analysis of the Women Survivors of the 1989–2003 Armed Conflict in Liberia* (Kampala, Uganda: Isis-WICCE, 2008) (Swiss et al. 1998).
83. Lydia Polgreen, "In First for Africa, Woman Wins Election as President of Liberia", *The New York Times*, 12 November 2005, http://www.nytimes.com/2005/11/12/world/africa/in-first-for-africa-woman-wins-election-as-president-of.html (Polgreen 2005).
84. Staff Reporter, "Charles Taylor Caught in Nigeria", *BBC News*, 29 March 2006 (Staff Reporter 2006).
85. Gang rape, providing for (Amending Title 26), An Act to Amend the New Penal Code Chapter 14 Sects. 14.70 and 14.71 and to provide for gang rape (see, http://www.liberlii.org/lr/legis/acts/grpft26322/).
86. Government of Liberia, "Ministry of Justice Liberia", Text and Pictures, *SGBV* (2016), http://moj.gov.lr/administration/sgbv/ (Government of Liberia 2016).
87. Agrast, Botero, and Ponce, "Rule of Law Index 2015", 6.
88. UN Peace Building Fund, "Liberia—United Nations Peacebuilding Fund", Text and Pictures, *Preventing A Relapse into Violent Conflict* (2015), http://www.unpbf.org/countries/liberia/ (UN Peace Building Fund 2015).
89. ABA, "American Bar Association: Defending Liberty Pursuing Justice", Text and Pictures, *Rule of Law Initiative: Liberia Programs* (2016), http://www.americanbar.org/advocacy/rule_of_law/where_we_work/africa/liberia/programs.html (ABA 2016).
90. Human Rights Watch, "Liberia: President Should Act on Rights Commission", Text and Pictures, *Human Rights Watch* (19 May 2010), https://www.hrw.org/news/2010/05/19/liberia-president-should-act-rights-commission (Human Rights Watch 2010).
91. Government of Liberia, "The Governance Commission: Republic of Liberia", Text and Pictures, *The Governance Commission, Its Mandate and Function* (2013), http://governancecommissionlr.org/page_info.php?&7d5f44532cbfc489b8db9e12e44eb820=MzIz (Government of Liberia 2013).
92. Government of Liberia, "Liberia Anti-Corruption Commission (LACC)", Text and Pictures, *About LACC* (2016), http://www.lacc.gov.lr/public/index.php (Government of Liberia 2016).

93. Government of Liberia, "The Law Reform Commission of Liberia: Law, Justice, Reform, Peace, Development", Government, *Home* (2016), http://liblrc.org/index.html (Government of Liberia 2016).
94. Government of Liberia, "Land Commission", Text and Pictures, *Home-Brochure* (2016), http://www.landlib.org/pg_img/brochure%20redone.pdf (Government of Liberia 2016).
95. LiberLII, "Liberia Legal Information Institute (LiberLII)", Text, *About LiberLII* (2016), http://www.liberlii.org (LiberLII 2016).
96. Government of Liberia, "Liberia Constitution Review Committee", Text and Pictures, *About CRC* (2016), https://www.facebook.com/LiberiaConstitutionReviewCommittee/about/?entry_point=page_nav_about_item&tab=page_info (Government of Liberia 2016).
97. Government of Liberia, "National Vision 2030", Government Policy (Monrovia, Liberia: Governance Commission, 2012), http://governancecommissionlr.org/doc_download/VISION%202030%20%20%20summary%20for%20the%20conference%20(25%20pgs)%20for%20GC%20%20Website.pdf?a4705305cd27e04fb1f66830e7e0ef9d=NjQ%3D (Government of Liberia 2012).
98. Truth and Reconciliation Commission of Liberia, "Truth and Reconciliation Report", Government Report (Monrovia: Government of Liberia, 19 December 2009), 347–350 (Truth and Reconciliation Commission of Liberia 2009).
99. RSCSL, "Special Court for Sierra Leone: Residual Special Court for Sierra Leone", Text and Pictures, *The Prosecutor vs Charles Ghankay Taylor* (2016), http://www.rscsl.org/Taylor.html (RSCSL 2016).
100. NDI, "The National Democratic Institute", Text, *House of Representatives and Senate Directories (Liberia)* (2016), https://www.ndi.org/node/16443 (NDI 2016).
101. Truth and Reconciliation Commission of Liberia, "Truth and Reconciliation Report", 350.
102. TRC, *Prince Johnson, Parts 1, 2, 3 and 4*, Video Recording (Monrovia, Liberia: TRC Hearing, 2008) (TRC 2008).
103. ICE, "Liberian Human Rights Violator Removed from US", Text, *US Immigration and Customs Enforcement*, accessed 1 September 2016, https://www.ice.gov/news/releases/liberian-human-rights-violator-removed-us (ICE 2016).
104. TRC, *George ES Boley, Parts 1–6*, Video Recording (Monrovia, Liberia: TRC Hearing, 2009) (TRC 2009).
105. Truth and Reconciliation Commission of Liberia, "Truth and Reconciliation Report", 359–361.
106. Nicholas Kristof, "Ellen Johnson Sirleaf and War Crimes?" Text and Pictures, *New York Times* (3 July 2009); Staff Reporter, "No

Apologies'—EJS Defends Family Appointment in Government", *Front Page Africa*, 30 March 2016, http://frontpageafricaonline.com/index.php/politics/86-no-apologies-ejs-defends-family-appointment-in-government; Staff Reporter, "Sirleaf 'Sorry' She Backed Taylor", *BBC News*, 12 February 2016, http://news.bbc.co.uk/2/hi/africa/7887117.stm (Kristof 2009).

107. Staff Reporter, "Sirleaf Starts to Form Government, Some Appointments Spark Protest", Text and Pictures, *IRIN* (14 February 2006), http://www.irinnews.org/news/2006/02/14/sirleaf-starts-form-government-some-appointments-spark-protest (Staff Reporter 2006).
108. United States of America v Jucontee Thomas Woewiyu 2014 (Indictment available at: https://www.ice.gov/doclib/news/releases/2014/140513philadelphia.pdf).
109. Truth and Reconciliation Commission of Liberia, "Truth and Reconciliation Report", 370.
110. UNDOJ, "Roy Belfast Jr., A/K/A Chuckie Taylor, Sentenced on Torture Charges", Text, *Immediate Press Release* (9 January 2009) (UNDOJ 2009).
111. Human Rights Watch, "Liberia".
112. Nancy Annan, "Violent Conflicts and Civil Strife in West Africa: Causes, Challenges and Prospects", *Stability: International Journal of Security & Development* 3, no. 1 (28 January 2014): 3, doi:10.5334/sta.da (Annan 2014).

Bibiliography

ABA. 2016. *American Bar Association: Defending Liberty Pursuing Justice*. Text and Pictures. *Rule of Law Initiative: Liberia Programs*. http://www.americanbar.org/advocacy/rule_of_law/where_we_work/africa/liberia/programs.html.

Abdul-Yekin, Kofi Ali. 2016. Who Are Our Law Makers in ECOWAS? Text and Pictures. *GhanaWeb Feature Article*, April 20, 2016. http://www.ghanaweb.com/GhanaHomePage/features/Who-are-our-law-makers-in-ECOWAS-432203.

African Commission. 2016. African Commission on Human and Peoples' Rights. Regional Organisation. *History of the African Charter*. http://www.achpr.org/instruments/achpr/history/.

African Union. 2015. Agenda 2063: The Future We Want for Africa—About Agenda 2063. Text and Pictures. *African Union: A United and Strong Africa*. http://agenda2063.au.int.

African Union Commission. 2015a. Agenda 2063: Framework Document—The Africa We Want. Text. *Addis Ababa: African Union*, September 2015. http://agenda2063.au.int/en/documents/agenda-2063-framework-document-ar-en-fr-po.

African Union Commission. 2015b. Agenda 2063: The Africa We Want. Popular Version. *Addis Ababa: African Union*, September 2015. http://archive.au.int/assets/images/agenda2063.pdf.

African Union Commission. 2016. Overview of Aspirations, Goals and Priority Areas of Agenda 2063. *African Union*, March 30, 2016. http://agenda2063.au.int/en/documents/overview-aspirations-goals-and-priority-areas-agenda-2063.

Agrast, Mark David, Juan Carlos Botero, and Alejandro Ponce. 2015. Rule of Law Index 2015. *Private Document*. Washington, DC: World Justice Project. http://worldjusticeproject.org/sites/default/files/roli_2015_0.pdf.

Aneme, Alemu. 2010. Introduction to the Norms and Institutions of the African Uniion. Text and Pictures. *Hauser Global Law School Program*, December 2010. http://www.nyulawglobal.org/globalex/African_Union.html.

Annan, Nancy. 2014. Violent Conflicts and Civil Strife in West Africa: Causes, Challenges and Prospects. *Stability: International Journal of Security & Development* 3 (1): 3. doi: 10.5334/sta.da.

Anonymous. 1962. Sanniquellie Conference. *International Organization* 62 (16): 444–446.

Anonymous. 2013. The Birth of the OAU. *New African* 528, (May), (2013): 132–137.

Araud, Gérard. 2013. UN Security Council, S/2013/759. Letter Dated 23 December 2013 from the President of the Security Council Addressed to the Secretary-General. UN Security Council, S/2013/759, December 23, 2013. http://www.securitycouncilreport.org/atf/cf/%7B65BFCF9B-6D27-4E9C-8CD3-CF6E4FF96FF9%7D/s_2013_759.pdf.

Awodola, Bosede. 2012. An Examination of Methods to Reintegrate Former Child Soldiers in Liberia. *Intervention* 10 (1): 30–40.

Bilak, Alexandra, Gabriel Cardona-Fox, Justin Ginnetti, Elizabeth Rushing, Isabelle Scherer, Marita Swain, Nadine Walicki, and Michelle Yonetani. 2016. *Global Report on Internal Displacement*. Geneva, Switzerland: Internal Displacement Monitoring Centre. http://www.internal-displacement.org/assets/publications/2016/2016-global-report-internal-displacement-IDMC.pdf.

Bingham, Tom H. 2007. The Rule of Law. *The Cambridge Law Journal* 66 (1): 67. doi:10.1017/S0008197307000037.

Bingham, Tom H. 2011. *The Rule of Law*. London, UK: Penguin.

Boateng, Osei. 2013. OAU and Western Penetration Efforts. *New African* 528 (May): 142–147.

Botero, Juan Carlos, and Alejandro Ponce. 2015. WJP Open Government Index™ 2015 | The World Justice Project. Washington, DC, March 20, 2015. http://worldjusticeproject.org/open-government-index.

Carvalho, Benjamin de, and Niels Nagelhus Schia. 2011. Sexual and Gender-Based Violence in Liberia and the Case for a Comprehensive Approach to the Rule of Law. *Journal of International Relations and Development* 14 (1): 134–141. doi:10.1057/jird.2010.26.

Commission on Human Rights. 2003. Report of the United Nations High Commissioner for Human Rights and Follow-up to the World Conference on Human Rights: Situation of Human Rights and Fundamental Freedoms in Liberia. Economic and Social Council Report. Geneva, Switzerland: United Nations Commission on Human Rights, August 12, 2003. http://www.refworld.org/docid/4090ffd40.html.

Community Computer Centre, and Directorate of Communication. 2016. Economic Community of West African States: From an ECOWAS of States to an ECOWAS of Peoples. Regional Organisation. *Home*. http://www.ecowas.int/.

Department of Peacekeeping Operations, and Officer of the High Commissioner for Human Rights. 2011. The United Nations Rule of Law Indicators: Implementation Guide and Project Tools. UN Report. Geneva, Switzerland: United Nations Publications. http://www.un.org/en/events/peacekeepersday/2011/publications/un_rule_of_law_indicators.pdf.

Directorate of Strategic Policy Planning. 2016. African Agenda 2063: General Briefing Kit. Powerpoint presented at the Agenda 2063, Addis Ababa, Ethiopia, March 30, 2016. http://agenda2063.au.int/en/sites/default/files/10-%20POWER-POINT%20PRESENTATION%20ON%20AGENDA%202063%2029March2016.pdf.

EAC. 2016. East African Community: One People, One Destiny. Text and Pictures. *EAC Organs*. http://www.eac.int/about/organs.

EACJ. 2016. The East African Court of Justice. Text and Pictures. *East African Court Of Justice*. http://eacj.org/.

ECOWAS. 2016. Community Court of Justice, ECOWAS. Regional Organisation. *List of Decided Cases from 2004 Till Date*, 2016. http://www.courtecowas.org/site2012/index.php?option=com_content&view=article&id=157&Itemid=27.

ECOWAS Court of Justice. 2010. Hissein Habre v. Republic of Senegal, Human Rights Watch (Court of Justice of the Economic Community of West African States 2010).

ECOWAS Court of Justice. 2012. Economic Community of West African States Court of Justice. Text and Pictures. *Community Court of Justice*. http://www.courtecowas.org.

Executive Office of the Secretary-General. 2016. United Nations and the Rule of Law. Text and Pictures. *United Nations and the Rule of Law*. https://www.un.org/ruleoflaw/.

Franceschi, Luis Gabriel. 2014. *The African Human Rights Judicial System: Streamlining Structures and Domestication Mechanisms Viewed from the Foreign Affairs Power Perspective*. Cambridge, UK: Cambridge Scholars Publishing.

Fynn, Veronica P. 2011. *Legal Discrepancies: Internal Displacement of Women and Children in Africa*. Kusterdingen, Germany: Flowers Books. https://www.amazon.com/Legal-Discrepancies-Internal-Displacement-Children/dp/1453873414.

Ginsburg, Tom. 2011. Pitfalls of Measuring the Rule of Law. *Hague Journal on the Rule of Law* 3: 269–280.

Gittleman, Richard. 1982. The African Charter on Human and Peoples' Rights: A Legal Analysis. *Virginia Journal of International Law* 22 (4): 667–714.

Government of Liberia. 2012. National Vision 2030. Government Policy. Monrovia, Liberia: Governance Commission. http://governancecommissionlr.org/doc_download/VISION%202030%20%20%20summary%20for%20the%20conference%20(25%20pgs)%20for%20GC%20%20Website.pdf?a4705305cd27e04fb1f66830e7e0ef9d=NjQ%3D.

Government of Liberia. 2013. The Governance Commission: Republic of Liberia. Text and Pictures. *The Governance Commission, Its Mandate and Function*. http://governancecommissionlr.org/page_info.php?&7d5f44532cbfc489b8db9e12e44eb820=MzIz.

Government of Liberia. 2016. Land Commission. Text and Pictures. *Home-Brochure*. http://www.landlib.org/pg_img/brochure%20redone.pdf.

Government of Liberia. 2016. Liberia Anti-Corruption Commission (LACC). Text and Pictures. *About LACC*. http://www.lacc.gov.lr/public/index.php.

Government of Liberia. 2016. Liberia Constitution Review Committee. Text and Pictures. *About CRC*. https://www.facebook.com/LiberiaConstitutionReviewCommittee/about/?entry_point=page_nav_about_item&tab=page_info.

Government of Liberia. 2016. Ministry of Justice Liberia. Text and Pictures. *SGBV*. http://moj.gov.lr/administration/sgbv/.

Government of Liberia. 2016. The Law Reform Commission of Liberia: Law, Justice, Reform, Peace, Development. Government. *Home*. http://liblrc.org/index.html.

Hoeffler, Anke. 2008. Dealing with the Consequences of Violence Conflicts in Africa. Oxford, England: African Development Bank Report, March 13, 2008. http://users.ox.ac.uk/~ball0144/consequences.pdf.

Human Rights Watch. 2010. Liberia: President Should Act on Rights Commission. Text and Pictures. *Human Rights Watch*, May 19, 2010. https://www.hrw.org/news/2010/05/19/liberia-president-should-act-rights-commission.

ICE. 2016. Liberian Human Rights Violator Removed from US. Text. *US Immigration and Customs Enforcement*. https://www.ice.gov/news/releases/liberian-human-rights-violator-removed-us. Accessed 1 Sep 2016.

Indiana University. 2004. The Liberian Constitutions. Text and Pictures. *The Declartion of Independence*. http://www.onliberia.org/con_declaration.htm.

Information and Communication Technology Division. 2016. Human Rights, Governance and Rule of Law. Text and Pictures. *United Nations Office for West Africa*. https://unowa.unmissions.org/Default.aspx?tabid=802.

International Justice Resource Center. 2012. Economic Community of West African States Court of Justice. *International Justice Resource Center*, September 5, 2012. http://www.ijrcenter.org/regional-communities/economic-community-of-west-african-states-court-of-justice/.

Isis-WICCE (Organization), Liberia, and West Africa Network for Peacebuilding. 2008. *A Situation Analysis of the Women Survivors of the 1989–2003 Armed Conflict in Liberia*. Kampala, Uganda: Isis-WICCE.

Jahn, Thaddeus C. B. 2014. The African Union: Organization of African Unity 2.0 or Regional Renaissance? *E-International Relations*, May 23, 2014. http://www.e-ir.info/2014/05/23/the-african-union-organization-of-african-unity-2-0-or-regional-renaissance/.

Kristof, Nicholas. 2009. Ellen Johnson Sirleaf and War Crimes? Text and Pictures. *New York Times*, July 3, 2009.

Lacina, Bethany, and Nils Petter Gleditsch. 2005. Monitoring Trends in Global Combat: A New Dataset of Battle Deaths. *European Journal of Population / Revue Européenne de Démographie* 21 (2–3) June 2005: 145–166. doi:10.1007/s10680-005-6851-6.

Legum, Colin. 1965. *Pan-Africanism: A Short Political Guide*. New York, NY: Frederick A Praeger. http://www.freedomarchives.org/Documents/Finder/Black%20Liberation%20Disk/Black%20Power!/SugahData/Books/Legum.S.pdf.

LiberLII. 2016. Liberia Legal Information Institute (LiberLII). Text. *About LiberLII*. http://www.liberlii.org.

Marcelo, Philip. 2013. Rebuilding Liberia: Child Soldiers and the Youth Problem in Liberia. *Providencejournal.com*, August 1, 2013. http://www.providencejournal.com/article/20130801/SPECIAL-REPORTS/308019903.

NDI. 2016. The National Democratic Institute. Text. *House of Representatives and Senate Directories (Liberia)*. https://www.ndi.org/node/16443.

Ntephe, Peter. 2012. Does Africa Need Another Kind of Law? Alterity and the Rule of Law in Sub-Saharan Africa. PhD Thesis, University of London, School of Oriental and African Studies. http://eprints.soas.ac.uk/13823/1/Ntephe_3376.pdf.

Polgreen, Lydia. 2005. In First for Africa, Woman Wins Election as President of Liberia. *The New York Times*. November 12, 2005. http://www.nytimes.com/2005/11/12/world/africa/in-first-for-africa-woman-wins-election-as-president-of.html.

Raz, Joseph. 1979. *The Authority of Law: Essays on Law and Morality*.Oxford: Oxford University Press.

RSCSL. 2016. Special Court for Sierra Leone: Residual Special Court for Sierra Leone. Text and Pictures. *The Prosecutor vs Charles Ghankay Taylor*. http://www.rscsl.org/Taylor.html.

SADC. 2016. Southern African Development Community: Towards a Common Future. Text and Pictures. *SADC Tribunal*. http://www.sadc.int/about-sadc/sadc-institutions/tribun/.

Sagoe-Moses, Lolan Ekow. 2013. The Well Runs Dry: The Socio-Economic Costs of Political Success—Pan-Africanism as a Quest for Racial Equality through National Independence. Bachelor Honours of Arts (Honours) Thesis, University of Virginia.

Shivute, Peter. 2008. The Rule of Law in Sub-Saharan African: An Overview. In *Human Rights and the Rule of Law in Namibia*, ed. Nico Horn and Anton Bösl, 213–219. Windhoek: Macmillan Namibia. http://www.kas.de/upload/auslandshomepages/namibia/HumanRights/shivute2.pdf.

Staff Reporter. 2006. Charles Taylor Caught in Nigeria. *BBC News*. March 29, 2006.

Staff Reporter. 2006. Sirleaf Starts to Form Government, Some Appointments Spark Protest. Text and Pictures. *IRIN*, February 14, 2006. http://www.irinnews.org/news/2006/02/14/sirleaf-starts-form-government-some-appointments-spark-protest.

Staff Reporter. 2016. 'No Apologies'—EJS Defends Family Appointment in Government. *Front Page Africa*. March 30, 2016. http://frontpageafricaonline.com/index.php/politics/86-no-apologies-ejs-defends-family-appointment-in-government.

Staff Reporter. 2016. Sirleaf 'Sorry' She Backed Taylor. *BBC News*. February 12, 2016. http://news.bbc.co.uk/2/hi/africa/7887117.stm.

Swart, Mia. 2015. *Can Regional and Sub-Regional African Courts Strengthen the Rule of Law in Africa?* Questions of Impact and Enforcement. In *Shielding Humanity*, ed. Olufemi Elias and Charles Jalloh, 705–725. Brill. http://booksandjournals.brillonline.com/content/books/b9789004293137_031.

Swiss, S, P. J. Jennings, G. V. Aryee, G. H. Brown, R. M. Jappah-Samukai, M. S. Kamara, R. D. Schaack, and R. S. Turay-Kanneh. 1998. Violence against Women during the Liberian Civil Conflict. *JAMA: The Journal of the American Medical Association* 279 (8): 625–629.

Tamanaha, Brian Z. 2004. *On the Rule of Law: History, Politics, Theory*. Cambridge, UK: Cambridge University Press.

Tate, Tony. 2004. *How to Fight, How to Kill: Child Soldiers in Liberia*. NGO Report. New York, NY: Human Rights Watch, February 5, 2004. https://www.hrw.org/reports/2004/liberia0204/liberia0204.pdf.

The African Union Commission. 2016. African Union. Text and Pictures. *History of the OAU and AU*. http://www.au.int/en/history/oau-and-au.

The World Justice Project. 2012. What Is the Rule of Law? *World Justice Project*, May 9, 2012. http://worldjusticeproject.org/what-rule-law.

Thompson, Edward Palmer. 1975. *Whigs and Hunters: The Origin of the Black Act*. New York, NY: Pantheon Books.
TRC. 2008. *George ES Boley. Prince Johnson, Parts 1, 2, 3 and 4*. Video Recording. Monrovia, Liberia: TRC Hearing.
TRC. 2009. *George ES Boley, Parts 1–6*. Video Recording. Monrovia, Liberia: TRC Hearing.
Truth and Reconciliation Commission of Liberia. 2009. Truth and Reconciliation Report. Government Report. Monrovia: Government of Liberia, December 19, 2009.
UN Peace Building Fund. 2015. Liberia—United Nations Peacebuilding Fund. Text and Pictures. *Preventing A Relapse into Violent Conflict*. http://www.unpbf.org/countries/liberia/.
UN Security Council. 2004. UN Secretary General Report: The Rule of Law and Transitional Justice in Conflict and Post-Conflict Societies. UN Document. Geneva, Switzerland: United Nations, August 23, 2004. RoL&TC-a1293.
UN Security Council. 2014. Report of the Secretary-General on the Activities of the United Nations Office for West Africa. UN Report. Geneva, Switzerland: United Nations Security Council. http://www.securitycouncilreport.org/atf/cf/%7B65BFCF9B-6D27-4E9C-8CD3-CF6E4FF96FF9%7D/s_2014_945.pdf.
UNDOJ. 2009. Roy Belfast Jr., A/K/A Chuckie Taylor, Sentenced on Torture Charges. Text. *Immediate Press Release*, January 9, 2009. https://www.justice.gov/archive/opa/pr/2009/January/09-crm-021.html.
UNHCR. 2016. Global Trends: Forced Displacement in 2015. UN Report. Geneva, Switzerland: United Nations High Commission for Refugees. http://www.unhcr.org/en-us/statistics/unhcrstats/576408cd7/unhcr-global-trends-2015.html.
United Nations General Assembly. 2012. Sixty-Seventh Session: Declaration of the High-Level Meeting of the General Assembly on the Rule of Law at the National and International Levels. In *Resolution Adopted by the General Assembly on 24 September 2012*. A/RES/67/1. Geneva, Switzerland: United Nations. http://www.un.org/en/ga/search/view_doc.asp?symbol=A/RES/67/1.
United Nations Human Rights. 2016. Measuring Justice and Rule of Law. Text and Pictures. *United Nations Human Rights Office of the High Commissioner*. http://www.ohchr.org/EN/NewsEvents/Pages/JusticeAndRuleOfLaw.aspx.
Viljoen, Frans. 2010. An Introduction to the Protocol to the African Charter on Human and Peoples' Rights on the Rights of Women in Africa. *Washington and Lee Journal of Civil Rights and Social Justice* 16 (1): 11–46.
Waldron, Jeremy. 2002. Is the Rule of Law and Essentially Contested Concept (in Florida?). *Law and Philosophy* 21 (2): 137–164.

Author Biography

Veronica Fynn Bruey is an award-winning scholar with an extensive interdisciplinary educational background in science, arts, public health and law from across four continents. A global researcher, Fynn Bruey, has conducted studies, taught, consulted on projects and spoken at international conferences in over 20 countries. She has published two books, two children's books, several chapters and peer-review journal articles. She is also the Founder and Editor-in-Chief of the Journal of Internal Displacement, the only scholastic platform dedicated to the plight of displaced peoples, globally. In 2014, Fynn Bruey was appointed a Senior Researcher of the Centre for Policy in Liberia, the only policy think tank in Liberia. She recently created a Law and Society's Collaborative Research Network called "Displaced Peoples", comprising 14 international academic experts. Currently, she teaches at Seattle University School of Law as an adjunct professor. Fynn Bruey is a born and bred Liberian war survivor.

CHAPTER 11

The African Dream: Attitudes and Prejudices in African Schools

David Nnanna Chukwukadibia Ikpo

1 Introduction

Tyranny snuck into the law, labelled itself Nigeria's Same-Sex Marriage Prohibition Act 2013 (Nigeria's anti-gay law) and has been running amok since then. Its original purpose as legislation is not clear besides sending a clear signal to the world that Nigeria has decided to further institutionalise inequality and has utter disregard for human rights commitments, both national and international. Unfortunately, it did succeed in consolidating the criminalisation of same-sex relations that was always been part of Nigeria's several criminal justice systems without cancelling out the death penalty obtainable under Sharia law in the North.[1] The anti-gay law is a federal legislation that has a wide coverage over all the criminal justice systems in Nigeria, prohibiting all forms of a public show of same-sex relations and support for same-sex relations concerned issues.[2]

D.N.C. Ikpo (✉)
Sexual Orientation Gender Identity and Expression Unit, Centre for Human Rights, University of Pretoria, Pretoria, Gauteng, South Africa
e-mail: snownspring@yahoo.com

A.C. Onuora-Oguno et al. (eds.), *Education Law, Strategic Policy and Sustainable Development in Africa*, DOI 10.1007/978-3-319-53703-0_11

The anti-gay law and its effects and implications are a violation of so many human rights protected on so many levels. The human rights violated are not just the rights of sexual and gender minorities but potentially those of everyone. This paper prefers the use of the term 'sexual and gender minorities' as opposed to Lesbian, Gay, Bisexual, Transgender, Intersex, Allies/Asexual (LGBTIA) because the former is more inclusive of the latter as well as other worded and 'unworded' sexualities, gender identities and expressions.

With a spotlight on prejudice and negative attitudes such as homophobia and transphobia (the fear of or dislike directed towards transgender people),[3] this paper broadly argues that the Nigeria's anti-gay law amounts to a gross violation of Nigeria's international commitment to guarantee the right to education of children and young persons in Nigerian schools.

2 Children and Young Persons in Nigerian Schools

A 'child' and young person for the purposes of this research are 'every human below the age of 18' and other young people above this age but not above 35 and are part of the Nigerian academic community.[4] The words 'school' and 'education' are very general words. They are quite incapable of an accurate and precise definition. School: 'an institution designed to provide learning spaces and learning environments for the teaching of students under the direction of teachers',[5] or 'an organisation that provides instruction…a source of knowledge'.[6] Education, by Nelson Mandela, has been argued to be a formidable means through which the world can be changed.[7]

Every day of the week, millions of people spend several hours as a 'captive audience in schools learning skills that will (should) enable them to function successfully in the society'.[8] As will be shown, for sexual and gender minorities who are part of the academic community, the more time they spend as audiences in these schools the more they are exposed to 'threats to their mental and physical health from their peers, teachers, and administrators'.[9]

Although the focus of this research deserves a multidisciplinary response to match the complex and multidisciplinary nature of the subject matter, this paper is mainly from the standpoint of human rights and legality in order to critically attend to these facets. To tackle this, this paper is split into five parts: this introduction; the human rights framework governing learning spaces; being gay and learning in Nigeria; legal analysis; and conclusions and recommendations.

3 The Human Rights Framework Governing Nigerian Schools

Nigeria is governed by several national and international human rights laws and structures amongst which include the following: International Covenant on Civil and Political Rights (ICCPR); International Covenant on Economic Social and Cultural Rights (ICESCR); International Convention on the Elimination of All Forms of Discrimination Against Women (CEDAW); Convention on the Rights of the Child (CRC); The African Charter on Human and Peoples' Rights (African Charter); The African Charter on the Rights and Welfare of the Child (ACRWC); African Youth Charter; and the Constitution of the Federal Republic of Nigeria 1999 (As Amended) (Nigerian Constitution). International treaties do not have the force of law until they have been domesticated.[10] Nigeria has domesticated the African Charter on Human and Peoples Rights.

The rights of children in Nigeria are specifically protected by the Child Rights Act which arguably draws inspiration from the CRC and the ACRWC. Section 1 of the Child Rights Act emphasises the principle of the best interests of the child as a primary consideration in all actions concerning the child undertaken by state and non-state parties.[11] Other primary considerations include the principles of non-discrimination; survival and development of the child; and the child's right to participation. The principle of the best interests of the child is also enshrined in African Charter on the Rights and Welfare of the Child as the primary consideration to be made in all actions concerning the child.[12] Invariably these rights enshrined therein apply to all spheres of the child's existence including his/her education, including its form and substance. In Nigeria, being a culturally conscious state, child education occurs in a wide range of places. However, for the purpose of this research, it shall be restricted to primary schools, secondary schools and Christian and Muslim worship places.

Education, as the primary preoccupation of Nigerian schools, by international standards, is a human right.[13] This right amongst other things includes the freedom of expression to give and receive information voluntarily; freedom of religion; freedom of association; the right to privacy;

and the right to dignity.[14] As such, in as much as the right to education is not a justiciable right within Chap. 4 of the Nigerian Constitution, these other rights as mentioned are salient aspects of the right to education. More so, on the argument of the minimum core approach, Nigeria is obliged to ensure that the core content of non-justiciable rights is realised. This core content is distilled into the features of availability, accessibility, adaptability, acceptability and the best interests of the student as a primary consideration.[15] These features shall be addressed subsequently. Nonetheless, they all hinge on the importance of recognition and protection of the human rights of children in the course of their education. And these are exactly what Nigeria's anti-gay law threatens.

4 The Legal Impact of the Anti-gay Law on Child Education in Nigeria

> 5 (2) A person who registers, operates or participates in gay clubs, societies and organisation, or directly or indirectly makes public show of same-sex amorous relationship in Nigeria commits an offence and is liable on conviction to a term of 10 years imprisonment.
>
> (3) A person or group of persons who administers, witnesses, abets or aids the solemnisation of a same-sex marriage or civil union, or supports the registration, operation and sustenance of gay clubs, societies, organisations, processions or meetings in Nigeria commits an offence and is liable on conviction to a term of 10 years imprisonment.[16]

Though there is no known jurisprudence on the application of these anti-gay legislative injunctions to Nigerian schools, the possibilities are endless. This deduction is reliably made on the basis of the increasing rate of homophobic attacks in Nigeria by both state and non-state actors.[17] The unsuitably intense and dire state of sexual minority rights in Nigeria also reflects in Nigerian schools and this is not in the best interest of children and young people who are in these schools. This is especially as discrimination on the basis of sexual orientation and gender identity, and expression has been reported to 'present the same risks of psychological and other harms as discrimination on the basis of race, religion or gender'.[18]

Addressing the scope of child rights to education under international law, six principal features have been deduced. They shall be discussed within the context of their being unjustly limited by Nigeria's anti-gay law:

4.1 Accessibility

This principle demands that learning spaces have to be within everyone's reach.[19] Generally, this refers to physical accessibility, economic accessibility and non-discrimination in the form and structure of the schools, as well as form and substance of what goes on in schools. The legal impact of Nigeria's anti-gay law is that it has made the sexual and gender minority rights discourse criminal, almost faceless and inaccessible on all levels. It makes the existence of sexual and gender minority information centres and their work inaccessible to the youths and children. It reduces the possibility of children and youths approaching such centres for fear of being labelled sexual and gender minorities. Also, it inhibits the chances of such topics being raised by teachers or students in schools for fear of falling within the bounds of criminality. As such what is almost unseen and unheard, almost does not exist and can barely be accessed.

Further, the unrecorded incidences of unpunished gay-bashing, harassment, intimidation, physical and mental abuse, and blackmail targeted at sexual and gender minorities within the academic community by exploitative and antagonistic members and non-members of the academic community, also are determining features in the social accessibility of the school by the members of sexual and gender minorities. If it is unsafe, it should be avoided, especially when the stigma and harassment gets in the way of making formal reports to the authorities, adequately benefitting from the learning environment and living and participating unthreatened as sexual and gender minorities.[20]

4.2 Availability

This principle generally applies to compulsory, inclusive, non-discriminatory and sufficient basic education as a necessity for the child's development and survival.[21] However, in consideration of the best interests of the child, what amounts to basic education varies from child to child. Admitting the universal needs of basic reading and writing skills for all children regardless of status, the importance of availability of learning materials cannot be overemphasised. 'The anti-gay law has an immediate and destructive impact on service provision sectors such as education'.[22] Sexual and gender minorities suffer the unavailability of learning materials that are both relevant and informative 'and the absence of any usual channels of community support that are open to heterosexuals'.[23]

This incapacity translates to their being socially excluded, stripped of their right to basic education and all chances of survival. This is more so where the school systems compel sexual and gender minorities, through oppressive and discriminatory curricula, to conform to heteronormative roles and identities, policing their compliance, increasing their vulnerability and reducing their access to vital (and sometimes life-saving) health and other information. In worse cases, this leads to violence (including sexual violence as a form of identity policing) against sexual and gender minorities.[24]

4.3 *Adaptability*

This principle demands that the training in the schools be flexible and conscious of the evolving dynamics of the child, changing societies and the relationship between all factors mentioned. There should be a thriving consciousness of the needs of the student within their specific social and cultural context. This also should be considered from the specific context of the child and not a one-size-fits-all method.[25] There is the need to include human rights education, preventive education on drug abuse, HIV/AIDS, social media, sex, sexuality and gender identity education as will be appropriate for the varying ages, levels of education and identity of the child.[26]

4.4 *Acceptability*

This principle attends to the form and content of the training ongoing in schools, that is what amounts to necessary, important and relevant in realising the child's best interest.[27] This also covers the school curricula, teaching methods and quality of education.[28] Also, it speaks to the importance of non-discriminatory consciousness and the need for regular of the diverse cultures and subcultures, identities and issues within the academic community in the spirit of safety, tolerance and progressive learning. As well, this should be conscious of and non-discriminatory towards the child's sexuality and gender identity and expression.[29]

5 The Best Interests of the Child

This is a dynamic principle with implications that are constantly evolving and must be determined on a case-by-case basis.[30] In other words, there is the need to take particular consideration of the 'personal context, situation and need' of each child. More importantly, it is the primary consideration demanded by law to underlay all actions by state and non-state parties (parents, guardians, teachers, school authorities) affecting children.[31] This includes amongst other things the eradication of all negative attitudes that impede the full realisation of the child rights. This principle encompasses the right to non-discrimination; the state duty to provide equal opportunities and protect the child's equal rights to make use of the opportunities available. Thus it serves a guide to the redress of inequality.

Further, the child's right to dignity comes into play. There is the need to ensure the growing stability of an environment that does not threaten, through the application of the principle of reasonable accommodation, making the school accessible and adaptable to the needs and identity of the child. The child has the right to be heard in matters that concern the child and the child's best interests which include, amongst things, the child's education, sexuality, gender identity and expression; the child's belonging to a minority or vulnerable group; the child's evolving capacities; safety and development, all taking into account the various degrees of vulnerability.[32] Consequently, the child's views and experiences should be reflected in legislation, rules, policies and arrangements affecting the child, to ground the legality of such legislation, rules and arrangement.[33]

As regards the compatibility of the principle of the best interests of the child with cultural norms and practices, the child is protected from forced compliance.[34] This is more so as in the event of conflict between culture and international human rights law concerning the child, the latter prevails.[35]

6 The Best Interests of the Student

It is fair to say that this principle is reflective of the best interests of the child principle, especially when the child is present and participating in learning, which is hard to rule out.[36] It includes the right of all students to non-discrimination.[37] It also includes the principle of academic freedom.[38] This means, amongst other things, the academic community, individually and/or collectively, has the liberty to express their opinions freely and to fulfil their functions without being unjustly curtailed by state or non-state actors.[39] This means to 'to enable the access and opportunity within limits of public order, professional ethics and social responsibility'.[40] This translates invariably to the effective participation of the academic community in public affairs.[41] Academic freedom also translates to the presence of libraries and the need to have, amongst other things, multidisciplinary material on sexualities and gender; the inclusion of sexualities and gender issues in the training of the members of the academic community, especially the teachers and healthcare staff; collaborations between schools and sexual and gender minority rights focused non-governmental organisations for the purposes of training and access to information and safe spaces for the members of the academic community.

The student has the right to be taught effectively according to global standards and in congnisance the right to non-discrimination on the grounds of sexuality and gender identity and expression by any member of the academic community; the right to access to guidance for studies and the right to express the child's views, even when they are contrary to the heternorm, and contribute to the content of the academic curricula. The state has the duty, in exercising executive, legislative and judicial powers, to protect the academic community in their exercise of their academic freedom, which is closely linked with the freedom of expression. This is exactly what Nigeria's anti-gay law defeats.

The legality of the anti-gay law has been contested from several angles. Nigerian academics question in 'A critical review of Nigeria's Same-Sex Marriage (Prohibition) Act' the constitutionality of the anti-gay law as well as the previous criminalisation in the Criminal Code, Penal Code and Armed Forces Act.[42] The authors also observe that none of the sanctions in the anti-gay law has the alternative option of a fine, and that the courts are not granted the discretion to impose punishments less than those stated in the law, which vary between 14 and 10 years depending on the offence.[43] They argue that homosexuality as a sexual orientation occurs naturally as such it falls within the category of 'circumstances of birth' a prohibited ground for discrimination in the Nigerian Constitution.[44] It is recognised that there is no constitutional limitation on the right to non-discrimination on prohibited grounds such as circumstances of birth; as such the anti-gay law is unconstitutional.[45] The argument also refers to unjust prohibition of sexual and gender minority focused or inclined institutions as a violation of the freedom of expression, an enforceable right in Nigeria. It furthers argues that the anti-gay law is not reasonably justifiable in a democratic society.

However, 'Same-Sex marriage versus human rights: the legality of the anti-gay and lesbian law in Nigeria' argues from the standpoint of justifying the anti-gay law on the basis of the Islamic faith and Nigerian cultural beliefs and practices.[46]

The article admits that the anti-gay law was passed into law for its perceived moral, spiritual and religious justifications.[47] The article argues that the idea of same-sex marriage has a negative impact on Nigerian religions, customs, norms and values and is contrary to the Nigerian version of human rights with roots in Nigerian culture and traditions. It restricts measuring the legitimacy of the anti-gay law against the requirement of compliance with national legislation and the Constitution. It argues that the Nigerian anti-gay law is 'legal and constitutional'.

But the legality of legislation in a democratic and secular state should not be based on the dictates of an isolated expression or perception of culture.

7 Being Gay (Sexual and Gender Minority) and Learning in Nigeria

In 2003, Bisi Alimi, an undergraduate student of the University of Lagos, Nigeria, was outed as gay by the university student newspaper during student government elections on campus.[48] Following this, he was expelled in 2004 and was denied his degree.[49] He spoke up on Fundi Iyanda's 'New Dawn' television show in 2004 in protest, and at this point, he voluntarily came out of the closet.[50] Consequences were felt: while Bisi Alimi received death threats and subsequently fled Nigeria for his safety, Funmi Iyanda's 'New Dawn' which was hosted by the Nigerian Television Authority (NTA) was cancelled.[51]

In July 2003, Davis Mac Iyalla, a lay minister in the Anglican church, was fired from his job as the Principal of St. John's Anglican Secondary School, Port Harcourt, Nigeria, for being gay.[52] Reverend Jide Rowland Macaulay, in the course of his regular visits to Nigeria, discovered that the Nigerian homosexual population needed a safe space. He began conversations with Nigerian gay men on a Yahoo group named 'African Gay Christians'. On his visit to Nigeria in September 2006, the House of Rainbow Fellowship kicked off in Oba Akran, Lagos.

On 1 December 2006, the House of Rainbow fellowship had their first meeting with 32 people in attendance. Unfortunately, the backlash commenced within weeks of the first meeting. The members of the fellowship started showing up for Sunday church service with broken noses owing to violent attacks meted out on them on their way to church. In January 2008, he started receiving death threats. Amongst these, Reverend Jide received a threat that he and his members shall be massacred in cold blood. These events are equally set against the context of strong opposition from Professor Augustus Olakunle Macaulay, Reverend Jide's father, who boldly supported the enactment of the bill into law.[53]

An anthology published in 2016 titled *Blessed Body: The secret lives of Nigerian Lesbian Gay Bisexual and Transgender* portrays the predominantly homophobic context of Nigerian schools. In a piece within the anthology titled 'Resurrection', homophobic tensions within Nigerian schools are clearly portrayed. Every member of the school was non-verbally recruited to police sexuality. The writer, a lesbian, in narrating an incident from her secondary days when she encountered another lesbian, writes 'I withdrew because we both would have been beaten into a pulp if we were caught in the act'.

The policing of student's perceived sexual orientation occurs through suspending them from school, enrolling them in religious exorcism sessions or changing the school or luring them into early marriage, without actually engaging with them to listen and to understand. In another piece titled 'Whips', the writer shows how homosexuality within the context of the Nigerian secondary school is seen as a sin worthy of retribution, an offence to be investigated and disgraced.

In 2015, Seun Idris, a Nigerian Muslim gay man and university student, came out on social media.[54] There were mixed responses to this from his classmates. While some admired and applauded him, some were curious and wanted to know more about his sexuality. Others simply wanted to oppress him for being gay. He was physically attacked at school and constantly attacked on Facebook. Pressure on the home front has been steadily increasing, from infliction of physical pain to mental pain through harsh name-calling, to confiscation of his phone and withdrawal of sponsorship for his education. He is being constantly policed by his parents to get a girlfriend.[55]

On 17 August, he shared a status on facebook which reads:

> Today, at school, I reported a very serious case–Death threats. I returned back to school on Monday, and I had gotten threats from two sets of people in two days. Some guys on Monday, and the other, today. I wouldn't have reported, but I needed to. The school authority should have something to do about this.
>
> Biola Adenuga is a good woman. She was in a hurry, but she listened to me. She told me to file a report to her, through one of the school's HODs. As I left her front, she called upon me and told me I'd be fine, and she's sorry for the inconvenience. She is phenomenal.

Uncle Jolaoso, Miss Joy, Miss Ednar, Tobi Kelani, the school's security men, and some other people were witnesses. I was raged and shivering. They were vulgar and aggressive. Nobody would support me. Damilola and Seyi were upstairs, and the news got to them late. They went downstairs, but those guys were gone. But I am assured.[56]

8 The Legal Impact of Nigeria's anti-gay Law

In 2015, a study was carried out by PEN Nigeria, PEN America and the Leitner Centre for International Law and Justice to review the impact of the anti-gay law on freedom of expression in Nigeria.[57] The study relies on sources such as interviews with writers, artists, activists and scholars, as well as media reports and other secondary sources. It argues that the anti-gay law: threatens self-expression by sexual and gender minorities; hinders the expression of support for sexual and gender minority rights; affects literary, artistic and cultural communication; inhibits free speech; erodes democracy by silencing what should be an open and informed democratic debate on wider issues relating to minority rights; and results in halting the incidences of sexual and gender minority friendly public gatherings. The study argues particularly that the anti-gay law inhibits freedom of expression and as such impacts on other indivisible human rights which include, amongst other things, 'access to housing, health care, physical security and the right to live with dignity'.

It argues that the anti-gay law poses a direct threat to prevention and treatment of HIV/AIDS. This in line with the argument that the anti-gay law creates a climate that not only affects access to education and health services by sexual and gender minorities, but also the general public.[58] The study is of the view that the provisions of the law are broad, vague and, as such, its consequences are far reaching. The study picks up the statement made by Navi Pillay, United Nations High Commissioner for Human Rights, on Nigeria's enactment of the anti-gay law: 'Rarely have I seen a piece of legislation that in so few paragraphs directly violates so many basic, universal human rights'.[59] In addition to its legalising discrimination, it implicitly legitimates violation of the rights of sexual and minority groups and individuals owing to their increased vulnerability.

With a focus on cultural rights, writing, thinking, association and public debate it argues that the freedom of expression refers to the liberty of an individual to 'inhabit and represent their own authentic identity and to share their experiences with others'. This includes, amongst other things, the right to self-autonomy, individual identity, its public portrayal as well as advocating for human rights through engaging in public discourse.

The study traces the history of the anti-gay law from 2006 to 2011 when it gathered the most support, and 2013 when it was finally passed.[60] The study shows that activists and political commentators consider the anti-gay law a distraction from the state's real problems.[61] In engaging with the law, it points that anti-gay law violates Nigeria's international human rights obligation to promote and protect the freedom of expression, association, assembly, the right to seek and impart information of all kinds, the right to privacy, liberty and security of person, the right to protection from arbitrary arrest, the right to equal protection of the law, freedom from discrimination, the right to the enjoyment of the highest attainable standard of physical and mental health, the right to participate in cultural life, as well as the right to effective judicial remedy in the event of human rights violations.[62]

It recognises that freedom of expression can be validly limited by the state through national legal frameworks.[63] However, this is provided that there must be a legal basis for the limitation, such as the possibility of threat to the state's safety and order. Also, such limitation must be measured against the requisite parameters of necessity, proportionality, and a link between the threat and the expression sought to be limited.[64] The study argues that Nigeria's anti-gay law wrongly finds the sexual and gender minority community a threat. It discusses an international standard for protection of sexual and gender minorities, the principle in *Toonen v Australia* that criminalising consensual same-sex relations is a violation of the right to privacy. It also mentions the 2014 African Commission resolution condemning violence against the lesbian, gay, bisexual, transgender and intersex community and human rights defenders, and the 2015 United Nations High Commissioner for Human Rights Report on violence and discrimination based on actual or perceived sexual orientation or gender identity, as a violation of international human rights law in which states were urged to repeal anti-gay laws.[65] The study discusses incidents of violations under the anti-gay law amongst which include the arrest of 21 men on 10 May 2015, by the Nigerian police, at a birthday party in Ibadan, alleging that the men were a group of homosexuals conducting an initiation of new members into a secret gay cult.[66]

The study shows that the anti-gay law unjustly curtails the freedom of writers and publishers in Nigeria by exposing them to criminality, extortion and blackmail as consequences of their contributing to the sexual and gender minority rights debate.[67] The anti-gay law reduces the spaces for free expression online as well and is 'a direct threat to HIV prevention and treatment'.

Human rights reports are of the stance that Nigeria's anti-gay law challenges the right to health by criminalising the outreach to sexual and gender minorities; is vaguely worded and is inconsistent with international and regional human rights obligations; challenges the freedom of expression of sexual and gender minorities, human rights organisations and writers; has led to blackmail, eviction, the arrest of 12 men in Kano in January 2015 and 21 men in Oyo in May 2015 (all of whom were released hours later) on homosexual charges, and over 200 cases of mob attacks on people perceived to be sexual and gender minorities prior to their being handed over to the police, across the country.[68] Also, it is reported in 2014 that the Assistant Commissioner of Police in Bauchi said that the police were in possession of a list of suspected sexual and gender minorities 'under surveillance' incidental to their profiling of criminals.[69]

9 Legal Analysis and the Aspiration Agenda 2063

Nigeria's anti-gay law is an unreasonable expansion of state power. In 2008, Amnesty International published a paper aimed at giving an analytic overview of the criminalisation of homosexuality.[70] It recognises that the protection of sexual and gender minority rights is well within the confines of international human rights law.[71] It discusses the effects of anti-sodomy laws as the institutionalisation of discrimination; creation of more opportunities for arbitrary exercise of law enforcement powers and disregard for global standards on all levels; systemic disadvantage of sexual and gender minorities; inaccessibility of judicial redress for human rights violations; legal constraints on sexual and gender minority focused or inclusive organisations to register, meet and operate; unjust limitation of the right to privacy; dehumanisation; and the violation of the right to life by the provision of the death penalty in anti-sodomy laws as a sanction.[72]

It explores the merits of decriminalisation of homosexuality as a contribution to evolution of the law and the society. However, it recognises the effect of the legacy of previous criminalisation as an antithesis to this progress that decriminalisation represents. It explores the several justifications for criminalisation such as morality, public health and protection.

It is also of the view that inclusion of transgender individuals, regardless of their sexual orientation, within the confines of anti-sodomy laws is erroneous.

It recognises, expanding on the principle in *Toonen v Australia* which prohibits discrimination on grounds of sexual orientation, state duties under international law to protect human rights by creating enabling legal environments such as protection through decriminalisation and enactment of anti-discriminatory laws inclusive of sexual orientation and gender identity as a prohibited ground for discrimination to prevent harm.[73] Further, it reiterates that 'the right to privacy must be regarded as suggesting some responsibility on the state to promote conditions in which personal self-realisation can take place'.[74] It links sexual and gender minority community rights to non-discrimination and privacy, and the principle of indivisibility of human rights to other rights, which include the freedom of opinion, as provided for in Article 19 of the Universal Declaration on Human Rights and the International Covenant on Civil and Political Rights.[75]

It argues that in a democratic society, the inclination of the majority to label minority sexual orientations and gender identities as immoral does not necessarily justify the dehumanisation of these minorities through oppressive anti-sodomy laws.[76] Further, in this light, it argues that the state embracing difference, dignity and equality does not mislead its citizens immorally but secures adherence to the rule of law by fostering tolerance and community.[77]

Besides the impact of human rights violation and the declining possibilities of democracy in Nigeria owing to the anti-gay law, it also leads to brain drain. Professionals, students, investors, entrepreneurs, artistes, teachers and families that fall within the scope of sexual and gender minorities, leave the country for fear of being violated.

On the ongoing conversations and concern about whether or not homosexuality is part of African cultures, religions and traditions, and whether or not Africa is ready for sexual orientation and gender identity and expression (SOGIE) rights, these as well require a multidisciplinary response, and it is in the best interests of the child that these conversations continue. Nonetheless, it is the argument of this research that no extent of majority inclination to a version of morality or perception of custom or religion justifies the violation of the rights of the child.

It is the argument of the law, as is evident in several claw back clauses, that freedoms and rights should be limited by national laws, public safety, morality, order and the rights of others. However, these limitations are unjust if they do not comply with global standards of international human rights law.[78] These standards amongst other things include the following questions: Do the limitations fall within the bounds of legality? Is the limitation compliant with international human rights law standards? Does the limitation have a lawful and useful purpose? Is it the last means of achieving such lawful purpose? Is the value of the target of the limitation greater or less than its disadvantages, in other words, will the human rights protected be greater or less than the human rights violated within the context of democracy?[79] And the limitation must not be discriminatory.

On the argument of public morality as valid limitation, it is observed that 'the concept of morals derives from many social, philosophical and religious traditions, consequently, limitation for the purpose of protecting morals must be based on principles from a single tradition', but a multiplicity of morals, as inclined to by the majority as well as the sexual and gender minority population.[80] This is line with the principles of the universality of human rights and non-discrimination. The anti-gay law fails in all these tests. Sexuality and gender identity and expression are incidents of a person's nature and such are inherent and natural as the diverse versions and expressions of racial identity.[81] They should not be unjustly policed by law, the state or non-state actors. The anti-gay law solves no problems. It has in fact, through the fostering of homophobia and transphobia, done more harm than good and a steady decline ensues.[82]

In consideration of the African Union's Agenda 2063, a long-term plan designed to direct the trajectory of Africa's development, the negative impact of anti-gay laws as discussed above are not a part of the envisioned continent.[83] This is especially as regards the goals of a prosperous Africa based on inclusive growth and sustainable development; An Africa of good Governance, Democracy, Respect for human rights justice and the rule of law; An Africa with strong cultural identity, common heritage, shared values and ethics; an Africa where development is people driven unleashing the potential of women and youth.[84] In the light of the goal of cultural identity common heritage and values in African Union Agenda 2063, it is important that the multiplicity of values, heritages, traditions, cultures and subcultures are considered and universality of tolerance and accommodation upheld. In as much democracy is about rule by the majority of the people, minority cultures and subcultures should not be swept under the carpet. This is so because even amongst the majority there are smaller pockets of minority groups and interests which still need to be attended to and protected. The widely spread Nigerian argument for the enactment of the anti-gay law is invalid one if it is set against the concept of good governance and democracy as it should be. A democracy that rests on the perceived religious or cultural inclination of the majority is not a democracy that will permit constitutional governance. This is because the constitution on which our democracy is based is not designed to protect and justify the rights of the just majority, as this may inevitably lead to mob justice.[85] The democracy as is pledged in the Constitution of the Federal Republic of Nigeria 1999 as amended is based on the acceptance of diversity and the inclusion of everyone. This is especially in the light of the goal of a youth-driven development. The status of our schools is reflective of the status of the legal and political context in which they are situated. If the wider society is set ablaze by anti-human rights and counter-productive laws such as Nigeria's anti-gay law, invariably the substance and form of the training in the schools are anti-human rights and counter-productive, the products can hardly vary.

10 Conclusions and Recommendations

This paper argues that Nigeria's anti-gay law interferes with the scope of Nigeria's obligation under international law to guarantee the right to education of everyone including sexual and gender minorities. And this interference stifles the realisation of Agenda 2063. Repealing the anti-gay law and providing for constitutional safeguards for the sexual and gender minority community, though a noble and inevitable aspiration, is easier said than done. This is especially as decriminalisation and availability of legal protections do not erase the increasing rate of sexual and gender minority rights violations; do not secure new socialisation of inclusion, tolerance; and do not build the community with inclusive cultural values, which is the Nigeria, the Africa, we want.

It is recommended that sexual and gender minorities within the academic community should as much as possible initiate, create and develop a thriving sub-community which will serve as a safe space not just for students, but academic and non-academic members who are both boldly out or closeted. This is important to build a momentum for the sexual and gender minority community to empower themselves. In as much as conversation with the rest of the world on sexual and gender identity and expression issues is important, such conversation could be unfairly dominated by intimidating jeering of the homophobic majority. It is in the best interests of this newly found safe space to serve as a haven to mentor, protect, sponsor, consolidate, strengthen and propel more participants for our side of the ongoing conversation, and as many events as may arise, serve as an avenue for healing and rebirth.

Harvey Milk, in the course of his inaugural celebrations as 'the first openly gay person to be elected to public office in California', said, 'The American Dream starts with neighbourhoods. If we wish to rebuild our cities, we must first rebuild our neighbourhoods'.[86] Is the African Dream dissimilar? Large-scale transformation and shifts begin from the grassroots, from the basic units that make up the society. Similarly, the journey towards important and necessary aspirations such as the Agenda 2063 should, as well, move from the core and most important sources of socialisation: the learning spaces and the schools, and must be targeted at the children and young people in the spirit of inclusion and non-discrimination. This is not so much because we need to recruit leaders for 2063 but to protect the interest of our children and young people from the destruction that comes with homophobia. The tyranny of the anti-gay law further denies our children safety, protection and preparation, pushing them into denial, cowardice criminality, exile to other more inclusive and tolerant systems, and will deny us Agenda 2063. This is not because we will not get there, but because the Africa that should then carry on may not be ready or, worse still, may not be here. If Ubuntu: the principle of 'I am because we are' is the African dream, as this research argues that it is, then let us insist on the universality of tolerance, inclusion and the importance of legal, political and social reconstructions of negative attitudes towards the sexual and gender minorities.

Notes

1. Nigerian Criminal Code S. 214 and 217; Nigerian Penal Code S. 130; Nigerian Armed Forces Act S. 81.
2. Same-Sex Marriage Prohibition Act S. 5.
3. http://www.lgbt.cusu.cam.ac.uk/resources/trans/tackling-transphobia/ (accessed 31 August 2016).
4. ACRWC art 3; African Youth Charter.
5. https://en.wikipedia.org/wiki/School (accessed 12 August 2016).
6. http://www.merriam-webster.com/dictionary/school (accessed 12 August 2016).

7. http://www.sowetanlive.co.za/news/mandela/2013/07/18/67-awesome-quotes-by-nelson-mandela (accessed 12 August 2016).
8. Rea Carey & Suman Chakraborty *Class president or 'just another suicide statistic': the effects of homophobic harassment on youth,* Geo. J. Gender & L.1, 125 (1999) (Carey and Chakraborty 1999).
9. Ibid.
10. Nigerian Constitution S 12(1).
11. Nigeria's Child Rights Act, sec 1; CRC art 3.
12. ACRWC art 4.
13. ICESCR arts 13 & 14; World declaration on Education for All art 1; CRC art 29(1); Part 1, para 33, 11, 80 Vienna Declaration and programme of action.
14. Fons Coomans *Identifying key elements of the right to education: a focus on core content* (2004) https://www.google.com/url?sa=t&rct=j&q=&esrc=s&source=web&cd=1&cad=rja&uact=8&ved=0ahUKEwjC1YGd78rQAhWIJ8AKHaU7BooQFggcMAA&url=http%3A%2F%2Fwww.crin.org%2Fen%2Fdocs%2FCoomans-CoreContent-Right%2520to%2520EducationCRC.pdf&usg=AFQjCNF81ckrAoUBzg2osdmWnxPJbMKykA&sig2=wTfX6EgcOyB7WNRNiinn6w (Coomans 2004).
15. United Nations Committee on Economic Social and Cultural Rights General Comment 13.
16. Anti-gay law S. 5(2)(3).
17. https://queerallianceni geria.wordpress.com/2016/02/05/nigeria-lgbti-rights-situation-report-2016/ (accessed 32 August 2016).
18. Academy of Science of South Africa Report on Diversity in Human Sexuality: Implications for policy in Africa 'What re are the Public health consequence of criminalising same-sex sexual orientations and attempting to regulate the behaviour/relationships related to some sexualities orientation?'; Fatou Marie Drame et al. Gay men and other men who have sex with men in west Africa: evidence from the field' Culture, health and sexuality, 15(sup 1) (2013) (Drame et al. 2013).
19. Fons Coomans *Identifying the key elements of the right to education: a focus on the core content.*; UN Committee on Economic Social and Cultural Rights General Comment 13.
20. Ibid., 9.
21. ICESCR art 13(2)(a); CRC arts 28–29.
22. Ibid., 18.
23. Ibid; Elis Berlan et al. *Sexual orientation and bullying among adolescents in growing up today study,* 46.4 Journal of Adolescent Health (2010) (Berlan et al 2010).
24. Ibid.
25. Ibid., 18.

26. Ibid.
27. Ibid.
28. Ibid.
29. Ibid.
30. General Comment 14.
31. Amanda Lloyd *A theoretical analysis of the reality of children's right in Africa: an introduction to the African charter on the rights and welfare of the child*, African Human Rights Law Journal 2 (2002) ACRWC art 4; Danwood Mzikenge Chirwa *The merits and demerits of the African charter on the rights and welfare of the child*, 10.2 International Journal of Children Rights (2002) (Lloyd 2002).
32. CRC art 12.
33. Alfred Chanda *Gaps in the law and policy in the implementation of the Convention on the Rights of the Child in Zambia*, 32 Zambia Law Journal 1 (2000) (Chanda 2000).
34. Ibid., 18.
35. ACRWC art 1(3); Frans Viljeon Supra-national human rights instruments for the protection of children in Africa: the convention on the rights of the child and the African charter on the rights and welfare of the child, 31.2 Comparative International Law Journal of South Africa (1998); ACRWC art 4(1); CRC art 3(1).
36. Ibid., 18.
37. ICESCR art 2(2), 3.
38. Ibid., 18; African Charter on Democracy, Elections and Governance art 3; Dar es Salaam Declaration art 6; Lima Declaration on Academic Freedom and Autonomy of Higher Education Institutions; Kampala Declaration art 7.
39. Ibid.
40. Ibid.
41. *Media rights agenda and others v Nigeria* (2000) AHRLR 200 (ACHPR 1998).
42. Ibid., 1; Anthony Nwazuoke & Chinedu Igwe *A critical review of Nigeria's same-sex marriage (prohibition) act*, 45 Journal of Law, Policy and Globalisation (2016).
43. Nigerian anti-gay law S. 5.
44. Nigerian Constitution S. 42(2).
45. Ibid., S. 42(3).
46. Magaji Chiroma & Awwal Ilyasu Magashi Same-Sex marriage versus human rights: the legality of the anti-gay and lesbian law in Nigeria, International Law Research (2015) (Chiroma and Ilyasu 2015).
47. Joseph Onuche, *Same-Sex Marriage in Nigeria: A Philosophical Analysis*, International Journal of Humanities and Social Science Vol. 3, No. 12 (2013) (Onuche 2013).

48. San Diego Gay and Lesbian News, *Gay Nigerian activist Bisi Alimi shares his compelling story.* http://sdgln.com/news/2010/08/10/bisi-alimis-gay-nigerian-story.
49. Ibid.
50. James Michael Nichols, *Meet the first and only man to ever publicly come out in Nigeria*, http://www.huffingtonpost.com/entry/boy-from-mushin-kickstarter_us_56d5ea33e4b0bf0dab338eaf.
51. True Team, *Bisi Alimi: human rights activists on the LGBT brain drain in Africa*', http://trueafrica.co/article/bisi-alimi-the-human-rights-activist-on-the-lgbt-brain-drain-in-africa/.
52. Manya Brachear, *Message to the episcopalians*, http://articles.chicagotribune.com/2007-06-04/news/0706040003_1_anglican-church-archbishop-peter-akinola-gay-man.
53. Mark Schoofs, *In Nigeria, a bill to punish gays divides a family*, http://www.wsj.com/articles/SB116855583547274450.
54. https://76crimes.com/2016/08/03/nigeria-coming-out-is-valuable-but-i-wish-i-hadnt/.
55. Ibid.
56. https://www.facebook.com/seun.idriss2/posts/1068903089857902.
57. PEN Nigeria, *Silenced voices threatened lives; the impact of Nigeria's anti-gay law on freedom of expression*, https://www.google.co.za/url?sa=t&rct=j&q=&esrc=s&source=web&cd=1&cad=rja&uact=8&ved=0ahUKEwjpyr_z_crQAhUJDMAKHWGsCS8QFggZMAA&url=https%3A%2F%2Fpen.org%2FNigeria-anti-LGBT-Laws&usg=AFQjCNGxm0UgJHBbyGjt-hWE81ghBfejAA&sig2=SF5NZ1EYKSk-eMvkyx3_Cw&bvm=bv.139782543,d.bGg.
58. Ibid., 17.
59. *UN Human Rights Chief Denounces 'Draconian' Anti-Homosexuality Law in Nigeria*, http://www.un.org/apps/news/story.asp?NewsID=46923#.WDvkzX3se5g.
60. *Nigeria: Reject 'Same Gender' Marriage Ban*, http://www.hrw.org/news/2009/01/26/nigeria-reject-same-gender-marriage-ban; Emmanuel Obidimma & Angela Obidimma, *The Travails of Same-Sex Marriage Relation Under Nigerian Law*, 17 J. L., Pol'y, & Globalization 42, 43 (2013).
61. Ayo Sogunro, *One More Nation Bound in Freedom*, https://ayosogunro.com/2015/10/01/nigeria-a-nation-bound-in-freedom-by-ayo-sogunro-2/.
62. ICCPR arts 2, 9, 17, 19, 21, 22; ICESCR art 12, 15; African Charter art 2–4, 10, 11, 16; Nigerian Constitution S. 17, 37, 39, 40.
63. ICCPR art 19(3); Sect. 45 Nigerian Constitution S. 45.
64. UN Human Rights Committee General Comment 34; http://chrgj.org/wp-content/uploads/2012/10/suppressing-protest.pdf.

65. African Comm. on Human and Peoples' Rights, Resolution on Protection against Violence and other Human Rights Violations against Persons on the Basis of Their Real or Imputed Sexual Orientation or Gender Identity, Resolution No. 275, May 2014, http://www.achpr.org/sessions/55th/resolutions/275/.
66. Colin Stewart *Twenty-One Young Men Arrested in Ibadan, Oyo State, Nigeria—A Case Report*, The Initiative for Equal Rights—Nigeria, https://76crimes.com/2015/05/21/nigeria-no-court-challenge-vs-alleged-police-misconduct/.
67. Unoma Azuah, *Extortion and Blackmail of Nigerian Lesbians and Bisexual Women*, in Nowhere to Turn: Blackmail and Extortion of LGBT People in Sub-Saharan Africa. https://iglhrc.org/sites/default/files/484-1.pdf.
68. Human Rights Watch *World report 2015*; Human rights watch *World report 2016*; Amnesty international *Amnesty international report 2014/2015: the state of the world's human rights*; Amnesty International *Amnesty international report 2015/2016: the state of the world's human rights.*
69. Ibid.
70. Amnesty International *Love, hate and the law: decriminalising homosexuality*, https://www.google.co.za/url?sa=t&rct=j&q=&esrc=s&source=web&cd=2&cad=rja&uact=8&ved=0ahUKEwiggfCAg8vQAhXpDsAKHcmnB00QFggfMAE&url=https%3A%2F%2Fwww.amnesty.org%2Fdownload%2FDocuments%2F56000%2Fpol300032008eng.pdf&usg=AFQjCNE535keYFofj3MwJt0oqyIgD0DYPA&sig2=acEU955nzbQ0kRetPG8yTw&bvm=bv.139782543,d.bGg.
71. Ibid.
72. Ibid.
73. *Toonen v Australia*, human rights committee communication No. 488/1992, CCPR/C/50/D/488/1992, 4 April 1994; Dudgeon v. UK, (1981) 4 EHRR 149; http://www.stonewallscotland.org.uk/information_bank/history__lesbian__gay/89.asp; http://www.isleofman.com/tourism/factfile/government.asp; *Lawrence v. Texas*, 539 U.S. at 18; Fijian Constitution http://www.servat.unibe.ch/law/icl/fj00000_.htm (accessed 25 August 2016); Constitution of Portugal, http://www.portugal.gov.pt/Portal/EN/Portugal/Sistema_Politico/Constituicao/; Constitution of South Africa, http://www.info.gov.za/documents/constitution/index.htm.
74. *National coalition for gay and lesbian equality v Minister of Justice* 1998 (1) SA 6.
75. Universal Declaration art 19; ICCPR art 19; Human Rights Watch, In a Time of Torture: The Assault on Justice in Egypt's Crackdown on Homosexual Conduct, HRW 2004, https://www.hrw.org/report/2004/02/29/time-torture/assault-justice-egypts-crackdown-homosexual-conduct; Human Rights Watch, India: Repeal Colonial-Era Sodomy

Law; Entrapment, Arrests Harm AIDS Prevention Efforts, 11 January 2006, http://hrw.org/english/docs/2006/01/11/india12398.htm.

76. Justice Stevens' dissenting opinion in *Bowers v. Hardwick*, 478 U.S. 186, cited in *Lawrence v. Texas* at 17. In *Toonen v. Australia*, the Human Rights Committee; para. 8.6.
77. *McCoska v The State* (2005) FJHC 500.
78. *Media rights agenda and others v Nigeria* (2000) AHRLR 200 (ACHPR 1998); UN Human Rights Committee General Comment 34.
79. Ibid.
80. Ibid.
81. http://nostringsng.com/nigerias-anti-gay-law-affects-nigerians/.
82. Ibid., 18.
83. https://www.google.co.za/url?sa=t&rct=j&q=&esrc=s&source=web&cd=3&cad=rja&uact=8&ved=0ahUKEwjJ2f3Jy-7OAhVCCsAKHY-cUDBcQFgglMAI&url=http%3A%2F%2Fagenda2063.au.int%2Fen%2Fsites%2Fdefault%2Ffiles%2F01_Agenda2063_popular_version_ENGs.pdf&usg=AFQjCNGqEIC65dAk_QJEu6jpeExzjPJg7Q&sig2=WxyId3in3Pv7ybS4zBhQtw&bvm=bv.131669213,d.d2s (accessed 31 August 2016).
84. Ibid.
85. http://dailypost.ng/2016/03/15/tiers-condemns-murder-of-akinnifesi-olubunmi-over-alleged-homosexualism/; http://nnannaikpo.blogspot.co.za/2016/03/for-olumide-and-us.html; https://www.change.org/p/president-of-the-united-states-the-14-year-jail-term-for-nigerian-lgbtq-must-be-rescinded.
86. Randy Shilts *The mayor of castro street* 192 (1982) (Shilts 1982).

Bibliography

Books

Blessed Body: The Secret Lives of Nigerian Lesbian Gay Bisexual and Transgender, Cooking Pot Publishing Nigeria (2016).

Shilts, Randy. 1982. *The Mayor of Castro Street*. United Kingdom: St. Martins Press.

International Human Rights Treaties

African Charter on Democracy, Elections and Governance.

African Charter on Human and Peoples' Rights.

African Charter on the Rights and Welfare of the Child.

African Youth Charter.
Convention on the Rights of the Child.
International Covenant on Economic Social and Cultural Rights.

International Human Rights Instruments

African Comm. on Human and Peoples' Rights, Resolution on Protection against Violence and other Human Rights Violations against Persons on the Basis of Their Real or Imputed Sexual Orientation or Gender Identity, Resolution No. 275.
Dar es Salaam Declaration.
Kampala Declaration.
Lima Declaration on Academic Freedom and Autonomy of Higher Education Institutions.
UN Committee on Economic Social and Cultural Rights General Comment 13.
UN Committee on the Rights of the Child General Comment 14.
UN Human Rights Committee General Comment 34.
UN Human Rights Committee General Comment 34.
Universal Declaration of Human Rights.

National Legislation

Constitution of Portugal.
Constitution of South Africa.
Constitution of the Federal Republic of Nigeria 1999 (As Amended).
Fijian Constitution.
Nigerian Armed Forces Act.
Nigerian Criminal Code.
Nigerian Penal Code.
Nigerian Same Sex Marriage Prohibition Act.
Vienna Declaration and programme of action.
World Declaration on Education for All.

Journal Articles

Academy of Science of South Africa. 2015. *Report on Diversity in Human Sexuality: Implications for policy in Africa 'What Are the Public Health Consequence of Criminalising Same-sex Sexual Orientations and Attempting to Regulate the Behaviour/Relationships Related to Some Sexualities Orientation?'.*
Berlan, Elis, et al. 2010. Sexual Orientation and Bullying Among Adolescents in Growing Up Today Study. *Journal of Adolescent Health* 46 (4): 366–371.

Carey, Rea, and Suman Chakraborty. 1999. Class President or 'Just Another Suicide Statistic': The Effects of Homophobic Harassment on Youth. *Geoorgetown Journal of Gender and the Law* 1: 125.

Chanda, Alfred. 2000. Gaps in the Law and Policy in the implementation of the Conventi on on the Rights of the Child in Zambia. *Zambia Law Journal* 32: 1–19.

Chiroma, Magaji, and Awwal Ilyasu Magashi. 2015. Same-sex Marriage Versus Human Rights: The Legality of the Anti-gay and Lesbian Law in Nigeria. *International Law Research* 4 (1): 11.

Chirwa, Danwood Mzikenge. 2002. The Merits and Demerits of the African Charter on the Rights and Welfare of the Child. *International Journal of Children Rights* 10 (2): 157–177.

Coomans, Fons. 2007. *Identifying the Key Elements of the Right to Education: A focus on the Core Content.* London: Child Rights Information Network.

Drame, Fatou Marie, et al. 2013. Gay Men and Other Men who have Sex with Men in West Africa: Evidence from the Field. *Culture, Health and Sexuality* 15 (Suppl 1): 7–21.

Lloyd, Amanda. 2002. A Theoretical Analysis of the Reality of Children's Right in Africa: An Introduction to the African Charter on the Rights and Welfare of the Child. *African Human Rights Law Journal* 2 (1): 11–32.

Nwazuoke, Anthony and Chinedu Igwe. 2016. A Critical Review of Nigeria's Same Sex Marriage (Prohibition) Act. *Journal of Law, Policy and Globalisation* 45.

Obidimma, Emmanuel, and Angela Obidimma. 2013. The Travails of Same-Sex Marriage Relation Under Nigerian Law. *Journal of Law, Policy and Globalization* 17: 42–43.

Onuche, Joseph. 2013. Same Sex Marriage in Nigeria: A Philosophical Analysis. *International Journal of Humanities and Social Science* 3 (12).

Viljeon, Frans. 1998. Supra-national Human Rights Instruments for the Protection of Children in Africa: The Convention on the Rights of the Child and the African Charter on the Rights and Welfare of the Child. *The Comparative and International Law Journal of Southern Africa* 31 (2): 199–212.

Case Law

Bowers v. Hardwick, 478 U.S. 186.

Dudgeon v. UK, (1981) 4 EHRR 149.

Lawrence v. Texas, 539 U.S. at 18.

McCoska v The State (2005) FJHC 500.

Media Rights Agenda and Others v Nigeria (2000) AHRLR 200 (ACHPR 1998).

National Coalition for Gay and Lesbian Equality v Minister of Justice 1998 (1) SA 6.

Toonen v Australia, Human Rights Committee Communication No. 488/1992, CCPR/C/50/D/488/1992, 4 April 1994.

Human Rights Reports

Amnesty International *Amnesty International Report 2014/2015: The State of the World's Human Rights.*

Amnesty International *Amnesty International Report 2015/2016: The State of the World's Human Rights.*

Amnesty International *Love, Hate and the Law: Decriminalising Homosexuality.* https://www.google.co.za/url?sa=t&rct=j&q=&esrc=s&source=web&cd=2&cad=rja&uact=8&ved=0ahUKEwiggfCAg8vQAhXpDsAKHcmnB00QFggfMAE&url=https%3A%2F%2Fwww.amnesty.org%2Fdownload%2FDocuments%2F56000%2Fpol300032008eng.pdf&usg=AFQjCNE535keYFofj3MwJt0oqyIgD0DYPA&sig2=acEU955nzbQ0kRetPG8yTw&bvm=bv.139782543,d.bGgAccessed 12 Aug 2016.

Human Rights Watch *World Report 2015.*

Human Rights Watch *World Report 2016.*

PEN Nigeria, *Silenced Voices Threatened Lives; the Impact of Nigeria's Anti-gay Law on Freedom of Expression.* https://www.google.co.za/url?sa=t&rct=j&q=&esrc=s&source=web&cd=1&cad=rja&uact=8&ved=0ahUKEwjpyr_z_crQAhUJDMAKHWGsCS8QFggZMAA&url=https%3A%2F%2Fpen.org%2FNigeria-anti-LGBT-Laws&usg=AFQjCNGxm0UgJHBbyGjt-hWE8lghBfejAA&sig2=SF5NZ1EYKSk-eMvkyx3_Cw&bvm=bv.139782543,d.bGg.

Internet Articles

Sogunro, Ayo. 2015. *One More Nation Bound in Freedom.* https://ayosogunro.com/2015/10/01/nigeria-a-nation-bound-in-freedom-by-ayo-sogunro-2/. Accessed 12 Aug 2016.

Azuah, Unoma. 2016. Extortion and Blackmail of Nigerian Lesbians and Bisexual Women. In *Nowhere to Turn: Blackmail and Extortion of LGBT People in Sub-Saharan Africa.* https://iglhrc.org/sites/default/files/484-1.pdf. Accessed 31 Aug 2016.

Brachear, Manya. *Message to the Episcopalians.* http://articles.chicagotribune.com/2007-06-04/news/0706040003_1_anglican-church-archbishop-peter-akinola-gay-man.

Coomans, Fons. 2004. *Identifying Key Elements of the Right to Education: A Focus on Core Content.* London: Child Rights Information Network.

http://www.lgbt.cusu.cam.ac.uk/resources/trans/tackling-transphobia/. Accessed 12 Aug 2016.

http://nostringsng.com/nigerias-anti-gay-law-affects-nigerians/. Accessed 12 Aug 2016.

https://www.facebook.com/seun.idriss2/posts/1068903089857902. Accessed 12 Aug 2016.

https://www.google.co.za/url?sa=t&rct=j&q=&esrc=s&source=web&cd=3&cad=rja&uact=8&ved=0ahUKEwjJ2f3Jy-7OAhVCCsAKHYcUDBcQFgglMAI&url=http%3A%2F%2Fagenda2063.au.int%2Fen%2Fsites%2Fdefault%2Ffiles%2F01_Agenda2063_popular_version_ENGs.pdf&usg=AFQjCNGqEIC65dAk_QJEu6jpeExzjPJg7Q&sig2=WxyId3in3Pv7ybS4zBhQtw&bvm=bv.131669213,d.d2s. Accessed 31 Aug 2016.

http://www.stonewallscotland.org.uk/information_bank/history__lesbian__gay/89.asp. Accessed 31 Aug 2016.

http://www.isleofman.com/tourism/factfile/government.asp. Accessed 31 Aug 2016.

http://www.servat.unibe.ch/law/icl/fj00000_.htm. Accessed 25 Aug 2016.

https://www.google.com/url?sa=t&rct=j&q=&esrc=s&source=web&cd=1&cad=rja&uact=8&ved=0ahUKEwjC1YGd78rQAhWIJ8AKHaU7BooQFggcMAA&url=http%3A%2F%2Fwww.crin.org%2Fen%2Fdocs%2FCoomans-Core-Content-Right%2520to%2520EducationCRC.pdf&usg=AFQjCNF81ckrAoUBzg2osdmWnxPJbMKykA&sig2=wTfX6EgcOyB7WNRNiinn6w. Accessed 31 Aug 2016.

http://www.sowetanlive.co.za/news/mandela/2013/07/18/67-awesome-quotes-by-nelson-mandela. Accessed 12 Aug 2016.

http://hrw.org/english/docs/2006/01/11/india12398.htm. Accessed 31 Aug 2016.

http://chrgj.org/wp-content/uploads/2012/10/suppressing-protest.pdf. Accessed 31 Aug 2016.

https://queerallliancenigeria.wordpress.com/2016/02/05/nigeria-lgbti-rights-situation-report-2016/. Accessed 12 Aug 2016.

http://dailypost.ng/2016/03/15/tiers-condemns-murder-of-akinnifesi-olubunmi-over-alleged-homosexualism/; http://nnannaikpo.blogspot.co.za/2016/03/for-olumide-and-us.html. Accessed 31 Aug 2016.

https://www.change.org/p/president-of-the-united-states-the-14-year-jail-term-for-nigerian-lgbtq-must-be-rescinded. Accessed 31 Aug 2016.

https://76crimes.com/2016/08/03/nigeria-coming-out-is-valuable-but-i-wish-i-hadnt/.

https://en.wikipedia.org/wiki/School. Accessed 12 Aug 2016.

http://www.merriam-webster.com/dictionary/school. Accessed 12 Aug 2016.

Nichols, James Michael. *Meet the First and Only Man to Ever Publicly Come Out in Nigeria*. http://www.huffingtonpost.com/entry/boy-from-mushin-kick-starter_us_56d5ea33e4b0bf0dab338eaf.

Schoofs, Mark. 2016. *In Nigeria, a Bill to Punish Gays Divides a Family* http://www.wsj.com/articles/SB116855583547274450. Accessed 31 Aug 2016.

Stewart, Colin. 2015. Twenty-One Young Men Arrested in Ibadan, Oyo State, Nigeria—A Case Report. *The Initiative for Equal Rights—Nigeria*, May 18.

https://76crimes.com/2015/05/21/nigeria-no-court-challenge-vs-alleged-police-misconduct/. Accessed 12 Aug 2016.
True Team *Bisi Alimi: Human Rights Activists on the LGBT Brain Drain in Africa*. http://trueafrica.co/article/bisi-alimi-the-human-rights-activist-on-the-lgbt-brain-drain-in-africa/. Accessed 31 Aug 2016.

Author Biography

David Nnanna Chukwukadibia Ikpo is a Nigerian lawyer, storyteller, blogger and author of Fimí sílẹ̀ Forever (a fictional novel that, among other things, explores homophobia and the negative impact of Nigeria's Same-Sex Marriage Prohibition Act 2013). He is presently at Centre for Human Rights, University of Pretoria, South Africa as a doctoral candidate and the Communications Officer in its Sexual Orientation Gender Identity and Expression (SOGIE) Unit. (Personal blog: http://nnannaikpo.blogspot.com).

CHAPTER 12

Realizing Maternal and Child Health Through Curbing the Barriers for Accessing Basic Education: Human Rights-based Options for Africa

Solomon Tekle Abegaz

1 Introduction

The biomedical dialect of "diagnose and treat" is not sufficient enough to foster the health and well-being of women and children.[1] It is rather firmly rooted in the social, political, economic, cultural, and environmental determinants of health. A failure to give the desired attention to these factors continues to be a cause of concern in Africa. More worryingly, this status quo *has* contributed to the unnecessary suffering and deaths of millions of children and women in the continent. Health outcomes resulting from adverse social and other determinants remain unaddressed. Equally, health disparities within and among countries have increased, and public health and medicine have continued to diverge.

S.T. Abegaz (✉)
College of Law and Governance Studies, Addis Ababa University,
Addis Ababa, Ethiopia
e-mail: solomomte@gmail.com

S.T. Abegaz
School of Law, University of Gondar, Gondar, Ethiopia

A.C. Onuora-Oguno et al. (eds.), *Education Law, Strategic Policy and Sustainable Development in Africa*, DOI 10.1007/978-3-319-53703-0_12

Drawing on Africa's past achievements and challenges, and looking ahead toward the next 50 years, the African Union (AU) adopts Agenda 2063 which envisions "an integrated, prosperous, and peaceful Africa, driven by its own citizens and representing a dynamic force in the international arena."[2] A common and shared set of seven aspirations has emerged from this vision which includes "improvement of habitats and access to basic necessities of life[3]; respect for human rights[4]; and creating opportunities for Africa's youth for self-realization, access to health, and education."[5]

This work aspires to reexamine that education has important social impacts on maternal and child health and underlines that curbing the barriers for girls' education has the potential to partly address the aspirations Africa sets down in its 2063 Agenda affecting the health well-being of women and children. In support of the link between education and health, researches reveal the link education has with reduced child and maternal deaths, improved child health, and lower fertility. Women with at least some formal education are more likely than uneducated women to use contraception, marry later, have fewer children, and be better informed of the nutritional and other needs of children. Also, education enables women to take decisions regarding health care, and the lack of it results the reverse.

The impact of education is one such determinant of maternal and child health outcomes in Africa. Not only that primary education empowers women but also improves the healthof them and their children.[6] Despite the importance of basic education, only in Africa the rate of illiteracy for people over 15 is 41%.[7] Low education is one of the challenges that prevent women from seeking health care and making the best choices for themselves and their children's health, resulting in delays and poorer health outcomes in the continent.[8] According to UNICEF, children are also at greater risk of dying before age five if they are born in rural areas, among the poor, or to a mother denied basic education.[9]

Nothing else degrades a human person as lacking complete mental or physical health. To address this threat, public health programs and strategies have made significant progress in reducing maternal and child mortality in many countries. Globally, the rate of under-five mortality has decreased by nearly half, from 90 deaths per 1000 live births in 1990 to 46 in 2013.[10] However, in the same time period, the decrease in newborn deaths has been significantly lower. Equally, maternal mortality continues to be a pressing challenge and many African countries failed to meet the targets set under the Millennium Development Goal (MDG)—Goal 5.

Since public health efforts designed to protect maternal and child health are not entirely successful, what additional measures have to be taken? This is what this work sets out to explore. It argues to counter and reverse the tide promoting "basic education as a commodity," there is a need to enforce a regional consensus within Africa on "basic education to women and girls care as a right" and tackling the barriers to realize this right. It seeks the social transformations indispensable to resolve the inequities found in education.

The premise of this work is simple—that the human rights laws dealing with basic education have an important role in ensuring a healthy and dignified life of women and children, while health improves learning potential. In summarized form, the argument is as follows: First, it should be reemphasized that the girl children in Africa are entitled to access to primary education enshrined under the various legal regimes. Second, this right has a significant impact on health outcome of women and children. Third, several factors including unmet enrollment levels, deficits in completion rates, challenges of quality education, gender gaps, accountability, and inadequate funding influence the full realization of the right, and such barriers should be abolished. My argument does not advance girls' basic education is the sole path for the betterment of health of these vulnerable groups in African societies, for improving health cannot be boiled down to just one underlying cause—education. However, I argue that ensuring the human right to basic education is one alternative pathway that can produce great benefits for groups that could hardly be considered privileged due to illiteracy.

2 Correlation of Education with Maternal and Child Health Gains

As highlighted in the introductory part, there is a strong correlation between primary education and improved child and maternal health. This section aims to analye the context in which this relation exists in greater detail. It answers how and why education improves health.

There appeared to be a complex web of factors connecting education with health. Some scholars argue against the direct link that education has in actually improving health by hypothesizing that "more schooling leads to better jobs, which in turn comes with better medical benefits."[11] This approach focuses education as a means for obtaining employment opportunity, where the latter in turn gives the capacity to literate people access to higher earning and medical health care. It is true that educated people are more likely to have health insurance. However, such education that led to better employment and health is often not primary education, where the latter is the focus of this work. Most importantly, the hypothesis fails to consider how primary education helps individuals or groups to make proper decisions affecting their health. It offers them to understand their health needs, follow instructions, advocate for themselves and their families, and communicate effectively with health providers.[12]

A disjuncture from the hypothesis in the foregoing, this work emphasizes the direct correlation between primary education and the enjoyment of healthy maternal and child lives. How does formal education impact health outcomes or what are the ways in which education influences same? First, in countries such as Peru, formal education of women has a profound effect on utilization of maternal health care services, mainly on the use of prenatal care and delivery assistance.[13] In this light, increasing girls' access to education improves maternal health. In Burkina Faso, mothers with secondary education are twice as likely to give birth more safely in health facilities as those with no education.[14] It has been estimated that an additional year of schooling for 1000 women helps prevent two maternal deaths.[15]

Second, increasing girls' education has positive effects on infant and child survival. A child born to a mother who can read is 50% more likely to survive past the age of five than a child born to an illiterate woman. In countries such as Indonesia, child vaccination rates are 19% when mothers have no education.[16] When mothers have at least a secondary school education, this figure increases to 68%. Africa is a continent where children continue to die unnecessarily in unacceptably high numbers.[17] Third, education is intertwined with the rate of infection of HIV. Basic education decreases a girl's or woman's risk for contracting HIV or transmitting HIV to her baby. A study in Uganda demonstrated that each additional year of education for girls reduces their chances of contracting HIV by 6.7%.[18] Also, a study in Zambia finds that HIV spreads twice as fast among uneducated girls. In a similar vein, according to the UNESCO's report, in Malawi, only 27% of women without any education know that HIV transmission risks can be reduced by taking drugs during pregnancy, but that figure rises to 59% for women with secondary education.[19]

Interestingly, human rights law also recognizes education as a human right is inextricably intertwined with the right to health. Both rights complement, enhance, and support each other. Veriava and Coomans argue that education is necessary for the enjoyment of other rights and freedoms.[20] The right to education improves health, while the right to health in turn improves learning potential of the right holder. The Committee on Economic, Social and Cultural Rights States that the right to health is closely related to, and dependent upon, the realization of other human rights including the right to education, food, and shelter which are important determinants of health.[21] Equally, the UN Human Rights Council underscores that a right-based approach to maternal and child survival and health depends on the realization of other rights to include the rights to food, education, and social security.[22]

Foregoing explains the links and benefits that education has with reduced child and maternal deaths, improved child health, and lower fertility, and, most importantly, that how these links are underscored in the work of relevant UN human rights bodies. But the important issue to the flag is how education is treated under human rights laws? The following section, hence, examines the normative basis for the right to basic education from global and regional law perspectives, and the obligations it places on State to realize the right.

3 The Normative Framework: The Right of Access to Primary Education

Primary education is understood as "the main delivery system for the basic education of children outside the family."[23] The human right to be able to read, write, and calculate is protected by international and national laws. These laws place an obligation on the State to realize girl children's right to education by delivering a range of services. It is important for policy-makers, planners, administrators, and education professionals who design, plan, and deliver these services to understand their international and constitutional obligations. In order to advocate for a sustained education service delivery, it is also important for education professionals, caregivers, children, and civil society have a clear understanding of every girls' basic education right and the State's obligations in realizing the right.

3.1 *The International Protection*

Education as a human rights issue has embedded its universal legacy. The right to basic education continues to receive significant attention at the international level through various international instruments.[24]

This right enjoys the extensive protection of international law and indeed rhymes its importance through various international instruments. Its official inclusion on the international agenda dates back to the founding of the Universal Declaration of Human Rights (UDHR 1948). The UDHR entrenched the right to education.[25] To date, this remains a foundational norm with regards to the right to education across all sectors in the international sphere. Apart from the UDHR, there is an array of other global instruments, giving effect to this right. This is inclusive of, among others, International Covenant on Economic, Social and Cultural Rights (ICESCR 1966), which obligates States to make primary education compulsory and free.[26] Other instruments include the Convention on the Elimination of all Forms of Discrimination against Women (CEDAW 1979), World Declaration on Education for all 1990, UNESCO Convention against Discrimination in Education.

Equally, the right to education is widely recognized in regional instruments. Protocol 1 of the European Convention for the Protection of Human Rights and Fundamental Freedoms provides that no person shall be denied the right to education.[27] It is also captured in the American Declaration of the Rights and Duties of Man (1948)[28] and the Protocol of San Salvador to the American Convention on Human Rights (1988).[29] In the African region, the right to education is entrenched in Article 17 of the African Charter on Human and Peoples' Rights (African Charter) (1981). Article 11(3) (a) of the African Charter on the Rights and Welfare of the Child (1990) also provides for the right to free and compulsory basic education.

The right in question has also secured attention in global social contracts that underline global development agenda. It is for this reason that the right to primary education was given explicit expression in the MDGs, MDG-2 in particular. Equally, obtaining a quality education is the foundation to improve people's lives and sustainable development—Sustainable Development Goal (SDG) 4.

The right has also attained recognition, in various formulations, in the national constitution of African countries. A paradigmatic example is that of the South African Constitution, which provides that:

1. Everyone has the right—
   (a) to basic education, including adult basic education; and
   (b) to further education, which the State, through reasonable measures, must make progressively available and accessible.

The explicit constitutional entrenchment in the above founded a greater regard for this right and a solid constitutional commitment to deliver quality basic education to the populace on the part of the State including the duty to take legislative and other measures.[30] South Africa thus is not only required not to interfere with an individual's enjoyment of the right, but the State is also obliged to provide basic education. The section below proffers a critical discussion on the content of the obligations that arise from the right to basic education in general.

3.2 State Obligations

In part, socioeconomic rights, such as education, health, and housing, impose positive duties on the State to take reasonable steps, within available resources, to achieve their progressive realization. In this light, these rights are often considered not to engage governments to implement them immediately—so as to ensure that States do provide for at least the minimum essential levels in respect of those rights and do not just attribute failures in respect thereof to a lack of resources. However, there are exceptions to the qualifying progressive realization. The right to basic education, including adult basic education, is by contrast unqualified and is therefore an absolute right.[31] Interestingly, South African jurisprudence in the area the right to basic education underscores that this right sets minimum obligations and is unqualified in terms of Section 29(1)(a) of the Constitution.[32]

The Committee on Economic, Social and Cultural Rights (Committee on ESCR), created in terms of CESCR, has prime responsibility for monitoring socioeconomic rights, including the right to education. In view of discharging this responsibility, the Committee is engaged in elaborating the meaning and obligations that the right to education entails. According to this treaty body, while the exact standard secured by the right to basic education may vary according to conditions within a particular State, education must exhibit the following features: availability, accessibility, acceptability, and adaptability. This four "A" scheme, considered below, is a useful device to analyze the content of the right to basic education and the corresponding obligations deriving from this unqualified right.

Availability, Accessibility, Acceptability, and Adaptability

According to the ESCR Committee,[33] availability requires that working educational institutions and programmes are available in sufficient quantity. It also requires "facilities at schools such as well-equipped classrooms, libraries, sanitation facilities for both sexes, safe drinking water, trained and well-paid teachers and teaching materials."[34] An accessible education, on the other hand, entails an education being available to all on the basis of the principle of non-discrimination, economic accessibility, and physical accessibility.[35] In terms of the principle of non-discrimination, education must exhibit a system where everybody is allowed in the classroom. Then again, economic accessibility implies that an affordable education for all at secondary and tertiary levels and a free education at primary level. In relation to physical accessibility, it is questionable whether the State is providing schools that are physically accessible where learners continue to walk distances of up to 8 km a day to get to school.[36]

Acceptability of education is premised an education of which the "form and substance, including curricula and teaching methods, are acceptable to students and in some cases to their parents; it should be relevant, culturally appropriate and of good quality."[37] It is argued that "the scope of the acceptability of basic education has been broadened in international human rights jurisprudence to include a system of education that seeks to protect the individual rights of learners on issues such as language rights, parental choice, and discipline of learners."[38]

Lastly, in terms of adaptability, "education has to be flexible so it can adapt to the needs of changing societies and communities and respond to the needs of students within their diverse social and cultural settings."[39] Put differently, States should adapt the education to the needs of the learners, the needs of society, and the job market. Adaptability entails mobile schools for nomadic groups or the more vulnerable segments of society.

Implementation of the forgoing scheme has a great impact to produce health and well-being of women and children, based on the premise access to girls' primary education improves maternal and child health. This is mainly because all national policies related to primary education compel the State and parents to send children to primary school. Sending children to primary school is not optional, but mandatory, therefore primary education that is sustained by an action plan is compulsory. In reality, Africa has made tremendous strides toward accessing universal primary education, increasing its net enrollment rate from 65% in 1999 to 83% in 2008.[40] However, the pace of progress is insufficient to ensure that all girls and boys will complete a full course of primary schooling.

The section that follows sets out to discuss the obstacles that militate against ensuring full response to the existing gaps in girls' education.

4 Barriers to Access to Girls' Education in Africa

According to encouraging sources, enrollment in primary education has continued to rise, reaching 89% in the developing world.[41] Despite the impressive results gained in expanding access over the past few decades, more than 100 million children are still deprived of access to primary education and fewer than half of all children worldwide participate in early childhood programmes.[42] Put differently, while it is acknowledged that African countries effort of legitimately advancing access and enjoyment of the right to basic education have been impressive in terms of legislative and other initiatives, it should also be noted that the same has been accompanied by non-exhaustive but critical and interconnected challenges discussed below.

4.1 Unmet Net Enrollment Levels

Africa has made tremendous strides toward achieving universal primary education, yet the current pace of progress of school enrollment in African countries is insufficient to ensure that all girls and boys will complete a full course of primary schooling. African countries have increased their net enrollment rate from 65% in 1999 to 83% in 2008. Indeed, this is the MDG where African countries have made the most progress. While a majority of African countries is set to achieve universal primary enrollment by the target date, far fewer countries met the goals for primary completion rates and young adult literacy rates. This partly explains that there are regional imbalances or inequities in enrollment to access primary education within Africa.

4.2 Deficits in Completion Rates

Despite a good performance by the majority of African countries toward universal primary school enrollment, this progress has yet to translate into commensurate primary completion rates. By no means, the end goal of basic education is enrollment despite its importance. This is precisely because "the focus of basic education must be on actual learning acquisition and outcome, rather than exclusively upon enrolment, continued participation in organized programs, and completion of certification requirements."[43] Evidence on net enrollment and completion rates, for selected African countries, shows that few countries have improved their rates since 2007.[44] However, some countries such as Chad, Congo, Eritrea, Namibia, and Tunisia have evidenced some decline in their primary completion rate since 2007.[45] The slow and in some cases regressive trend is caused by a range of dynamics. First, the primary school entry age is higher than the formal age required in many African countries. This increases peer pressure on older students to enter the labor market prior to completing the primary school cycle.[46] Second, a major setback in Africa is the unequal access to education services, which affects low-income households, weakens retention and learning outcomes, undermines the quality of education, and increases grade repetition. In North Africa, the percentage of children out of school improved from 3% in 1999 to 2% in 2008. However, in the rest of Africa, the percentage of children out of school grew marginally from 43% in 1999 to 46% in 2008, which translates that there were 31 million children who were school-aged but not enrolled in school in Africa (excluding North Africa).[47]

4.3 Challenges of Quality of Education

The concept of quality of education is elusive. In an attempt to capture its meaning, a World Bank-sponsored study identifies in terms of the strong relationship between students' cognitive achievement and the provision of inputs features.[48] It identified five major in-school areas for improving the quality of education—improving curriculum; increasing learning materials; increasing instructional time; improving teaching; and increasing the capacity of students.[49] These are research inputs which are focused generally on materials such as textbooks, desks, and blackboards as well as teachers and students.

In Africa, the challenge of quality of primary education continues to loom large. While the gains in enrollment had been quite impressive in many parts of the world, including the sub-Saharan African region, low quality and high dropout rates led to the perception that many of the children left school without having obtained a sustainable level of basic reading, writing, and numeracy skills.[50] The rising concern with education quality was strongly reflected in the protocols of the World Conference on Education for All held in Jomtien, Thailand in 1990 and the World Education Forum held in Dakar, Senegal in 2000. It was perceived that ensuring education quality is a necessary complement to educational access and hence quantity and quality had to go hand in hand.[51]

4.4 *Primary Education Gender Gap*

The gender gap between girls and boys in accessing primary education has been narrowed in Africa over the past few decades. However, too many girls do not complete a full educational cycle and millions of girls in Africa were forced to be out of school. Girls face particular obstacles throughout their schooling, including the costs of **schooling, early marriage, safety, particularly in transport, and sexual violence.** More broadly, **girls' education in Africa is still faced with inequalities and gender-based discrimination inherent in their society**. Education for girls is also affected by school building, sanitation facilities, the hiring of women teachers, and teacher pay for women. Statistics show that "for every 100 boys out of school, there are still 117 girls in the same situation."[52] Building the knowledge necessary to combat disease, eradicate poverty and hunger, and ensure environmental sustainability will be impossible unless these gaps are addressed in the African continent.[53] As a result, millions of children and women will continue to die needlessly, placing the rest of the SDGs at risk.

4.5 *Gaps in Accountability*

It is argued that accountability is central in a human rights-based approach to health or other socioeconomic rights.[54] Focussing on judicial accountability, Skelton underscores the recent focus of South African courts concerning the right to education to address issues including availability and accessibility.[55] She further analyzed the approach advanced by the Constitutional Court of South Africa in interpreting the right to basic education—as a right that is not subject to progressive realization taking, by way of example, the case of *Juma Musjid*.[56] In this case, the Constitutional Court, inter alia, interpreted "Unlike some of the other socio-economic rights, this right (the right to basic education) is immediately realizable. There is no internal limitation requiring that the right be 'progressively realised' within the available resources subject to 'reasonable legislative measures'."[57]

Although there are positive trends in recent years in judicializing socioeconomic rights in other African countries including the right to education, there remains to be challenges in enforcing these rights before courts.[58] Kamga was right when he raises concerns about the importance of judicial accountability in the realm of the right to basic education, and how challenges of justiciability of the right owing to lack of standing in court for private individuals, the lack of constitutional remedies in case of a violation of rights, and weak separation of powers as a factor that militate against the realization of the right basic education in the Cameroonian context.[59] Many African countries constitutions mainly include socioeconomic rights in "Directive Principles of States Policy." As such, the justiciability of those rights tends to be uncertain, which is partly the cause of concern for courting the right in question.

5 Concluding Remarks and the Way Forward

Girl's and women's access to education and health information are human rights. It seemed self-evident. All African States have also ratified the UN CRC and, except a few of them,[60] are parties to the ACRWC at the same time. Clearly, both of these instruments raise an obligation on them to ensure primary education to be free of charge and subjected to a detailed implementation plan and comply with the 4 A's. Constructed around the premise that education has a correlation with the African women's and children's health, this chapter mainly identifies that implementation of these obligations, more specifically ensuring the right to primary education, has a huge impact to make in fostering the well-being of vulnerable women and children. In this way, African countries have the potential to achieve the several aspirations postulated in their 2063 Agenda.

However, the current State universal primary education in Africa or that of sub-Saharan Africa is fraught with challenges of implementation, despite the impressive achievements gained over the past one decade in expanding access. These challenges must not hold ground and need to be addressed. The following proposals can be considered. First, African countries must continue to uphold the idea that ensuring universal primary education is an unfinished agenda and requires continued effort to ensure every child receives an education compulsorily and freely. Adequate budgetary measures must be placed to ensure that education inputs such as textbooks, desks, and blackboards as well as teachers are available and accessible in sufficient number and quality. In this connection, African countries must intensify partnerships with key partners in the education for all initiatives, such as UNICEF to help mobilize resources toward the education goal; to help countries with policy, data, capacity-building, and financial support; and to help them improve the efficiency of their resources. Second, African countries must guarantee a "safe, supportive learning environment" as key a condition for keeping girls in school and ensuring their successful education. In particular, gender-based violence must be addressed by education policy at several levels: from prevention to **identify and address the issue of violence, criminalization of acts of violence and** raise the legal marriage age, and combat early marriages. Third, with respect to mechanisms of implementation and enforcement of the right to basic education, South Africa seems to take the lead in Africa, principally with regards to the extent of judicial enforcement. Hence, other African countries have a lot to learn from the South African experience which, as expressed by the South African Constitutional Court, is that the right to basic education should be "understood as immediately realisable, unlike other socio-economic rights." Not only in the realm of the judiciary, but it is also highly imperative for all spheres of government (local, provincial and national) in Africa to commit and ensure access to basic education as a guaranteed right. In this light, resolute political focus on primary education is a remedy in the prime to achieve learning success in quality *basic education* for all.

Notes

1. See Claudia Kessler and Verena Renggli, "Health Promotion: Concepts and Practices: A Key Issue Paper Focusing on the Relevance for International Cooperation" (Basel: Swiss Center for International Health, 2011), 5. Accessed July 13, 2016: http://www.medicusmundi.ch/de/schwerpunkte/chronische-krankheitendieglobaleepidemie/gesundheits-foerderung-und-praevention-1/health-promotion-concepts-andpractices/atdownload/file (Kessler and Renggli 2011).
2. The African Union Commission, *Agenda 2063: The Africa We Want* (Banjul: The African Union Commission, September 2015), 11 (The African Union Commission 2015).
3. Ibid., Aspiration 1 of *Agenda 2063.* The remaining four African Aspirations are: An integrated continent, politically united and based on the ideals of Pan Africanism and vision of Africa's Renaissance (Aspiration 2); A peaceful and secure Africa (Aspiration 4); Africa with a strong cultural identity, common heritage, values and ethics (Aspiration 5); and Africa as a strong, united, resilient and influential global partner and player (Aspiration 7).

4. Ibid., Aspiration 3 of *Agenda 2063.*
5. Ibid., Aspiration 6 of *Agenda 2063.*
6. John Strauss and Duncan Thomas, "Human Resources: Empirical Modeling of Household and Family Decisions," *Handbook of Development Economics 3*, (1995): 1883–2023; Pinar Mine Güneş, "The Role of Maternal Education in Child Health: Evidence from a Compulsory Schooling Law," GCC Working Paper Series (2013): 1–44; John C. Caldwell, 'Education as a Factor in Mortality Decline: An Examination of Nigerian Data," *Population Studies* 33, (1979): 395–413; Albino Barrera, 'The Role of Maternal Schooling and its Interaction with Public Health Programs in Child Health Production', *Journal of Development Economics* 32, (1990): 69–91 (Strauss and Thomas 1995; Pinar 2013; Caldwell 1979; Barrera 1990.
7. Christof Heyns and Magnus Killander, 'Compendium of Key Human Rights Documents of the African Union' (Pretoria: Pretoria University Law Press, 2013), 486 (Heyns and Killander 2013).
8. Paragraph 74 of the Technical Guidance on the Application of a Human Rights-Based Approach to the Implementation of Policies and Programmes to Reduce and Eliminate Preventable Mortality and Morbidity of Children Under-Five Years of Age (June 30, 2014). Accessed August 13, 2016: http://www.ohchr.org/Documents/Issues/Children/TechnicalGuidance/TechnicalGuidancereport.pdf.
9. USAID, *A Promise Renewed: Ending Preventable Child and Maternal Deaths* (New York: USAID: 2012), 6 (USAID 2012).
10. UNICEF, "UN Inter-agency Group for Child Mortality Estimation Report 2014: Levels and Trends in Child Mortality" (New York: USAID, 2014), 10. Accessed July 1, 2016: http://www.childmortality.org/files_v17/download/UNICEF%202014%21GME%20child%20mortality%20Report_Final.pdf (UNICEF 2014).
11. Nathan Collins, "Why Does Education Improve Health? It's complicated". Accessed June 10, 2016: https://psmag.com/why-does-education-improve-health (Pacific Standard 2015).
12. Dana P. Goldman and James P. Smith, "Can patient self-management help explain the SES health gradient?" *Proceedings of National Academy of Sciences*, (2002): 10929–10934 (Goldman and Smith 2002).
13. Health Transit Review 2, no. 1 (1992): 49–69 (Health Transit Review 1992).
14. UNESCO, *EFA Global Monitoring Report: Reaching the Marginalized* (Paris: UNESCO, 2010). Accessed July 23, 2016: http://unesdoc.unesco.org/images/0018/001866/186606E.pdf (UNESCO 2010a).
15. Lawrence Summers, "Educating All the Children *Policy Research Working Papers Series*" (Washington, DC: World Bank, 1992) (Summers 1992).

16. UNESCO, *Education Counts: Towards the Millennium Development Goal* (Paris: UNESCO, 2010). Accessed July 16, 2016: http://unesdoc.unesco.org/images/0019/001902/190214e.pdf (UNESCO 2010b).
17. Ibid.
18. Damien De Walque, '*How Does the Impact of an HIV/AIDS Information Campaign Vary With Educational Attainment? Evidence From Rural Uganda*" (Washington, DC: The World Bank, 2004) (De Walque 2004).
19. UNESCO, *Education Counts.*
20. Faranaaz Veriava and Fons Coomans, "The Right to Education," in Danie Brand and Christof Heyns (eds.). *Socio-economic Rights in South Africa* (Pretoria: Pretoria University Law Press, 2005), 57. See, also, Manfred Nowak, "The Right to Education," in Asbjorn Eide et al. (eds.). *Economic, Social and Cultural Rights: A Textbook* (2001), 245; Katarina Tomasevski 'Removing Obstacles in the Way of the Right to Education' *Right to Education Primers* no. 1 (2001): 8–9. Accessed June 21, 2016: http://www.right-to-education.org (Veriava and Coomans 2005; Nowak 2001; Tomasevski 2001).
21. Paragraph 3 of the Committee on Economic, Social, and Cultural Rights General Comment 14, The Right to the Highest Attainable Standard of Health, 08/11/2000, E/C.12/2000/04.
22. See for instance, Paragraph 24 of the Technical Guidance on the Application of a Human Rights-Based Approach to the Implementation of Policies and Programmes to Reduce And Eliminate Preventable Mortality and Morbidity of Children Under-Five Years Of Age (June 30, 2014). Accessed August 13, 2016: http://www.ohchr.org/Documents/Issues/Children/TechnicalGuidance/TechnicalGuidancereport.pdf.
23. Committee General Comment 13 of the ESCR paragraph 9.
24. Mashele Rapatsa and Nicholas Matloga, "The Right to Basic Education in South Africa: Lessons from *Section 27 and Others v Minister of Education and Another* (2012) ZAGPPHC 114," *Mediterranean Journal of Social Sciences* 5, no. 27 (2014): 1123 (Rapatsa and Matloga 2014).
25. See article 26.
26. See article 13(2).
27. See article 2, Protocol 1.
28. See article 12.
29. See article 13.
30. South Africa has taken laudable steps to give effect to the realization of the basic right to primary education, although further action is required to fulfil the right for all children in the country. For a comprehensive engagement see, for instance, Lorette Arendse 'The Obligation to Provide Free Basic Education in South Africa: An International Law Perspective' *ER/PELJ 14, no. 6* (2011): 97–127. Also, to apprehend how

the South African Constitutional Court has analyzes basic education as a human right, see the case of *Section 27 and Others v Minister of Education and Another* (24565/2012) [2012] ZAGPPHC114.

31. Veriava and Coomans, 62.
32. Ibid., 64.
33. General Comment 13 of the ESCR Committee paragraph 6(a).
34. Serges A Kamga, "Realising the Right to Primary Education in Cameroon," *African Human Rights Law Journal* 11, no. 2 (2011): 174 (Kamga 2011).
35. General Comment 13 of the ESCR Committee paragraph 6(b).
36. *The Star* (January 17, 2002).
37. General Comment 13 of the ESCR Committee paragraph 6(c).
38. Veriava and Coomans, 71.
39. Ibid., paragraph 6(d).
40. "Assessing Progress in Africa toward the Millennium Development Goals, 2011", Accessed July 20, 2016: http://www.afdb.org/fileadmin/uploads/afdb/Documents/Publications/Goal2%20Eng.pdf.
41. Ibid.
42. UN Chronicle, "Improving maternal health through education: Safe motherhood is a necessity," Vol. XLIV, no. 4 (December 2007). Accessed July 23, 2016: https://unchronicle.un.org/article/improving-maternal-health.
43. The World Declaration on Education for All, Adopted in Jomtien in 1990, Article 4. See, also, Articles 1 and 5 of this Declaration. This document is not a legally binding.
44. "Assessing Progress in Africa toward the Millennium Development Goals, 2011" (n. 40 above).
45. Ibid.
46. Ibid.
47. Ibid.
48. Martaine E. Lockheed and Andiaan M. Verspoor, *Improving Primary Education in Developing Countries* (Washington, DC: World Bank, 1991) (Lockheed and Andiaan 1991).
49. Ibid.
50. Daniel Sifuna and Nobuhide Sawamura, "Challenges of Quality Education in Sub-Saharan Africa-Some Key Issues" (2011), 1–12. Accessed July 22, 2016: http://home.hiroshima-u.ac.jp/cice/wp-content/uploads/2014/03/4-1-13.pdf (Sifuna and Sawamura 2011).
51. Ibid.
52. UNICEF, "Goal: Achieve Universal Primary Education". Accessed August 12, 2016: http://www.unicef.org/mdg/education.html (UNICEF 2016).
53. Ibid.

54. See, for instance, Helen Potts, "Accountability and the Right to the Highest Attainable Standard of Health" (Colchester: University of Essex, 2008), 17; Flavia Bustreo et al. *Women's and Children's Right to Health: Evidence of Impact of Human Rights*' (Geneva: WHO; 2013), 13 and 74; Solomon Abegaz, "A Rights Based-Approach to Reducing Child Mortality in Ethiopia" (LLD thesis, University of Pretoria, South Africa, 2016), 292–314 (Potts 2008; Bustreo 2013; Abegaz 2016).
55. Ann Skelton, "South Africa", in Ton Liefaard and Jaap E. Doek (eds), *Litigating Children's Rights: The UN Convention on the Rights of the Child in Domestic and International Jurisprudence* (The Netherlands: Springer, 2014), 25 (Skelton 2014).
56. *Governing Body of the Juma Musjid Primary School v Essay NO* (Centre for Child Law as Amicus Curiae) 2011 (8) BCLR 761 (CC).
57. Ibid., paragraph 37.
58. See, for instance, John Mubangizi, "The Constitutional Protection of Socio-Economic Rights in Selected African Countries: A Comparative Evaluation," *African Journal of Legal Studies* 2, no. 1 (2006): 1–19 (Mubangizi 2006).
59. Kamga, "Realising the Right to Primary Education in Cameroon", 186–192 (Kamga 2011).
60. As of early 2016, only Central African Republic, Sao Tome and Principe, Tunisia, Somalia, Saharawi Arab Democratic Republic, South Sudan, and Democratic Republic of Congo are not ratifying countries of the ACRWC. See, ACERWC "Ratifcation Data," accessed August 12, 2016: http://www.acerwc.org/ratification-data/ (ACERWC 2016).

Bibliography

Books and Others

Abegaz, Solomon. 2016. A Rights Based-Approach to Reducing Child Mortality in Ethiopia. LLD thesis, University of Pretoria, South Africa. 292–314.

ACERWC. 2016. Ratification Data. http://www.acerwc.org/ratification-data/. Accessed 12 Aug 2016.

Arendse, Lorette. 2011. The Obligation to Provide Free Basic Education in South Africa: An International Law Perspective. *ER/PELJ* 14 (6): 97–127.

Barrera, Albino. 1990. The Role of Maternal Schooling and its Interaction with Public Health Programs in Child Health Production. *Journal of Development Economics* 32: 69–91.

Bustreo, Flavia, et al. 2013. *Women's and Children's Right to Health: Evidence of Impact of Human Rights*. Geneva: WHO.

Caldwell, John C. 1979. Education as a Factor in Mortality Decline: An Examination of Nigerian Data. *Population Studies* 33: 395–413.
Committee on Economic, Social, and Cultural Rights General Comment 14, The Right to the Highest Attainable Standard of Health, 08/11/2000, E/C. 12/2000/04.
Committee on Economic, Social, and Cultural Rights General Comment 13, The Right to Education (Art. 13), Document E/C. 12/1999/10.
De Walque, Damien. 2004. *How Does the Impact of an HIV/AIDS Information Campaign Vary With Educational Attainment? Evidence From Rural Uganda*. Washington, DC: The World Bank.
Goldman, Dana P., and James P. Smith. 2002. Can Patient Self-management Help Explain the SES Health Gradient? *Proceedings of the National Academy of Sciences of the United States of America* 99 (16): 10929–10934.
Health Transit Review. 1992. 2:1 49–69.
Heyns, Christof, and Magnus Killander. 2013. *Compendium of Key Human Rights Documents of the African Union*. Pretoria: Pretoria University Law Press.
http://www.childmortality.org/files_v17/download/UNICEF%20 2014%2IGME%20child%20mortality%20Report_Final.pdf.
Kamga, Serges A. 2011. Realising the Right to Primary Education in Cameroon. *African Human Rights Law Journal* 1 (2): 174.
Kessler, Claudia, and Verena Renggli. 2011. *Health Promotion: Concepts and Practices: A Key Issue Paper Focusing on the Relevance for International Cooperation*, Basel: Swiss Center for International Health.
Lockheed, E. Martaine, and M. Verspoor Andiaan. 1991. *Improving Primary Education in Developing Countries*. Washington, DC: World Bank.
Mubangizi, John. 2006. The Constitutional Protection of Socio-Economic Rights in Selected African Countries: A Comparative Evaluation. *African Journal of Legal Studies* 2 (1): 1–19.
Nowak, Manfred. 2001. The Right to Education. In *Economic, Social and Cultural Rights: A Textbook*, vol. 245, ed. Eideet Asbjorn et al. The Netherlands: Springer.
Pacific Standard. 2015. Why Does Education Improve Health? It's complicated. https://psmag.com/why-does-education-improve-health. Accessed 10 June 2016.
Pinar, Mine G. 2013. The Role of Maternal Education in Child Health: Evidence from a Compulsory Schooling Law. GCC Working Paper Series: 1–44.
Potts, Helen. 2008. *Accountability and the Right to the Highest Attainable Standard of Health*. Colchester: University of Essex.
Rapatsa, Mashele, and Nicholas Matloga. 2014. The Right to Basic Education in South Africa: Lessons from *Section 27 and Others v Minister of Education and Another* (2012) ZAGPPHC 114. *Mediterranean Journal of Social Sciences* 5 (27): 1123.

Sifuna, Daniel, and Nobuhide Sawamura. 2011. Challenges of Quality Education in Sub-Saharan Africa-Some Key Issues. http://home.hiroshima-u.ac.jp/cice/wp-content/uploads/2014/03/4-1-13.pdf. Accessed 22 July 2016.

Skelton, Ann. 2014. "South Africa" in Liefaard. In *Litigating Children's Rights: The UN Convention on the Rights of the Child in Domestic and International Jurisprudence*. ed. Ton and E. Doek Jaap, vol. 25. The Netherlands: Springer.

Strauss, John and Duncan Thomas. 1995. Human Resources: Empirical Modeling of Household and Family Decisions. *Handbook of Development Economics* 3: 1883–2023.

Summers, Lawrence. 1992. Educating All the Children *Policy Research Working Papers Series*. Washington, DC: World Bank.

The African Union Commission. 2015. *Agenda 2063: The Africa We Want*. Banjul: The African Union Commission (September 2015).

The Office of High Commissioner for Human Rights, "Technical Guidance on the Application of a Human Rights-Based Approach to the Implementation of Policies and Programmes to Reduce and Eliminate Preventable Mortality and Morbidity of Children Under-Five Years of Age" (June 30, 2014). http://www.ohchr.org/Documents/Issues/Children/TechnicalGuidance/TechnicalGuidancereport.pdf. Accessed 13 Aug 2016.

The World Declaration on Education for All, Adopted in Jomtien in 1990.

Tomasevski, Katarina. 2001. Removing Obstacles in the Way of the Right to Education. *Right to Education Primers* 1. http://www.right-to-education.org. Accessed 21 June 2016.

UN Chronicle. 2007. Improving Maternal Health Through Education: Safe Motherhood is a Necessity, vol. XLIV, no. 4 (December 2007), https://unchronicle.un.org/article/improving-maternal-health. Accessed July 23, 2016.

UNDP. 2012. Assessing Progress in Africa toward the Millennium Development Goals. http://www.afdb.org/fileadmin/uploads/afdb/Documents/Publications/Goal2%20Eng.pdf. Accessed 20 July 2016.

UNESCO. 2010a. *EFA Global Monitoring Report: Reaching the Marginalized*, Paris: UNESCO. http://unesdoc.unesco.org/images/0018/001866/186606E.pdf. Accessed 23 July 2016.

UNESCO. 2010b. *Education Counts: Towards the Millennium Development Goal*, Paris: UNESCO.

UNICEF. 2016. Goal: Achieve Universal Primary Education. http://www.unicef.org/mdg/education.html. Accessed 12 Aug 2016.

UNICEF. 2014. *UN Inter-agency Group for Child Mortality Estimation Report 2014: Levels and Trends in Child Mortality*, New York: USAID. Accessed 1 July 2016.

USAID. 2012. *A Promise Renewed: Ending Preventable Child and Maternal Deaths*. New York: USAID.

Veriava, Faranaaz, and Coomans Fons. 2005. The Right to Education. In *Socio-economic Rights in South Africa*, ed. Danie Brand and Christof Heyns, vol. 57. Pretoria: Pretoria University Law Press.

Cases

Governing Body of the Juma Musjid Primary School v Essay NO (Centre for Child Law as Amicus Curiae) 2011 (8) BCLR 761 (CC).

Section 27 and Others v Minister of Education and Another (24565/2012) (2012) AGPPHC114.

Author Biography

Solomon Tekle Abegaz (LL.B, LL.M) (Addis Ababa) (LL.D) (Pretoria) is currently an Assistant Professor of law at the School of Law of University of Gondar, in Gondar, Ethiopia, and lectures on a part-time basis at the College of Law and Governance Studies, Addis Ababa University, in the same country. He formerly served as legal counsellor at Ethiopian Airlines Group and taught law again on a part-time basis at Rift Valley University in Ethiopia. He has published articles and commentaries including in the area of children's and women's rights. His research area is international human rights and international air law.

Index

A.C. Onuora-Oguno et al. (eds.), *Education Law, Strategic Policy, and Sustainable Development in Africa*, DOI 10.1007/978-3-319-53703-0

The manufacturer's authorised representative in the EU is Springer Nature Customer Service Centre GmbH, Europaplatz 3, 69115 Heidelberg, Germany. If you have any concerns regarding our products, please contact ProductSafety@springernature.com

Printed and bound by CPI Group (UK) Ltd, Croydon, CR0 4YY
30/09/2026
02225439-0009